*Hemispheric Indigeneities*

# Hemispheric Indigeneities

*Native Identity and Agency in Mesoamerica, the Andes, and Canada*

Edited by
MILÉNA SANTORO
and
ERICK D. LANGER

*University of Nebraska Press*
LINCOLN & LONDON

Portions of chapter 7 originally appeared in *Radio Fields: Anthropology and Wireless Sound in the 21st Century*, ed. Lucas Bessire and Daniel Fisher (New York: New York University Press, 2012).

Portions of chapter 8 originally appeared in *Earth Politics: Religion, Decolonization and Bolivia's Indigenous Intellectuals*, by Waskar Ari (Durham: Duke University Press, 2014).

The text of Réal Junior Leblanc's *Nanameshkueu/Earthquake* in chapter 9 is reproduced courtesy of Wapikoni Mobile.

Library of Congress Control Number: 2017056172

Set in Minion Pro by E. Cuddy.

To my parents, Bruce and Rolande Andrews, who encouraged my interest in the indigenous peoples of Canada's West Coast during my formative years.

—Miléna

To my host mother and father in Bolivia, Luís Sánchez and Adela Abella de Sánchez, who made me love a corner of the world I would never have considered otherwise.

—Erick

# CONTENTS

# ILLUSTRATIONS

# ACKNOWLEDGMENTS

This volume is the result of the extraordinary opportunity to organize a symposium ambitiously titled "Becoming Indigenous, Asserting Indigeneity" at Georgetown University in the spring of 2013. This symposium was funded by the Americas Initiative of Georgetown College under the deft and congenial leadership of Dr. John Tutino and assisted in its organization by Kathy Gallagher, whose logistical skills were invaluable in making our event a success. We are also indebted to Dr. Chester Gillis, who, during his tenure as dean of Georgetown College, maintained support for the Americas Initiative, thus allowing this interdisciplinary and collegial working group to continue offering a monthly outlet for our scholarly exchanges. We are also extremely fortunate to have brought together an outstanding group of indigenous and nonindigenous scholars who participated in the two-day symposium and have since most graciously performed the revisions necessary to turn our shared exchanges and research into this book. They have shown both patience and faith in us as we sought the right publisher and shepherded the book through this four-year process and into its current form.

We also wish to thank our partners at the University of Nebraska Press, in particular Matthew Bokovoy and Heather Stauffer. They have believed in us and have responded to our every query most generously along the way. We are grateful as well to have had such excellent outside readers and copyeditors, whose comments and suggestions helped make this a better book.

Summer funding from Georgetown's Faculty of Languages and Linguistics assisted Miléna Santoro in the preliminary stages of developing her research on indigenous filmmaking in Canada. Miléna would like to thank Alanis Obomsawin, Wapikoni Mobile, Jeff Barnaby, and John Christou at Prospector Films for graciously according permission to use the images included in her contribution to this volume, as well as for responding so positively when contacted for interviews or answers to her questions.

This volume has provided the opportunity for some exceptional collaborations and dialogues, and we, the editors, feel fortunate indeed to have not only learned a lot from this meeting of minds but also developed a friendship that might never have happened had it not been for the spirit walk of this work. Our sincere thanks to all our colleagues, friends, and family who have inspired and accompanied us on this journey.

# Introduction

ERICK D. LANGER WITH MILÉNA SANTORO

T he idea of a book exploring the concept of indigeneity in the Americas came from a symposium titled "Becoming Indigenous, Asserting Indigeneity" that Miléna Santoro and I organized on March 15, 2013, under the auspices of the Americas Initiative of Georgetown College at Georgetown University.[1] While the issues we hoped our participants would explore were not predetermined, our guiding question was how the idea of *indigeneity* has changed over time in different contact zones and contexts. We defined *indigeneity* as characteristics that indigenous peoples in the Americas took on to define themselves during crucial historical periods. Because of the focus of the symposium, most of the participants were historians, though scholars in anthropology and film studies were also included. We invited some of the foremost authorities of Mesoamerican, Andean, and Canadian indigenous peoples, including when possible scholars of indigenous origin, to participate in our symposium and contribute to this project.

This book takes as its point of departure the idea that indigeneity is a historical construct and a social positioning that has perpetually changed and continues to change even today. As many contributors to this book argue, it is best to look at and define indigeneity as a process rather than a static category. In fact, a number of contributors use the term *becoming Indian* to describe how terms and identities shifted over time. Many studies have dealt with this process both empirically and theoretically, especially in the discipline of anthropology.[2] The authors of this volume have used some of these theoretical constructs but mostly focus on empirical case studies that illustrate the ways in which conceptions of indigeneity varied over time and in different regions.

The book itself is organized temporally and thus has an explicit historical dimension. The concept of indigeneity in the case of the Americas is closely tied to colonialism, as only the irruption of Europeans into the hemisphere led to the creation of the *indigenous* category. The book is thus organized into three periods: the colonial period; the nineteenth century, when new nations emerged to take the place of the colonies; and the twentieth century. As the book demonstrates, over time the concept of *the Indian* varied widely, and the changes that occurred were large and important. This book is not alone in being intentionally more heavily weighted toward the present than the more distant past. We want to show how indigeneity changed over time by emphasizing that the idea of who Native peoples were, and how their self-definition as indigenous changed, is not rooted just in a deep past but continues to evolve in the present.

Starting with the invasion of Europeans (who also brought some Africans), the vast colonial period is one that saw major transformations. This period forms the backbone of the transformations indigenous societies suffered through their interactions with the interlopers. While in the Andes and Mesoamerica the Spanish were able to conquer most large-scale societies commonly known as the Aztec and Inca empires, the French and then the English had more complex and less dominant roles among the indigenous groupings in what later became known as Canada.[3] The colonial period is more difficult to delimit for Canada since the process of becoming an independent nation was much more gradual. Nonetheless, we use *the colonial period* to refer to something arguably similar across the Americas, extending essentially from contact with Europeans up to the early nineteenth century. Despite possible quibbles about periodization, for indigenous peoples such issues as the profound economic impact of European commercial demand and the catastrophic demographic impact of the introduction of new diseases to which indigenous populations had little or no immunity were common among all regions. The ability of the Spanish empire to rule and extract surplus from the indigenous populations during the colonial period differs from that of the North American experience, where European populations remained relatively small, were less urban, and resorted to mostly indirect methods to access indigenous resources over vast expanses of territory where colonial powers had limited effective presence.

It is well understood that the idea of *indios*, a term Christopher Columbus used for the Native peoples he encountered in the Americas, is an artificial one. The term emerged from Columbus's profound navigational error, since he thought he had landed on the eastern coast of Asia or its environs. Before Europeans arrived on the scene, Native peoples in the Americas obviously did not think of themselves as Indians. That term, *indios*, only became possible with the European conquest. It created an entirely new category— the natives of a hemisphere unknown to Europeans—and created a distinction for these peoples as separate from their conquerors. After all, the Europeans had to figure out who these new peoples were—some, such as the Franciscan José de Acosta, thought that they might be one of the Lost Tribes of Israel (Acosta [1590] 2009).[4] In the end, the European interlopers lumped these highly diverse peoples into a single category for their own convenience and as a means to rule over them, in typical imperial fashion. This did not mean, as Susan Kellogg and Susan Ramírez argue in their chapters, that any given indigenous group used this term, at least not until relatively late in the colonial period.

However, within decades after the conquest, many Native peoples began to adopt this terminology themselves, at least in relations with the colonial overlords, since using it often appeared to be in their best interest. By using that term they could access more favorable systems of justice—at least in the Spanish case—and be accepted as human beings. For the most part, the peoples who had lived in peasant empires and city-states such as the Mexicas of Mexico, the Mayas of Yucatán, and the Incas of South America, eventually submitted to Spanish rule over a period of time. They entered into a tributary relationship with the conquerors and yet maintained much of their local autonomy, though they had to convert to Christianity and accept that the Spaniards reorganized their societies. In the Andes, for example, this meant pulling together different groups and "reducing" them into new towns, with a church in one corner of the central plaza, an administrative building, and a jail. They also forged a new way of thinking about themselves and adjusted, often in complicated ways, to their new colonial masters. It is remarkable that this system was able to subsist for three centuries, disturbed only by a few large rebellions (but many local ones). The key to the relative success of the colonial system resided in great part in the relative autonomy that most indigenous villagers could maintain.

However, many indigenous peoples did not accept the Europeans as their overlords. In 1701, about forty indigenous tribes signed the Great Peace of Montreal with the French colonial authorities, an indication of the French diplomatic strategy with their indigenous adversaries that clearly implies the former conferred equal negotiating status to the latter. Historians have noted the French colonizers' difference of approach from their Spanish peers, although admittedly the Great Peace did not prevent future conflict between the parties. Elsewhere in the Americas, however, while mostly sedentary peasant societies quickly fell to the conquerors (though there were holdouts even there, such as some of the Mayas or the Chiriguanos), the Spanish had a much harder time with peoples who were not peasants and were more mobile. Indigenous peoples such as the Mapuches or Araucanians of South America and the Apaches of North America, among many others, refused to submit to the colonial polities. They were *indios*, of course, but also classified as savages, or *bárbaros*, often seen as beyond the pale of "civilization" (a loaded term in itself, defined to include only non-natives of the Americas).[5] In the Iberian and French empires, such "savages" were to be civilized mainly through converting them to Christianity. In the case of the French, in areas of what would become Canada where there was a minimal or nonexistent colonial structure, the great race between the British and French colonial empires made it necessary for the French to accept indigenous groups into their alliance structures in ways the British, who had a much greater demographic presence, did not.

There is much literature on indigenous groups' fascinating transformation from defining themselves as different from all others to accepting themselves as *indios* or Indians; readers will find much of this in the first section of the book. This creation of "Indians" occurred fairly quickly after contact, but the idea of what constituted indigenousness and how it was acted upon and perceived changed over time, both because of actions by indigenous peoples and the interaction with the colonial and then later national states. The essays on the colonial period in this book illuminate these important issues and transformations in self-perception.

As a number of our contributing authors argue, *indigeneity* was first defined as a fiscal category—at least in the Spanish colonial realm—but it was also much more than that. Presumably, among the Spanish, the Indians who formed part of the population of their empire represented the Indian Republic—the *república de indios*—in counterdistinction to the Republic of Spaniards. As Susan Kellogg and Susan Ramírez show, the conception of indigeneity within the indigenous communities was quite different than the Spanish categories imposed upon them. Nevertheless, the indigenous community members were forced to pay tribute to the Crown, whereas other colonial subjects usually did not.[6] Of course, the colonial authorities could not maintain this neat bifurcation for very long; the mixing of Spanish and indigenous peoples, as well as Africans, complicated matters very quickly. By independence in the early nineteenth century in the former Spanish possessions and new republics, the new revolutionary elites abolished Indian tribute and, in the Andes, the special forced mining labor regime, the *mita*. In Mexico Indian tribute disappeared completely. However, in Peru, Ecuador, and Bolivia, the government hastily reintroduced the Indian tribute because of fiscal pressures, thus reemphasizing the fiscal nature of the indigenous category. The Peruvian and Ecuadorian government abolished this special tax on its indigenous population by the mid-nineteenth century, whereas in Bolivia it subsisted into the late nineteenth century. However, as Luis Granados points out, the way the elites and the government defined indigenous peoples in Mesoamerica kept them in pretty much the same place socially as before. By contrast, Erick Langer's chapter shows that in the Andes at least, the indigenous population was able to take the lead in the economic development of the region for a number of decades.

The French experience in Canada was different yet again, in that the French colonial government acknowledged race mixture, with the recognition of a new category, that of the Métis, initially a product of the union of French men and indigenous women. In the English territories, especially in western Canada, these unions were also common. The Métis category existed in addition to the other indigenous groups that presumably did not intermix with Europeans. When the English took over the French dominions in 1763, *Métis* described peoples who mostly intermarried with other Métis. The historian David McNab, a Métis himself, highlights some of the identity issues encountered by Métis peoples in his autobiographical postface to this volume.

The treatment of the Métis and their recognition as an indigenous category in Canada differed from the Latin American experience. In the Spanish realms mestizos generally were not considered indigenous; in fact, they did not fit into *república de indios* or *españoles* model. Although it varied and many mestizos were absorbed into Spanish or indigenous societies, the Spanish colonial government saw them as potentially dangerous populations that might be beholden to their indigenous brethren but were an interstitial group and thus suspect. In any case, the Spanish authorities never contemplated distinguishing them as a special indigenous category, nor did the mestizos, many of whom wanted to belong to Spanish and not indigenous society and be counted as such. When by the eighteenth century the Spanish attempted to categorize all the different types of race mixture, they had artists draw up *casta* paintings that tried to show visually the different combinations that race mixture could include—including mixing with the Afro-descendants. However, they never were effectively able to incorporate conceptually the ever-growing mestizo population, especially in urban centers.[7]

By the late nineteenth century, the situation in the hemisphere had changed dramatically for indigenous peoples again. Governments and large landowners took away vast swaths of the lands in most regions that autonomous indigenous peoples had controlled, on what the states called frontiers. The usurpation of land also occurred with those peasant communities (mostly in Spanish America) that had been integrated into the new national societies. Large estates—called haciendas—often took over indigenous lands, as governments prohibited communal properties, and opened up these territories for sale to nonmembers of the community. This had a tremendous impact in the largely peasant societies of Mesoamerica and the Andes. As important, if not more so, is that governments finally had the technology and the resources to invade the lands of indigenous peoples who had remained autonomous from the colonial states. Thus, people such as the Araucanians and the Mapuches of the Southern Cone, the Apaches and Comanches of North America, and many other tribal peoples lost their autonomy and land. As a result, they were crammed onto reservations that were a small portion of their former territories, if indeed they were permitted to stay in their ancestral areas at all. Ultimately, the northern deserts of Mexico and the prairie plains of North America fell under the jurisdiction of the state and were opened up to colonization by nonindigenous groups. The rubber boom in the Amazon region also wreaked havoc on indigenous people, who were often killed or forced to work as rubber tappers or prostitutes.

Canada remained a colonial unit of Great Britain in the nineteenth century, although after Canadian Confederation in 1867, the newly formed dominion was relatively autonomous. By contrast, when the populations of Mesoamerica and the Andes went through fierce independence struggles that devolved into civil wars (from about 1809 to 1825), the consequence was political autonomy of the new nation-states, though with greatly weakened institutions. European powers interfered, especially in Mexico. The economic ties between the Andes and Mesoamerica with western Europe faded but strengthened again by the end of the nineteenth century. The late nineteenth century was thus a dark period in the indigenous history of the hemisphere. Social Darwinism marginalized indigenous peoples by asserting their inferiority. Governments and local nonindigenous elites took away resources, especially land, from indigenous peoples at an accelerating rate. Autonomous indigenous peoples lost their territories as settlers and national troops invaded. Indigenous communities were wiped out in many regions, and the reservations set up in Canada, as well as in the United States, Chile, and Argentina, were on the most marginal lands that neither the church nor any descendant of Europeans wanted. The process was similar to that of the second wave of imperialism, when industrialized countries took over peoples and territories in Africa, Oceania, and Asia in a mad dash to acquire as many colonies as possible. In many ways, the late nineteenth and early twentieth centuries were the nadir for indigenous peoples throughout the world, with the Americas representing an important if unfortunately exemplary case.

Only in the late twentieth century did these tendencies reverse somewhat. In Canada movements where indigenous peoples began redefining themselves as First Nations began to gain traction, and their successes included the designation of Métis as an indigenous people. In the Constitution Act of 1982, Canada formally recognized the Métis as a separate group of indigenous heritage, along with other First Nations. In Spanish America indigenous movements such as the Zapatistas took off in Mexico, as well as in the Andes, where strong indigenous movements emerged, especially in Ecuador and Bolivia. The official rejection of racism in the aftermath of World War II, the creation of nongovernmental agencies that aided indigenous causes, and the passing of the United Nations International Labour Organization Resolution 169, which defined and codified indigenous rights in 1989, all served to aid the reversal of fortunes of indigenous peoples in the hemisphere. However, indigenous peoples still remain among the poorest people in the hemisphere and, in most cases, did not recoup the land and other resources that they had lost only a century before.

This book's essays look in more detail into many of the processes described above. While there are many important studies of indigeneity throughout the world—there are people defined as natives or Aboriginal peoples from Asia to Africa to Australia—this project concentrates on the Americas.[8] What does it mean for people in this hemisphere to be indigenous? Each chapter in this book answers this question a bit differently, and in fact, it is a question that is more difficult to answer than might first appear. For example, Marisol de la Cadena has shown that in twentieth-century Peru, the Cuzco elites, who prided themselves in their European heritage, claimed to speak a more pure Quechua, the indigenous language the Incas spoke, than the indigenous population in the countryside surrounding the city (de la Cadena 2000). Who was Indian if the elites appropriated for themselves the indigenous language? It is with an awareness of this kind of complexity, and a desire to explore nuances, that many of the authors in this book speak about "becoming indigenous." While our contributors are not the first to posit this, their work affirms that indigeneity is a historically positioned category that has evolved over time and is closely related to and affected by power relations.

The tension many scholars feel in using the various terms for indigenous peoples is evident in this book as well. We have respected the variable deployment of the terms that our contributors use in this text, in part because it reflects the inevitable and productive distinctions between regions, time periods, and intellectual traditions. The discontinuous process of creating "Indians," as several of the contributors to this volume argue, constantly made for circumstances that changed the relative placement of Native peoples in the Americas vis-à-vis other peoples and the state. The research presented here shows how this process varied across geographical and cultural regions as well as time.

Given the vastness of our topic, we also wanted to provide a geographical and temporal context that would permit each scholar to elaborate on an important aspect of indigeneity. It was impossible to do justice to every important region in the Americas; this volume would have become excessively unwieldy. We had to leave out many regions, such as the Amazon, about which many interesting studies have proliferated, especially in the last two decades.[9] We decided instead to concentrate on three core regions where indigenous peoples were relatively numerous. These regions were Mesoamerica, the Andes, and the North American territory now largely falling within the borders of Canada. Each one of these regions has had and continues to have distinctive indigenous cultures and is governed by nation-states that have permitted the inclusion of indigenous peoples in different ways.

The three regions we focus on offer a number of similarities in addition to their historical differences with respect to the status and treatment of indigenous peoples. Both Mesoamerica and the Andes were conquered and ruled by the Spanish at about the same time. After independence in the early nineteenth century, Mesoamerica and the Andes divided into different states, though most of Mesoamerica remained mainly united under the Mexican state. Only the far southern parts—Guatemala, El Salvador, Nicaragua, and Honduras—broke off from Mexico. For its part Canada was partially conquered by the French and then later by the British. Formal independence in Canada really only came in the twentieth century, but the region remained one country, unlike the Andes or Mesoamerica. In all of these regions, a large diversity of indigenous groups existed with widely different material and political cultures, population sizes, and languages, but of course all of these have been profoundly and negatively impacted by colonization.

In this volume, we decided not to include the United States for a host of significant reasons. First of all, the United States and its treatment of indigenous peoples is well known, and so U.S. Native studies has its own programmatic biases that relate mostly to U.S. concerns and to the issue of a strong state and highly complex legislation, at least since the nineteenth century. The impression one gets when dealing with indigenous peoples and the state in the United States is that legislation looms large, at the expense of most other issues. For Canada, Mesoamerica, and the Andes, that is significantly less the case, as the essays that follow show, and moreover, these regions offer an important countervailing set of examples that we feel deserve to be considered comparatively, without requiring an automatic evocation of the already abundant literature on the U.S. case. We in no way wish to discourage comparative studies that include indigenous peoples in the United States, but in the pursuit of fostering a greater hemispheric dialogue on indigeneity, we felt we could make a more original and compelling contribution to knowledge by bringing together specialists on regions that spark new and even surprising insights and connections. And indeed our participants echoed our sentiments, since for many of them our symposium was the first time their research had rubbed shoulders with that of scholars from the other two regions we focus on in this systematic way.

A second and no less important point is that indigenous populations relative to the non-Indian population are higher in the regions we discuss. Admittedly, even attempting to count who is an

Indian or not is difficult, since the criteria vary widely from country to country. That said, some common measures are useful for the purpose of rough demographic estimates. While in Canada about 4 percent of the total population identifies as indigenous, such areas as the Northwest Territories contain about 37 percent who identify as indigenous. In Mexico about 15 percent of the population is considered indigenous, with the largest number in the south. The highest proportion of indigenous people in Mesoamerica lives in Guatemala, with around 40 percent. In the Andes, Bolivia ranges from 40 to 60 percent indigenous, Ecuador around 25 percent, and Peru around 30 percent. In turn, in the United States only 1.7 percent identified as Native American in the 2010 census. In Brazil, the largest Amazonian country, less than 1 percent count themselves as natives, though admittedly the amount of indigenous territory in the Amazon is large.[10] These figures give a rough sense of how relatively significant the indigenous population is in the different regions and nations of the hemisphere. Another associated issue is that the economic dynamism of indigenous peoples in the nineteenth century can be emphasized for certain regions within the Americas in ways that have not yet been tried for the United States. We are sure others can and will address this in due course.

Perhaps most important, however, is that by excluding the United States, we can better highlight comparisons of Mesoamerica and the Andes with Canada, something that, to our knowledge, has not been systematically presented before. Indeed, Canadian First Nations have often been left out of anthologies and interpretations of indigeneity, though arguably the interactions between the First Nations and the state in Canada are not only some of the most interesting but also among the most significant developments in indigenous self-assertion and sovereignty today.

If the early twentieth century saw a continuation of many of the disastrous trends and treatment affecting indigenous peoples since first contact, it is nonetheless during this contemporary period that indigenous peoples started to fight back and achieve a measure of success. In the Andes indigenous leaders organized to maintain their lands and even to try to regain them through legal means. Both in the Andes and Mesoamerica, sporadic indigenous rebellions proved largely ineffective in regaining autonomy and often led to greater loss of land, though at times the threat of further violence slowed its acquisition by outsiders. The mid-twentieth century brought about a focus more on class than on ethnicity in Latin America, effectively masking many ethnic vindication efforts through class-based organizations. The period of effective indigenous activism and the high point of indigenous movements in the Americas generally occurred in the late twentieth century. Throughout the region, as democracy and neoliberalism took hold in Latin America and class identity after the fall of the Soviet Union appeared to be outmoded, ethnic movements surged. In Canada as elsewhere in the Americas, the quincentenary of Columbus's voyage in 1992 brought about the mobilization of indigenous groups to protest the many lingering injustices that indigenous peoples have suffered over the past five hundred years. These transcontinental protest movements transformed national politics in many countries and placed indigenous demands on the front burner for some of them. The self-perception of indigenous peoples was also enhanced by such protests and examples of political efficacy. They felt themselves more powerful and capable of inducing political and cultural change. One of the most important consequences was the election of Evo Morales as president of Bolivia in 2006, the first president who campaigned on and identified himself as indigenous and as a fighter for indigenous rights.[11]

Within this tripartite temporal framework, the volume at hand makes a number of important contributions. First of all, in all cases, the chapters examine the issue of indigeneity from the indigenous perspective. This is important, since the creation of the concepts of the Native, the indigenous person, and community is only accomplished through the comparison with non-Natives. Many have made this point, given that indigeneity itself is a social construct and varies over time and in different regions (Sturm 2002; Graham and Penny 2014; de la Cadena and Starn 2007). By contrast with much of the existing scholarship, however, our chapters engage mainly with indigenous self-perceptions.

Although each chapter stands on its own, reading from the first to the last will provide the reader with insights that show both temporal and geographic changes. We organized the chapters in such a way as to be implicitly comparative, making possible an understanding of the issues of how people adapted to being indigenous in each society and across time. Thus, while during the colonial period the imperial authorities attempted to create a framework of domination, indigenous peoples were quite creative in adapting for their own uses the presumed strictures imposed from outside and in many cases made those strictures their own. The book also shows the significance of the nineteenth century, when indigenous peoples began to use the many remaining colonial institutions for their own ends. The nineteenth century thus ends up being a crucial period, one that made it possible to understand the contemporary issues we address in our third and final section. One cannot jump just from the colonial period (as many still do) to today and try to explain the actions of the twentieth and twenty-first centuries. For example, as Karl Hele shows, the treaties signed and implemented in Canada during the nineteenth century set in stone relations that persist even now between the state and indigenous groups. In the Andes it was only possible for liberal elites to gain control of the economy by crushing the commercial vitality of the Andean peoples of the first fifty-odd years after independence in the 1820s, and again, this has had a determinant effect through the present.

The volume also takes to task the frequent misconception that indigenous peoples were mostly victims and were unable to forge their own destiny. While there were clearly limits to what Natives could do, they were continually defining and redefining their own place in the social hierarchy as structures changed. Perhaps most important, what mattered was how the indigenous peoples in Mesoamerica, the Andes, and Canada organized themselves internally to survive and live as well as they could manage. This was not just the case with the indigenous movements in the last few decades, as Lynn Stephen shows for southern Mexico and Waskar Ari-Chachaki for Bolivia, but also in earlier periods. Indeed, as Miléna Santoro argues, indigenous peoples in Canada have achieved important gains in shaping their own images through film, a contemporary example of adapting the practices of the colonizer's culture in pursuit of artistic sovereignty and cultural integrity. Thus, the volume takes issue with the still prevalent idea that indigenous peoples are mainly poor and rural or that they are disempowered rather than active social agents who shape themselves and their world.

### Presenting the Book's Chapters

The colonial period section first features a chapter by Susan Kellogg, who examines the changing concepts of indigeneity in the context of scholars who study the Nahuas or Mexicas in Central Mexico during the colonial period. In Nahuatl, there is no term for *indio*. Kellogg shows us how the Nahua see ethnicity not in the European context but in the context of communities and belonging to certain kin groups. In turn, Susan Ramírez sees the term *Indian* as a Western construct. Instead, she argues that *ancestralities* might be a better term, since Andean peoples thought of their community, or *ayllu*, as hierarchically nested relatives. Ayllu affiliations were most important, similar to what Kellogg highlights in Mesoamerica. Ramírez shows *indio* was a term that only appeared in the seventeenth century among the Andean peoples she studied and was a word that had an urban rather than rural origin.

In the third chapter of part 1, David McNab takes the reader through the history of the Mi'kmaq people from the sixteenth to the eighteenth century. He describes how the Mi'kmaq interacted with both French and British authorities, both of which saw these peoples as "savages" even if they resided on their own lands. However, the Mi'kmaq were only resisting the usurpation of their lands and considered that they, like all others, should be treated as human beings. Later legislation almost completely erased the Mi'kmaq from the map in legal terms, though they remained in their ancestral home of Newfoundland. McNab's essay thus offers a contrasting case study that reveals the legal ramifications of how colonial authorities defined and circumscribed certain indigenous peoples in Canada.

The initial chapter of part 2 on the nineteenth century again starts with Mesoamerica. Luis Granados takes on the idea of the indigenous of Mexico and Guatemala and shows how the idea of the Indian changed and yet essentially remained the same in what he calls *gattopardismo*. He traces the category of Indian from a political and fiscal category to a racial one by the late nineteenth century. In the twentieth century, "Indianness" became a concept that had revolutionary potential once anthropologists began to examine indigenous peoples and measure their capacity for rebellion. Indigeneity and its definition was closely tied to the development of the state in Mesoamerica and while there were many conceptual changes, the people that were to be analyzed and dominated remained the same, marginalized human beings.

Erick Langer's chapter on Andean peoples in the nineteenth century changes the debate to economic factors and questions our notions of economic development. He shows how indigenous peoples from the Andean highlands emerged from the independence struggles relatively autonomous and with the weak state were able to control their own economies to an extent not possible in the colonial period. As a result, they prospered and were the engines of the Andean economy. Only in the late nineteenth century, once the Creole elites were able to plug into the increasingly vibrant Atlantic economy, were they able to discipline the peasants and impoverish them. They did so through the appropriation of indigenous lands and by marginalizing them within the national imaginary. It was only then that Indians began to be thought of as inherently poor.

Karl S. Hele, himself an Anishinaabe scholar, takes up the theme of how indigenous peoples in Canada went from being a "nation" to becoming indigenous. Focusing on the Sault region along the border of Canada and the United States around the Great Lakes, Hele shows how different conceptions of who was an Indian in Canada and the United States led to the inclusion or exclusion of people and access to fishing and other rights in the region. He illustrates the mutability of ethnic categories during the nineteenth century and the freezing of these categories in the second half of the nineteenth century as a result of treaties with indigenous peoples and between the United States and Canada.

In part 3 Lynn Stephen goes directly to the late twentieth century to demonstrate how indigenous peoples in southern Mexico, Guatemala, and Nicaragua have asserted their rights with or without the approval of the state. She asserts that self-determination of indigenous identity has been at the heart of indigenous movements in the region since 1992. These movements have been able to attain self-definition and agency through peace treaties with the government, through the creation of radio stations (many not legally licensed), through the administration of justice, and through control of territory. The Zapatistas of Chiapas are only one of various groups that have been able to create a new assertiveness among indigenous groups in Mesoamerica.

Waskar Ari-Chachaki, who is Aymara and grew up in Bolivia, delves into the first half of the twentieth century with his discussion of the Alcaldes Mayores Particulares, a small but highly influential multiethnic indigenous group in Bolivia that had its heyday from the 1930s to the 1950s. He documents how they tried to resist the reclassification of Indians as peasants in the aftermath of the Bolivian Revolution of 1952 and how many finally turned to religion, a version of the indigenous Andean one and then the Baha'i faith, as a means to resist the incorporation of their indigenous heritage into a nation that the government imagined as mestizo and peasant.

Miléna Santoro analyzes films made by indigenous peoples in Canada from the 1960s onward. She takes up the concept of *visual sovereignty*, proposed by Michelle Raheja, that describes the impetus felt by indigenous peoples to assert their identities creatively through film. At first, with support from the National Film Board of Canada, First Nations filmmakers made mainly documentaries, but by the 1990s they were creating fictional stories of their peoples on film, showing a great sophistication in their often subversive treatment of stereotypical Natives and interactions with nonindigenous peoples as well. Santoro's chapter demonstrates how state support for indigenous cultural production can lead to the revitalization of certain communities and linguistic groups, and provide inspiration for multiple generations of indigenous artists.

To conclude the book, we offer a more personal essay, Métis historian David McNab's autobiographical recollection, "Travels of a Métis through Spirit Memory, around Turtle Island, and Beyond." In his meditation on what it means to be indigenous, McNab considers his journey into knowledge of his family's heritage and his own identity in North America, which some Canadian First Nations peoples refer to as Turtle Island, evoking one of the indigenous origin stories of the birth of this continent and its inhabitants. In an episodic narrative that echoes the island trope of his title, McNab confronts the obstacles facing many who must try to find their place in the complex legal, educational, and cultural framework of Canada, which tends to impose a narrative and definition of indigenous identity and history that precludes Native ways of knowing, or what McNab calls *spirit memory*.

In many indigenous cultures, turtles are symbolic figures that are associated with teaching, memory, and history, so it is fitting that McNab, as a scholar-teacher, connects implicitly with this aspect of indigenous mythology. But his style, which diverges from the linear Cartesian argumentation of the other chapters in this volume, does unsettle the conventions of an academic anthology, just as his hybrid Métis identity challenges the categorization to which many indigenous peoples continue to be subjected. We include his autobiographical testimony precisely because it has this exemplary ontological value and also because it opens up the academic discourse on indigeneity to fundamental questions like "What does it mean to be indigenous or become indigenous, for those who are?" or "What would an indigenous autohistory offer that is different from traditional historical narratives, and what difference can this alternative story make in our understanding of the hemisphere that indigenous and nonindigenous peoples have shared since the arrival of Europeans?"[12]

McNab's memories and experiences show the importance of connections to the past and to each other in the development of our identity and, perhaps, point the way to an increasingly open and dialogic approach to thinking and writing about indigenous peoples, identity, and history. We hope that the spirit of his story underscores for our readers the importance of seeking out truths that are not always contained in scholarly or legal documents, such as the truth of a generously shared life. These truths can draw attention to and contextualize the experiences of indigenous peoples, particularly their self-realization and their growing self-assertion, that continue to shape the social and cultural realities of this hemisphere. We know there is much work still to be done to understand such dynamics, and we look forward to the continuing dialogue across indigenous studies communities and among indigenous and no-indigenous scholars, teachers, and students for whom indigenous peoples and their survival constitute a privileged font of human interest and new knowledge.

The chapters described above take different viewpoints, but they all contribute to our understanding of indigeneity in the Americas in new ways. In each region—Mesoamerica, the Andes, and Canada—indigenous peoples have lived and felt their ethnic identity as distinct from others. But what these essays show is that being indigenous has changed over time, and that self-identification within the relationship indigenous peoples have with the state (and the economy), as well as with various forms of cultural expression, was most important in the development of these differing self-conceptions. Because of this fluidity, the concept of indigeneity will continue to be problematic. In the end, that is a good thing because exploring this nuanced and contextually dependent issue challenges us to think about indigenous peoples in new ways that can be constructive and can help us understand the problems and potential of this designation in the Americas and beyond.

## Notes

1. We are deeply thankful to John Tutino, the director of the Americas Initiative, who helped plan the symposium and provided the resources for it.

2. Indigeneity is defined as a relational, emergent, contextual category, and in this our volume echoes much previous scholarship. Some of the theoretical advances in this area include Hill 1996; Urban and Sherzer 1991; Wade 2010; Maybury-Lewis 2002; Warren 1978; Warren and Jackson 2002; and Kuenzli 2013.

3. There were other important political units, such as the Tarascan state and the Maya city-states, among others, in Mesoamerica.

4. While Acosta's theory was popular, it was not universally accepted. His near-contemporary, Bernabé de Cobo, disputed Acosta's assertions (Cobo [1653] 1979). For a discussion of this debate, see Prieto 2010.

5. See, for example, Weber 2005.

6. It is slightly more complicated than that, but essentially only people recognized as indigenous peoples and living in peasant communities were required to pay this tax.

7. The issue of *mestizaje* is extremely complex, and it is impossible to do justice to the topic in a paragraph. For an excellent discussion, see Wade 2010. For casta paintings, see Katzew 2004.

8. For elsewhere in the world, see, for example, Hodgson 2011 and Li Murray 2000.

9. See, for example, Ramos 1998 and Garfield 2001.

10. To a certain extent, counting indigenous populations is like comparing apples and oranges because of the different criteria used to do so. However, the numbers provided give an approximate idea of the weight of indigenous populations.

11. President Alejandro Toledo of Peru (2001–2006) also identified himself as indigenous but did not run on a platform that emphasized indigenous rights.

12. The term *autohistory* is from Sioui 1991, an essay originally published in French in Quebec.

## Bibliography

Acosta, José de. (1590) 2009. *Natural and Moral History of the Indies*. Edited by Jane Mangan. Duke University Press.

Cobo, Bernabé. (1653) 1979. *History of the Inca Empire: An Account of the Indians' Customs and Their Origin, Together with a Treatise on Inca Legends, History, and Social Institutions*. Translated and edited by Roland Hamilton. Austin: University of Texas Press.

de la Cadena, Marisol. 2000. *Indigenous Mestizos: The Politics of Race and Culture in Cuzco, Peru, 1919–1991*. Durham: Duke University Press.

de la Cadena, Marisol, and Orin Starn. 2007. *Indigenous Experience Today*. Oxford: Berg.

Garfield, Seth. 2001. *Indigenous Struggle at the Heart of Brazil: State Policy, Frontier Expansion, and the Xavante Indians, 1937–1988*. Durham: Duke University Press.

Graham, Laura R, and H. G. Penny. 2014. *Performing Indigeneity: Global Histories and Contemporary Experiences*. Lincoln: University of Nebraska Press.

Hill, Jonathan D. 1996. *History, Power, and Identity: Ethnogenesis in the Americas, 1492–1992*. Iowa City: University of Iowa Press.

Hodgson, Dorothy L. 2011. *Being Maasai, Becoming Indigenous: Postcolonial Politics in a Neoliberal World*. Bloomington: Indiana University Press.

Katzew, Ilona. 2004. *Casta Painting: Images of Race in Eighteenth-Century Mexico*. New Haven: Yale University Press.

Kuenzli, E. Gabrielle. 2013. *Acting Inca: Identity and National Belonging in Early Twentieth-Century Bolivia*. Pittsburgh: University of Pittsburgh Press.

Li Murray, Tania. 2000. "Articulating Indigenous Identity in Indonesia: Resource Politics and the Tribal Slot." *Comparative Studies in Society and History* 42, no. 1: 149–79.

Maybury-Lewis, David. 2002. *Indigenous Peoples, Ethnic Groups, and the State*. Boston: Allyn and Bacon.

Prieto, Andrés I. 2010. "Reading the Book of Genesis in the New World: José de Acosta and Bernabé Cobo on the Origins of the American Population." *Hispanófila* 158: 1–19.

Ramos, Alcida Rita. 1998. *Indigenism: Ethnic Politics in Brazil*. Madison: University of Wisconsin Press.

Sioui, Georges E. 1992. *For an Amerindian Autohistory: An Essay on the Foundations of a Social Ethic*. Translated by Sheila Fischman. Montreal: McGill-Queen's University Press.

Sturm, Circe. 2002. *Blood Politics: Race, Culture, and Identity in the Cherokee Nation of Oklahoma*. Berkeley: University of California Press.

Urban, Greg, and Joel Sherzer. 1991. *Nation-States and Indians in Latin America.* Austin: University of Texas Press.

Wade, Peter. 2010. *Race and Ethnicity in Latin America.* London: Pluto Press.

Warren, Kay B. 1978. *The Symbolism of Subordination: Indian Identity in a Guatemalan Town.* Austin: University of Texas Press.

Warren, Kay B., and Jean E. Jackson, eds. 2002. *Indigenous Movements, Self-Representation, and the State in Latin America.* Austin: University of Texas Press.

Weber, David J. 2005. *Bárbaros: Spaniards and Their Savages in the Age of Enlightenment.* New Haven: Yale University Press.

*Hemispheric Indigeneities*

# 1

## First Contacts, First Nations

# The Early Colonial Origins of Indigeneity in and around the Basin of Mexico

SUSAN KELLOGG

While the concept of indigeneity has its roots in the colonial period, the large and growing literature on indigeneity rarely addresses that era.[1] When it does so, the viewpoint that Donna Lee Van Cott has expressed suggests how scholars of contemporary Native peoples see the colonial period. She writes: "Colonial systems [across Latin America] relegated Indians to the bottom of the social, economic, and political hierarchy through a web of tribute and labor responsibilities alongside 'protections' such as special legal status (often as minors), exemption from military service, and inalienable land rights" (1994, 4). Taking this perspective even further in discussion of Mexico in the same edited collection, Julio Tresierra asserts that "the indigenous movement was organized to resist the European invasion. The rejection of the invasion and the subsequent process of colonization, which degraded Indians and their culture, led the movement to extremes of collective immolation as an option that was considered preferable to the denial of liberty" (1994, 153). This picture of colonial indigenous populations as internally undifferentiated, hopelessly oppressed, even potentially self-immolating is fundamentally at odds, however, with the trends of scholarship on Mesoamerican colonial indigenous cultures focused on indigenous-language documents, especially those in Nahuatl, that began in the 1950s.

Scholarship attempting to trace the history of colonial Mesoamerican indigenous peoples and cultures through indigenous-language documents has its roots in the 1950s and 1960s in the work of Angel María Garibay and Miguel León-Portilla.[2] But the 1980s and especially early 1990s represent a transformative period historiographically due to the work of James Lockhart and his students. Lockhart published his landmark book, *The Nahuas after the Conquest*, in 1992. Even if Charles Gibson's seminal book, *The Aztecs under Spanish Rule*, made somewhat greater use of indigenous-language texts than is sometimes recognized, Lockhart's book represented a definitive break with Gibson's broad approach to "Indians" and the viewpoint interpreting the conquest as leading to chaos, exploitation, and disaster for Native peoples.[3] That view was also well represented in León-Portilla's classic, *The Broken Spears*, a book still read today.[4] *The Nahuas after the Conquest* represented not just a shift in naming, as *Aztecs* became *Nahuas*, it also challenged many assumptions about the so-called Aztecs and ushered in the use of new terminologies relating to the sociopolitical structures (e.g., the *altepetl* [kingdom]), forms of expression (e.g., annals), and definitions of identity (e.g., Nahuas) across the Basin of Mexico. It is hard, I think, to overstate just how important this scholarship, christened the New Philology, has been in enhancing historical knowledge about central Mexican Native peoples.[5]

This largely historiographical essay examines the idea of colonial indigeneity by looking at the changing use of key words: *Aztec* to *Nahua*, *tribe* to *ethnicity*, and *Indian* to *indigenous*. I first review the concepts Lockhart and others employ in their definitions and discussions of identity, focusing particularly on concepts of group self-identity and ethnicity.[6] I then examine the concept of indigeneity and ask, given that the roots of indigeneity indeed lie in the colonial period, what colonialists might contribute to a discussion of the origins of a broad conception of indigenous identity. I argue that those who fell into this identity category themselves recognized it and made use of the category to navigate an evolving plural social system that deeply influenced indigenous societies throughout the colonial period, even if the term *indio* appeared only in selected contexts. Colonial indigenous and mestizo (people of indigenous and Spanish descent) writers of late sixteenth- and early seventeenth-century central Mexico gave voice to a kind of discourse of *indigenismo* (indigenism) or what might be better termed *indianismo* (indianism). I delve into the writing of the most Spanish-identified of these writers, Diego Muñoz Camargo, himself a mestizo, to explore the emergence of sixteenth-century discourse of indianismo. This idea represented an ideology and defense of Indianness but never coalesced into a coherent political movement even as it underlay local strategies of defense of autonomy and land as I describe later in the essay.[7]

### From *Aztec* to *Nahua* and *Tribe* to *Ethnicity*

Whereas Charles Gibson asserted unequivocally the utility of the concept of "Aztec civilization" to describe the "Indians" of the Basin of Mexico, even as he noted it had "no very precise meaning" (1964, 1), Lockhart stated that he preferred the term *Nahuas*, "a name they sometimes use themselves and the one that has become current today in Mexico, in preference to Aztecs."[8] He rejected the use of *Aztecs* because "it implies a kind of quasi-national unity that did not exist, it directs attention to an ephemeral imperial agglomeration, is attached specifically to the preconquest, and by the standards of the time, its use for anyone other than the Mexicas (the inhabitants of the imperial capital, Tenochtitlan) would have been improper even if it had been the Mexica's primary designation, which it was not" (Lockhart 1992, 1). In Lockhart's writings, just as *Aztecs* became *Nahuas*, *tribes* became *ethnicities* and *Indians* became *indigenous*. These usages became ubiquitous as Lockhart and other ethnohistorians sought less negative, less value-laden terminologies to better understand the worldviews of Native peoples. This turn toward a much deeper engagement with the mentalities of Native peoples went hand in hand with an emphasis upon the use of indigenous-language sources in Nahuatl to examine the development of colonial society and culture across the Basin of Mexico and beyond.[9]

The rejection of the term *indio* was derived not only from the search for less pejorative terminology but was also grounded in the usages for self-identity found in Nahuatl documents themselves. In his seminal 1982 article "Views of Corporate Self and History in Valley of Mexico Towns," Lockhart observed about the texts he was analyzing from the Chalco area, examples of *títulos primordiales* (primordial titles), "Nowhere in the texts is any derivative of the Spanish word *indio* used, nor is anyone called by any other term that could be translated as 'Indian.'" He noted, too, that a community's self-identification was always based on "the name of the local ethnic-political entity" (1982, 383).[10] In *Nahuas after the Conquest*, Lockhart further emphasized the irrelevance of the word *indio*, arguing that "Spanish documents, and even Spanish translations of Nahuatl documents, make repeated use of the term Indian (*indio*), but rarely do we find it in Nahuatl documents, not even in the very ones whose translations use the word. The significant subject of the evolution of indigenous corporate self-definition must be worked out exclusively from Nahuatl-language sources" (1992, 8).[11]

Lockhart and the New Philologists generally place considerable emphasis on analyzing the internal workings of indigenous community and society. This was because their goal was to shift the emphasis away from "a community's relations with the outside" toward "viewing *individual* Indians as well as the community, and *internal* as well as external relations" (emphasis in original; Anderson, Berdan, and Lockhart 1976, 1). While acknowledging interactions among "Europeans, Africans, and Indians," Lockhart asserts that "almost nothing in the entire indigenous cultural ensemble was left untouched, yet at the same time almost everything went back in some form or other to a preconquest antecedent" (1992, 4–5).

Lockhart's writings, based on voluminous reading and translation of Nahuatl documents, vividly capture the pre-Hispanic roots of colonial Nahua sociopolitical organization, land tenure practices, spirituality, and cultural expressions. They furnish a highly detailed view of the inner workings of Nahua kingdoms across the Basin of Mexico. Spanish conquerors, priests, officials, institutions, germs, and practices are present, but it is Nahua institutions, communities, practices, and people that lie at the center of the analysis, described with a level of detail that any ethnographer would envy. Yet the granular nature of this painstaking analysis leaves Spanish influence operating in vague ways that imply a figurative kind of autonomy for Nahua communities, culture, and people, harking back at times to the idea of the closed corporate community.[12] In the transition from *Aztecs* to *Nahuas*, with local, community-based identities nestled within this broad linguistically defined identity, the dominant idea appears to be that no idea of a broader collectivity beyond either the localized group or the linguistic identity existed. Yet in both Nahuatl- and Spanish-language documentation produced by indigenous and mestizo writers, there is terminology that recognizes an emerging racially stratified society and that addresses the need at times to acknowledge a broader collectivity of indigenous people. I will return to the question of a collective indigenous self-identity as the last of four issues in relation to the concepts of self-identity that scholars of the colonial Basin of Mexico commonly use.

The first idea I want to explore is that if the usage of *Aztec* by Gibson and others is something of an abstraction, so too is the term *Nahua*. The word *Nahua* as an identifier of a linguistically based cultural category has many advantages, first and foremost because it reminds us of the language spoken by a large number of the inhabitants of the basin in 1519 when Europeans first arrived. Sahagún's informants, for example, referred to Nahuas as those who spoke the Nahuatl language ("iehoantin in naoatlatolli"; FC 1961, Bk. 10, 175). But the word *Aztec*, a term of cultural identity still used by archaeologists as well as by students and the general public, did not come out of nowhere. It was a term of self-identity evidently used by the Mexicas quite early in their history. The *Codex Aubin*, for example, tells us that it was the Azteca who emerged from Chicomoztoc (Place of Seven Caves) and settled in Aztlan (Place of the White Heron). As the Azteca left Aztlan, having been ordered by their deity Huitzilopochtli to search for new home, he gave them a new name, Mexica (1980, 12, 14). Thus, *Azteca* (or *Aztlaneca* as it appears in some sources) was a term of self-identity likely used by the Mexicas in their early years.[13]

So how did *Aztec* come to serve as the name for the broader linguistic and cultural grouping? While Robert Barlow in his 1945 essay "Some Remarks on the Term 'Aztec Empire'" asserts that the broader usage was an artifact of later, eighteenth-century colonial history offered up by Francisco Javier Clavijero and then popularized by William H. Prescott (1943), an examination of Clavijero's writings suggests that while he occasionally referred to *los aztecas*, he far more often used the word *mexicanos* to designate the Mexicas and used phrases such as "las otras naciones de Anáhuac" (the

other nations of Anáhuac) when referring more broadly to the
Nahuatl-speaking inhabitants of the Basin of Mexico.[14] It would
thus appear that it was Prescott who was largely responsible for
turning the Mexicas and related peoples into Aztecs, a usage that
then became popular, especially but not only in English-language
writings. Still, as Frances F. Berdan points out, Alexander von
Humboldt also used the term, and his writings were widely read
though did not—I would argue—have the same impact among
historians and a broader public that Prescott's did. (Berdan 2014,
xvii). Even while acknowledging the need for a general term, just
as *Aztec* suggests "a kind of quasi-national unity that did not exist"
(Lockhart 1992, 1), so perhaps does the generic term *Nahua* imply
a kind of cultural uniformity, like the word *Maya*, which under-
states variation among Nahuatl-speaking peoples past and present.[15] The terms *Aztec* and *Nahua*, both reflecting some indigenous
(or emic) usage, more predominantly give voice to an etic perspective.[16] That is, they are useful general terms that emerged primarily from the discourse of scholars to refer to peoples who speak
a common language or closely related languages and who had
similar, though far from identical, cultural practices and intense
political interactions in the late Postclassic period. Neither term
adequately conveys how these peoples thought about and named
their own identities in most political or social contexts. Ethnohistorians have, however, also argued that localized "ethnic" identities were central to the worldviews of Nahuatl-speaking peoples.
Lockhart, for example, defined the altepetl as an "*ethnic* kingdom"
in several places (1991a, 9; 1992, 14; 1993, 22; my emphasis), an idea
to which I will return.

Yet at the same time, while the treatment of the Nahua as a uni-
tary linguistic-cultural category and Nahuatl as the overwhelm-
ingly dominant language in the Basin of Mexico in 1519 downplays
the cultural variations among Nahuatl-speaking peoples past and
present, it has tended also to efface cultural and linguistic variations in and around the basin that existed in 1519 and exist even now.
This is the second issue. Not only, for example, were the Ñahñu (or
Otomí, another term for both a people and language) an important cultural minority with a lengthy history of their own, but other

languages and cultural patterns existed before and after the coming of Europeans.

The Ñahñu, speakers of an Otomanguean rather than Uto-Aztecan language (the family of languages to which Nahuatl belongs), themselves believed their origins lay in caves in the region of Xilotepec, northwest of the basin, so their origin story was not the same as that of the Nahuatl-speaking groups of the basin. They may, in fact, have been one of the first groups who migrated to the basin from Tollan after its fall. There they founded the kingdom of Xaltocan where, eventually, Tepanecas of Azcapotzalco conquered them. They were then ruled first by the Tepanecas, then by the Mexicas. Ñahñu also lived around Xilotepec and the Valley of Toluca. Eventually some left these areas for Michoacán; others were resettled by the Tlaxcaltecas along their western border with the Triple Alliance powers. Other linguistic and cultural groups to the north and west (to take just one nearby basin area), also speaking Otomanguean languages, including the Matlatzinca and Mazahua, could be found in and around the basin.[17] The main point here is that concentration on Nahuatl language and culture has overwhelmed some sense of the linguistic, cultural, and historical complexity of the population of the basin and its surrounding areas.

Point number three: Something else that gets downplayed is the tangled and complex nature of ethnicity, even among Nahuas. The entities Gibson called "tribes," some fourteen of them, constituted the peoples of the Basin of Mexico proper. The names he gave included the Olmeca, Xicalanca, Tolteca, Chichimeca, Teochichimeca, Otomí, Culhuaque, Cuitlahuaca, Mixquica, Xochimilca, Chalca, Tepaneca, Acolhuaque, and Mexica, with the first five having become "extinct, absorbed, or expelled" by 1519. The others "constituted the basic ethnic divisions at the time of the Spanish conquest" (Gibson 1964, 9). But the word *tribe* as Gibson used it is now recognized as "limiting and inaccurate" (Umberger 2008, 92), its usage highly problematic. Before touching upon the question of whether ethnicity is the word that best captures Postclassic Mesoamerican notions of higher-level self-identity beyond the community, especially for the region under discussion here, it should be recognized that a general transition away from the word *tribe* toward *ethnicity* or *ethnic*

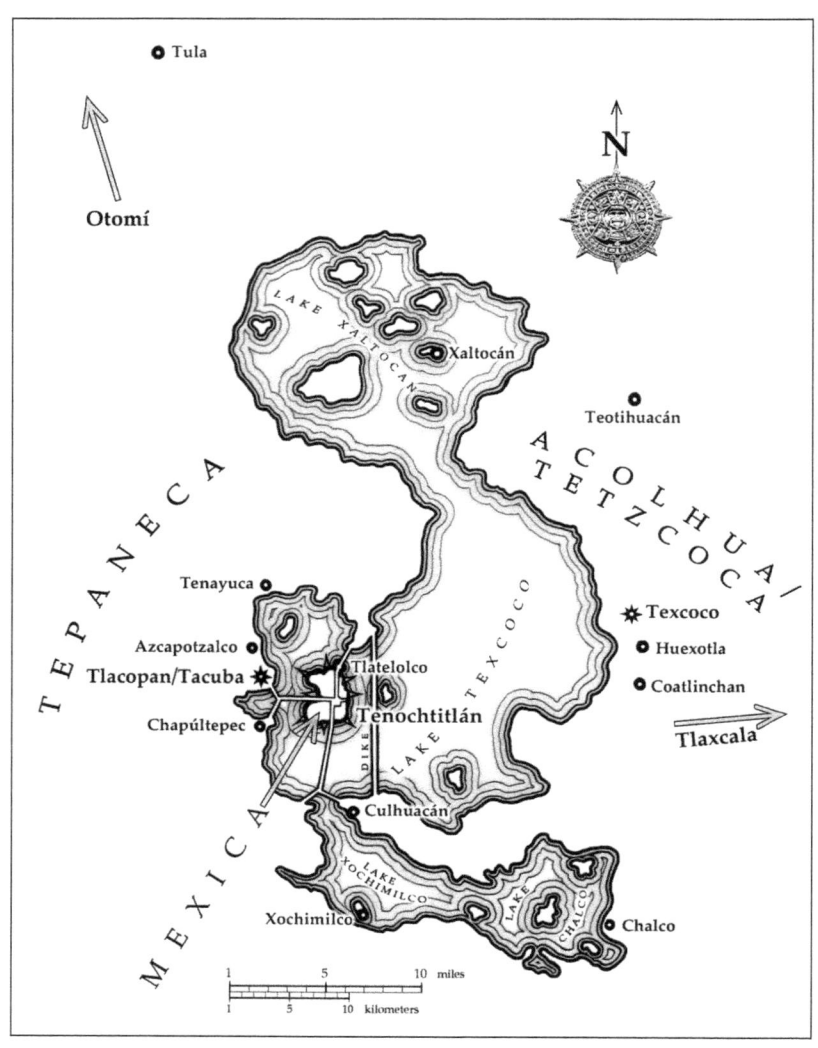

MAP 1. The Basin of Mexico and beyond. Cartography by Mark Van Stone.

*group* substituted, took place among anthropologists and ethnohistorians. Beginning in the 1970s these scholars rejected the "colonialist," "pejorative," and "atavistic" assumptions embedded in a word that came from the Latin, *tribus*, "meaning barbarians at the border of empire" (Cohen 1978, 384).

Using the terms *ethnicities* and *ethnic groups* is not, however, value- or assumption-free. In part this is because what ethnicity is and how it should be defined remains an unsettled matter among anthropologists and sociologists. They are divided by the issue of whether ethnic identities are primordial, rooted in ancient cultural differences that persist, or instrumental, that is, created in situations of resource competition or inequity (Barth 1969; Cohen 1978; Comaroff 1987; Stone 1996; Stephen 1996; Ward 2001; Stark and Chance 2008). Also, the word *ethnic* carries implications or associations of modernity and universality that a simple shift in terminology ignores (Cohen 1978, 384).

Specifically for the basin region of Mesoamerica, studies of the meanings of higher-level self-identity do not support the idea that ethnicity, however defined, whether as common heritage, as either self-described or as attributional (Stark and Chance 2008; Barth 1969; also see Comaroff 1987), or even as a combination of both (Brumfiel 1994) underlays large-scale group identities. Both Emily Umberger and Frances Berdan argue that, for Nahuas (by which they really mean Mexica) in defining identity, *place* was central. Membership in the polity, which most often was an altepetl but could also be a region, defined identity more so than did ethnicity, yet Umberger and Berdan both argue that the concept of ethnicity had some relevance (and this may be as precise as we can be) to group identities in the late Postclassic period (Umberger 2008, 70–73, 103; Berdan 2008, 130–32; also see Terraciano 2001, ch. 9; Olko 2012; Horn, 2014).

Most of the basin's *altepeme* (plural of altepetl) were multiethnic (Berdan 2008, 109, 116, 128, 131; also see Hodge 1984; Carrasco 1971, 366; Leibsohn 1994, 162). Altepeme were actually multiethnic in three ways. One, widely recognized, was that the lower-level altepeme units, the *calpolli* and *tlaxilacalli* might themselves be of differing origins. The second was that nobilities were themselves of mixed origins because of the practice of interdynastic hypogamy, wherein a high-level ruler gives a daughter to a subordinate ruler of the different altepetl, and interdynastic hypergamy, wherein a high ruler takes a daughter of a lower-ranking altepetl (Carrasco 1984, 45, 54). There is no particular reason to think that marriages across ethnic lines did not, on occasion, also occur among lower-ranked nobility as well as among commoners (Carrasco 1971, 367; also see Carrasco 1976a; Carrasco 1976b; Ward 2001, 422–30). Third, codices and chronicles suggest that the nobles and commoners of an altepetl were conceived of as descended from different heritage groupings, commoners from the Chichimeca and nobles from Tolteca *and* Chichimeca (Umberger 2008, 72). Thus, the idea of an altepetl as an ethnic state is at odds with the nature of the mixed groups that constituted the populations of these kingdoms.[18]

The kingdom or city-state should not be understood, therefore, to have been coterminous with ethnic identity. Identities rooted in *place* and those based upon *ethnicity*, or what could also be called heritage identity, derived from the particular tale of migration and noble class formation told by the various basin groups that existed in 1519, were not equivalent, yet both existed. For some individuals these were coterminous, but for many—nobles and commoners—they were not. The mixing of heritage-based identities within kingdoms constituted a purposeful action of statecraft within altepeme in which "different groups lived together in separate enclaves" (Umberger 2008, 72). Beyond the individual altepetl, that the "ethnically" mixed marriages of high rulers helped create a sort of pan-"ethnic" ruling group across the basin should also be recognized (Smith 2003, 60). This practice should be regarded, in part, as a political strategy that helped produce the shifting alliances in which late Postclassic dynasties involved themselves, shifting alliances that would ultimately prove key to European conquest and colonial governance.

Like other early preindustrial states, the kingdoms and confederations of the late pre-Hispanic Basin of Mexico were thus highly ethnically diverse. They constitute examples of *plural societies*. R. D. Grillo argues that preindustrial plural societies can be defined as "polities where there coexist people who with varying degrees of consciousness and with varying consequences believe they are 'different' from each other in their way of life, their language, their religion, their historic identity" (1998, 5). He observes that the Aztec empire existed as a loosely organized example of a plural society focused on extraction of tribute and the gathering of bodies for sacrifice but did not constitute a plural polity seeking to incorporate or establish cultural hegemony over or homogenization across its imperial domain. Conquest and colonialism would introduce a different kind of pluralism, colonial pluralism, into Mesoamerica, particularly among its basin societies where the impact was first felt. A new category of identity, indio, came into being as a colonial system of pluralism developed.

J. S. Furnivall, who wrote about colonialism in Southeast Asia (Burma and Java), first developed the idea of pluralism and saw it as based *in* colonialism. He maintained that colonialism gave rise to a new kind of heterogeneity in which groups "mix but do not combine. . . . . There is a plural society, with different sections of the community living side-by-side, but separately, within the same political unit. Even in the racial sphere there is a division of labor along racial lines" (1948, 304). For Furnivall, colonial plural societies were artificial conglomerations, held together by their segmented economies. The concept was then refined by M. G. Smith, who argued that in a culturally plural nation, different sectors of the population practice different forms of kinship and marriage, property ownership and labor, religion, and manifest distinct forms of political organization. "The culturally differentiated sections will differ in their internal organization, their institutional activities, and their system of beliefs and values," but for Smith, political and social domination by a powerful minority was essential for maintaining the plural system (Smith 1965, 14; Smith 1971; also see Grillo 1998, 6–8; Yannakakis 2008, 14–18; Colby and van den Berghe 1969, vii, 1–13). Colonial New Spain with its hierarchically organized *sistema de castas* (caste system), rooted in relations of domination and subjugation formalized as the ranking of and differing legal positions of ethnoracial groupings, can be described as an example of colonial pluralism in both Furnivall's and Smith's terms.

### From *Indio* to *Indigenous*

In this context, let us again consider the lack of use of the term *indio* in Nahuatl sources; this leads us to the fourth identity-related issue. Does this lack mean that indigenous people lacked a consciousness of what was both a legal and social status on the part of indigenous people? If Nahuas did not generally adopt the word *indio* to refer to themselves as individuals or any collectivity, how can we approach the question of whether any broad notion of a collective identity existed beyond the level of the local community? This question is especially important because, as Gibson and Lockhart argue, notions of identity linked to heritage traditions largely faded away. They lingered on in the writings of such colonial indigenous or mestizo writers as Chimalpahin, Alvarado Tezozómoc, and Alva Ixtlilxóchitl (Gibson 1964, 30–31) but otherwise became irrelevant to the organization of daily life, focused as it was on the altepeme or the local communities (*calpolli* or *tlaxilacalli*) that constituted them. For Lockhart, colonial indigenous group self-identity, largely reflecting a pre-Hispanic state of affairs, manifested itself in the altepeme as each "imagined itself a radically separate people" (1992, 15).[19]

Nahuas and others of the basin and beyond, however, could not avoid the reality of their legal and social position, even if in daily life, especially in more rural areas, Native language, culture, and officials mediated Spanish demands for labor, requirements to adhere to a new belief system, changes in land use, and new forms of goods and money. In the words of John Chance: "There is no reason to doubt that the indigenous peoples of colonial central Mexico and elsewhere in Mesoamerica knew that in the eyes of the Spanish they were indios and stigmatized as inferior beings" (2008, 139; also see Gruzinski 1988, 49).[20] The existence of colonial policies, oversight, and officials impinged upon crucial components of Native everyday life—labor, land, political organization, and worship—and thus must have been keenly felt in both urban and rural areas. One way we know that such impingements had an impact is through the immense body of legal documentation that evidences how New Spain's Native peoples, beginning in the Basin of Mexico, contested both officials' actions and colonial policies.

Spanish usage of the word *indio* flattened indigenous distinctions of class, place of origin, and heritage, so it makes some sense that Natives did not adopt a word that was so at odds with their own ways of defining social identities. Given that local traditions shaped how Native people responded, it stands to reason that only slowly did a consciousness develop, along with a terminology, to deal with the indigenous as a totality. However that transpired, we do know that such an awareness *did* evolve among indigenous leaders and indigenous and mestizo intellectuals. The argument can be made that some degree of consciousness of "indio" identity existed as early as the 1530s in central New Spain, where indigenous leaders, broadly speaking, enthusiastically embraced those aspects of Spanish law that allowed indigenous individuals and communities to defend themselves, their properties, and rights (Borah 1983, 40; Kellogg 1995, 9, 37; Ruiz Medrano 2010, 31; also see Owensby 2008; Yannakakis 2013).

This embrace helped produce a rich body of cases, detailed in codices as well as pages and pages of archived judicial records, in which Native litigants contested Spaniards as well as each other. The legal encounters influenced the complex webs of identity spun by the colonial indigenous: identity with the community, which was frequently though not always the entity that engaged with the colonial legal system, and identity with the broader legal and social status, "indio." This status, rooted in the concept of the two republics, especially that of the república de indios, carried legally defined rights and obligations used by individuals and communities to deal with the many civil, criminal, even religious issues that such communities or individuals pursued over the course of the colonial period (Hanke 1948; MacLachlan 1974; Borah 1983; Menegus Bornemann 1991; Kellogg 1995; Owensby 2008; Owensby 2011; Yannakakis 2008; Ruiz Medrano 2010; O'Hara 2010).[21]

If the starting point for legal action was generally the local community, knowledge about how to interact with a growing body of law pertaining to indios spread widely across the colonial Mesoamerican indigenous world, beginning in the Basin of Mexico. Spanish officials such as Viceroy Antonio de Mendoza fostered this development by ordering that royal edicts concerning Native practices be broadcast to Nahua pueblos (communities) and their Native inhabitants in their language to ensure they were understood (Sell and Kellogg 1997). The Spanish *procuradores* (legal practitioners) who made a living off of Indian litigation, no doubt encouraged it as well (Kellogg 1995, 14–21; Ruiz Medrano 2010, 48–61). But officials who played a leading role in bringing complaints and who, on occasion, testified against colonial officials during *residencias* (investigations carried out at the end of an official's time in office) and indigenous intermediaries who helped prepare documents were the people most responsible for the explosion in litigation. They communicated information about how to litigate within and beyond community borders. Indigenous nobles from across the Basin of Mexico complained, for example, about the *oidor* (judge) Lorenzo de Tejada, during the *residencia* conducted in the mid-1550s (Ruiz Medrano 2008, 3, 8–9).[22] Using the legal system became a learning experience about legal and social status, and information about the juridical status with its attendant rights and obligations spread far and wide. This observation does not mean that "indio" became the primary component of indigenous identity. Rather, it suggests awareness on the part of the indigenous that such a legal status existed in the minds and institutions of Spaniards and that the status could be mobilized when it proved useful for Native communities and individuals to do so.

Another kind of evidence suggests that a notion of collective status or identity slowly developed. We see it in the writings of indigenous and mestizo intellectuals who memorialized the heritage traditions and the histories of the particular altepetl about which they wrote, even as these became less relevant in the colonial world. In the sixteenth century, while Nahuatl documents rarely used terms that refer broadly to indigenous people, such terms did exist. For example, the phrase *nican titlaca*, meaning "we people here," is used for the broad collectivity of Native people, distinct from Spaniards, which could include both nobles, commoners, even non-Nahuas (Lockhart 1992, 115–16; Lockhart 1993, 13–14, 23). By the seventeenth century, however, as indigenous and mestizo chronicler-historians began to produce their own histories of altepeme and narrations of conquest, a colonial indigenous vocabulary of a broader self-identity emerged.[23]

These writers bore witness to the formation of New Spain's colonial plural society. For example, the word *timacehualtin*, "we macehualli," begins to show up. It appears in the writings of Chimalpahin, a Nahua commoner born in Amecameca Chalco who moved to Mexico City in 1594, where he served as the *fiscal* of a small church, San Antonio Abad (Schroeder 1991, 7–15). A brilliant, apparently self-taught man, perspicacious observer, and prolific and eloquent historian, he wrote histories that focused on Chalco, Tenochtitlán, Tlatelolco, Tetzcoco, and other nearby altepeme in the early seventeenth century. His Nahuatl-language histories focused on particular communities, but at times he mentioned the indigenous population broadly, using the words *titlaca* (we people) or *timacehualtin* (Lockhart 1992, 115–16; Schroeder 1994, 89). At one point, for example, he reflected at length on the complex nature of mestizaje, seeming to suggest there were three groups of human beings. He referred to "our bodies as divided into three kinds," presumably indigenous, Spanish or European, and African, yet focused on those who contributed to the creation of mestizos, those being Spaniards and "we local people" (Chimalpahin 1965, 2:22; Chimalpahin 1998, 228–31; Lockhart 1992, 384–85; Schroeder 1994, 86).

If Chimalpahin were the only indigenous chronicler to use such phraseology, we might conclude that his usage was idiosyncratic. But he was not alone. Tlaxcalteca chronicler Don Juan Buenaventura Zapata y Mendoza, who wrote in the mid-seventeenth century and like Chimalpahin in Nahuatl, also used the word *indio* (*itiotzin*, as he spelled it) some dozen times (Townsend 2010a, 162; for the text, see Reyes García and Martínez Baracs 1995, 36, 386, 458, 500, 520, 536, 554, 560, 600, 604). His preference for the word *indio* over *macehualli* likely relates to his continuing reliance on that latter term to mean *commoner*, so that only once did he expand the word *macehualli* to mean indigenous people broadly (Lockhart 1992, 509n99; Townsend 2010a, 163). As a general descriptor of an emerging identity, "neither the traditional word for 'commoner' nor the word for 'person of a certain altepetl' would do for him: he needed a more inclusive rubric" (Townsend 2010a, 164). Zapata y Mendoza used the term to express a sense of indigenous identity, in contrast to that of Spaniards, especially when he wanted to talk about both the Native nobles *and* commoners of the Tlaxcalteca altepetl; his occasional notes on conflicts between Spaniards and "Indians" imply an indigenous critique, even though his usage usually denoted "a social category, nothing more" (Townsend 2010a, 161–68).

Another Tlaxcalteca chronicler wrote in similar fashion: the mestizo Diego Muñoz Camargo. Born from the union of conquistador Diego Muñoz and an unknown indigenous woman around 1529, Muñoz Camargo married a Native noblewoman of Tlaxcala, Leonor Vázquez (Gibson 1950; Vázquez 1986). Through his marriage he gained access to status and property in the altepetl, participated in a number of business interests in cattle and salt especially, and held a number of important positions in the altepetl's governance. These positions included *teniente* (deputy), official interpreter (the position that saw him tapped to travel to Spain in 1584 to help Tlaxcalteca nobles lobby Felipe II for various privileges), and *procurador* (a low-level legal advocate). While serving in these positions he chronicled the history, geography, and culture of this complex altepetl from its beginnings through the period of the Tlaxcalteca alliance with Cortés and the Spaniards (Carrera Stampa 1945; Gibson 1950; Vázquez 1986; Reyes García 1998; Acuña 1981; Acuña 2000).

Tlaxcala's alcalde mayor, Alonso de Nava, commissioned Muñoz Camargo to prepare the *relación geográfica* (geographic report) for the altepetl. Both the preparation and subsequent history of the manuscript differentiate it from most of the other relaciones geográficas written in the late sixteenth century; that is, it was separated from the others (because it was hand-delivered to the king of Spain, unlike others) and because its organization and themes varied from most others (Acuña 2000, 20–23). This text was completed by 1585 and given to Felipe II. It stayed in Spain in the royal library until the latter part of the eighteenth century when it ended up first in the collection of a Scottish doctor, William Hunter, and then at the University of Glasgow, where it remains today under the title *Descripción de la ciudad y provincia de Tlaxcala* (Acuña 2000, 15–17).[24] The closely related text that carries the title *Historia de Tlaxcala* was based on the *Descripción*. The *Historia* actually consists of Muñoz Camargo's own draft of the *Descripción* (the king having received a copy), a draft on which he continued to work for much of the rest of his life (Acuña 2000, 19). In these texts Muñoz Camargo touches upon issues of identity: his own, that of the alte-petl of Tlaxcala, and that of the indigenous people he chronicles.

### A Spanish-Identified Mestizo's Discourse of Indianismo

Unlike Zapata y Mendoza, Muñoz Camargo felt no great sense of identity with the Tlaxcaltecas, quite the opposite actually. He pur-posefully styled himself an outsider to the ways of life and beliefs he chronicled. If Zapata y Mendoza's writing reflects the strongly held feelings and views of local patriotism of a colonial noble who participated in the governance of his community, holding the gov-ernorship and other offices (Townsend 2010a, 151–53), Muñoz Cam-argo's sense of personal identity lay in the opposite direction. Like many mestizo children of high-ranking Spanish fathers, he likely was illegitimate, raised by his father and Spanish stepmother, and therefore came to have a strong sense of identification with the Spanish. The Tlaxcalteca woman who bore him seems not to have been of high birth but had some kind of relationship with the elder Muñoz because, in addition to Diego, another son—Juan—was also born to that union (Gibson 1950, 199–200; Vázquez 1986, 11–12). Whenever or however this anonymous woman disappeared from Diego's life, he spent his childhood among Spaniards and received an excellent education.

Both his family life and education, so different from that of either Chimalpahin or Zapata y Mendoza, inclined Muñoz Camargo— despite his marriage—toward a Hispanic identification that is revealed in his texts, not so much by his discussion of his own life or ancestry but by the way he narrates disparate incidents from his childhood. These brief tales provide the reader with a glimpse into how he thought about himself. He recalled one occasion that took place when he was about six or seven years old in Mexico City, when he was running around with other boys, "sons of Spaniards," and one boy was grabbed by some young indigenous men, never to be seen again (Muñoz Camargo 2000, 274). He also wrote about how, at the age of ten or eleven, when Cabeza de Vaca and his surviving companions returned from their famous travels, Spanish officials entrusted him with teaching the more than thirty indios who had accompanied them Christian doctrine and prayers so they could be converted (2000, 128). He appears, as Germán Vázquez observes in his introduction to an edition of the *Historia*, "so integrated into Castilian culture that, in spite of his Indian blood, he was accepted into the highest levels of New Spain's government" (1986, 13). When he refers to Spaniards he often calls them "nuestros españoles" (our Spaniards) or "los nuestros" (ours; see 2000, 43, 75, 261), and on occasion refers to "nuestro modo" (our way) or "nuestras costumbres" (our customs; 2000, 47, 198), seeming to fully embrace his identification with the Spanish colonizers.

At the same time, he critiques indios as people and scorns a number of indigenous ways of being and doing. For example, he refers to some as "simple minded with little understanding . . . comparable to irrational animals . . . like a Spanish child of eight or ten years" (2000, 77). For Muñoz Camargo indigenous gods were demonic, indigenous religious belief was idolatrous; as people they were cowardly and cruel in their ways of making war, lacking reason and honor. He attacked even the Tlaxcalteca nobility as lazy and desirous of honors and status they did not deserve (2000, 176). Although these "indios" or "naturales" (terms he uses interchangeably) spoke languages that Muñoz Camargo acknowledged as complex, expressive, and, in the case of the Nahuatl spoken by the Mexicas, as of the purest and highest status (2000, 208), and although they had, he observes, a legal system that produced orderly societies (2000, 78), his indios were not the pre-Hispanic proto-Christians of another writer of mixed origins, Fernando Alva Ixtlilxóchitl.[25]

Even the Tlaxcalteca alliance with Spaniards during the conquest seemed suspicious to Muñoz Camargo. He viewed the alliance as undertaken by nobles not just to maintain their own status but to enable them to "die as fighting men" (2000, 176). Whereas Alva Ixtlilxóchitl tried to equate indigenous and European histories, cultural practices, and social organization, Muñoz Camargo did not, instead portraying Spaniards, their beliefs, and forms of government as clearly superior. Nonetheless, his understanding of Tlaxcala's political organization and the group identities and histories that constituted the indigenous sector of his profoundly bifurcated world—even as he acknowledged the multiracial society of the late sixteenth-century Basin of Mexico region—reflects indigenous ways of thinking about political organization, history, and group identities.[26]

It must first be observed that this *relación geográfica*, while written in Spanish, was filled with Nahuatl terminology, as its author carried out the task of describing to the colonizers Tlaxcala's geography, people, and ways of life. Place-name etymologies abound in the Nahuatl vocabulary he provides, as do names of peoples, titles for governing positions, and some vocabulary relating to deities and religious practices.[27] What is noticeable in Muñoz Camargo's discussions of places and peoples is the vocabulary he uses for political and social organization. This is not a tale of indigenous "cities" and "empires" like that told by Alva Ixtlilxóchitl. Instead Muñoz Camargo describes a region, a *provincia, señorio* or *reino* (province or kingdom), loosely organized into a confederation of four *cabeceras*, the "head towns" that Charles Gibson described at length (1964, 33–57, 188–94), each with its ruling house and subject communities.[28] Only rarely does Muñoz Camargo refer to Tlaxcala as a city (2000, 35–36). He refers often to the "province" of Tlaxcala structured around its ruling houses and provides histories of the rulerships of the four descent lines that governed the communities of the province. This description is strikingly close to the complex altepetl organization described by Lockhart and others, with each of the *cabeceras* constituting an altepetl (a word Muñoz Camargo does not use), structured around a *casa de mayorazgo*, (a lordly or noble house; 2000, 177), with the entire region or province constituting a complex altepetl.[29]

Along with his description of Tlaxcala's political organization, the author also describes the structure of leadership and peoples of the region, the Basin of Mexico, and beyond. In a passage on the structure of rulership, Muñoz Camargo writes that he "does not want to use the word 'cacique'" because "this is foreign language and not native, because it is from the islands of Cuba and Santo Domingo and Hispaniola, cacique, that is to say, *tecuhtli, piltlatoani*, that is 'principal lord and leader' of whichever rulership or state that he held." He defines the word *tlatoani* as "supreme lord," a leader whose orders are obeyed like those of an emperor or king (2000, 67). As much as he admired the Spanish language, "nuestra lengua castellana," (2000, 82), in this and other passages he rejects the imposition of terms that Spaniards brought with them from the Caribbean, preferring to use and explain the relevant Nahuatl vocabulary.

We also get a sense of the plural identity—the complex mix of community identity, heritage identities, and language groups—that made up the region of Tlaxcala, the basin, and its surrounding area as well as some of the history of these peoples before the arrival of Spaniards as he understood it. The main groups Muñoz Camargo speaks of are the Tlaxcaltecas, the Mexicanos Culhuaques, the Tepanecas, and Tetzcocanos (or Acolhuacanenses as he sometimes calls them). As in the *Florentine Codex*'s discussion of the peoples of this area, place, history, and language constitute meaningful ways of categorizing group identities in both the immediate and more distant past. In his descriptions of peoples and history, Muñoz Camargo appears to rely on diverse and conflicting indigenous oral historical traditions (vaguely mentioning songs and metaphors; see, for example, 2000, 117), not ones he has studied carefully like Fernando Alva Ixtlilxóchitl. Muñoz Camargo refers almost solely to the writings of Spaniards, mostly priests, as his sources of written information.[30] But he discusses a variety of indigenous historical traditions through which he describes the older stratum of basin population, especially the Otomis. Also mentioning what might be termed the Seven Caves tradition, Muñoz Camargo emphasizes the migration of the Chichimeca-descended groups as key to the history of the Tlaxcaltecas (with little mention of the Tolteca component of the region's groups and settlements). He also reports on the founding of Tenochtitlán (which he claims was founded by, as he calls them, Tecpanecas), with none of these traditions reconciled into any linear historical narrative (2000, 117–21). He complicates his historical assertions further with the idea, seemingly gleaned from Fray Diego Durán's writings though he does not mention Durán as a source, that indios derived, ultimately, from Hebrews, mentioning on occasion their Judaic practices (2000, 128–29, 196).[31]

Thus, like Zapata y Mendoza, Muñoz Camargo occasionally uses the word *indio* to describe the indigenous population of a community (2000, 58, 83, 85, 233), though never to describe *pre-Hispanic* indigenous peoples; workers assigned to labor through *repartimiento* (2000, 59, 87); or an indigenous collectivity broader than that of an altepetl's, pueblo's, or even region's population (2000, 77, 128–29, 196, 236, 274). Even for this most Spanish-identified of colonial mestizo writers, the term *indio* therefore did not serve as a way to think about or classify group identity as it existed in the pre-Hispanic era. Instead, the term proved convenient as a collective ethnoracial descriptor in the new colonial plural society. Its usage signaled his recognition of the indigenous component of a basin population in which new peoples had settled, changing the nature of basin's demography. Muñoz Camargo's terminology also signaled his awareness of the bifurcated nature of daily life and governance in the still very indigenous altepetl of Tlaxcala.[32] Does his terminology constitute a kind of colonial indigenismo or indianismo as I referred to it earlier in this essay?

Let me make clear that this was not an indigenismo of purposeful political actions that reflected strategizing at higher levels of political organization such as the national and international levels described in Lynn Stephen's chapter in this volume. I argue rather that this emerging indianismo articulated the recognition of a broad, legally defined identity and recorded indigenous agency at the community level (altepetl, pueblo, even sometimes barrio, urban, or rural) to create the space for local autonomy wherever possible. The broader legal and more localized cultural identities were thus closely connected, inseparable even, as colonial society with its plural components took shape.[33]

Several elements of this colonial indianismo can be identified in the writings of such indigenous and mestizo authors as Chimalpahin, Juan Bautista Pomar, Hernando Alvarado Tezozómoc, and Alva Ixtlilxóchitl. Here I examine these elements in Muñoz Camargo's writing. First, he recognizes an indigenous identity that spans diverse Native groups in varying regions, speaking diverse languages, and with diverse living arrangements and belief systems. Second, he offers criticism of Spanish actions during or after the conquest of Tenochtitlán, a veiled criticism to be sure, but fault-finding nonetheless that reflects a kind of critical perspective from an indigenous point of view about the conquest. Third, Muñoz Camargo portrays agency as action at the local level, not only in showing that a particular group was an essential ally in the Spanish but also that the same group embraced Christianity early and voluntarily.

As noted above, Muñoz Camargo recognized the idea of an "indio" identity, several times using the term in both the *Descripción* and *Historia* to refer to a broad collectivity of Native peoples. What about the theme of critique? Because Muñoz Camargo's assessment of indigenous (i.e., Tlaxcalteca) culture as well as colonial indigenous leadership could perhaps best be described as savage indictment of both, can an element of critique be found in this writer's effusively celebratory stance on the conquest?[34]

Three criticisms of the conquest surface in Muñoz Camargo's account. For one thing, he points out that the arrival of Spaniards led to wars, property destruction, and a loss of social order (2000, 39, 75–76, 77–78). In a passage reminiscent of Fray Toribio de Benavente Motolinía's discussion of the plagues, real and metaphorical, that the Spaniards brought to the indigenous population (1971, 21–31), Muñoz Camargo discusses the negative impact of disease, detailing what he sees as the causes of depopulation: wars and migration, the spread of disease (especially measles, which he says was brought by a slave or servant of Pánfilo de Narváez), and the taking of Indian slaves to gold mines, which meant an unhealthy traversing of different climates and new lands (2000, 75–76). He further observes that the Spaniards' severe punishment of Indians who lacked judgment or wisdom also led to increased mortality (2000, 77–78). Such demographic and social dislocations led to the disordering of Tlaxcalteca society; he describes its social order turned upside down (quoting a lamentation, he refers to "las cosas del mundo revueltas"), with those of "low birth" serving in Tlaxcala's government while nobles were becoming poor (2000, 98). Second, he mourns the destruction of books, pictures, and chronicles, that is, the historical records of the altepetl, as Christian zeal led to burning or other kinds of destruction of evidence of idolatry. Such records also contained information, especially about Native origins, that to his frustration was lost (2000, 98, 112–13).

And, third, on the subject of idolatry, as devout a Christian as Muñoz Camargo portrayed himself to be, he traced the conversion process as it unfolded in Tlaxcala and portrayed the difficulties the first friars encountered in the region. In the passages on the conversion of the rulers by Cortés in 1519, Muñoz Camargo reveals the difficult path toward understanding the idea of one supreme deity and the growing comprehension of the notion that the old gods could no longer be worshiped (2000, 249–52). He recognizes that this process had actually gone slowly in fits and starts and that neither the local populace nor their leaders knew what to make of the early friars, seeing them as poor miserable creatures, perhaps even as crazy (2000, 211). He describes leaders telling the common people to allow these strange men to voice their ideas so that perhaps their craziness or illness would pass. He points out, too, that at times of popular celebration, the friars would yell and cry, these "men without sense who instead of seeking out pleasure looked only for sadness" (2000, 211). If not directly critical of the military conquest and spiritual project of conversion in his own harshly negative assessment of Native people, Muñoz Camargo pointed out some of the negative consequences of conquest and colonization. The *Descripción* shows that the evangelization project—even in Tlaxcala, an early center for missionizing—went slowly and faced real difficulties, with the church's early representatives seen as incomprehensible, ridiculous, even pitiful figures.

Yet Muñoz Camargo also highlights how Cortés and his band of invaders relied upon the Tlaxcaltecas as their most essential allies. He portrays the Tlaxcaltecas as initiating the alliance through both kinship and conversion. When Cortés and his men reached Tlaxcala in August of 1519, the Tlaxcalteca rulers—in Muñoz Camargo's version—immediately provided gifts of precious jewels, textiles, and food as well as three hundred women to serve Cortés as servants. Seeing that the Spaniards took to the women, the rulers soon gave their own daughters in the hopes that any children born of relationships between Spaniards and these women would create ties of consanguinity (2000, 242–43). The leaders and Cortés then give a series of orations in which Cortés, according to Muñoz Camargo, demanded that the Tlaxcaltecas abandon their false gods and declare themselves to be Christians (2000, 245–46).[35] The leaders responded by agreeing to be baptized, with the alliance proceeding, in this version, based upon Tlaxcalteca agency.

What the text omits, as observed by literary scholar Salvador Velazco, is the role military conflict between the Spanish and the Tlaxcaltecas played in the formation of this alliance. Sixteenth- and seventeenth-century accounts by Cortés, Díaz del Castillo, López de Gómara, Andrés de Tapia, as well as that of Alva Ixtlilxóchitl— who consulted the lost indigenous account about Tlaxcala of Tadeo de Niza de Santa María—all describe a conflict provoked by the Tlaxcaltecas (Cortés 1993, 175–78; Díaz del Castillo 1982, 119–28; López de Gómara 1986, 123–29; de Tapia in Vázquez 1988, 87–91; Alva Ixtlilxóchitl 1975, 2:208–9). As the Spaniards neared the alte-petl, the Tlaxcaltecas engaged them in battle, with fierce fighting occurring on several days in late August and early September of 1519. In each battle the Tlaxcaltecas withdrew and, according to the Spanish accounts, decided—especially after witnessing the fierce treatment Spaniards meted out to Otomí allies of the Tlaxcalte-cas—to engage in peace talks with Cortés. This Tlaxcalteca attack is completely elided in Muñoz Camargo's account, with a voluntary early conversion taking the place of conquest to explain the alli-ance between the Tlaxcaltecas and Spanish (Velazco 2003, 163–68).

Arguing that this scene of orations that accompanied the bap-tism of the four Tlaxcalteca tlatoani never occurred, Velazco notes that in substituting an image of Tlaxcala as a "converted republic" for a "conquered republic" (2003, 179), Muñoz Camargo gave voice to the interests of the nobles and leaders of the altepetl, articulating their desire to maintain status and privileges in words that bear a similarity to those of the *relaciones de méritos y servicios* (reports of merits and services) that both Spaniards and Natives used to seek rewards, promotions, and privileges (Velazco 2003, 194; also see MacLeod 1998; Adorno 1989; Restall 2003, 11–13; Restall and Fernández-Armesto 2012, 8–15).

Aside from promoting what were at base the material interests of the Tlaxcalteca nobility, of which his own wife was a member, these ideas about the Tlaxcaltecas as willing Christian converts and partners of Cortés in the conquest express a notion of auton-omy that is similar to the claims of local autonomy made in both lawsuits as well as many *títulos primordiales*. Stephanie Wood says about the títulos and codices that she has analyzed that they often convey "essentially indigenous concerns of territoriality and community autonomy" (2003, 145). But claims of property rights and autonomous community self-governance, as Charles Gibson argued long ago, required assertions of a history of autonomy and freedom from coercion and exploitation: "The legal advantage for Indians . . . lay in a pretense of more communality in pueblo form than was in fact the case" (1964, 299). Thus the ability to assert local agency and autonomy, whether in títulos or in a Spanish-language text like that of Muñoz Camargo's *Descripción*, was inextricably linked to an *Indian* legal identity that allowed for the contestation of claims in courts that indigenous people had little control over but in which their legal rights as indios provided the basis for their claims.[36] These notions of autonomy constituted powerful legal fictions, but they were fictions nonetheless.

The indianismo of a writer like Diego Muñoz Camargo expressed both concepts of a collective Indian identity, legal and cultural, as well as localized forms of community identity, agency, and rights, especially but not only the status and privileges of Native nobles as well as community access to land and labor. Even Tlaxcalteca commoners relied upon their legal rights as indios when they pushed for the expulsion of Muñoz Camargo and other mestizos residing in the altepetl in 1587 or 1588, based upon unspecified abuses by Muñoz Camargo and the Tlaxcalteca leaders with whom he was allied (Archivo General de la Nación, Indios, Leg. 5, no. 574, 228v–29r [1589]).[37]

## Conclusion

Despite Muñoz Camargo's efforts to identify with the Spanish cultural heritage of his father, his writings—especially the *Descripción*—manifest significant amounts of indigenous cultural influence. This essay contends that the heterogeneity of themes and language in Diego Muñoz Camargo's writing marks it as a mestizo rather than a Hispanic or Creole chronicle, as some have argued.[38] More important for the argument about colonial plural identities made here is the idea that group identities were plural and flexible in both the pre-Hispanic and colonial periods, and Muñoz Camargo's writings, particularly the *Descripción*, provide evidence of these plural and flexible identities as they evolved in the sixteenth century. The focus on the local as constituting the primary and essential identity that survived into the colonial period and beyond in the historiography ignores the existence of multiple and malleable identities beyond the local before and after the arrival of Spaniards. The content and uses of identity categories certainly shifted. There is no doubt that the pejorative legal category and social identifier "indio" never became the sole or even predominant category through which Nahua peoples in and around the Basin of Mexico identified themselves (see Susan Ramírez's chapter in this volume for a similar argument about Andean indigenous identities).

But the complex of ideas apparent in Diego Muñoz Camargo's writings, what I have called indianismo, with its recognition of a collective indigenous identity (one recognized by such other chroniclers as Chimalpahin and Zapata y Mendoza), represents what has been designated an ethnography of cultural hybridization (Adorno 1994, 401). Muñoz Camargo's discourse captured a changing world in which ethnoracial identities were emerging and in which the formation of the two republics undergirded a highly unequal colonial world in which Native communities could only exercise limited kinds of agency and autonomy. While always realized more in the legal realm than in lived experience, the notion of two republics supported the formation of a concept of indianismo rooted in the contrasting identities and sets of rights implicit in Spanish and indigenous identities. However acculturated Muñoz Camargo's own sense of identity and historical consciousness was, his writings describe a moment of identity recollection and formation in which older forms of collective identity beyond the level of the community were fading and the new identity, indio, was developing profound legal, political, and cultural consequences.

If today's Nahuas recognize themselves as such (or as mexicaj or mexicanos, other terms some use for this broader identity), they continue to identify with their local communities. But they also recognize a kind of connection—especially around ritual practices—with other indigenous groups and a difference between themselves and local mestizo communities and peoples as well as a profound social distance from the national Mexican culture (Sandstrom 2000; Sandstrom 2008; Good 2000; see also Friedlander 1975; Cortés Ruiz 1989; Dehouve 1994; Dehouve 1995; and Schryer 1990). Acting locally was and perhaps still is connected to indigenous collective thinking, even if the names and definitions of community and ethnic identities change over time in the Basin of Mexico, indeed in Mesoamerica as a whole.

## Notes

1. In addition to major works on indigenism in Latin American that include Stavenhagen 1988; Stavenhagen and Ituralde 1990; Perry 1996; Brysk 2000; Maybury-Lewis 2002; Niezen 2003; Langer 2003; and Jackson and Warren 2005, the concept of indigeneity in the Americas receives greater attention in several recent collections, especially Mallon 2011; Castellanos et al. 2012; and Graham and Penny 2014. For Mexico, see Taylor 2009; for ethnographic approaches see Metz 2006 and Canessa 2012. Several authors observe that contemporary trends in usages of *indigenous* and *indigeneity*, even as they capture current political ideas and movements globally among indigenous peoples, also flatten ethnic and gender distinctions. Stephen 2005 (see especially chapters 3, 5, 8–10); Speed, Hernández Castillo, and Stephen 2006; and Graham 2014 all make this point. Perrone-Mosés 2014 explores some of the colonial contradictions of ethnicity and indigeneity.

2. Garibay and León-Portilla began the shift away from the use of *Aztec* toward *Nahua*, but, especially in their early works, they still drew a distinction between Nahuatl-language texts and speakers and "Aztec culture," defined widely (in and around the basin, in works like Garibay K. 1953, 32) or narrowly (Mexica-focused, as in León-Portilla 1956, 1–2). León-Portilla argued, however, that the language was closely tied to the culture and philosophy (worldview) of the Nahuas (1956, 2–4).

3. For Lockhart's insightful analyses of Gibson's writings see 1991b; 1992, 3, 6, 449.

4. See the interchange between Schwaller (2009) and León-Portilla (2009) on the meaning of the phrase *broken spears*.

5. See Restall 2003 for an overview of the New Philology. Lockhart appears to have first used the term in his essay "Charles Gibson and the Ethnohistory of Postconquest Central Mexico" (1991b, 78). He later defined it as "center[ing] on indigenous-language texts, though including any other likely source of information as well, and combines career pattern research where possible with a philology not unlike that of the classicists" (1999, 366).

6. By *self-identity*, I refer to the broad kind of concept rooted in self-image as discussed by J. H. Elliott in his introductory essay to Canny and Pagden (1987) on identity formation in the Atlantic world and in Pagden's essay in the same volume on the formation of identity in Spanish America. Both Elliott and Pagden reference colonial elite identity formation, but in the same volume Stuart Schwartz, while concentrating on how Portuguese colonists began to have a sense of incipient Brazilian identity,

speculates that there is, for colonial Brazilians of color, "an unwritten history of colonial identity that at present cannot be reconstructed. It is one no less valid than that we have traced" (1987, 50). For a clear and insightful overview of the issues faced by Latin American historians dealing with the themes of individual and group identity, see Fisher and O'Hara 2009.

7. Literary scholars use the terms *indianismo* and *indigenismo*, the former to refer to "romantic-inflected" nineteenth-century texts that "portrayed the indio in a sentimental light and was noticeably silent regarding the indigenous population's social, economic, and political marginalization," especially in Mexico, Guatemala, and Andean countries. Indigenismo, on the other hand, "takes a critical position with respect to the dominant society and accuses it of exploiting and debasing indigenous people and their cultures" (Coronado 2009, 7). Also on indianismo, see Queiroz 1962 and Cornejo Polar 1980. Both terms can also be used to refer to twentieth- and twenty-first-century political movements of indigenous peoples (see chapters by Stephen and Ari-Chachaki, this volume). Two other sets of related terms appear in this essay, *mestizo/mestizaje* and *nation/national*, that I cannot fully interrogate, given my focus on *Aztec/Nahua*, *tribe/ethnicity* and *Indian/indigenous*. The terms *mestizo* and *mestizaje* can carry biological and cultural meanings. As peoples, languages, and cultures came into contact with each other, not only did Mesoamericans and Spaniards experience new economic and political realities and develop new social and cultural, especially religious, patterns, but artists and writers of indigenous, Spanish, and mixed heritages represented these new realities and patterns in visual and written texts. Memory and identity—communal and individual—come into play in such texts as I explore later in this chapter through writings by one particular mestizo writer. The other set of terms that appear in places is *nation* and *national*. In some cases, especially Lockhart's usage of "quasi-national" on p. 29 and Dueñas's use of "Indian nation" in note 23 herein, a supra-ethnic indigenous identity is implied; in other cases the usage refers to the modern nation-state, often culturally plural. A number of these terms are insightfully discussed in Wickstrom and Young 2014.

8. Gibson 1964 as well as Keen 1971 used the term *Aztec* very broadly (covering the valley or Basin of Mexico) as did Moreno 1971 and Caso 1982. More recently, Michael E. Smith (1996; 2008) has defined it as including an even larger area, to include "valleys east, south, and west," beyond the Basin of Mexico (2008, 15). Others have carefully limited its use, generally referring to the Mexicas or explaining why and when they use it more broadly to refer to those of the Triple Alliance confederation, or the Nahuatl-speaking peoples in the basin region (see, for example, Wolf 1959; Soustelle 1961; Davies 1973; Berdan 1982).

9. In addition to citations in Restall 2003 for relevant English-language literature, see Martínez 1984; García Martínez 1987; C. Reyes García 2000; Fernández Christlieb and García Zambrano 2006; and Navarrete Linares 2011.

10. Works on títulos, beyond Wood 2003, include Wood 1991; Gibson 1964; Lockhart 1991; Haskett 1992; Gruzinski 1993; Florescano 1994; Oudijk and Romero Frizzi 2003; López Caballero 2003.

11. Also see Lockhart, 1991a, 9; Lockhart, 1993, 13. Other work that articulates this point of view includes Haskett 1992; Wood 1991; Wood 2003; and Chance 2008.

12. See Wolf 1957 and 1959 for the earliest articulations of this concept. Lockhart's idea of "Double Mistaken Identity," defined as the way in which "each side takes it that a given form or concept is essentially one already known to it, operating in much the same manner as in its own tradition, and hardly takes cognizance of the other side's interpretation" (1992, 445) represents another way of describing indigenous autonomy.

13. Other sources that narrate these events, sometimes using the name Aztlaneca, include the *Codex Azcatitlan*, the *Códice Boturini*, the *Historia de los mexicanos por sus pinturas*, the *Anales de Quauhtitlan*, the *Crónica mexicayotl*, the *Mapa Sigüenza*, as well as chronicles by Alva Ixtlilxóchitl and Torquemada. For discussions of these sources see Barlow 1945 and Boone 2000, chs. 7 and 8.

14. For examples of his use of *Azteca*, see Clavijero 1945, 1:173, 218, 220; for a reference to Anáhuac, see 1945, 4:276. He also used the word *mexicano* (and *perulero*) to refer broadly to the indigenous population of New Spain (and Peru); see 1945, IV: 275.

15. This is not to say that no variation is recognized. Lockhart wrote about an east-west divide in relation to the naming and structure of lordly houses (the *teccalli* or *tecpan*, "lord's location" or, by extension, "lord's house," 1992, 102–9, 506n60). Also see Pizzigoni 2007 on regions and subregions of Nahua culture and language in the Toluca Valley area. Archaeologists also have written about the variations in size (geographic and demographic) of Nahua kingdoms as well as their variations in political structure, religious practice, and the self-defined identities of those who constituted these altepeme (Hodge 1984; Hodge and Smith 1994; Smith 2008). On variation among contemporary Nahua groups, see Good 2000 and Sandstrom 2000.

16. Emic usages or perspectives are those that come out of the language and cultural perspective of people or groups; etic usages are those that emerge from observers (see Harris 1976 for definitions and discussion). Also see Luis Granados, this volume, on imposed terminologies in Mesoamerica.

17. On the Ñahñu, see Soustelle 1937; Carrasco 1950; Manrique 1967; and Lastra 2006. On the Matlatzinca, see Quezada 1972 and García Castro 1999. For the Mazahua (Jñatjo), see Iwanska 1971; Sandoval Forero 1997; and Sánchez Blas 2007. Both Davies (1980, 74–79) and M. E. Smith (1984, 155–66, 175–76) have discussed the connections among migration, group identity, and variable languages early in the Postclassic in the basin area.

18. It should be noted, however, that Lockhart himself recognized that even small altepeme were themselves confederations of distinct and competing ethnic groups (1992, 27). Also on Nahuas and ethnicity, see Horn 1997, 19–23, 30–33, 42–43, and note that Schroeder (1994, 82) and Horn (1997, 19) follow the idea of the altepetl as an ethnic polity; others, Haskett for example, use a definition that does not tie the altepetl to ethnicity. He calls the altepetl a "regional state" (1991, 3); also see García Martínez 1998 and Florescano 2009.

19. Also on colonial Nahua senses of group identity, see Wood 2003, especially ch. 1.

20. On early images and uses of the term *indio* in early New Spain, see Vázquez 1991; Rozat 2002; Ramírez Zavala 2011, especially 1643–46.

21. On the república de indios especially, see Borah 1983, 29–54; Menegus Bornemann 1991, chs. 5–7; Yannakakis 2008, 14–18; O'Hara 2010, 31–39.

22. On the role of indigenous intermediaries in colonial Oaxaca, see Yannakakis 2008.

23. Dueñas discusses the political implications of the Andean notion of an "Indian nation" in seventeenth- and eighteenth-century colonial Peru (2010: 197–201, 225–26).

24. It is this text, in both its facsimile and transcribed editions, on which I focus in this essay.

25. On Fernando Alva Ixtlilxóchitl's life and writings, see Brian 2014; Townsend 2014; Brokaw and Lee 2016.

26. Fully aware of the different types of people populating his world, Muñoz Camargo refers at one point, to people in Tlaxcala's marketplace as "Spaniards[,] . . . Indians, mestizos, negros and mulatos" (2000, 46).

27. On Muñoz Camargo's emphasis on Nahuatl as the source of names for New World phenomena as well as the language constituting an expressive system he admired, see Miller 2008.

28. There has been much debate over how many noble houses constituted the complex altepetl of Tlaxcala, with Muñoz Camargo himself providing different numbers ranging from two to four (2000, 35–38, 165), combined with disagreement over whether the four noble houses identified first by Motolinía represented the pre-Hispanic political structure of the region or constituted an artifact of colonial rule (1971, 246–47; also see Baber 2005, 28–31 for an excellent summary of this debate).

29. On the structures of complex altepetl, see Lockhart 1991; Lockhart 1992, 20–28; Schroeder 1991, 42–44; Horn 1997, 30–31, 43; and Pizzigoni 2012, 6–7.

30. The Spanish writers mentioned include Olmos, Sahagún, Mendieta, Motolinía, Díaz del Castillo, Francisco de Terrazas, and López de Gómara. For Native sources, in addition to the songs and metaphors, he mentions Tlaxcalteca poet Tequanitzin Chichimecatl Tecuhtli, and he was familiar with the *Lienzo de Tlaxcala* (Carrera Stampa 1945, 105–6; Vázquez 1986, 28–36; Verlinden 1994, chs. 3 and 4; and Kranz 2010, 53–54).

31. See Velazco on whether he might have read Durán (2003, 145).

32. Velazco refers to the "bipolarity that informs his discourse" (2003, 154).

33. My argument about a discourse of indianism is similar to, yet broader than, discussions of the idea of *tlaxcaltequidad*, a "unique ethnopolitical identity . . . a self-understanding rooted in the idea that Tlaxcalans, as willing Christians and participants in the Spanish conquest, were not defeated subordinates in Catholic New Spain but its victorious architects" (Villela 2012, 4; also see Cuadrillo 2004 for the development of the idea of *tlaxcaltequidad*). For colonial discourses about Tlaxcala's governance, see Lockhart, Berdan, and Anderson 1986; Haskett 2008, Martínez Baracs 2008; Townsend 2010b; Baber 2005, 2010; Kranz 2010; Krug and Townsend 2011; and McEnroe 2012.

34. In this he differs considerably in both the tone and substance from other writers, especially Chimalpahin and Alva Ixtlilxóchitl, who celebrate many aspects of indigenous ways of life and whose criticisms of Spaniards, while veiled, seem more apparent. For the usage in the *Historia* see 1972, 178, 180, 223–24, 249, 255, 265, 272–73.

35. See Velazco 2003, 166.

36. Also see McNab's essays, this volume, on the importance of court claims for establishing both rights and identities in a very different cultural context.

37. For the royal *cédula* the commoners succeeded in obtaining, its text along with

relevant discussion of this order of expulsion (probably never carried out), see Mörner and Gibson 1962, with the text of the order for the expulsion of Diego Muñoz Camargo, on 567–68.

38. This issue has been a subject of debate among literary scholars. Mignolo 1982, 1987; Vázquez 1986; and Florescano 1999, 262–65 emphasize the influence of Spanish sources and forms of writing history on Muñoz Camargo's writings. Adorno 1994; Verlinden 1994; Velazco 2003, ch. 2; and Miller 2008 emphasize the heterogeneity and hybridity of those same writings. Also see Lienhard 1983 on the general nature of *crónica mestiza*.

## Bibliography

Acuña, René. 1981. "Estudio preliminar." In *Descripción de la ciudad y provincia de Tlaxcala de las Indias y del Mar Océano para el buen gobierno y ennoblecimiento dellas, by* Diego Muñoz Camargo and René Acuña, 9–47. Facsimile edition. Mexico City: UNAM.

———. 2000. "Estudio preliminar." In *Descripción de la ciudad y provincia de Tlaxcala de las Indias y del Mar Océano para el buen gobierno y ennoblecimiento dellas*, by Diego Muñoz Camargo and René Acuña. San Luis Potosí: El Colegio de San Luis, Gobierno del Estado de Tlaxcala.

Adorno, Rolena. 1989. "The Warrior and the War Community: Constructions of the Civil Order in Mexican Conquest History." *Dispositio* 14: 225–46.

———. 1994. "The Indigenous Ethnographer: The 'Indio Ladino' as Historian and Cultural Mediation." In *Implicit Understandings: Observing, Reporting, and Reflecting on the Encounters between Europeans and Other Peoples in the Early Modern Era*, edited by Stuart B. Schwartz, 378–402. Cambridge: Cambridge University Press.

Alva Ixtlilxóchitl, Fernando de. 1975. *Obras historicas*, edited by Edmundo O'Gorman. 2 vols. Mexico City: UNAM.

Anderson, Arthur J. O., Frances Berdan, and James Lockhart, trans. and eds. 1976. *Beyond the Codices*. Berkeley: University of California Press.

Archivo General de la Nación, Indios, Leg. 5, no. 574 (1589).

Baber, Jovita. 2005. "The Construction of Empire: Politics, Law and Community in Tlaxcala, New Spain, 1521–1640." 2 vols. PhD diss., University of Chicago.

———. 2010. "Empire, Indians, and the Negotiation for the Status of City in Tlaxcala, 1521–1550." In *Negotiation within Domination: New Spain's Indian Pueblos Confront the Spanish State*, edited by Ethelia Ruiz Medrano and Susan Kellogg, 19–44. Boulder: University Press of Colorado.

Barlow, Robert H. 1945. "Some Remarks on the Term 'Aztec Empire.'" *The Americas* 1: 345–49.

Barth, Fredrick. 1969. Introduction. In *Ethnic Groups and Boundaries: The Social Organization of Cultural Difference*, edited by Fredrik Barth, 9–38. Boston: Little, Brown.

Berdan, Frances. 1982. *The Aztecs of Central Mexico: An Imperial Society*. New York: Holt, Rinehart and Winston.

———. 2008. "Concepts of Ethnicity and Class in Aztec-Period Mexico." In *Ethnic Identity in Nahua Mesoamerica: The View from Archaeology, Art History, Ethno-*

*history, and Contemporary Ethnography*, edited by Frances F. Berdan, John K. Chance, Alan R. Sandstrom, Barbara Stark, James Taggart, and Emily Umberger, 105–32. Salt Lake City: University of Utah Press.

———. 2014. *Aztec Archaeology and Ethnohistory*. New York: Cambridge University Press.

Boone, Elizabeth Hill. 2000. *Stories in Red and Black: Pictorial Histories of the Aztecs and Mixtecs*. Austin: University of Texas Press.

Borah, Woodrow. 1983. *Justice by Insurance: The General Indian Court of Colonial Mexico and the Legal Aides of the Half-Real*. Berkeley: University of California Press.

Brian, Amber. 2014. "The Original Alva Ixtlilxochitl Manuscripts at Cambridge University." *Colonial Latin American Review* 23: 85–93.

Brokaw, Galen and Jongsoo Lee, eds. 2015. *Fernando de Alva Ixtlilxochitl and His Legacy*. Tucson: University of Arizona Press.

Brumfiel, Elizabeth M. 1994. "Ethnic Groups and Political Development in Ancient Mexico." In *Factional Competition and Political Development in the New World*, edited by Elizabeth M. Brumfiel and John W. Fox, 3–13. Cambridge: Cambridge University Press.

Brysk, Allison. 2000. *From Tribal Village to Global Village: Indian Rights and International Relations in Latin America*. Stanford: Stanford University Press.

Canessa, Andrew. 2012. *Intimate Indigeneities: Race, Sex, and History in the Small Spaces of Andean Life*. Durham: Duke University Press.

Carrasco, Pedro. 1950. *Los otomies, cultura e historia prehispánicas de los pueblos mesoamericanos de habla otomiana*. Mexico City: UNAM.

———. 1971. "Social Organization of Ancient Mexico." In *Handbook of Middle American Indians, Archaeology of Northern Mexico*, vol. 10, edited by Gordon F. Ekholm and Ignacio Bernal, 349–75. Austin: University of Texas Press.

———. 1976a. "The Joint Family in Ancient Mexico: The Case of Molotla." In *Essays on Mexican Kinship*, edited by Hugo. G. Nutini, Pedro Carrasco, and James M. Taggart, 45–64. Pittsburgh: University of Pittsburgh Press.

———. 1976b. "Los linajes nobles del México antiguo." In *Estratificación social en la Mesoamérica prehispánica*, edited by Pedro Carrasco, J. Broda, Frederic Hicks, Yolanda Gonzalez Torres, Marina Anguiano, and Matilde Chapa, 19–36. Mexico City: INAH.

———. 1984. "Royal Marriages in Ancient Mexico." In *Explorations in Ethnohistory: Indians of Central Mexico in the Sixteenth Century*, edited by H. R. Harvey and Hanns Prem, 41–82. Albuquerque: University of New Mexico Press.

Carrera Stampa, Manuel. 1945. "Algunos aspectos de la *Historia de Tlaxcala* de Diego Muñoz Camargo." In *Estudios de historiografía de la Nueva España*, edited by Ramón Iglesia, 91–142. Mexico City: El Colegio de México.

Castellanos, M. Bianet, Lourdes Gutiérrez Nájera, and Arturo J. Aldama, eds. 2012. *Comparative Indigeneities of the Américas: Toward a Hemispheric Approach*. Tucson: University of Arizona Press.

Chance, John K. 2008. "Indigenous Ethnicity in Colonial Central Mexico." In *Ethnic*

*Identity in Nahua Mesoamerica: The View from Archaeology, Art History, Ethno-history, and Contemporary Ethnography*, edited by Frances F. Berdan, John K. Chance, Alan R. Sandstrom, Barbara Stark, James Taggart, and Emily Umberger, 133–49. Salt Lake City: University of Utah Press.

Chimalpahin Cuauhtlehuanitzin, Domingo Francisco de San Antón Muñon. 1965. *Die Relationen Chimalpahin's zur Geschichte Mexico's.* Edited by Günter Zimmerman, 2 vols. Hamburg: Cram, De Gruyter.

———. 1998. *Las ocho relaciones y el memorial de Colhuacán.* Edited by Rafael Tena. México DF: Consejo Nacional para la Cultura y las Artes.

Clavijero, Francisco. 1945. *Historia Antigua de México.* 4 vols. Mexico City: Editorial Porrúa.

Cohen, Ronald. 1978. "Ethnicity: Problem and Focus in Anthropology." *Annual Review of Anthropology* 7: 379–404.

Colby, Benjamin N. and Pierre L. van den Berghe. 1969. *Ixil Country: A Plural Society in Highland Guatemala.* Berkeley: University of California Press.

Comaroff, John L. 1987. "Of Totemism and Ethnicity: Consciousness, Practice, and the Signs of Inequality." *Ethnos* 52: 301–23.

Cornejo Polar, Antonio. 1980. *Literatura y sociedad en el Perú, la novela indigenista.* Lima: Losontay.

Coronado, Jorge. 2009. *The Andes Imagined: Indigenismo, Society, and Modernity.* Pittsburgh: University of Pittsburgh Press.

Cortés, Hernan. 1993. *Cartas de Relación.* Edited by Ángel Delgado Gómez. Madrid: Clásicos Castalia.

Cortés Ruiz, Efraín and María Cristina Suárez y Farías. 1989. *Estudios Nahuas.* Mexico City: INAH.

Cuadrillo, Jaime. 2004. *Las Glorias de la república de Tlaxcala: o la conciencia como imagen sublime.* Mexico City: UNAM, Museo Nacional de Arte, INBA.

Davies, Nigel. 1973. *The Aztecs: A History.* New York: Putnam.

———. 1980. *The Toltec Heritage: From the Fall of Tula to the Rise of Tenochtitlán.* Norman: University of Oklahoma Press.

Dehouve, Danièle. 1994. *Entre el caiman y el jaguar: los pueblos indios de Guerrero.* Mexico City: CIESAS.

———. 1995. *Hacia una historia del espacio en la montaña de Guerrero.* Mexico City: Centro de Estudios Mesoamericanos y Centroamericanos, CIESAS.

Díaz del Castillo, Bernal. 1982. *Historia verdadera de la conquista de la Nueva España.* Edited by Carmelo Sáenz de Santa María. Madrid: Instituto "Gonzalo Fernández de Oviedo," UNAM, Universidad Rafael Landívar.

Dueñas, Alcira. 2010. *Indians and Mestizos in the "Lettered City": Reshaping Justice, Social Hierarchy, and Political Culture in Colonial Peru.* Boulder: University Press of Colorado.

Elliott, John H. 1987. "Introduction: Colonial Identity in the Atlantic World." In *Colonial Identity in the Atlantic World, 1500–1800*, edited by Nicholas Canny and Anthony Pagden, 3–13. Princeton: Princeton University Press.

Fernández Christlieb, Federico, and Ángel Julián García Zambrano, eds. 2006. *Ter-*

*ritorialidad y paisaje en el altepetl del siglo XVI*. Mexico City: Fondo de Cultura Económica, Instituo de Geografía de la UNAM.

Fisher, Andrew B., and Matthew D. O'Hara. 2009. "Introduction: Racial Identities and Their Interpreters in Colonial Latin America." In *Imperial Subjects: Race and Identity in Colonial Latin America*, edited by Andrew B. Fisher and Matthew D. O'Hara, 1–37. Durham: Duke University Press.

Florentine Codex. 1961. *Florentine Codex*, Book X. Compiled by Bernardino de Sahagún, translated by Charles E. Dibble and Arthur J. O. Anderson. Santa Fe and Salt Lake City: School of American Research and University of Utah.

Florescano, Enrique. 1994. *Memoria mexicana*. Mexico City: Fondo de Cultura Económica.

———. 1999. *Memoria indígena*. Mexico City: Taurus.

———. 2009. *Los orígenes del poder en Mesoamérica*. México DF: Fondo de Cultura Económica, Arqueología Mexicana.

Friedlander, Judith. 1975. *Being Indian in Hueyapan: A Study of Forced Identity in Contemporary Mexico*. New York: St. Martin's Press.

Furnivall, J. S. 1948. *Colonial Policy and Practice*. Cambridge: Cambridge University Press.

García Castro, René. 1999. *Indios, territorio y poder en la provincia Matlatzinca: la negociación del espacio politico de los pueblos otomianos, siglos XV-XVII*. Mexico City: CONACULTA-INAH.

García, Hildeberto. 1984. *Tepeaca en el siglo XVI*. Mexico City: CIESAS.

García Martínez, Bernardo. 1987. *Los pueblos de la sierra*. Mexico City: El Colegio de México.

———. 1998. "El altepetl o pueblo de indios. Expresión básica del cuerpo político mesoamericano." *Arqueología Mexicana* 6: 58–65.

Garibay K., Angel María. 1953. *Historia de la literatura náhuatl*. 2 vols. Mexico City: Editorial Porrúa.

Gibson, Charles. 1952. *Tlaxcala in the Sixteenth Century*. New Haven: Yale University Press.

———. 1964. *The Aztecs under Spanish Rule*. Stanford: Stanford University Press.

Good, Catharine. 2000. "Indigenous Peoples in Central and Western Mexico." In *Supplement to the Handbook of Middle American Indians*, vol. 6, *Ethnology*, edited by John D. Monaghan, 120–49. Austin: University of Texas Press.

Graham, Laura R. 2014. "Genders of Xavante Ethnographic Spectacle: Cultural Politics of Inclusion and Exclusion in Brazil." In *Performing Indigeneity: Global Histories and Contemporary Experiences*, edited by Laura R. Graham and H. Glenn Penny, 305–50. Lincoln: University of Nebraska Press.

Graham, Laura R. and Penny, H. Glenn, eds. 2014. *Performing Indigeneity: Global Histories and Contemporary Experiences*. Lincoln: University of Nebraska Press.

Grillo, R. D. 1998. *Pluralism and the Politics of Difference: State, Culture, and Ethnicity in Comparative Perspective*. Oxford: Clarendon Press.

Gruzinski, Serge. 1988. "The Net Torn Apart: Ethnic Identities and Westernization in Colonial Mexico, Sixteenth–Nineteenth Century." In *Ethnicities and Nations: Pro-*

*cesses of Interethnic Relations in Latin America, Southeast Asia, and the Pacific*, edited by Remo Guidieri, Francesco Pellizzi and Remo Guidieri, 39–56. Austin: University of Texas Press.

———. 1993. *The Conquest of Mexico: The Incorporation of Indian Societies into the Western World, Sixteenth-Eighteenth Centuries*. Translated by Eileen Corrigan. Cambridge, UK: Polity Press.

Haskett, Robert. 1991. *Indigenous Rulers: An Ethnohistory of Town Government in Colonial Cuernavaca*. Albuquerque: University of New Mexico Press.

———. 1992. "Visions of Municipal Glory Undimmed: The Nahuatl Town Histories of Colonial Cuernavaca." *Colonial Latin American Review* 1: 1–36.

Hanke, Lewis. 1949. *The Spanish Struggle for Justice in the Conquest of America*. Philadelphia: University of Pennsylvania Press.

Hodge, Mary. 1984. *Aztec City-States*. Ann Arbor: University of Michigan, Museum of Anthropology.

Hodge, Mary, and Michael E. Smith, eds. 1994. *Economies and Polities in the Aztec Realm*. Albany: Institute for Mesoamerican Studies, SUNY Albany.

Horn, Rebecca. 1997. *Postconquest Coyoacan: Nahua-Spanish Relations in Central Mexico, 1519–1650*. Stanford: Stanford University Press.

———. 2014. "Indigenous Identities in Mesoamerica after the Spanish Conquest." In *Native Diasporas: Indigenous Identities and Settler Colonialism in the Americas*, edited by Gregory D. Smithers and Brooke N. Newman, 31–78. Lincoln: University of Nebraska Press.

Iwanska, Alicja. 1971. *Purgatory and Utopia: A Mazahua Indian Village of Mexico*. Cambridge MA: Schenkman Publishing Company.

Jackson, Jean E., and Kay B. Warren. 2005. "Indigenous Movements in Latin America, 1991–2004: Controversies, Ironies, New Directions." *Annual Review of Anthropology* 34: 549–98.

Keen, Benjamin. 1971. *The Aztec Image in Western Thought*. New Brunswick: Rutgers University Press.

Kellogg, Susan. 1995. *Law and the Transformation of Aztec Culture, 1500–1700*. Norman: University of Oklahoma Press.

Kranz, Travis Barton. 2010. "Visual Persuasion: Sixteenth-Century Tlaxcalan Pictorials in Response to the Conquest of Mexico." In *The Conquest All Over Again: Nahuas and Zapotecs Thinking, Writing, and Painting Spanish Colonialism*, edited by Susan Schroeder, 41–73. Brighton: Sussex University Press.

Krug, Frances, and Camilla Townsend. 2007. "The Tlaxcala-Puebla Family of Annals." In *Sources and Methods for the Study of Post-conquest Mesoamerican Ethnohistory*, edited by James Lockhart, Lisa Sousa, and Stephanie Wood. Eugene: University of Oregon Wired Humanities Project. http://whp.uoregon.edu/Lockhart/index.html/.

Langer, Erick D., ed. 2003. *Contemporary Indigenous Movements in Latin America*. Wilmington DE: SR Books.

Lastra, Yolanda. 2006. *Los otomies: su lengua y su historia*. Mexico City: UNAM.

Leibsohn, Dana. 1994. "Primers for Memory: Cartographic Histories and Nahua Identity." In *Writing without Words: Alternative Literacies in Mesoamerica and the Andes*, edited by Elizabeth Hill Boone and Walter D. Mignolo, 161–87. Durham: Duke University Press.

León-Portilla, Miguel. 1956. *La filosofía Nahuatl, estudiada en sus fuentes*. Mexico City: Ediciones Especiales del Instituto Indígena Interamericano.

——. 2009. "Response to John F. Schwaller." *The Americas* 66: 252–54.

Lienhard, Martin. 1983. "La crónica mestiza en México y Perú hasta 1620: apuntes para su estudio histórico literario." *Revista de Crítica Literaria Latinoamericana* 17: 105–15.

Lockhart, James. 1982. "Views of Corporate Self and History in Some Valley of Mexico Towns, Late Seventeenth and Eighteenth Centuries." In *The Inca and Aztec States*, edited by George A. Collier, Renato Rosaldo, and John D. Wirth, 367–93. New York: Academic Press.

——. 1991a. "Postconquest Nahua Society and Culture Seen through Nahuatl Sources." In *Nahuas and Spaniards: Postconquest Central Mexican History and Philology*, 2–22. Stanford and Los Angeles: Stanford University Press and UCLA Latin American Center Publications.

——. 1991b. "Charles Gibson and the Ethnohistory of Postconquest Central Mexico." In *Nahuas and Spaniards: Postconquest Central Mexican History and Philology*, 159–82. Stanford and Los Angeles: Stanford University Press and UCLA Latin American Center Publications.

——. 1992. *The Nahuas after the Conquest: A Social and Cultural History of the Indians of Central Mexico, Sixteenth through Eighteenth Centuries*. Stanford: Stanford University Press.

——. 1993. *We People Here: Nahuatl Accounts of the Conquest of Mexico*. Berkeley: University of California Press.

——. 1999. "A Historian and the Disciplines." In *Of Things of the Indies: Essays Old and New in Early Latin American History*, 333–67. Stanford: Stanford University Press.

Lockhart, James, Frances Berdan, and Arthur J. O. Anderson, trans. and eds. 1986. *The Tlaxcalan Actas: A Compendium of the Records of the Cabildo of Tlaxcala (1545–1627)*. Salt Lake City: University of Utah Press.

López Caballero, Paula. 2003. *Los títulos primordiales del centro de México*. Mexico City: Consejo Nacional para la Cultura y las Artes.

López de Gómara, Francisco. 1986. *La conquista de México*. Edited by José Luis de Rojas. Madrid: Historia 16.

MacLachlan, Colin M. 1974. *Criminal Justice in Eighteenth-Century Mexico: A Study of the Tribunal of the Acordada*. Berkeley: University of California Press.

MacLeod, Murdo. 1998. "Self-Promotion: The *Relaciones de Méritos y Servicios* and Their Historical and Political Interpretation." *Colonial Latin American Historical Review* 7: 229–68.

Mallon, Florencia, ed. 2012. *Decolonizing Native Histories: Collaboration, Knowledge and Language in the Americas*. Durham: Duke University Press.

Manrique C., Leonardo. 1969. "The Otomí." In *Handbook of Middle American Indians*, vol. 8, edited by Robert Wauchope and Evon Z. Vogt, 682–722. Austin: University of Texas Press.

Martínez Baracs, Andrea. 2008. *Un gobierno de indios: Tlaxcala, 1519–1750*. Mexico City: Fondo de Cultura Económica, Fideicomiso Colegio de Historia de Tlaxcala, CIESAS.

Maybury-Lewis, David, ed. 2002. *The Politics of Ethnicity: Indigenous Peoples in Latin American States*. Cambridge MA: Harvard University David Rockefeller Center for Latin American Studies.

Menegus Bornemann, Margarita. 1991. *Del señorio a la república de indios: el caso de Toluca, 1500–1600*. Madrid: Ministerio de Agricultura, Pesca, y Secretaria General Técnica.

McEnroe, Sean. 2012. *From Colony to Nationhood in Mexico: Laying the Foundations, 1560–1810*. New York: Cambridge University Press.

Metz, Brent E. 2006. *Ch'orti'-Maya Survival in Eastern Guatemala: Indigeneity in Transition*. Albuquerque: University of New Mexico Press.

Mignolo, Walter. 1982. "Cartas, crónicas, y relaciones del descubrimiento y la conquista." In *Historia de la literatura hispanoamericana*, vol. 1, *Época colonial*, edited by Luis Iñigo Madrigal, 57–125. Madrid: Ediciones Cátedra.

———. 1987. "El mandato y la ofrenda: *la Descripción de la Ciudad y Provincia de Tlaxcala*, de Diego Muñoz Camargo, y las relaciones de Indias." *Nueva Revista de Filología Hispánica* 35: 451–84.

Miller, Marilyn. 1997. "Covert *Mestizaje* and the Strategy of 'Passing' in Diego Muñoz Camargo's *Historia de Tlaxcala*." *Colonial Latin American Review* 6: 41–58.

Mörner, Magnus, and Charles Gibson. 1962. "Diego Muñoz Camargo and the Segregation Policy of the Spanish Crown." *Hispanic American Historical Review* 42: 558–68.

Motolinía, Toribio de Benavente. 1971. *Memoriales o Libro de las cosas de la Nueva España y de los naturales de ella*. Edited by Edmundo O'Gorman. Mexico City: UNAM.

Muñoz Camargo, Diego. 1972. *Historia de Tlaxcala*. Edited by Alfredo Chavero. Facsimile of 1892 edition. Guadalajara: Biblioteca de Facsimiles Mexicanas.

———. 1998. *Historia de Tlaxcala*. Edited by Luis Reyes García. Tlaxcala, México: Gobierno del Estado de Tlaxcala, CIESAS, Universidad Autónoma de Tlaxcala.

———. 2000. *Descripción de la ciudad y provincia de Tlaxcala*. Edited by René Acuña. San Luis Potosí: El Colegio de San Luis, Gobierno del Estado de Tlaxcala.

Navarrete Linares, Federico. 2011. *Los orígenes de los pueblos indígenas del Valle de México: los altépetl y sus historias*. Mexico City: UNAM.

Niezen, Ronald. 2003. *The Origins of Indigenism: Human Rights and the Politics of Identity*. Berkeley: University of California Press.

O'Hara, Matthew D. 2010. *A Flock Divided: Race, Religion, and Politics in Mexico, 1749–1857*. Durham: Duke University Press.

Olko, Justyna. 2012. "El 'otro' y los estereotipos étnicos en el mundo Nahua." *Estudios de Cultural Náhuatl* 44: 165–98.

Oudijk, Michel R., and María de los Ángeles Romero Frizzi. 2003. "Los títulos primordiales: un género de tradición mesoamericana: Del mundo prehispánico al siglo XXI." *Relaciones* 24: 17–48.

Owensby, Brian P. 2008. *Empire of Law and Indian Justice in Colonial Mexico*. Stanford: Stanford University Press.

———. 2010. "Pacto entre rey lejano y súbditos indígenas. Justicia, legalidad y política en Nueva España, siglo XVII." *Historia Mexicana* 61: 59–106.

Perrone-Moisés, Beatriz. 2014. "Performed Alliances and Performative Identities: Tupinambá in the Kingdom of France." In *Performing Indigeneity: Global Histories and Contemporary Experiences*, edited by Laura R. Graham and H. Glenn Penny, 110–35. Lincoln: University of Nebraska Press.

Perry, Richard J. 1996. . . . *From Time Immemorial: Indigenous Peoples and State Systems*. Austin: University of Texas Press.

Pizzigoni, Caterina. 2007. "Region and Subregion in Central Mexican Ethnohistory: The Toluca Valley, 1650–1760." *Colonial Latin American Review* 16: 71–92.

———. 2012. *The Life Within: Local Indigenous Society in Mexico's Toluca Valley, 1650–1800*. Stanford: Stanford University Press.

Prescott, William H. 1943. *Conquest of Mexico*. Garden City NY: Blue Ribbon.

Quezada, Noemí. 1972. *Los matlatzincas: época prehispánica y colonial hasta 1650*. Mexico City: INAH.

Queiroz, Maria José de. 1962. *Do indianismo ao indigenismo nas letras hispanoamericanas*. Belo Horizonte: Imprensa da Universidade de Minas Gerais.

Ramírez Zavala, Ana Luz. 2011. "Indio/Indígena, 1750–1850." *Historia Mexicana* 60: 1643–81.

Restall, Matthew. 2003. *Seven Myths of the Spanish Conquest*. New York: Oxford University Press.

Restall, Matthew, and Felipe Fernández-Armesto. 2012. *The Conquistadors: A Very Short Introduction*. New York: Oxford University Press.

Reyes García, Cayetano. 2000. *El Altépetl: Origen y desarrollo: construcción de la identidad regional náuatl*. México: El Colegio de Michoacán.

Reyes Garía, Luis, and Andrea Martínez Baracs, eds. 1995. *Historia chronológica de la Noble Ciudad de Tlaxcala por Don Juan Buenaventura Zapata y Mendoza*. Tlaxcala: Universidad Autónoma de Tlaxcala.

Rozat, Guy. 2002. *Indios imaginarios e indios reales en los relatos de la conquista de México*. Xalapa: Universidad Veracruzana.

Ruiz Medrano, Ethelia. 2010. *Mexico's Indigenous Communities: Their Lands and Histories, 1500–2010*. Translated by Russ Davidson. Boulder CO: University Press of Colorado.

Sánchez Blas, Joaquín. 2007. *Estudio histórico de la zona mazahua*. Toluca: Instituto Mexiquense de Cultura.

Sandoval Forero, Eduardo. 1997. *Población y cultura en la etnorregión mazahua (jañtjo)*. Mexico City: Universidad Autónoma del Estado de México.

Sandstrom, Alan R. 2000. "Contemporary Cultures of the Gulf Coast." In *Supplement to the Handbook of Middle American Indians*, vol. 6, *Ethnology*, edited by John D. Monaghan, 83–119. Austin: University of Texas Press.

———. 2008. "Blood Sacrifice, Curing, and Ethnic Identity among Contemporary Nahua of Northern Veracruz, Mexico." In *Ethnic Identity in Nahua Mesoamerica: The View from Archaeology, Art History, Ethnohistory, and Contemporary Ethnography*, edited by Frances F. Berdan, John K. Chance, Alan R. Sandstrom,

Barbara Stark, James Taggart, and Emily Umberger, 150–82. Salt Lake City: University of Utah Press.

Schroeder, Susan. 1991. *Chimalpahin and the Kingdoms of Chalco.* Tucson: University of Arizona Press.

———. 1994. "Looking Back at the Conquest: Nahua Perceptions of Early Encounters from the Annals of Chimalpahin." In *Chipping Away on Earth: Studies in Prehispanic and Colonial Mexico in Honor of Arthur J. O. Anderson and Charles E. Dibble*, edited by Eloise Quiñones Keber, 81–94. Lancaster CA: Labyrinthos.

Schryer, Frans J. 1990. *Ethnicity and Class Conflict in Rural Mexico.* Princeton: Princeton University Press.

Schwaller, John F. 2009. "Broken Spears or Broken Bones: Evolution of the Most Famous Line in Nahuatl." *The Americas* 66: 242–52.

Schwartz, Stuart B. 1987. "The Formation of a Colonial Identity in Brazil." In *Colonial Identity in the Atlantic World, 1500–1800*, edited by Nicholas Canny and Anthony Pagden, 15–50. Princeton: Princeton University Press.

Smith, Michael E. 1984. "The Aztlan Migrations of the Nahuatl Chronicles: Myth or History?" *Ethnohistory* 31: 153–86.

———. 1996. *The Aztecs.* Malden MA: Blackwell.

———. 2003. *The Aztecs*, 2nd ed. Malden MA: Blackwell.

———. 2008. *Aztec City-State Capitals.* Gainesville: University Press of Florida.

Smith, M. G. 1965. *The Plural Society in the British West Indies.* Berkeley: University of California Press.

Soustelle, Jacques. 1937. *La famille Otomi-pame du Méxique central.* Paris: Institut d'Ethnologie.

———. 1961. *The Daily Life of the Aztecs on the Eve of the Spanish Conquest.* Translated by Patrick O'Brian. New York: Macmillan.

Speed, Shannon, R., Aida Hernández Castillo, and Lynn M. Stephen, eds. 2006. *Dissident Women: Gender and Cultural Politics in Chiapas.* Austin: University of Texas Press.

Stark, Barbara L., and John K. Chance. 2008. "Diachronic and Multidisciplinary Perspectives on Mesoamerican Ethnicity." In *Ethnic Identity in Nahua Mesoamerica: The View from Archaeology, Art History, Ethnohistory, and Contemporary Ethnography*, edited by Frances F. Berdan, John K. Chance, Alan R. Sandstrom, Barbara Stark, James Taggart, and Emily Umberger, 1–37. Salt Lake City: University of Utah Press.

Stavenhagen, Rodolfo. 1988. *Derecho indígena y derechos humanos en América Latina.* Mexico City: El Colegio de México.

Stavenhagen, Rodolfo, and Diego Iturralde, eds. 1990. *Entre la ley y la costumbre: el derecho consuetudinario indígena en América Latina.* Mexico City: Instituto Indigenista Interamericano.

Stephen, Lynn. 1996. "The Creation and Re-creation of Ethnicity: Lessons from the Zapotec and Mixtec of Oaxaca." *Latin American Perspectives* 23: 17–37.

———. 2005. *Zapotec Women: Gender, Class, and Ethnicity in Globalized Oaxaca*, 2nd ed. Durham: Duke University Press.

Stone, John. 1996. "Ethnicity." In *The Social Science Encyclopedia*, 2nd ed., edited by Adam Kuper and Jessica Kuper, 260–63. London: Routledge.

Taylor, Analisa. 2009. *Indigeneity in the Mexican Cultural Imagination: Thresholds of Belonging*. Tucson: University of Arizona Press.

Terraciano, Kevin. 2001. *The Mixtecs of Colonial Oaxaca: Ñudzahui History, Sixteenth through Eighteenth Centuries*. Stanford: Stanford University Press.

Townsend, Camilla. 2010a. "Don Juan Buenaventura Zapata y Mendoza and the Notion of a Nahua Identity." In *The Conquest All Over Again: Nahuas and Zapotecs Thinking, Writing, and Painting Spanish Colonialism*, edited by Susan Schroeder, 144–80. Brighton: Sussex University Press.

———. 2010b. *Here in This Year: Seventeenth-Century Nahuatl Annals of the Tlaxcala-Puebla Valley*. Edited and Translated by Camilla Townsend. Stanford: Stanford University Press.

———. 2014. "Introduction: The Evolution of Alva Ixtlilxochitl's Scholarly Life." *Colonial Latin American Review* 23: 1–17.

Tresierra, Julio C. 1994. "Mexico: Indigenous Peoples and the Nation-State." In *Indigenous Peoples and Democracy in Latin America*, edited by Donna Lee Van Cott, 187–210. New York: St. Martin's Press.

Umberger, Emily. 2008. "Ethnicity and Other Identities in the Sculptures of Tenochtitlan." In *Ethnic Identity in Nahua Mesoamerica: The View from Archaeology, Art History, Ethnohistory, and Contemporary Ethnography*, edited by Frances F. Berdan, John K. Chance, Alan R. Sandstrom, Barbara Stark, James Taggart, and Emily Umberger, 64–104. Salt Lake City: University of Utah Press.

Van Cott, Donna Lee. 1994. "Indigenous Peoples and Democracy: Issues for Policymakers." In *Indigenous Peoples and Democracy in Latin America*, edited by Donna Lee Van Cott, 1–22. New York: St. Martin's Press.

Vázquez, Germán. 1986. "Introducción." In *Historia de Tlaxcala*, by Diego Muñoz Camargo, edited by Germán Vázquez, 7–67. Madrid: Historia 16.

———. (Andrés de Tapia). 1988. *La conquista de Tenochtitlan, Relación de algunas cosas de las que acaecieron al muy ilustre señor don Hernando Cortés*. Madrid: Historia 16.

Vázquez, Josefina Zoraida. 1991. *La imagen del indio en el español del siglo XVI*. Xalapa: Universidad Veracruzana.

Velazco, Salvador. 2003. *Visiones de Anáhuac: reconstrucciones historiográficas y etnicidades emergentes en el México colonial: Fernando de Alva Ixtlilxóchitl, Diego Muñoz Camargo y Hernando Alvarado Tezozómoc*. Guadalajara: Universidad de Guadalajara.

Verlinden, Marianne. 1994. "Relación geográfica o Historia de Tlaxcala: La escritura mestiza de Diego Muñoz Camargo." PhD diss., Tulane University.

Villella, Peter B. 2012. "Indian Lords, Hispanic Gentlemen: The Salazars of Colonial Tlaxcala." *The Americas* 69: 1–36.

Ward, Thomas. 2001. "Expanding Ethnicity in Sixteenth-Century Anahuac: Ideologies of Ethnicity and Gender in the Nation-Building Process." *MLN* 116: 419–52.

Wickstrom, Stefanie, and Philip D. Young. 2014. "Introduction to Key Concepts." In

*Mestizaje and Globalization: Transformations of Identity and Power*, edited by Stefanie Wickstrom and Philip D. Young, 3–19. Tucson: University of Arizona Press.

Wolf, Eric. 1957. "Closed Corporate Peasant Communities in Mesoamerica and Central Java." *Southwestern Journal of Anthropology* 13: 1–18.

———. 1959. *Sons of the Shaking Earth*. Chicago: University of Chicago Press.

Wood, Stephanie. 1991. "The Cosmic Conquest: Late-Colonial Views of the Sword and Cross in Central Mexican *Títulos*." *Ethnohistory* 38: 176–95.

———. 2003. *Transcending Conquest: Nahua Views of Spanish Colonial Mexico*. Norman: University of Oklahoma Press.

Yannakakis, Yanna. 2008. *The Art of Being In-Between: Native Intermediaries, Indian Identity, and Local Rule in Colonial Oaxaca*. Durham: Duke University Press.

———. 2013. "Indigenous People and Legal Culture in Spanish America." *History Compass* 11: 931–47. DOI: 10.1111/hic3.12096.

# 2

# Existing Ancestralities and the Failure of Colonial Regimes

SUSAN ELIZABETH RAMÍREZ

Most, if not all, schoolchildren learn that Christopher Columbus sailed the ocean blue in 1492. What is usually left out is that Columbus erred in thinking to the end of his life that he had reached the East Indies, the so-called Spice Islands. Thus, his generic name for the peoples he encountered, the Indians or los indios, was his legacy and a misnomer that is still commonplace to this day.

In the Americas, the word *Indian* became synonymous with *other* but changed in meaning and use over time. In referencing non-Europeans, *Indian* became charged with the connotation of difference and subordination. The category of Indians came to refer to individuals who spoke a Native language, dressed in recognized Native garb, wore their hair long (except a few groups, like the Incas, also known as the Cuzcos, and some Amazonians, who wore their hair short), consumed Native foods and drink (such as maize, potatoes, guinea pigs, quinoa, and *chicha* or maize beer), and were subject to obligations to the state, such as labor service. In Peru in 1613–14, the category included *indios de la China* (Filipinos), *indios de la India de Portugal* (Indians from the subcontinent under the sway of the Portuguese), and *indios de la Xapon* (Japanese; Contreras [1613] 1968). The group might also be divided into *indios de paz* (peaceful Indians) and *indios de guerra* (warlike Indians) who were captured in a "just war" and could be legally enslaved, branded, and sold (Lowry 1991, 31; van Deusen 2015, 147–68). In time, the members of the class became defined theoretically as free subjects of the king with continuing tribute obligations to the state. The inevitable racial mixing of colonial times, however, meant that it soon lost its exclusivity, as society sometimes designated persons of mixed blood as "indios" if they lived in Native societies, spoke a Native language, and shared in Native culture.

"Indian," however, is not a label that the overwhelming majority of Andean native Americans routinely used to identify themselves, even at the end of the colonial era. The purpose of this essay is to show that "Indian" remained a Western construct and category, defined by those of European blood to group certain "others." Andean Natives did not begin to appropriate it as a generic category and conceptualization of self until the middle of the seventeenth century. Then it was employed almost exclusively by a numerically tiny group of elite Native officials and intellectuals living in Lima, the administrative capital city of the viceroyalty of Peru, for achieving political ends. Consequently, if judged by sheer numbers, most Andeans did not "become Indians," did not consciously put themselves in that category, during the colonial era, but this does not imply that they were deficient in a means of self-representation. Their identities remained deeply rooted in their ancestral religious beliefs, and their associated practices and cultures, a heritage that I call their ancestralities.[1]

To support this argument, I first outline the traditional bases of Native identities before the arrival of the Spanish in 1532 as a backdrop for sketching the impact that Spanish presence and governance had on Native self-perceptions. Despite the fragmentation and forced relocation caused by *encomienda* grants, the imposition of a foreign god and religion, demographic decline, resettlement in new towns, and interactions with Spanish colonial officials in rural areas, the Natives clung to their ancestral lineage identities and continued to practice their rites, often clandestinely. A few leaders and intellectuals, most living close to power, learned to use the term *indio* to further political ends, but the vast majority of the Native population never embraced the term. Thus, the colonial effort to segregate them into an undifferentiated group failed, except on paper.

### Pre-Hispanic Ancestralities

Before the Cuzcos expanded their jurisdiction to embrace other peoples, members of over eighty ethnicities or chiefdoms (*cura-*

*cazgos*), each with its distinctive dress and ethnic gods, lived scattered and interspersed from southern Colombia through Ecuador and Peru into Chile, Bolivia, and northwestern Argentina (Rowe 1946, 186–92 and map 3). Members of one ethnic group and its lineages, however large or small, lived next to and among subjects of other chiefs, sometimes many days' walk away from each other. This so-called *ocupación salpicada* (scattered or splattered occupation) or the occupation of an archipelago of ecological niches, as conceptualized by John V. Murra, guaranteed an ethnic group basic subsistence needs (Ramírez 2005, 226 on *ocupación salpicada*; Murra 1972).[2] In the Andean mountains, this vertical pattern of land use implied growing diverse varieties of crops on separate plots of ground. So if, for example, a field of potatoes became blighted and destroyed at one location, the family or lineage could harvest potatoes from elsewhere. If the maize fields wilted on the flood plain, the maize at higher elevations might survive. Maize grew in warmer areas than most potatoes, so kin with more maize than potatoes could, if necessary, exchange with kin who had more potatoes than maize. Or those with maize or potatoes from the western flanks of the Andean mountains might exchange these products for brightly colored feathers or wild honey with kin living in warmer climes on the eastern slopes.

Each ethnicity consisted of a varying number of lineages or *ayllus* (also called *parcialidades*, "parts of a whole"), *guarangas* (lineages with a thousand households), and *pachacas* (lineages with a hundred households), each with its own name and a leader subordinate to a paramount chief or *curaca*. One ethnic group might encompass a dozen or more lineages. Kinship-bound lineage members believed that they descended from a common ancestor. Lineages remembered notable fathers and grandfathers as cultural heroes who were particularly generous or who had made singular contributions to the well-being of the group, and, in time, deified them. On important ceremonial occasions, their stories were retold and sung; and descendants removed their mummies or images from their crypts to celebrate them. Thus, worship of the ancestors, even those several generations removed, reinforced the lived genealogical links and further united the ayllus into ethnicities (Abercrombie 1998, 341).

Andeans venerated their ancestors, as modern Bolivian *originarios* still did into the twentieth century (see Ari-Chachaki in this volume), because they believed that dead relatives did not die in the absolute, Western sense but journeyed to another world from which they continued to influence the lives and fortunes of their living kin. For that reason, attendants interred curacas with their personal effects, wives, and servants so that they would continue to be comfortable in the other world. Relatives buried other deceased relatives nearby in caves, niches in walls or rocks, and crypts in places that served as ceremonial centers, which the Spanish later called *pueblos viejos* (Ramírez 2005, 124–25, 151, 178, 188–91, 203, 220, 231, 234). There, the mummy bundles of the ancestors remained accessible and could be easily removed for ceremonial occasions. They were carried during ritual dancing and given food and drink offerings. Some served as oracles, answering questions of import to the living. With accurate prognostications, reputations grew, giving rise to increasing numbers of gift-bearing devotees and believers, further consultations, and additional honors.

But because many generations of the foreparents occupied the other world, Andeans imagined that it was crowded and that food and drink shortages occurred. For that reason, the living sacrificed guinea pigs and other animals, llama knuckles, corn cakes, and *chicha* to keep them content. If the ancestors remained happy, the living could anticipate fertility and bountiful harvests. If they became discontent, their kin expected drought, floods, blight, earthquakes, and worse. Periodic ceremonies of supplication or praise (for their bounty) for the departed reinforced the identity of folk with their leaders who functioned as chief organizers and celebrants on these occasions (Duviols 1986; Ramírez 2005, especially ch. 4).

Andean society associated the status and prestige of any given lord with the number of followers who owed him service when summoned. The more subjects a lord claimed, the higher his rank. Recognized titles and symbols on or around a lord's person indicated his position. Such attributes of power included his name and the manner he was addressed; his costume and iconic headdress; the height and elaboration of his stool or seat; his genealogy; the numbers of his wives and escorts; and whether or not his subjects carried him in a hammock or litter (Martínez Cereceda 1988; Martínez Cereceda 1995).

As time passed, distances increased, and the subjects of one lord increased in number faster than those of another, rankings shifted, sometimes to the point that one segment (be it a lineage or larger) asserted its independence. The lineage fragmented. If it continued to grow, it could come to rival its larger counterparts or rise even higher if success in battle or other trial indicated a powerful spiritual backing. With such pressures and memories relatively short, identities were flexible and changing. The identity of a given lord would immediately situate followers' status and power in the socio-religious and political hierarchy and determine the relationship with neighbors, regardless of where they homesteaded.

Any given lord's status also correlated directly with society's expectation of hospitality, reciprocity, and redistribution: the higher the standing, the greater the liberality of his feasting and gifts.[3] This equation proved self-reinforcing because the larger the number of followers, the more labor a lord managed and the larger the amounts of surplus for display and ritual indulging his people produced. The number of a lord's wives proved an informal index of their expression of respect and superiority; he distributed beer at his gatherings because he had the wives who brewed it. This beer served as the essential, mildly intoxicating drink necessary for negotiating, sacrificing, hosting, and celebrating. Thus, it was expected that a *curaca (de guaranga)* with a thousand subject families would provide a more sumptuous feast than a lesser chief (for example, a *curaca de pachaca* of a hundred households) with a smaller following. A corollary is that the higher-ranked lords would provide more help and protection in times of need than a lower-ranking authority with limited kin and ally networks. The more sumptuous a lord's gatherings, the more satisfying his hospitality and gifts, the more following he attracted (Ramírez 2005; Muñoz Arveláez 2015).

Thus, the identity of each ethnic group and lineage centered on their veneration of the ancestors and the blood ties that they represented. Celebration of the past with stories and songs, sacrifices and ritual feasting and dancing, organized and orchestrated by the lord, helped define and solidify the group. The ancestors determined who succeeded in power by favoring one contender over another in intra-ethnic tests, among brothers, for example. Claim of an ancestral god's favor added luster that distinguished a genealogy, a memorialized kinship memory that served as a charter to rule. Thus, a group's religious belief and observance provided their identity and gave the lord his legitimacy to rule. The group's continuing ability to recognize and appease the ancestors, under the direction of their lord, supported the fertility and bounty of the group's activities, that is, whether couples were fertile, animals reproduced, seeds sprouted, and waters yielded fish (Ramírez 2005, ch. 4).

The Cuzcos were one of the scores of chiefdoms in the southern highlands of modern Peru. They claimed to descend from the union of the sun, their father, and their mother, the moon. At one crucial point in their history, another ethnic group, the Chancas, challenged the Cuzcos for the title of sons of the sun. In the subsequent war, the sun favored the Cuzcos. They in turn interpreted this victory as a mandate and began to unite other ethnicities, often using force, and after the groups in the path of their expansion learned of their reputation for ruthlessness and victory, invitation, negotiation, and diplomacy established—sometimes resentful—alliances. Despite lingering antagonisms, the Cuzcos ultimately claimed hegemony over peoples living throughout the Andean region. This jurisdictional empire was not conceived of as a territorial whole with clear marked, recognized, and defended borders. Instead, it was an unstable assemblage of over eighty ethnic groups, each with its own traditions and often speaking a distinctive language or dialect (Rowe 1946, 186–92). Unlike the Nahuas, described by Kellogg in this volume, the Cuzcos attempted to construct from these diverse peoples, which were allowed to keep their own customs and ancestral devotions, a megalineage based, often tenuously, on personal ties of kinship, loyalty, and service, reinforced by sun worship and associated religious beliefs; a common, sometimes imposed, language; and the principles of hospitality, reciprocity, and redistribution (Ramírez 2005; 2008).

To this end and to build their empire, the Cuzcos replaced defeated and uncooperative ethnic lords with loyal administrators. To minimize resistance, the ruler, known to his followers by his title el Cuzco, split recalcitrant and potentially troublesome ethnic groups, forcing a portion to relocate and settle among loyal peoples, and sent "missionaries" to teach all non-Cuzco subjects the Quechua language and the proper manner to celebrate the sun (ANP/DI, l. 6, c. 75, 1623, 29v–30). The Cuzco confirmed in office the rulers of those groups who recognized the inevitable, joined the alliance peacefully, and, sometimes, were rewarded with tangible signs of privilege, like a particularly fine tunic, a seat, or the privilege of being carried in a litter. The Cuzco might also accept a female relative of a curaca as a secondary bride, and the lord might be highly honored with a daughter or sister of the Cuzco to take as a principle wife. This exchange visualized the relationship between the ruling group and its subordinates and promised the birth of future generations that would be close blood relatives of the dominant lineage. Such exchanges within this biologically defined empire also established expectations of service and loyalty from the subordinates, be it for forces to defeat another enemy, to build an irrigation ditch, to terrace a mountainside, to maintain the infrastructure of roads and bridges, to transmit messages, to carry the Cuzco's litter, or to make him cloth. In return, the overlords recognized obligations to support allies in times of crisis in the form of food, clothing, or other necessities when the crops failed or an earthquake or flood destroyed households and livelihoods (Ramírez 2005; 2008).

These ties and thus the foundations of the pan-ethnic, relationship-defined empire remained tenuous, fickle, and fraught with negotiations and constant difficulties, especially at times of succession. Because reciprocity was, to a certain extent, undefined, it was sometimes hard to gauge and live up to expectations. Meager rewards gave a ruler a bad reputation as stingy and hoarding and could and did lead to abandonment, resistance, and revolt. Better than expected distributions made people sing of a ruler's generosity and magnanimity and praise his father, the sun. Such personal attentions to ethnic-political relations had the Cuzco and his court traveling to visit his followers, where he was reported to don at times the headgear and dress of a given ally and even dance for one of their ancestral heroes, a rightfully recognized extraordinary honor. Failure to renew such ties led to fissuring and shrinkage in the number of loyal followers.

A loss of followers was undesirable because power, strength, and the Native concept of wealth were defined and gauged by numbers of subjects, as it was in the *curacazgo*. Blood ties usually proved more stable than alliances based on gift-giving or fear, but either way both giver and receiver usually recognized that cooperation served the interests of all. The Cuzco, as the highest ranking authority, had the greatest number of followers who would respond when called. The entire megalineage was organized hierarchically. Ethnic groups might number in the thousands and lineages in the hundreds, depending on definitions and historically remembered parentage. A lord of a thousand families proved constrained in his reciprocity and redistribution compared to a lord of ten thousand and so forth because without labor natural resources had no use.

Religion infused the culture at all levels of these relational societies and the empire. People continued in their belief that their ancestors determined not only the outcomes of planting but even the outcomes of war. Foes carried the representations of their gods onto the battlefields. The outcome established the hierarchy of the lords as well as their deities. Thus, one worshiped his or her father, grandfather, and great-grandfather, while recognizing a higher-ranking lord and worshiping his ancestral gods because they were all linked in the past by kinship. Ultimately, all venerated the sun. Genealogy and religion, and fissuring and alliance, defined the size of this solar congregation and established the right to rule. The empire, then, was the ayllu writ large, an encompassing lineage and sun-worshiping assembly, united eventually and ideally by blood to act together and cooperate under one law (Ramírez 2005).

Analogous to the situation described by Karl Hele in this volume in which the Anishinaabe in the Sault region were defined as one single unified group yet were in reality several autonomous communities, the claimed unity of the Cuzcos' empire was more apparent than real. In 1532 as they made their way south along the coast, Francisco Pizarro and his band heard that the Sañas had revolted against the Cuzcos just before their arrival (Ramírez 1996, 7; Ramírez 1990; Betanzos [1551–57] 2004, 270; ART/CoR, 30-IV-1576). Pabur, the lord of another ethnicity in the Spaniards' path, made it known that Atahualpa, one brother in the succession war being waged at the time, had killed many of Pabur's followers for his failing to give the Cuzcos' ruler the expected recognition (Jerez [1534] 1917, 28). Pizarro took advantage of latent discontent to assemble his own Native followers and allies. Thus, the fratricidal civil war between the half-brothers Atahualpa and Guascar over succession benefited Pizarro and attests to the structural weaknesses of the Native empire. Corroborating this is Sabine MacCormack's finding that sun worship quickly disappeared after 1532, underscoring the shallowness of Cuzco hegemony over its subordinate ethnicities and its failure to meld all into a more homogeneous subject base. What remained were the ethnic ancestors, the founders and contributors to their living kin, and the religious beliefs and practices and material culture they inspired that had predated interactions with the Cuzco forces. Such was the scenario, ideally, on the eve of the Spanish invasion. Identities were flexible and situational, based on genealogy and kinship and the perceived power of the group and its gods. They were limited only by living memories of the past. Thus, these Andean peoples, who the Spanish defined as infidels, pagans, and even uncivilized brutes, were under close examination highly organized and logical in their conceptualization of power and society (MacCormack 1991).

## Ancestralities versus the Spanish Colonial State

The Spanish invaded in 1532 with a religious justification. Dr. Palacio Rubios prepared a summary statement to that effect in 1512. Called the *requerimiento* (requirement) because it was required to be read to non-Christian, usually non-Spanish-speaking foes, the document demanded that listeners accept the Christian god and Spanish domination or be subject to war, confiscation of goods, and enslavement. This, in time, became the basis of "the colonial project," one aspect of which was transforming the Indians, the pagans, infidels, and heathens, into good Catholics and loyal subjects of the Spanish Crown. In the process, they were to be taught "human customs" (Lowry 1991, 3). Because the listeners did not understand Spanish and might be too far away to hear the *requerimiento* read, the ritual amounted to the Spanish speaking to themselves to ease their conscience and quell the fear that their souls might be eternally dammed for their actions (Tibesar 1957, 115–16; Wernke 2007, 152).

To facilitate indoctrination and control, the Spanish Crown allowed governors to divide the Native population and entrust its administration to persons who had served the king. Pizarro granted to his followers Native curacas and the people who were subject to them, often without clear or verified knowledge of the number of subjects. Thus, some early grantees (*encomenderos*) learned that they benefited from the labor of ten thousand families (for instance, Melchior de Verdugo, encomendero of the Cajamarcas), while others had to be content with a few hundred.[4]

The grant of labor or encomienda explicitly obligated the Spanish conquerors who received the coveted trusteeships to provide protection and religious instruction for their charges. Compliance with the latter condition proved uneven in the first few decades of Spanish colonial hegemony because there were not enough regular and secular clergy to catechize all. Franciscans, Augustinians, Mercedarians, and Dominican regulars arrived first on the scene (Cieza de León [1548–50] 1998, 178–79, 297, 394, 397). Other religious orders came later. They tended to be concentrated in Lima, the city of Cuzco, and other large towns, but gradually their presence permeated more rural areas, though they never covered them all, even in the eighteenth century (ART/CoCompulsas, l.265, c. 3046, 17-XII-1784). The Franciscans, for example, arrived sometime before 1551 in Chiclayo, on the north coast, yet the nearby peoples of Mórrope and Pácora remained unbaptized ten years later (Rubiños y Andrade [1782] 1936, 300). The Jesuits settled in Juli in the late 1570s. But missions were not established in the Chaco until the second half of the eighteenth century (Saeger 1985). Beside their small numbers, the early missionaries faced language barriers, complicated by a high-level policy debate on whether or not to preach in the Native languages or to teach the Natives Spanish (Frances 2006). Ultimately, missionaries ignored scores of ethnic languages and learned Quechua and Aymara, using these two as lingua francas to spread the Christian message. Simultaneously, the missionaries invented ways to communicate, improvising methods to explain otherwise unintelligible Western concepts. They used the word

FIG. 1. The revered seated Christ. Source: Jaye and Mitchell 1999, 17. Courtesy of the Huntington Free Library, Bronx, New York.

*supay* that originally meant "spirit" or "angel for a devil," despite the fact that Domingo Santo Tomás had defined *supay* in 1560 as "good angel" (*alliçupa* or *ángel bueno*) or "bad angel" (*manaalliçupa* or *ángel malo*). To express concepts they drew pictorial catechisms that, for instance, expressed Christ's divinity by showing him seated on a chair that hovered in the air above parishioners, emulating the pre-Hispanic practice of prostrate or squatting subjects looking up at a seated authority (see the top line of figure 1;Santo Tomás [1560] 1951, 40). In this illustration from a catechism text, the first line of the picture prayer represents Christ in an elevated circle, seated on a chair above a kneeling figure. Yet concepts like grace and the trinity remained poorly or incompletely understood into the nineteenth century (Rubiños y Andrade [1782] 1936; Silverblatt 1987, 178; Jaye and Mitchell 1999).

Native conversions implied more than acceptance of the Christian god. Some Natives at first accepted baptism and the Spanish god as another of many that they venerated (Wernke 2007, 154).[5] But Christianity also implied learning how the Spanish defined the concepts of good, evil, sin, morality, and modesty. This usually necessitated, sooner or later, learning a modicum of Spanish; accepting Spanish categories (for example, separating the political, religious, social, and economic from one another, instead of fusing them and considering the political, economic, and social all aspects of the religious); re-fashioning dress codes; and, for some men, choosing one wife from many to wed, and thus determining which children would be "legitimate" (Rubiños y Andrade [1782] 1936, 301). Concurrently, Natives accepted some imported foods (such as beef, chicken, wheat, and grapes) and many material items (such as household furnishings, including tables and chairs; Foster 1960; Super 1988). In short, colonialism was not just a change in masters and god but was the acceptance of some new cultural elements.[6]

High indigenous mortality rates and reports of abuses led to debates over Native status and policy affecting their well-being. Reports of unemployed Spaniards wandering the countryside, taking advantage of Native hospitality that provided visitors with food, drink, and housing while teaching them "bad customs" worried Iberian authorities (Ramírez 1986, 47–48). As one element of a solution, the Crown mandated the official segregation of the Natives from the Spanish, envisioning a New World society divided into the república de españoles (commonwealth of Spaniards) and the república de indios (commonwealth of Indians). The repúblicas were to be residentially segregated and separately governed. This plan, unlike that of the Cuzcos, implied the disregard of Native ethnic difference. Under the Spanish, all Natives were subject to similar treatment. They were to become Europeanized and to be treated as one homogeneous group.

The Crown mandated that other aspects of the plan to protect the Natives be introduced nearly simultaneously. The first, in the 1560s and 1570s, required Natives to leave their ancestral homes and the many plots of land they tilled to be forcibly resettled in a town, sometimes far from their original homes and ceremonial centers, patterned on the Spanish city ideal of a grid of perpendicularly intersecting streets around a central square. The church, municipal hall, and curaca's lodgings faced the plaza. Each was to have its own municipal government, traditional leaders, and corporately held lands. In theory, these *reducciones*, as the new Native towns were called, concentrated the previously scattered Native population for ease of indoctrination and control. The newly appointed *corregidor de indios* or Spanish governor was a second innovation. This official served as a royal representative with jurisdiction over a given number of ethnicities. He worked with ethnic lords to collect tribute and supervise work obligations, thus taking away day-to-day control over the Native labor force from the encomendero and his agents, some of whom were accused of bad treatment and exploitation of their charges (Keith 1971; Ramírez 1978; Mumford 2012; Huertas Vallejos, n.d.).

The reducciones began in the 1560s and were extended throughout the Andean kingdom by Viceroy Francisco de Toledo in the 1570s. Some representative statistics on the effects of this initiative are shown in table 1. The numbers are striking and speak of the enormous concentration of the indigenous population. The Cajamarcas, for example, moved from over 500 hamlets and homesteads into 22 new Native towns. In total, Spanish inspectors resettled over 1,700 separate hamlets and settlements belonging to various ethnic groups into 354 reducciones. Toledo envisioned the reducciones as the bases of parishes (*doctrinas*, defined demographically as 400 households each) and mandated that each new settlement be situated far from the ancestral mortuary centers (*pueblos viejos*, or "old towns") where ethnic groups traditionally revered their ancestors and past. This, he believed, would be a deterrence to continued ancestor worship and "idolatry" in general (AGI/AL 123; AL 29; Mumford 2012; Ramírez 2005, 50–51, 252–53; Armas Medina 1952, 122; Adrián 1997, 242–43; MacCormack 1985, 353; Levillier 1935, 246–52).

Table 1. Reducciones

| Date | Name of people | Original number of settlements | Number of reducciones |
|------|----------------|-------------------------------|-----------------------|
| 1557 | Huamangas | 676 | 252 |
| 1567 | Cajamarcas | 500+ | 22 |
| 1570s | Aullagas-Uruquillas | 19 | 3 |
| 1570s | Punas | 28 | 2 |
| 1570s | Killaka-Asanaqis | 21 | 4 |
| 1570s | Chacallas | 41 | 6 |
| 1572 | Yucayes | no data | 4 |
| 1573 | Colesuyus | 226 | 22 |
| ≤1586 | Huarochiris | 200 | 39 |

*Sources:* Abercrombie 1998, 238; ANP/DI, l. 6, c. 75, 1623, 11, 16, 21v; Ulloa 1909, 332–47; MacCormack 1985, 453; Rostworowski 1983, 25; Rostworowski 1977, 84–85; Rostworowski 1970, 171; Rostworowski 1993, 205; AGI/AL 123; Polo 1906, 471; Huertas Vallejos, n.d., 4.

Spanish elites sometimes influenced the location of the new towns. They recommended new sites to the inspector far from traditional habitats in the hope that the productive lands thus vacated would be available for themselves (AGI/AL 132, 4; Ramírez 1978). The new lands assigned to the reducciones were supposedly closer to their new settlements, but while perhaps nearer they often turned out not to be as fertile as the old (ART/CoR, l. 157, c. 301, 14-XII-1595, 6–6v, 11v). The Spanish assigned these lands to an ethnicity as a corporation, fixating it in place, and threatening the pre-Hispanic custom of occupying any piece of unoccupied ground for however long it was bountiful and useful. Open access to any empty common ground ended (Ramírez 1996, ch. 3).

The Spanish met reluctance and resistance to such moves with threats of burning Native homes and removal by force. In sum, this policy, to the extent that it was effectively implemented, modified or destroyed Native subsistence strategies and fixed Natives in place. The Spanish decreed that Natives could no longer roam the countryside visiting relatives and trading services or goods, cultivating distant plots or using unique resources freely, or making pilgrimages to ancient shrines and important ancestral oracles. Further, they did not mobilize to serve far-removed lords. Travel likely implied movement to work for the Spanish (Abercrombie 1998, 250, 252; Santillán [1563] 1968, para. 82, pp. 131–32; Levillier 1924, 163–66, 174, 181; Lissón y Chaves 1944, 2:9, 618–19; Altman and Butler 1994, 496).

The reducción policy and appointment of corregidores occurred at the same time that the tribute system was changing. Under the Cuzco regime, service was defined as labor and assigned as tasks. Collective labor often was carried out with a festive air, because the work potentially benefited the group (Abercrombie 1998, 225; Morales 1977; Wachtel 1977; Ramírez 1996, ch. 4; Ramírez 2005, 42–43). Once the task was done, the Natives owed nothing more. After 1532 encomenderos inherited the labor service of the Cuzcos. Spanish decrees defined tribute-payers as able-bodied men of 17 to 47, later standardized at 18 to 50. But because the Natives did not calculate time or age in years, both younger and older men found themselves included in the ranks of the tribute-obligated. In addition, encomienda labor was originally meant to support the encomenderos' household. But a lack of supervision meant that, until President Pedro de la Gasca mandated that tribute lists specify what services and goods each group owed in 1549, no one controlled what the encomenderos requested. Even after the written tribute lists existed, viceroys provided no oversight and no enforcement—except sporadically, when a high Spanish official came to inspect a population and its administration (AGI/J 454–55). By the 1560s labor requirements were being replaced with lists of specific goods and values in silver coin. The Spanish Crown prohibited Natives from providing personal service to the encomendero, replacing it with periodic and rotating service to specific sectors of the growing Spanish economy (Ramírez 1996, ch. 4).

Viceroy Toledo made two more changes. First, he mandated that goods increasingly be valued in currency and that the Natives be given the choice of whether or not to deliver goods or money. Further, tribute was assessed individually, no longer by lineage (Ramírez 1996, ch. 4). Such changes gradually pushed Natives to enter into the money economy in the cities, at the mines, and on agricultural estates. The sum total of these changes "destructured" (to use a concept coined by Nathan Wachtel [1977]) Native society and reduced the lords to salaried tribute collectors and labor organizers, liaisons, and brokers, intermediaries between the república de españoles and the república de indios.

However, in the countryside, such policy attempts to create a homogeneous group of Indians did not often take hold even in part. In response to the reducción initiative, the curacas of Chérrepe on the north coast sued in royal courts to nullify Toledo's decrees, hoping to gain the right for at least some of the lineage to remain near their ancestral *pueblo viejo*, Noquique (Ramírez 1979). Murra reports that ethnic groups tried to bribe royal officials to prevent removal (Murra 1970, 9; Andrien 1991, 128). Others acquiesced and built homes in reducción towns, only to melt away later to continue living near their scattered fields and sacred ancestral shrines (Abercrombie 1998, 283; Doyle 1988, 265; Espinoza Soriano 1981, 125; Cock 1976–77, 101; Flores and Gutierrez 1992, 203; Saignes 1987, 111; Hart 1983, 48; Duviols 1986, 102, 403). They returned, on occasion, to appear before the priest in church on important feast days and celebrations, but overall, many early reducciones were failures (AGI/J 458, 942v).

Natives also resisted the church's efforts to change their habits. Despite some earnest efforts by missionaries and priests, relatives routinely disinterred the preserved bodies of family members buried in the churches or churchyards to place them in their traditional burial centers. In some highland villages, Native builders working on church walls embedded sacred representations of their ancestral spiritual forces above the altars, so that worship in the church continued Native veneration of their traditional gods (Duviols 2003, 192, 194, 696, 699, and 707). Furthermore, ancestor worship continued, as the records of idolatry trials show, out of Spanish sight on the north and central coasts and the central and southern highlands to at least the end of the eighteenth century (Larco 2008; ART/ CoCompulsas, l.265, c. 3046, 17-XII-1784; Duviols 1986 and 2003; Salomon 1987; Polia Meconi 1996; Polia Meconi 1999; Sánchez 1991).

Somewhat more common were the Natives who eventually participated—directly or indirectly—in the market economy to satisfy the need for silver to pay tribute. In the sixteenth century, curacas formed work parties of their subjects and offered them to city dwellers in return for silver, which they then handed over to the encomendero or corregidor. Eventually, some individuals offered their labor to others or sold what they produced to earn their tribute payment directly. But such participation grew slowly and sporadically, as individuals feared nonpayment of wages or being cheated, and language remained a barrier to quotidian communication. Temporary labor for the Spanish in the mines, on agricultural estates, and in the cities exposed Natives to the market economy. Some stayed on as wage laborers, eventually losing contact with their lineages (Bakewell 1984).

Such contact resulted in some acculturation, but Hispanization was an uneven process outside the two major colonial cities of Lima and Cuzco. Even within one group, the curacas and important lords had most occasions to interact with encomenderos, colonial officials, and priests, so they became the first to learn Spanish. Already in the second half of the sixteenth century, lords on the north coast hired tutors to teach their sons to read and write (Ramírez 2003). In the early seventeenth century, the state institutionalized such family efforts with two schools to instruct the sons of lords to be effective intermediaries between the Spanish and their Native followers (Alaperrine Bouyer 2002; Alaperrine Bouyer 2007). Native lineage authorities were conspicuous at mass, even though many continued to lead ancestral rites out of Spanish view (Duviols 1986; Ramírez 2005, ch. 4, especially p. 137). They coordinated tribute labor and payment. A few traveled to Lima or even Spain to petition the court. They changed so that, as Granados discusses for Mesoamerica in this volume, they could remain the same and in place, the pivotal nexus between the two theoretical colonial republics (Puente Luna 2010).

Thus, in the provinces, ancestral lineage identities and their complex of religious practices, political rites, and cultural attributes continued strong, despite the reducciones; the presence of royal officials, priests, and friars; and changes in the tribute system that pressured them to participate actively in the colonial economy. Even where two or more ethnic groups were settled together in one reducción, they often remained geographically and ritually segregated with distinctive, recognizable dress. Thus, the lineages of Sinto and Collique were "reduced" to a new Native town called Chiclayo with a Franciscan mission on the main square (Ramírez 2002, 69). Each occupied one side of a main street. Based on the sixteenth-century censuses of Cajamarca, Rostworowski and Remy describe such reducciones as *pueblos compartidos* (shared towns) because they included members of several separate lineages. Near Lima, the settlement of La Magdalena included Natives from the lineages of Maranga, Guatca, Guala, Lima, and Amancaes. The lords of each people retained authority over their kin and subjects, and each group maintained vestiges of their separate socioreligious identity which lasted throughout the colonial period (Lowry 1991, 65; Rostworowski and Remy 1992).[7]

Yet never in any colonial documentation did the Sintos or Colliques refer to themselves as Chiclayanos. They normally did not represent themselves as Sintos or Colliques either. Instead, they identified themselves and were recognized by their lineage affiliation within an ethnic group. Near Chiclayo, in the reducción of Lambayeque, eleven ayllus (del cacique, la de segunda, Huerta, Efquem, Yanaconas, Calencec, Yencala, Olleros, Gigloc, Corñan, and Jacap) lived in spatially segregated neighborhoods in 1765, but informants remembered that years ago, there had been many more (ANCR/1765). The baptismal and marriage records of Lambayeque attest to the persistence of these identities. The names of thirty-two indigenous lineages, not including those listed as others, Spaniards, slaves, and unknown, appear between 1615 and 1797 in a sampling from the colonial records in the parish office. Most have indigenous names. Some names identify the rank of the lord: *del cacique* (of the chief), *de la segunda* (of the second person in charge), and *principales* (nobles). Others grouped by occupational specialty: *olleros* (potters), named from 1615 to 1769; *chicheros* (maize beer brewers), identified between 1646 and 1796; *huseros* (spindle whorl makers), present from 1651 to 1700; *pintores* (painters of cloth), noted from 1693 to 1698; and *liseros* (fishermen), reporting from 1707 to 1797. Some of these specialists also appear individually or as lineages in documentation from the 1560s (Ramírez 2007, 264). Individuals used these identities or were recognized by them before the priests who baptized their babies and married them and before the royal authorities who considered their petitions and received their testimonies. Such ayllu affiliation remained the principal mode of self-identification into the second half of the seventeenth century within forty leagues of the capital city (Duviols 2003, 340).

## Becoming Indians

The Spanish colonial plan and process of "becoming Indians" (i.e., where Natives consciously referred to themselves as "Indian," thus eschewing their usual lineage identities, their ancestralities) proved more successful in the major urban centers. Indeed, Lynn Lowry's research shows that starting about the middle of the seventeenth century, Native lords and intellectuals of several different ethnicities began to use the term *Indian* in the phrase *la nación indica*. Despite what some might expect to see, the origins of a wider ethnic consciousness did not start in the neighborhood of Santiago de Cercado, or El Cercado for short, that was founded in 1570 on the other side of the river from the capital city as a hospice to house temporary workers (*mitayos*) and other Native immigrants from the provinces on short visits to Lima. Originally built for transients who lived there under the tutelage of the Jesuits, El Cercado became eventually the home of Native servants and artisans, fishermen, laborers, market vendors, and gardeners from many different lineages from all over the realm. The exclusivity of El Cercado did not lead them to overcome their varied ancestral identities (Lowry 1991, 68, 126; Charney 1998, 380).

Instead, Lowry posits that a broader sense of self originated in another settlement, San Lázaro. This marginal parish attracted Natives, free blacks, and eventually even Spaniards, especially after the bridge was built in the early seventeenth century. She writes that "during the 17th century, the Indians of this parish, more autonomous than those of the Cercado, became the core of a new 'Indian Nation.' Significantly, it was here, where they lived in proximity to peoples of all races, not in the Cercado where they lived apart and somewhat buffered from Spanish society by Jesuit paternalism, that Indians developed a sense of pride in their separate status" (Lowry 1991, 89). Interaction with a wider range of different peoples that they saw as "others," argues Lowry, fed an evolving and encompassing collective identity that weakened ethnic and lineage differentiation.

Paul Charney and Lowry, in research that overlaps, trace the advent of a new "Indian" consciousness to the shared activities of *cofradías* (religious brotherhoods), *gremios* (craft guilds), a Native militia, and the emergent influence of Native intellectuals. Native cofradías organized processions, pageants, celebrations, and masses on the feast days of their patron saints and acted as mutual aid societies for their members. In this latter capacity, they buried the dead; delivered charity to members, orphans, the imprisoned, and the sick, and paid for masses for dead members and their dependents and other souls in purgatory with donated funds, initiation fees, and legacies. They also reinforced common devotions, thus helping to socialize members (Lowry 1991, 149–50; Charney 1998, 382–83). Participation in cofradía activities brought prestige and power and sharpened management skills. Native gremios that do not appear in the records until the late seventeenth and eighteenth centuries were sometimes organized as cofradías as well as occupational groups, for example of fishermen and shoemakers. In addition to the activities listed above, they examined and licensed craftsmen, oversaw the quality of products, and settled disputes among members. Some of these gremios restricted membership, meetings, and office holding to *indios de nación*, the Indian nation. Both institutions helped overcome the divisions of immigrants to the city and their social welfare functions fostered a growing consciousness of self and belonging (Lowry 1991, 149, 153; Charney 1998, 382–88).

The Native militia already functioned in the first decade of the seventeenth century. Documents mention infantry commanders: a captain of the Cañares, a captain of the natives of Lima, and a captain of the Indians of El Cercado. By 1622 high-ranking captains officered ten companies of infantrymen. These companies led the parade when Viceroy Conde del Chinchón made his official entrance into Lima and continued to appear on ceremonial occasions throughout the eighteenth century (Lowry 1991, 154–55).

But the process of overcoming ancestralities or ancestor-based identities was slow and irregular. Each ethnic group still used unique symbols and insignias and performed group-specific dances that distinguished them from others and reinforced corporate identity in celebrations described from 1555 to 1659. By the middle of the seventeenth century, however, persons of multiple ethnicities were portraying the Incas as symbols of a nascent collective identity. In the second half of the seventeenth century, a claim to Inca blood brought prestige. Knowledge of Inca history spread with the increased use and dissemination of the chronicled history and literature. Increasingly in the eighteenth century, Native immigrants to the capital saw the pageants and plays in the plaza and the streets with the Incas reimagined as the leaders of a pan-Andean identity. Thus, slowly a "revival" and "reimagining of all things Inca" became a harbinger of when the Incas became the symbols of an emerging collective identity (Lowry 1991, 265–75; Charney 1998, 382).

Intellectuals and reformers spearheaded this increasing awareness. Don Carlos Chimu, Don Vicente Mora Chimo, and the mestizo Fray Calixto Tupac Ynga traveled to Spain to present manifestos listing Native grievances to the king. In the 1640s Don Carlos Chimu, an alleged cacique of Lambayeque who acted as a representative of a group of cooperating caciques, complained about abuses and mistreatment, including those that occurred during a land title inspection (*visita de la tierra*). He presented a petition, which, when reviewed by the council, resulted in the viceroy's establishing a special court to review cases and sending an inspector to return usurped Native lands. Don Vicente Mora Chimo, a cacique of Chicama (on the north coast), presented five reports complaining of mistreatments to the king between 1722 and 1732. Fray Calixto Tupac Ynga likewise wrote and sent manifestos listing Native grievances to the royal peninsular court and Ferdinand VI in the mid-eighteenth century, when talk of nationalism and self-determination was heard in Europe. His secret meetings with

Native elites after his return to America, however, ended with his imprisonment and banishment (Lowry 1991, 275–79).

Other Natives who appealed to the king for redress of Native grievances went even further. Don Antonio Collatopa, a cacique of Cajamarca and a descendant of the Cuzco Viejo or Guayna Capac, the purported twelfth emperor, wrote another declaration drawn up by several caciques, including Don Carlos Apoalaya, a cacique of Hanan Guanca. The Council of the Indies reviewed it in 1664 and ordered the viceroy to take action. In 1666 when the colonial government failed to find constructive remedies to their complaints, the Native elite, including some caciques and at least two captains of the Lima Native militia (a saddler and a shoemaker) began planning a revolt. In subsequent clandestine meetings, they discussed burning the city, flooding it by diverting canal water, and killing all Spaniards. Factionalism and disagreements led to a betrayal, and the leaders were detained, adjudicated, and sentenced to be hanged, drawn, and quartered. The one leader who escaped to the highlands schemed there with other Natives of Huarochirí and Yauyos to attack settlers in the area. They too were betrayed but only after they had torn down bridges, cutting off food supplies to Lima and killing a lieutenant of the Corregidor of Jauja (Lowry 1991, 279–82).

These protests and later revolts in 1742 (headed by Juan Santos among the Tarmas), 1750 (involving Captain Francisco García Jiménez, alias Francisco Inca, among the Huarochirí Natives), and another in 1750 among the Saña and Lambayeque, fostered a degree of unity and revealed collective strength. Lowry asserts that Native reformers and revolutionaries alike wanted self-determination, a demand that still echoed in twentieth-century Bolivia (see Ari-Chachaki's chapter in this volume). They used the phrase *Indian nation* in their written protests and lawsuits starting in the mid-seventeenth century. Indicative of their strength, unity, and growing shared conscience was a major court case filed in 1763 by the Native *cabildo* (town council) of Lima for the right of replacing two Spanish *procuradores de naturales*, Crown attorneys who represented Natives, with their own. Although Natives continued to be divided sometimes by ethnicity and jealousies, they used the phrase *comun de la nación Yndica* in their petition (Lowry 1991, 282–87).

Thus art, lawsuits, petitions, public displays, and rebellions helped forge a sense of self that used Inca history as a basis to end peninsular tutelage and advocate for equality with the Spanish (Lowry 1991, 288–89). Native leaders employed the phrase *nación indica* as spokesmen, probably reckoning that if they claimed to speak for all the "others," they would project more clout in authorities' eyes than if they were to speak in the name of one lineage or another. Thus, the phrase served political purposes. Its use reflected more expediency than a wholesale change in identity. Native leaders and intellectuals employed it in the viceregal capital and on the peninsula to further their causes. Its limited use did not necessarily mean that the elite and the tribute-payers unanimously identified and used pan-Incanism as a substitute for their original ancestral identity among themselves.

**The Futility of Colonial Impositions**

This urban phenomenon reveals a continuum in the process of "becoming Indian," that is, consciously identifying oneself as within the imposed Indian category. Living the Spanish ideal of a Hispanized loyal and devout Catholic subject of the king (like Don Melchor Carlos Ynga, pictured in figure 4) proved strongest in the capital city and became weaker and weaker in the countryside (Charney 1998, 378–79). This sequence is illustrated poignantly in the early seventeenth-century drawings of Felipe Guaman Poma de Ayala, a Hispanized Native chronicler, a few of which are reproduced in figures 2–4.

They show (in ascending order and power) how Native dress changed at different levels of the Native hierarchy and increasing interactions with the Spanish: the higher the rank of the authority, the greater his interaction with the Spaniards, and the more European his dress appears. In figure 2, the minor lord of ten families wears sandals and is clothed in garments decorated with Andean symbols. On the front of his tunic are centered *tocupu* (square designs). Such designs are interpreted by some scholars as representing the four divisions of the Inca empire. Over his shoulder is slung a bag for his supply of coca leaves, which he chews and offers to his fellows. The rosary in his left hand indicates his Christian baptism, a requisite condition in Spanish eyes for holding any position of Native authority. In figure 3, a lord of a hundred families (a *curaca pachaca*) still wears a sleeveless tunic of Native design, but his hat loses Native symbols and the coca bag disappears. He also appears to wear shoes instead of sandals. Don Melchor Carlos Ynga's portrait (in figure 4) shows him in a Spanish-style jacket, cloak, ruff, and boots, with a hat devoid of Andean symbols. His bearded face and short-cropped hair suggest a non-Native identity.

Such changes in dress and grooming, while keeping in mind the rural-urban and distance-from-power continuum, reveal a transformation. The lord of ten families interacted with his subjects and other Native lords above him but probably never attended court, even at the provincial level. Neither did the *curaca pachaca*, lord of one hundred families, though he would have had sporadic relations with the corregidor who would need reminding of the lord's Catholic devotion. Don Melchor Carlos, in contrast, represented himself as indistinguishable, at least in superficial appearance, from a Spaniard. His aspect was a transformative performance, following Beatriz Perrone-Moisés (2014), that underscored the fact that he considered himself as equal to the Spanish, thus lessening the contextual relevance of his birth.

The Spanish imperial project, then, to reduce all Natives to a unified, homogenous group, did not occur, except rhetorically and in an embryonic, unstable, and temporary form. But even when ancestralities were momentarily overcome and common cause recognized, antagonisms and jealousies often ultimately undercut Native hopes for unity, change, and redress.

Outside of Lima, to the end of the colonial era, ancestral identities remained the norm. The majority of the Native populace continued to speak such traditional languages as Quechua, Aymara, Mochik, Culle, Sec, or others. Ancestor worship survived, despite the fact that some attended mass, took the sacraments, and even buried their dead in the church or churchyard (at least temporarily). More and more Natives moved to reducciones as round-ups and force were continued periodically throughout the colonial era. As tribute was standardized, more and more participated in the monetary economy, and communities continued to appeal to colonial

FIG. 2. Mandoncillo de 10 Indios. Source: Guaman Poma de Ayala (1613) 1936, f. 753.

FIG. 3. Mandoncillo de 100 Indios. Source: Guaman Poma de Ayala (1613) 1936, f. 751.

## PRINCIPES
## DONMELCHORCARLOS

ynga                    principeauqui ynga

conestos principes habla el señor vey enperadoryssabelanqui
encomienda de santiago — quieredezirprincipe·a
uqui ynga capacchuri enla ley desiereyno delosyns
ytodosusnietos ydecien dientes son principes delos
yns ensugeneracion ylley mud del s. vey enperador
tienen — yns deencomienda ellos ellas —

FIG. 4. Melchor Carlos Ynga. Source: Guaman Poma de Ayala (1613) 1936, f. 739.

courts to counter injustices. But despite these changes and repeated adversities, few adopted the identifier *indio*. This is reflected in colonial records when petitioners, witnesses, and parents continued to identify themselves by ayllu or *parcialidad* into the late eighteenth century.[8]

The least acculturated lived far from the cities (Altman and Butler 1994, 492). They sustained links to their past longer (Charney 1998, 380; Berliner 2005, 206). Charney's research found that cofradías in the rural areas around Lima commonly functioned as covers of "organized heresy," a euphemism for what the Spanish considered continued ancestor worship and idolatry (Charney 1998, 395). James Saeger's investigations on the Guaycuruans of the Gran Chaco from 1743 to 1810 concluded that the missions were limited successes. The Native habits changed little under Jesuit tutelage (Saeger 1985, 494, 502–3, 506, 513, 516). And Antonine Tibesar notes that missions did not permanently change Native culture in the *montaña* (jungle) (Tibesar 1957, 118).

When used, the word *indio* suited Native ends to further their own interests in limited contexts. It was situational and conjunctural. It did not necessarily imply more than a colonial expedient. Its use remained uneven: more in the city and less in the countryside. Indianness or indigeneity remained a function of a practical, self-conscious use and the partial adaptation of urban culture and Spanish values. Thus, "becoming Indian," accepting the imposed term "Indian" as a personal identifier, remained largely an unfinished process even at the end of the Spanish colonial era.

## Notes

1. The phrase "becoming Indian" appears elsewhere. See, for example, Jackson (1991), who uses it in relation to the agency of contemporary South American lowland Native groups, and Maybury-Lewis (1991), who features it in a similar vein in his overview of evolving national policy toward "Indians" and their reactions in Chile, Argentina, and Brazil. Further readings on the topic include Hodgson 2011 and Sturm 2011.

2. By the mid-seventeenth century, Native groups were described as becoming "mixed up" or "scrambled" (*revueltos*), among those of other lineages (Mills 1994, 44; Duviols 1986, 168).

3. For an example of the practice of indigenous gift-giving feasts in Canada, see Seguin 1986.

4. For example, the encomendero of Chérrepe had two hundred tribute-paying families in 1564. The encomendero of Íllimo had three hundred in 1541. See Ramírez 1978; Ramírez 1996, 27–29, for more examples on the north coast; Rostworowski and Remy 1992 on Cajamarca; Puente Brunk, 1992 for the viceroyalty as a whole.

5. Rubiños y Andrade (1782) 1936, 315 relates that in 1658 even Spanish-speaking Natives (*indios ladinos*) still believed that the Christians worshiped three gods. The priest Don Augustín Fernández Delgadillo asked Pedro Quevedo, "hubiese sido uno de los más ladinos, y racionales que entonces tenía Mórrope" (who was one of the most Hispanicized and rational persons who lived in Mórrope), if he believed in God. Quevedo asked which one he was asking about, so Delgadillo asked him how many gods he thought there were. Quevedo replied: "Señor . . . tu me has enseñado, y los demás curas, que el Padre es Dios, el Hixo, es Dios, y el Espíritu Santo es Dios, y siendo tres personas distintas, son tres dioses distintos." (Sir . . . you and the other priests have taught me that the Father is God, the Son is God, and the Holy Spirit is God, and being three distinct persons, they are three distinct gods.)

6. The Spanish also accepted new foods, textiles of cotton and wool, etc. That story is beyond the focus of this study.

7. Wernke reports that in Yunque (Colca Valley near Arequipa in southern Peru), villagers in 1988 still recognized divisions of people settled there in the reducción movement. These divisions are reflected in their burial patterns organized by ayllu (Wernke 2007, 174–75).

8. See the registers of births and marriages in the Archivo Parroquial de Lambayeque.

# Bibliography

## Abbreviations

AGI/AL    Archivo General de las Indias/Audiencia de Lima
AGI/J    Archivo General de las Indias/Justicia
ANP/DI    Archivo Nacional del Perú/Derecho Indígena (now Archivo General de la Nación)
ANCR    Archivo Notarial de Carlos Rivadeneira, Lambayeque
APL    Archivo Parrochial de Lambayeque
ART/Co    CompulsasArchivo Regional de Trujillo (now Archivo Regional de La Libertad)/Corregimiento Compulsas
ART/CoR    Archivo Regional de Trujillo (now Archivo Regional de La Libertad)/Corregimiento Residencias

Abercrombie, Thomas A. 1998. *Pathways of Memory and Power: Ethnography and History among an Andean People*. Madison: University of Wisconsin Press.
Adrián, Monica. 1997. "El espacio sagrado y el ejercicio del poder: Las doctrinas de Chayanta durante la segunda mitad del siglo 18." In *Anuario del Archivo y Biblioteca Nacionales de Bolivia* (Sucre): 239–55.
Alaperrine Bouyer, Monique. 2002. "Saber y poder: La cuestión de la educación de las elites indígenas." In *Incas e indios cristianos: Elites indígenas e identidades cristia-*

*nos en los Andes coloniales*, edited by Jean-Jacques Decoster, 145–67. Cusco: Centro de Estudios Regionales Andinos "Bartolomé de las Casas."

——. 2007. *La educación de las elites indígenas en el Perú colonial*. Lima: Instituto Francés de Estudios Andinos.

Altman, Ida and Reginald D. Butler. 1994. "The Contact of Cultures: Perspectives on the Quincentary." *American Historical Review* 99, no. 2: 78–503.

Andrien, Kenneth J. 1991. "Spaniards, Andeans, and the Early Colonial State in Peru." In *Transatlantic Encounters: Europeans and Andeans in the Sixteenth Century*, edited by K. J. Andrien and Rolena Adorno, 121–48. Berkeley: University of California Press.

Armas Medina, Fernando de. 1952. "Evolución histórica de las doctrinas de indios." *Anuario de Estudios Americanos* 9: 101–29.

Bakewell, Peter. 1984. *Miners of the Red Mountain: Indian Labor in Potosi, 1545–1600*. Albuquerque: University of New Mexico Press.

Berliner, David C. 2005. "The Abuses of Memory: Reflections on the Memory Boom in Anthropology." *Anthropological Quarterly* 78, no. 1: 197–211.

Betanzos, Juan de. (1551–57) 2004. *Suma y narracion de los Incas*. Madrid: Ediciones Polifema.

Charney, Paul. 1998. "A Sense of Belonging: Colonial Indian Cofradías and Ethnicity in the Valley of Lima, Peru." *The Americas* 54, no. 3: 379–407.

Cieza de León, Pedro de. (1548–50) 1998. *The Discovery and Conquest of Peru*. Translated and edited by Alexandra Parma Cook and Noble David Cook. Durham: Duke University Press.

Cock, Guillermo. 1976–77. "Los kurakas de los Collaguas: Poder político y poder económico." *Historia y cultura* 10: 95–118.

Contreras, Miguel de. (1613) 1968. *Padron de los In[di]os que se hallaron en la ciuda[d] de los Reyes de Piru [ . . . ]*. Lima: Seminario de Historia Rural Andina, Universidad Mayor de San Marcos.

Doyle, Mary Eileen. 1988. "The Ancestor Cult and Burial Ritual in Seventeenth- and Eighteenth-Century Peru." PhD diss., University of California–Los Angeles.

Duviols, Pierre. 1986. *Cultura Andina y represión*. Cuzco: Centro de Estudios Rurales Andinos.

——. 2003. *Procesos y visitas de idolatrías: Cajatambo, siglo XVII*. Lima: Pontificia Universidad Católica del Perú.

Espinoza Soriano, Waldemar. 1981. *La destrucción del imperio de los Incas*. Lima: Amaru Editores.

Flores Espinoza, Javier, and Gutiérrez, Laura. 1992. "Dos documentos sobre los Jesuitas en Huarochirí." *Boletín del Instituto Riva Agüero* 19: 201–16.

Foster, George. 1960. *Culture and Conquest: America's Spanish Heritage*. Chicago: Quadrangle.

Frances, J. Michael. 2006. "Language and the 'True Conversion' to the Holy Faith: A Document from the Archivum Romanum Societatis Iesu, Rome, Italy." *The Americas* 62, no. 3: 445–53.

Guaman Poma de Ayala, Felipe. (1613) 1936. *Nueva coronica y buen gobierno*. Paris: Institut d'ethnologie.

Hart, Elizabeth Ann. 1983. "Prehistoric Political Organization on the Peruvian North Coast." PhD diss., University of Michigan–Ann Arbor.

Hodgson, Dorthy. 2011. *Being Maasai, Becoming Indigenous: Postcolonial Politics in a Neoliberal World*. Bloomington: Indiana University Press.

Huertas Vallejos, Lorenzo. "Introducción al estudio de los centros poblados." Accessed March 1, 2013. http://peru.inka.free.fr/Runapacha/.

Jackson, Jean E. 1991. "Being and Becoming an Indian in the Vaupés." In *Nation-States and Indians in Latin America*, edited by Greg Urban and Joel Sherzer, 131–55. Austin: University of Texas Press.

Jaye, Barbara H., and William P. Mitchell, eds. 1999. *Picturing Faith: A Facsimile Edition of the Pictographic Quechua Catechism in the Huntington Free Library*. Bronx: Huntington Free Library.

Jerez [also Xerez], Francisco de. (1534) 1917. *Las relaciones de la conquista*. Lima: Sanmartí y Ca.

Keith, Robert G. 1971. "*Encomienda*, Hacienda, and *Corregimiento* in Spanish America." *Hispanic American Historical Review* 51, no. 3: 431–46.

Larco, Laura. 2008. *Más allá de los encantos: Documentos sobre extirpación de idolatrías Trujillo (siglos XVIII–XX)*. Lima: Instituto Frances de Estudios Andinos.

Levillier, Roberto, ed. 1921–26. *Gobernantes del Perú: Cartas y papeles, siglo 16*. Madrid: Sucesores de Rivadeneyra.

———. 1935. *Don Francisco de Toledo: Supremo Organizador del Perú*. Madrid: Espasa-Calpe.

Lissón y Chaves, Emilio. 1943–46. *La iglesia de España en el Perú*. 4 vols. Sevilla: Escuela de Estudios Hispano-Americanos.

Lowry, Lyn Brandon. 1991. "Forging an Indian Nation: Urban Indians under Spanish Colonial Control (Lima, Peru, 1535–1765)." PhD diss., University of California–Berkeley.

MacCormack, Sabine G. 1985. "The Heart has Its Reasons: Predicaments of Missionary Christianity in Early Colonial Peru." *Hispanic American Historical Review* 65, no. 3: 443–66.

———. 1991. *Religion in the Andes: Vision and Imagination in Early Colonial Peru*. Princeton NJ: Princeton University Press.

Martínez Cereceda, José Luis. 1988. "Kurakas, rituales e insignias: Una proposición." *Histórica* 12, no. 1: 61–74.

———. 1995. *Autoridades en los Andes, Los atributos del señor*. Lima: Pontificia Universidad Católica del Perú.

Maybury-Lewis, David. 1991. "Becoming Indian in Lowland South America." In *Nation-States and Indians in Latin America*, edited by Greg Urban and Joel Sherzer, 207–35. Austin: University of Texas Press.

Mills, Kenneth. 1994. *An Evil Lost to View: An Investigation of Post-Evangelisation Andean Religion in Mid-Colonial Peru*. Liverpool: University of Liverpool.

Morales, Adolfo de. 1977. *Repartimiento de tierras por el Inca Huayna Capac*. Cochabamba: Departamento de Arqueología, Universidad Mayor de San Simón.

Mumford, Jeremy. 2012. *Vertical Empire: The General Resettlement of the Indians in the Colonial Andes*. Durham: Duke University Press.

Muñoz Arbeláez, Santiago. 2015. *Costumbres en disputa: Los muiscas y el Imperio español en Ubaque, siglo XVI*. Bogotá: Universidad de los Andes.

Murra, John Victor. 1970. "Current Research and Prospects in Andean Ethnohistory." *Latin American Research Review* 5, no. 1: 3–36.

———. 1972. "El control vertical de un máximo de pisos ecológicos en la economía de las sociedades andinas." In *La visita de la Provincia de León de Huánuco en 1562*, vol. 2, by Íñigo Ortiz de Zúñiga, 427–76. Huánuco: Facultad de Letras y Educación, Universidad Nacional Hermilio Valdizán.

Perrone-Moisés, Beatriz. 2014. "Performed Alliances and Performative Identities." In *Performing Indigeneity*, edited by Laura R. Graham and H. Glenn Penny, 110–35. Lincoln: University of Nebraska Press.

Polia Meconi, Mario. 1996. "Siete cartas inéditas del Archivo Romano de la Compañía de Jesús, 1611–13: Huacas, mitos y ritos Andinos.'" *Antropológica* (Lima) 14: 209–59.

———. 1999. *Cosmovisión religiosa Andina en los documentos inéditos del Archivo Romano de la Compañía de Jesús, 1581–1752*. Lima: Pontificia Universidad Católica del Perú.

Polo, José Toribio. 1906. "Un Convento Franciscano." *Revista histórica* (Lima) I: 466–85.

Puente Brunke, José de la. 1992. *Encomienda y encomenderos en el Perú*. Sevilla: Excma, Diputación Provincial de Sevilla.

Puente Luna, José Carlos de la. 2010. "Into the Heart of the Empire: Indian Journeys to the Hapsburg Royal Court." PhD diss., Texas Christian University.

Ramírez, Susan Elizabeth. 1978. "Chérrepe en 1572: Un análisis de la Visita General del Virrey Francisco de Toledo." *Historia y cultura* 11: 79–121.

———. 1986. *Provincial Patriarchs: Land Tenure and the Economics of Power in Colonial Peru*. Albuquerque: University of New Mexico Press.

———. 1990. "The Inca Conquest of the North Coast: A Historian's View." In *The Northern Dynasties: Kingships and Statecraft in Chimor*, edited by Michael E. Mosely and Alana Cordy-Collins, 507–37. Washington DC: Dumbarton Oaks Research Library and Collection.

———. 1996. *The World Upside Down: Cross Cultural Contact and Conflict in Sixteenth-Century Peru*. Stanford: Stanford University Press.

———. 2002. *El mundo al revés: Contactos y conflictos transculturales en el Perú del siglo XVI*. Lima: Pontificia Universidad Católica del Perú.

———. 2003. "New Data on Education in Colonial Peru before 1700." Paper read at the International Congress of Americanistas, Santiago de Chile.

———. 2005. *To Feed and Be Fed: The Cosmological Bases of Authority and Identity in the Andes*. Stanford: Stanford University Press.

———. 2007. "It's All in a Day's Work: Occupational Specializationon the Peruvian North Coast, Revisited." In *Craft Production in Complex Societes: Multicraft and Producer Perspectives*, edited by Izumi Shimada, 262–80. Salt Lake City: University of Utah Press.

———. 2008. "Negociando el imperio: El estado Inca como culto." *Bulletin de l'Institut Français d'Études Andines* 37, no. 1: 5–18.

Rostworowski [de Diez Canseco], María. 1970. "El repartimiento de Doña Beatriz Coya, en el Valle de Yucay." *Historia y cultura* 4: 153–267.

———. 1977. "Las etnias del Valle del Chillón." In *Etnia y sociedad, 21–98*. Lima: Instituto de Estudios Peruanos.

———. 1983. "Esquemas Religiosos." In *Estructuras Andinas del Poder: Ideología religiosa y política*, 1–96. Lima: Instituto de Estudios Peruanos.

———. 1993. "La macroetnías en el ámbito andino." In *Ensayos de Historia Andina*, 201–18. Lima: Instituto de Estudios Peruanos.

Rostworowski [de Diez Canseco], María, and Pilar Remy. 1992. *Las visitas a Cajamarca, 1571–72/1578*. 2 vols. Lima: Instituto de Estudios Peruanos.

Rowe, John H. 1946. "Inca Culture at the Time of the Spanish Conquest." In *Handbook of South American Indians*, vol. 2, edited by Julian H. Steward, 183–331. Washington DC: U.S. Government Printing Office.

Rubiños y Andrade, Justo Modesto. (1782) 1936. "Un manuscrito interesante." *Revista histórica* 10, no. 3: 289–363.

Saignes, Thierry. 1987. "De la borrachera al retrato: Los caciques andinos entre los legitimidades (Charcas)." *Revista Andina* 5, no. 1: 139–70.

Salomon, Frank. 1987. "Ancestor Cults and Resistance to the State in Arequipa, ca. 1748–54." In *Resistance, Rebellion, and Consciousness in the Andean Peasant World, Eighteenth Century*, edited by Steve J. Stern, 148–65. Madison: University of Wisconsin Press.

Sánchez, Ana. 1991. *Amancebados, hechiceros y rebeldes (Chancay, siglo XVII)*. Cuzco: Centro de Estudios Regionales Andinos "Bartolomé de las Casas."

Santillán, Hernando de. (1572) 1968. "Relación del origen, descendencia, política y gobierno de los Incas (c. 1563–72)." In *Crónicas peruanas de interés indígena*, edited by Francisco Estete Barba, 97–150. Madrid: Ediciones Atlas.

Santo Tomás, Domingo. (1560) 1951. *Lexicon o vocaulario de la lengua general del Perú*. Lima: Instituto de Historia.

Saeger, James S. 1985. "Another View of the Mission as a Frontier Institution: Guaycuruan Reductions of Santa Fe, 1743–1810." *Hispanic American Historical Review* 65, no. 3: 493–517.

Seguin, Margaret. 1986. "Understanding Tsimshian 'Potlash.'" In *Native Peoples: The Canadian Experience*. R. Bruce Norrison and C. Roderick Wilson, eds. Toronto: McClelland and Stewart. 473–500.

Silverblatt, Irene. 1987. *Moon, Sun, and Witches: Gender Ideologies and Class in Inca and Colonial Peru*. Princeton: Princeton University Press.

Sturm, Circe. 2011. *Becoming Indian: The Struggle over Cherokee Identity in the Twenty-first Century*. Santa Fe: School of American Research Press.

Super, John C. 1988. *Food, Conquest, and Colonization in Sixteenth-Century Spanish America*. Albuquerque: University of New Mexico Press.

Tibesar, Antonine. 1957. "The Franciscan *Doctrinero* versus the Franciscan *Misionero* in Seventeeth Century Peru." *The Americas* 14, no. 2: 115–24.

Ulloa, Luis. 1909. "Documentos del Virrey Toledo." *Revista Histórica* 2: 332–47.

van Deusen, Nancy E. 2015. *Global Indios: The Indigenous Struggle for Justice in Sixteenth-Century Spain*. Durham: Duke University Press.

Wachtel, Nathan. 1977. *Vision of the Vanquished: The Spanish Conquest of Peru through Indian Eyes, 1530–70*. New York: Barnes and Noble.

Wernke, Steven A. 2007. "Analogy or Erasure?: Dialectics of Religious Transformation in the Early 'Doctrinas' of the Colca Valley, Peru." *International Journal of Historical Archaeology* 2, no. 2: 152–82.

# 3

# "We Do the Same Thing among Ourselves"

## Becoming Indigenous in Atlantic Canada

DAVID T. MCNAB

W hat did "becoming indigenous" mean in the fifteenth to eighteenth centuries, and what does it mean in the early twenty-first century?[1] In Atlantic Canada since the fifteenth century, becoming indigenous has meant that indigenous people were human beings who saw themselves as equal to Europeans. When the Mi'kmaq said to the French trader Nicolas Denys, who settled in the region of Acadia for some thirty years and chronicled his observations of its Native peoples and landscapes, "we do the same thing among ourselves," they were echoing the fact that they were original people of their territories. Among themselves, indigenous people were neither friend nor foe, nor saw themselves as "savages" or any other category devised by European science. Indigenous people were complex, multidimensional beings who could not be categorized as something colonial or as mere appendages of European empires. As such, they resisted things colonial and fought back against these European empires. They have survived as indigenous human beings in the Atlantic world to this day. Research into the Mi'kmaq community (on which this chapter is based) became part of my experiences beginning in the spring of 1978, when I first visited Conne River. Later, the Federation of Newfoundland Indians asked me to be an expert witness on the history and the existence of the Mi'kmaq (variously spelled *Micmac*, *Migmaw*, and *Mi'gMaq*) people on the island of Newfoundland, in a 1992 court challenge on Canada's constitution (1982).

I was asked to investigate the history of the Mi'kmaq, specifically referring to the question whether they existed on the island before the nineteenth century. The old story about the history of indigenous people of Newfoundland was that the Beothuk (a separate people who resided in the north and the eastern parts of the island of Newfoundland), who were known by Europeans as the "red Indians," became extinct when then the last one passed away in 1829. The Mi'kmaq only came to the island in the late eighteenth century from Cape Breton and mainland Nova Scotia. When Newfoundland, formerly a British colony, joined the Confederation of Canada in 1949, the indigenous people were literally penciled out of the negotiations, and thus the Mi'kmaq did not receive status as "Indians" under the Indian Act, nor did they receive the reserves normally associated with such a status. No research was undertaken at that time to show whether or not any "Indians" still existed on the island. In 1984 after review of the history of the Conne River Mi'kmaq, the Mi'kmaq people on the southeast coast received status and a reserve, thirty-five years after the fact. My doctoral dissertation research on indigenous policy of the British Empire, completed in 1978 at the University of Lancaster, figured in the latter decision in 1984.

This early research was the reason I was chosen to be an expert witness in the 1992 constitutional challenge. I completed my five-hundred-page expert's report in August 1996. Since the court case still remains a live one, I have not received permission to publish it in its entirety. However, the result of this and other work has had an impact through negotiations, and the remaining eight communities, numbering now about 100,000 persons out of a total population on the island of 500,000, are today currently registering as Indians under federal self-government legislation (these negotiations unfortunately did not include land for reserves). So as one can readily see, the issue of the precolonial aspects of becoming Indigenous has a long history in Atlantic Canada, going back at least to the fifteenth century, if not before, and stretching down to this day. This overview of European representations of Mi'kmaq since the time of the first European visits shows that Europeans have understood or interpreted Mi'kmaq variously as friends, allies, foes, and savages. Mi'kmaq, however, have retained agency and acted strategically.

## Who Were the Indigenous People of Newfoundland?

The indigenous people—Mi'kmaq, Beothuk, Wuastukwiuk, or Maliseet—in what became Atlantic Canada were known to themselves as the "people of the sunrise" (see Santoro, chapter 9 in this volume). Their territories also included parts of present-day northeastern United States. The history of the Mi'kmaq nation in present-day Atlantic Canada is based on the oral tradition of the *Sayewedjikik*, the Ancients. Their history intersects with that of the Wuastukwiuk, also known as the Maliseet people, and it also informs that of the Beothuk (McNab 2001, 85). The Mi'kmaq nation's stories have been handed down through generations of Mi'kmaq families and communities to form their oral tradition and histories. The Mi'kmaq nation has its own rich and diverse history as well as its own historians, including their elders (Paul 1993, 5–6).

The Mi'kmaq people were reputed to have been known, by the name the French gave to them, as allies. However, this appellation reflects the European perceptions of them. It is instructive that the word the Mi'kmaq used to describe themselves was *El'nu*, meaning "true men" in the Mi'kmaq language (much like the Anishinaabe, "the original people"; see Hele, chapter 6 in this volume). The late Olive Dickason wrote that the Mi'kmaq "were probably the Toudamans of Cartier, and were certainly the Souriquois of Lescarbot; they were also called Tarratines, a reference to their trading proclivities" (Dickason 2009, 87). They were not "savages," as European Nations and their writers had often demonized them, using their "scientific" categories. Nor were they categorized as friends or foes (Jaenen 1976, 153–89). As the French trader Nicolas Denys wrote in 1670, the Mi'kmaq people told him that they did the "same thing among themselves" as human beings, with all of the variations that people have always had (McNab 2006, 47–48). Using categories based on European "scientific" knowledge has proven a flawed methodology, since the European explorers and colonists were unable to understand indigenous oral traditions' experiential complexities (see Granados, chapter 4 in this volume).

## What Were the Mi'kmaq Territories in Atlantic Canada?

The Mi'kmaq territory includes the present-day Atlantic region in modern Canada as well as parts of Maine. This territory also includes the Mi'kmaq district of Ktaqamkuk, meaning the place of fog or the foggy lands, which includes Cape Breton Island and the island of Newfoundland. Their territory includes the islands and peninsulas and the surrounding waters in the Gulf of the Saint Lawrence (Tanner and Henderson 1992, 132–33). The water was and is their lifeblood—the element that sustains and restores the land. These places that make up their territory shape their lives and their history (Speck [1922] 1981, 12–13).

The Mi'kmaq nation's oral tradition is told by the people of their nation and includes their stories and their history. Nevertheless, some of these stories, however incomplete, have been told and written down by nonindigenous people. For the Mi'kmaq of Newfoundland, a few of these stories were told to Frank Speck (1881–1950), an American ethnologist who was also a Mohegan-Pequot/Innu and who visited them at Conne River, Badger's Brook, and Saint George's Bay in the summer of 1914. Speck included information on the Mi'kmaq and their oral tradition in his reports to the federal Anthropological Survey of Canada, which deposited them in the Victoria Museum in Ottawa (now the Canadian Museum of History). They were also included in Speck's study entitled *Beothuk and Micmac* (1922), a work that is, in fact, more about the Mi'kmaq than about the Beothuk. These peoples were neighbors and friends, and their families frequently intermarried (Jaenen 1976, 25–26). It was a custom as well as part of their lived experience for centuries (Bartels 1991, 43–51).

Speck noted that the Mi'kmaq oral tradition presents the nation's ancient roots as on the island of Newfoundland. Speck records that their knowledge is "from remote times. They speak of a branch of their people called *Sa'yewe'djki'k*, 'ancients,' . . . and to corroborate this they give an old nomenclature of landmarks in various parts of the island in Micmac" (Speck [1922] 1981, 26–27). The Mi'kmaq relations with the Beothuk were in the best tradition of neighbors, characterized for the most part by peace and friendship. Like most neighbors, sometimes they quarreled. Speck observed this Mi'kmaq tradition that "their ancestors lived in amicable contact with the Beothuk, whom they designate *Meywe'djik*, 'red people.' This period of friendly relationship interests us now because during that time we may surmise some culture borrowing and blood intermixture to have taken place" (Speck [1922] 1981, 28). Speck thus suggests they were practicing the indigenous ritual of sharing—the concept represented by the dish with one spoon that became embodied in the Covenant Chain of Silver, which was codified in English at least as early as the seventeenth century. Speck, as an indigenous person, had an insider's vision of the Mi'kmaq people and understood and recorded their oral history and traditions. As an ethnologist, he also repeats the written records and lets his reader choose. He was one of a few who tried to show history, traditions, and customs from an indigenous perspective. As such, Speck was critical to my research and to the success of the Mi'kmaq charter litigation.

**Friends and Neighbors**

Speck highlighted the close relationship through intermarriage of the Mi'kmaq and the Beothuk right into the early twentieth century. This is related through the Mi'kmaq oral tradition as well as being supported by Speck's own fieldwork. This is the story of Santu—"The Case of Santu"—who Speck noted died in 1919. Santu was likely not the only Beothuk to have lived past 1829 and into the twenty-first century. Speck noted that Santu was a Beothuk whose family history could be traced back to at least the early nineteenth century (Speck [1922] 1981, 55–68). With his understanding of the Mi'kmaq oral tradition, Speck also gives no credence to the written historical record that had developed through the influence of John Peyton, a white Newfoundlander, who suggested that the Mi'kmaq had been mercenaries for the French imperial government and were as such responsible for the apparent demise and the seeming extermination of the Beothuk (Speck [1922] 1981, 47–48). Speck wrote down the "Ancient Place-Names in Newfoundland," thereby illustrating the depth of the oral tradition and knowledge of the land by the Mi'kmaq people (Speck [1922] 1981, 138–39).

A Mi'kmaq historian, Daniel N. Paul, has indicated that the Mi'kmaq territory is divided into seven districts. Holding authority over all the districts was a grand chief, who was one of the chiefs of the seven districts and was chosen grand chief by the other citizens. Each district was made up of small villages that contained between fifty and five hundred people. The number of villages in each district is unknown. The total Mi'kmaq population has been estimated to be over one hundred thousand people before it was decimated by European diseases. Paul has also noted that each village had a local chief. District council meetings were held and brought together all the local chiefs. Among other items, the agenda would be to "readjust the hunting and fishing territories and to satisfy other administrative and political needs" (Paul 1993, 5–6). In addition, there was a grand council with a grand chief selected from the peers of that council. The district chief of the Foggy Lands (Cape Breton Island and the island of Newfoundland) was grand chief of that council (Paul 1993, 7–8). Their political organization was tied directly to the lands and its uses through this decision-making process. Paul, as a Mi'kmaq historian, knows his oral history and traditions and completely contradicts the European thought and version of events in Mi'kmaq history. As such, he once again gives their history agency and complements the words of Speck.

### Sustainable Mi'kmaq Economies

The Mi'kmaq nation and ancestors have long been recognized by European nations and empires as politically independent and sovereign. Having a separate government based on their own customs and culture, they have been self-governing. Their economy at the time of first contact and afterwards was mixed and diverse. It still is. It was a maritime economy and culture. Their fishing grounds are located both offshore and on the inland rivers and lakes. This is not to exclude their hunting grounds, including their trapping territories, and the places where they continue to gather a variety of products. Their natural resource harvesting included such traditional activities as fishing, hunting, trapping, and gathering vegetal and other products as well as horticulture, which was practiced wherever possible.

Another indigenous historian of the Mi'kmaq nation, Bill Wicken (Six Nations of the Grand River), has interpreted the seasonal migrations of the Mi'kmaq people. He has argued that the Mi'kmaq communities inhabited ecologically varied zones. He has argued that as they came into contact with Europeans in different ways and at

different times, their individual experience cannot be characterized similarly and thus any alterations in economy and seasonality
cannot be applied to all of the Mi'kmaq communities, which, let us
recall, were located throughout much of the northeastern maritime
region of Canada and New England. Wicken's work has underlined
the notion that the Mi'kmaq inhabited river valleys and harbors.
Wicken explained that into "each of these harbours flows streams
and rivers whose waterways provide access to the interior and to the
panorama of rivers, lakes and ponds which characterize the interior of southwestern Nova Scotia. Significantly, this region has the
largest concentration of fresh water in all of Nova Scotia, thus making it possible to move through the interior from one coast to the
other" (Wicken 1992, 4). Wicken, like Speck, Dickason, McNab, and
Paul, has provided a deep understanding of the varied terrain the
Mi'kmaq inhabited and the varied customs their lifestyle encompassed, which could not legitimately be categorized monolithically
given their regional variations. This was critical to other litigation
about Mi'kmaq treaties in which Wicken, as an indigenous historian, has participated as an expert witness.

### Mi'kmaq Encounters with Europeans

The Mi'kmaq's uses of their territory were observed by the first European newcomers, Basque, Portuguese, Dutch, and French fishermen and traders, who encountered them in the fifteenth and early in
the sixteenth century.[2] These encounters first occurred in Mi'kmaq
waters (McNab 1996, 1–2). Trade and the transatlantic transport of
indigenous people followed this cultural congruence. For example,
in the "Chronicle of Eusebius," which was first published in Paris
in 1512, it was reported as early as 1509 that

> Some savages have been brought from that island which is called New
> foundland, to Rouen, (in 1509, by the French ship, Bonaventure,—six
> in all) with their canoes, their clothes and their arms. They are of the
> colour of soot (fulginei), have thick lips, are tattooed on the face with
> a small blue vein from the ear to the middle of the chin, across the
> jaws. . . . Canoes are made of the bark of a tree. With one hand a man
> can place it on his shoulders. . . . Their food is of cooked meat, and

their drink, water. They have no kind of money, bread, or wine. They go naked or else in the skins of animals, bears, deer, seal-calves, or the like. (Howley [1915] 1974, 7)

The Beothuk covered their bodies with red ocher and were known as a result as the Red Indians. The Mi'kmaq people did not color themselves entirely in red, but they tattooed themselves. Dickason, in her *The Myth of the Savage*, has corroborated this finding and has told of the fate of the Mi'kmaq people who were taken to France: "Six of these men quickly succumbed on arriving in Normandy, but the seventh was sent to the court of Louis XII as an object of curiosity." On Sunday October 16, 2016, I visited Versailles and saw the Grand Canal, the place where later the Mi'kmaq showed off their canoes and their prowess at canoeing before Louis XIV. This example of indigenous people visiting Europe, returning to Turtle Island, and telling and retelling their own stories about Europe and Europeans, is repeated over and over again in the sixteenth, seventeenth, and eighteenth centuries (Dickason, 1984, 209–10).[3]

The Mi'kmaq nation has had a presence in Atlantic Canada at least since the fifteenth century and well before the arrival of the Basque, Portuguese, Dutch, Breton, and French newcomers. John Cabot is usually given credit for the European discovery of the north Atlantic area, but not for the Mi'kmaq nation. Based on the Icelandic sagas and archaeological evidence at L'Anse aux Meadows on the Northern Peninsula, the Norse were the first European visitors to the island, at least five hundred years earlier (Oleson 1963, 128–40). Often overlooked, the Dutch also participated in the trade with the Mi'kmaq (Hart 1959, 13–14). In addition, there have been archival and archaeological discoveries at Red Bay in present-day Labrador. It has shown that Basque fishermen and traders had many encounters with the Mi'kmaq and other indigenous people at least as early as the sixteenth century.

The Basque archival and other related records illustrate that the Mi'kmaq people were residing on the southern and western coasts of Newfoundland when the Basque fishermen and traders arrived (Bakker 1991c, 1–19). The Basques are a particularly reliable source of information for the Mi'kmaq. Like the Mi'kmaq, they were fishermen and traders. Their encounters have been documented in written and archival records, especially through the use of the Basque language in the trade language used by the Mi'kmaq. Linguist Peter Bakker has identified at least two early written sources that showed the relationship between the Basque and the Mi'kmaq. The first of these is a "Spanish chronicle" that was "written by a man who was born in the Basque country." Bakker has also noted another uncovered Scottish source (Bakker 1996, 21–24). This linguistic situation testifying to early European influences was described in the early 1600s by Marc Lescarbot, who stated that "the language of the coast tribes is half-Basque" (Lescarbot [1618] 1968, 394–95). A later source, dating from 1710 but based in earlier documentation, summarizes the relationship between the Basque and the Mi'kmaq in this way:

> When the Basques first started fishing for cod and whales in the Gulf of St. Lawrence, they made friends with the Indians of this area, and traded with them, especially with a nation called Eskimos, who have always been hostile to other nations. Since their languages were completely different, they created a lingua franca composed of Basque and the different languages of the Indians, by means of which they could understand each other quite well; the settlers of the French colonies in Canada and from the northern part of Acadia [which included Newfoundland in 1710], found this language already well established when they arrived. (Bakker 1991c, 5)

This framework continued when French fishermen, traders, and settlers came to the shores of Atlantic Canada after the fifteenth century.

### The French as Allies since the Early Sixteenth Century

The French had an extensive degree of contact with the Mi'kmaq nation, arising out of their desire to trade in fish and fur along the coasts of the Mi'kmaq territory. Trade came before settlement; the flag followed the traders. The French approach was a mutually advantageous maritime one (Jaenen 1991, 79–116). The written record left by the French is thus replete with references to the Mi'kmaq people. This situation was different from the English legacy of empire in the north Atlantic (Marshall 1996, 7–23). The presence of the Mi'kmaq nation and people within the Mi'kmaq territory and adjacent waters can be documented from the French written records (McNab 1996). The French were primarily interested in fish, though further inland, they were interested in fur (Innis [1930] 1970, 9–22). They had the technology to fish and to dry their catch (Innis [1940] 1978, 11–29, 34). However, they lacked the Mi'kmaq nation's traditional ecological knowledge of its territory (McNab 2006, 47–56). Thus, the French were at a distinct disadvantage both on water and particularly on land. Moreover, they did not have the technology for hunting fur-bearing animals for sustenance or trade (see Hele, chapter 6 in this volume, for the French impact on Sault Sainte Marie).

The commercial impact of these European newcomers was profound for the Mi'kmaq nation. Trade increased the bounty harvested from the land in the short term. But with the arrival of John Cabot in 1497, more than five hundred years ago now, the newcomers also brought devastation through disease and alcohol (Paul 1993, 38–39). The French took an inordinate interest in the Mi'kmaq, even to the extent of taking them back to France as exotica (Dickason 1984, 209). Peter Martyr, another European observer, also did not give a very pleasing account of the manners and customs of the Mi'kmaq in 1516 (Howley (1915) 1974, 1–5).

One of the first Frenchmen to encounter the Mi'kmaq was Jacques Cartier, who made his first voyage to North America in 1534 (Cook 1993, 1–2). After visiting the island of Newfoundland and Labrador in early June of 1534, Cartier remarked on the "wilderness" that he saw all around him. He saw the indigenous people he met as a part of that wilderness, as "savages" (Cook 1993, 10). The following year, Cartier sailed west to Chaleur Bay. Here, he met many more Mi'kmaq, who had already encountered Europeans: "We caught sight of two fleets of savage canoes that were crossing from one side of Chaleur Bay to the other, which numbered in all some forty or fifty canoes. . . . These were joined by five more of those that were coming in from the sea, and all came after our longboat, dancing and showing many signs of joy, and of their desire to be friends, saying to us in their language: Napou tou daman asurtat, and other words which we did not understand" (Cook 1993, 20). It is important to recognize the Mi'kmaq's ability to travel by shallop or by canoe across wide stretches of open water, such as Chaleur Bay in the Gulf of Saint Lawrence, especially to trade. Cartier observed that the Mi'kmaq "bartered all they had to such an extent that all went back naked without anything on them; and they made signs to us that they would return on the morrow with more skins" (Cook 1993, 21). The early trading alliance, and the Mi'kmaq willingness to ally with the French, thus had its foundation in early July of 1534.

The remainder of the sixteenth century witnessed great changes for the Mi'kmaq nation with the addition of the fur trade to their economy (Cook 1993, 52–54). In addition, it was clear that this trade did not always include white settlement and so land was not an immediate issue (Cook 1993, 51). It was only later that the British Empire and its ethos attempted to write the Mi'kmaq nation out of its own history (MacKenzie 1984, 1–2). It is one of the shortcomings of both the French and the English historical records that the Mi'kmaq were seen merely as "savages" (Jaenen 1991, 79–80). Indigenous historians had understood Mi'kmaq agency and customs in the past. Only a few Europeans did so, such as Nicolas Denys and Samuel de Champlain.

Early in the seventeenth century, the English explorer Bartholomew Gosnold encountered a Basque-made fishing shallop manned by eight Mi'kmaq somewhere off the New England coast. By this time, after more than one hundred years of contact with French, Breton, and Basque fishermen, the Mi'kmaq also used European vessels as well as their own canoes. The Mi'kmaq would borrow European-made fishing shallops while the French fishermen were drying their catch on the shore. When these shallops were left on shore after the fishing had ceased for the season, the Mi'kmaq would continue to use the boats the Europeans left behind.

Nicolas Denys observed the Mi'kmaq use of the shallop in his work *The Description and Natural History of the Coasts of North America (Acadia)*, published in Paris in 1672. Denys lived with the Mi'kmaq on Cape Breton Island as well as mainland Nova Scotia and New Brunswick. One of Denys's sons married a member of the Mi'kmaq nation. Denys reported on the basis of his experiences for over fifty years that

> If they [the Mi'kmaq] have always the liberty of frequenting the ships, it will still be worse in the future. For their skins are not worth so much as they have been. To obtain as much drink as they have had, it will

be necessary for them to use force, as they have already done with the ships which they have found alone, something which is happening rather often. They have already threatened [European vessels], and in the case of a little ship, which they found alone in a harbour, they have forced her to give them some [alcohol]. And they have plundered boats which were at the distant fishery. This is the return of all that which they have learned. (Denys 1908, 450–51)

I will return to Denys's importance later. For now, we can note that his account shows the Mi'kmaq were knowledgeable seamen employing their own canoes as well as French and other European shallops which they acquired from the European fishermen. At LaHave, Nova Scotia, then called La Hève by the French, Chief Messamouet "was an accomplished shallop sailor and was apparently visiting the French settlement at Sainte Croix. He had spent time in France prior to 1580" (Whitehead 1991, 22). In other words, this activity was not at all unusual. It was an extension of traditional Mi'kmaq maritime interests, and it appears the Mi'kmaq had been doing this for well over two hundred years (Brereton (1906) 1934, 330).

Early in the seventeenth century, Champlain, in his "Of Savages or Voyage of the Sieur de Champlain Made in the Year 1603," refers to the Mi'kmaq presence: "On the east side is an island called St. Lawrence [Cape Breton Island], where lies Cape Breton; and where a tribe of savages, called the Souriquois [Mi'kmaq], winter. Passing the strait of the island of St. Lawrence, and ranging the cost of Acadia, one enters a bay which comes as far as the said copper mine" (Champlain [1922] 1971, 170). Champlain also entered into one of the first treaties with an indigenous nation in 1613. The council proceedings were held near Brewer, Maine, at the "land between the Kenduskeag and the Penobscot" Rivers (Champlain [1922] 1971, 170). Champlain was prepared for the treaty-making process. This may indicate that he had already entered into a treaty with the Mi'kmaq nation. He had brought along two Mi'kmaq interpreters, who were not identified in his text. He was aware of the significance of the treaty protocol of the giving of presents and of feasting with his indigenous interlocutors before and after the treaty-making. Here he reiterated that the Mi'kmaq

made them [the French] understand, whereat they [the Mi'kmaq] signified that they were well satisfied, declaring that no greater benefit
could come to them than to have our friendship; and that they desired
us to settle in their country, and wished to live in peace with their enemies, in order that in future they might hunt the beaver more than
they had ever done, and barter these beaver with us in exchange for
things necessary for their usage. When he had finished his speech, I
made them presents of hatchets, rosaries, caps, knives, and other little
knick-knacks; then we separated. The rest of this day and the following night they did nothing but dance, sing, and make merry, waiting
the dawn, when we bartered a certain number of beaver-skins. (Champlain [1922] 1971, 293–96)

This was one of the first of many treaties between the French and
indigenous nations. As reported by Champlain, this was a treaty-
making process which was indigenous in its protocol. It would eventually include the Covenant Chain of Silver as the treaty framework
of the two-row wampum (Jennings 1985, 127–53).

There were other more perceptive French recorders, such as Marc
Lescarbot. Lescarbot was born "about 1570," "at Vervins near Laon."
He was trained as a lawyer in Paris. One of his clients was Jean de
Biencourt, Seigneur de Poutrincourt, Champlain's business partner.
Lescarbot, using his connections, went to New France in 1606–7
and stayed at Port Royal, where he came to meet members of the
Mi'kmaq nation (Lescarbot [1618] 1968, ix–xi). Lescarbot was aware
of the significance of the Mi'kmaq nation. He wrote in his history
of New France of the good relations that the Mi'kmaq had established with the French: "Having received an abundant supply of
wine and other creature comforts by the 'Jonas,' [a ship] and having from the first wisely established most friendly relations with
the Indians, who brought in a profusion of fish, game, and ven-
ison, the little band of settlers seem to have had a jolly time of it
during the winter. They accompanied the Indians in their hunting
expeditions, encamped with them in the forest, invited the chiefs to
their table, and regaled the squaws and children with bread and bis-
cuit" (Lescarbot [1618] 1968, 10, 58–59). Father Pierre Biard, a Jesuit
missionary who was in the region almost eighty years after Cart-

ier, in 1611–12, also provided perceptive accounts of the Mi'kmaq. These descriptions are heavily colored by Biard's Catholic interests (Delage [1985] 1993, 59–60). One has to look carefully at the indigenous places and people being described by Europeans to ascertain if there is any true understanding in the descriptions. Frequently, Europeans were wholly ignorant on these people and the places they visited, and thus they entirely missed indigenous agencies. You had to live in these places and get to know indigenous people over many years to develop such an understanding.

## The Mi'kmaq and Nicolas Denys

One of the finest French depictions that we have of the Mi'kmaq was written by the Frenchman Nicolas Denys (1598–1688), whose chronicles were cited earlier. He was known as La Grande Barbe, the name given to him by the Mi'kmaq (MacBeath 1966, 256–59). Denys lived with the Mi'kmaq in their territories in present-day Acadia for more than fifty years. He was a merchant, an adventurer, a fisherman, and a fur trader (Denys 1908, 256–59). Denys was born in 1598 at Tours, France, which was then "a textile town of almost 20,000 inhabitants and the judicial and ecclesiastical center of its region" (Denys 1908, 65). He arrived in the Mi'kmaq territory in 1633. With the exception of a year or two in Paris (1670–72), to publish his *Description and Natural History of the Coasts of North America (Acadia)*, he lived most of his life in Acadia. He was "well established at Saint Peters [on Cape Breton Island] and Nepisiguit, two admirable centres for the Indian trade and the fishery" (Denys 1908, 13). He died in 1688, not in France but at a Mi'kmaq place— beside Winpekijawik, meaning "rough water," which is descriptive of the Bay of Chaleur (the present-day site of Bathurst, New Brunswick)—and was likely buried beneath a willow tree overlooking the water (Denys 1908, 61).

Denys's *The Description and Natural History of the Coasts of North America (Acadia)* shows he understood that the territories of the Mi'kmaq nation were also those known by the French as Acadia. Its landscape had its own indigenous memory (Denys 1908, 240). As a result of his more than fifty years' experience living with the Mi'kmaq in their territories, he was for the most part able to accept his French perspective and attempted to overcome it by depicting the Mi'kmaq nation and its citizens with an empathetic, human dimension. Though ostensibly a direct agent of the French empire in North America, nevertheless Denys did not try to force French religion or culture on the indigenous inhabitants, by contrast with the French missionaries.

His *Description* is a perceptive and questioning account of his perspectives on Acadia in the seventeenth century (MacBeath 1966, 259). Written at Winpekijawik sometime between 1669 and 1671, this work is both exploration literature and, at times, intensely autobiographical (Chabot 1966, 351–59). Written in two volumes, Denys explained his purpose in writing this *Description* "of the most beautiful part of New France" in his self-deprecating "Notice to the Reader" (Denys 1908, 89). The first volume, *Geographical Description of the Coasts of North America*, is travel literature and describes the landscape of the Mi'kmaq territories. Except for his digressions about specific events of his own life, it follows, in its general geographical descriptions, the writings of Champlain. It also has authentic and accurate evocations of local features that Denys obviously knew intimately based on his direct experiences. The second volume, *Natural History of the People, of the Animals, of the Trees and Plants of North America, and of Its Diverse Climates*, drawn largely from his memory, is intensely more fascinating for his descriptions of natural history and of the Mi'kmaq and their traditional practices (Innis [1930] 1970, 74–76).

Denys was always careful to delineate Mi'kmaq life before their encounter with Europeans compared to their situation in the seventeenth century. For example, he was very impressed by the Mi'kmaq's abilities as hunters, devoting an entire chapter to it. Denys had an excellent grasp of their family life, education, and social organization. Observing the children, he noted that they were

> not obstinate, since [the adults] give them everything they ask for, without ever letting them cry for that which they want. The greatest persons give way to the little ones. The father and the mother draw the morsel from the mouth if the child asks for it. They love their children greatly. They are never afraid of having too many, for [their children]

are their wealth. The boys aid the father, going on the hunt, and help in the support of the family. The girls work, aiding the mother; they go for the wood, for the water, and to find the animal in the woods. After the latter is killed they carry it to the wigwam.

Denys knew the Mi'kmaq people, having lived with their families, and his own family had become part of an indigenous family and clan. Kinship was all-important. Indeed, "all my relations" were paramount in understanding and living with them in their territory:

There is always some old woman with the girls to conduct them and show them the way, for often these animals which it is necessary to go and find are killed at five or six leagues from the wigwam, and there are no beaten roads. The man will tell only the distance of the road, the woods that must be passed, the mountains, rivers, brooks, and meadows, if there are any on the route, and will specify the spot where the animal will be, and where he will have broken off three or four branches of trees to mark the place. This is enough to enable them to find it, to such a degree that they never fail, and they bring it back. (Denys 1908, 404–5)

Denys also referred to their seasonal round of activities and the sustainability of their natural resource activities. He paid close attention to the significance of their history. Their oral traditions, he observed,

have thus developed into a custom of the recital of their genealogies, both in the speeches they make at marriages, and also at funerals. This is in order to keep alive the memory, and to preserve by tradition from father to son, the history of their ancestors, and the example of their fine actions and of their greatest qualities, something which would otherwise be lost to them, and would deprive them of a knowledge of their relationships, which they preserve by this means; and it serves to transmit their [family] alliances to posterity. On these matters they are very inquisitive, especially those descended from the ancient chiefs; this they sometimes claim for more than twenty generations, something which makes them more honoured by all the others. (Denys 1908, 410)

Likewise, these stories were also important in many other ways: "They composed stories which were pleasing and spirited. When they told one of them, it was always as heard from their grandfather." Some of these stories made it appear that they had knowledge of the Deluge, and of matters of the ancient law. Like most indigenous people, they had a sixth sense that enabled them to survive and a sense of humor that informed the moments of storytelling that were vital to their collective well-being: "When they made their holiday feasts, after being well filled, there was always somebody who told one so long that it required all the day and the evening with intervals for laughing. They were great laughers. If one was telling a story, all listened in deep silence; and if they began to laugh, the laugh became general" (Denys 1908, 418–19). Wampum, used as a mnemonic device for remembering stories, was also known and highly prized (Denys 1908, 414–15).

The Mi'kmaq had a multidimensional seasonal economy that created a surplus of wealth. Integral to this bounty was their trade with other nations, including European nations. Yet Denys noted the ill effects of trade with the French, primarily through the disease of alcoholism, among others (Denys 1908, 449–50). He knew much about Mi'kmaq culture, customs, and economy (MacBeath 1966, 256–59). He never questioned the Mi'kmaq ownership or indigenous title and land rights over their territories (Steele 1994, 246–47). It is clear that the Mi'kmaq respected Denys, and they may have adopted him. His son married one of them. They told stories about him. They let him fish and hunt and trade with them. The Mi'kmaq showed him their ways and shared their knowledge.

In Denys's *Description*, he seldom makes comparisons with France or with French society. Instead he describes the Mi'kmaq as human beings conflicted between their lifeways before their encounter with Europeans and their situation in the seventeenth century. Denys makes no attempt to romanticize or glorify them or their country. He chose to spend fifty-three of his ninety years with them, and he died with them in their territory (Steele 1994, 59–79). One of the long-term effects of Mi'kmaq sovereignty is that their indigenous title and their treaties still exist. These issues have not been addressed to this day (Tanner and Henderson 1992, 131–66). Denys would have agreed with a recent Mi'kmaq assessment that they "were not the savages" (Paul 1993, 1–2).

## The Mi'kmaq and the French Empire in the Eighteenth Century

By the turn of the eighteenth century, French writers were no longer interested in description of Mi'kmaq people or their economy; they were now more concerned with the Mi'kmaq's role as French allies in the struggle with Britain. Baron de Lahontan, for example, noted: "The three principal savage nations that live upon the Coasts of Acadia, are the Abenakis, the Mikemak, and the Canibas. There are some other erratic nations, who go and come from Acadia to New England, and go by the names of Mahingans, Soccokis and Openango. The first three (having fixed habitation) are entirely in the interest of the French; and I must say that in time of war, they gall the English colonies with their incursions, so much, that we ought to take care to perpetuate a good understanding between them and us" (Lahontan [1703] 1905, 328). Like Lahontan, many writers of the eighteenth century were interested in delineating political boundaries. These writers are specific with regard to group identification. Jean Palairet's description of the island of Newfoundland is particularly revealing: "The natural inhabitants of this Island are Indians like the Canadians. However, we only are acquainted with the coasts of this Island, where we dry our codfish, and we have no knowledge of the people of the interior" (Palairet 1756, 66). This is not the only reference to the Mi'kmaq people as "Canadians" or a "nation related to the Canadians" (Palairet 1756, 57).

Since at least the fifteenth century, the Mi'kmaq were viewed, like other indigenous nations, mythically as "savages," "sauvages," or "wild men," part and parcel of the "wilderness" (Dickason 1984, 61–62). With both the passage of time and increased knowledge by the French in the seventeenth century, this perception gave way to one of the Mi'kmaq people as clever fishermen, knowledgeable guides, outstanding hunters and gatherers, and astute traders, though wont to use trickery at times. Ignorance was gradually replaced by respect for the Mi'kmaq as human beings.

New imperial forces from Europe intruded in the eighteenth century. The balance between the Mi'kmaq nation and the French empire shifted. Dale Miquelon has written that the official demarcation of French imperial policy arrived when, on May 31, 1701,

"Canada was thereby given a new imperial mission quite different from its traditional and still continuing one of being a source
of raw materials and a market for French manufactures. The barrier was intended to prevent the British colonies in North America
from increasing in economic, political, and strategic value" (1987,
1). In all of this imperial strategy and European power politics, the
Mi'kmaq nation continued to keep its "complete independence"
both in terms of territoriality and its sovereignty (Miquelon 1987, 2).

In this imperial process, the Mi'kmaq nation was a victim of the
Treaty of Utrecht. In 1713 the French empire, without consulting
or notifying its First Nation allies, relinquished its alleged rights
to the island of Newfoundland except for the French shore, leaving the Mi'kmaq nation alone to defend itself. The port and the
large naval base at Placentia on the island of Newfoundland were
abandoned for the fortress of Louisbourg. The flag and permanent
European settlement followed trade in fish and fur. Settlement,
as well as disease and depopulation, was a gradual appendage of
European imperialism. Concomitant with this imperial policy in
the nineteenth and twentieth centuries was the attempt to assimilate indigenous children through forced schooling or residential
schools (Dickason 1984, 273–78). Although these attempts at cultural genocide ultimately failed, the result was a short-term disaster for the Mi'kmaq nation.[4]

### The Mi'kmaq Nation's Treaty-Making Process

The Mi'kmaq nation's treaty-making process with the French was
one of mutual support in times of peace and war. The French let the
Mi'kmaq nation into their councils and into their decision making. For the French it was a practical and a necessary relationship
to enable them to continue living in North America in the seventeenth century, as well as to provide protection from the British
Empire. And yet there was, as may be expected, a wide divergence
in the principles and concepts embodied in the treaties and their
meanings and interpretations (Johnston 1982, 155–75).

One Mi'kmaq historian has described the Mi'kmaq nation's
general perspective on the treaty-making process in the following
manner: "The Micmac believed that treaties worked out between

adversaries were binding. The tenets of their civilization demanded strict personal integrity when entering into agreements with others. They felt that, if they failed to act with integrity, their reputation and honor would be forever tarnished. From this perspective, the treaties could only be altered through mutual consent" (Paul 1993, 69). There was thus enormous potential for misunderstanding. In addition to the many cultural differences between the Mi'kmaq nation and the European empires, there were also differences in language. Many of the concepts in the indigenous treaty-making process had no concomitant or equivalent principles for Europeans (McNab 1992, 27–28).

The Mi'kmaq believed that for Europeans the process of treaty-making had "an entirely different meaning: they were entered into as a matter of convenience and would only last until one side or the other decided it would be to its best advantage to disregard them. This philosophy caused much warfare and misery among the European peoples. When the same philosophy was applied to their inter-governmental exchanges with the Micmac, a people unschooled in the intricacies of European intrigue and treachery, the result was disastrous for the Tribe" (Paul 1993, 69). The treaty-making process ultimately brought no long-term peace or friendship for the Mi'kmaq nation. This experience was not dissimilar to that of other indigenous nations elsewhere in Canada (see Hele, chapter 6).

An account of the relations between the Mi'kmaq nation and the French can also be found in Métis historian Olive Dickason's work. Dickason made extensive use of European records. She made several points that help us to understand why the Mi'kmaq got along better with the French than they did with the English. She contrasted the English desire for land for white settlement with the French desire for resources. In fact, the French and Mi'kmaq relationship became strong as European goods were exchanged for furs, and the Mi'kmaq welcomed the French presence. The second point Dickason makes concerns the French missionaries: "The French held a trump card in this contest to win Amerindian loyalties: their missionaries . . . . The effectiveness of these missionaries stemmed at least in part from the fact that traditionally, among Amerindians, the most highly respected leaders were also shamans" (Dickason 1984, 9). In short, before the European empires invaded North America in the sixteenth and the seventeenth centuries, land had never been the reason for warfare.

French treaty-making differed in many ways from English approach. The French did not make treaties for land and natural resource uses that involved "land surrenders." They made treaties for trade and other purposes. The French, who came in smaller numbers with the purposes of fishing and trading, had all the land they needed (O'Callaghan 1856, 775–88). The French were interested in making treaties for such other purposes as peace, protection, and trade. Indigenous citizens were useful to the French because they raided British settlements, as they did in Newfoundland in 1705, 1706, and 1708. These raids created an outrage among the local colonial populations, who demanded protection from the British. These actions forced the British to deploy the Royal Navy in North America. By asking their Mi'kmaq allies to raid British settlements, the French were able to devote fewer men and fewer munitions to their own colonial effort. Another reason that France needed the indigenous nations as military allies was that they needed indigenous knowledge as well as skills and experience, especially as guides, hunters and fishermen. Without these advantages, the French could not have survived in North America until the mid-eighteenth century (Miquelon 1987, 51–52).

The Mi'kmaq historical perspective on the Treaty of Utrecht is likewise instructive. It stresses Mi'kmaq resistance to the treaty and its implementation. Mi'kmaq historian Daniel Paul has described it in these terms: "The Micmac were a free and independent people who had not given their consent to the transfer of their territory or to the extinguishment of their independence and freedoms. The hour the French abandoned their loyal allies to the revenge of the British without consultation, and placed the territorial rights of these same allies into question is one of the darkest moments in the French colonial activities in the Americas" (Paul 1993, 71). One year after the treaty was signed, the French still had not yet told the Mi'kmaq nation what had happened in Utrecht, Holland. The Mi'kmaq were still attacking British ships on the high seas. It was reported to the French governor, Philippe de Rigaud Vaudreuil, in

May 1714 that there was a "breach of the treaty of peace [Utrecht] and commerce committed by Indians under French government upon a British trading vessel at Beaubassin. Enclosed letter from Pere Felix, giving the Indians' excuse, i.e. that they did not know that the treaty was concluded between the two crowns, or that they were included in it. The Indians come from Richibucto" (Paul 1993, 72). In 1715, two years after Utrecht was signed, the Mi'kmaq found out from British officers what had been done to them. In response, they protested to the French governor at Louisbourg. The latter replied that Louis XIV "knew full well that the lands on which he tread, you possess them for all time. The King of France, your Father, never had the intention of taking them from you, but had ceded only his rights to the British Crown." But the trust and respect between the French and the Mi'kmaq had been broken by the actions of the French Crown (Paul 1993, 72). And yet the citizens of the Mi'kmaq nation continued to resist the attacks of the British Empire. The truth was that the Mi'kmaq nation was never conquered, and thus they were recognized in the Treaty of Paris that was signed by the French and the British empires after the Seven Years' War—once again a truly European war. Thus, the Mi'kmaq still survive as a people and as an indigenous nation within Canada.

### The Treaty of Boston of 1725

One of the results was the treaty entered into at Boston on December 15, 1725, between the British Crown and the Abenaki, Maliseet, and Mi'kmaq nations. The latter ratified the treaty on behalf of the Mi'kmaq nation, according to the custom of treaty-making of the day. The Treaty of Boston ended a long decade of war between the British and the Mi'kmaq and other indigenous nations that had begun in response to the Treaty of Utrecht. The raiding of British ships by Mi'kmaq forces continued until the treaty was ratified on September 24, 1728, in Nova Scotia.

The Boston Treaty was made at a public council meeting according to the protocol of the treaty-making process of the indigenous nations. The treaty document was in the form of an "agreement" that reflected the Treaty of Utrecht and the ten years of war that had occurred. The treaty was not a surrender of indigenous title or rights but a reaffirmation of the Covenant Chain to put an end to a decade of war. The treaty did not include provisions for lands or natural resource activities of the Mi'kmaq nation. It only included those for trade by the white settlers with the Mi'kmaq and noninterference in the local affairs of the white government of Nova Scotia by the Mi'kmaq nation. The treaty promised compensation to the white settlers if there were any more raids on their ships or settlements by the Mi'kmaq. Notably and finally, the treaty was ratified within the homeland of the Mi'kmaq nation—at Annapolis Royal—in 1728 (Canadian Government 1992, 198–204). Significantly, no consideration of any kind, presents or monies or reserves, flowed to the Mi'kmaq nation as a result of the signing or the ratification of the Treaty of Boston.

As some commentators have observed, the Treaty of Boston did not put an immediate end to the resistance movement of the Mi'kmaq nation thereafter. Dickason observed that this "Mi'kmaq war" was not over:

> The peace treaty was a blow to the French, and their immediate reaction was to disclaim that the English-Indian War had been of any concern to them. . . . The treaties called for counter-measures, especially as the allies were complaining that the all-important gift distributions often did not have enough goods to go around. The budget for this purpose was steadily increased; by 1756 it had reached 37,000 livres, a figure that did not include "extra-ordinary expenses" entailed when employing Amerindians. Promises of gifts were no longer acceptable; the allies would be led only when they had goods on hand. What had started as a matter of protocol to cement alliances and trade agreements had ended as a means of subsistence for Amerindians and a form of protection for the French. (Dickason 2009, 159–60)

The protocol referred to above was, of course, at least in part, a medium of exchange to renew the treaty.

A Mi'kmaq historian has a different view of the 1725 treaty. This is partly a result of the fierce war that had been waged by the Mi'kmaq without the benefit or the assistance of the French empire. The treaty was one-sided. It was in the English language. No interpreters or translators appear to have been present. The treaty was dictated to the Mi'kmaq nation. Daniel Paul caught the Mi'kmaq nation's spirit and the intent of this treaty: "Given British attitudes, the treaty-making process would not be responsive to Micmac needs and aspirations. The treaties would mainly serve British interest and not those of the Micmac. When questioning the wisdom of the tribe's entrance into this treaty with the British, one can only conclude that it was an act of desperation. The people probably saw it as the last avenue open to them to preserve a measure of their territory, independence, and freedom." From the Mi'kmaq perspective, the treaty was soon thrown into disrepute by the behavior of the British officials who did not act "in an honourable manner and [who they thought should] refrain from having any further designs upon their territories and their assets" (Paul 1993, 76–85). As a result, the Treaty of Boston of 1725 has not been seen as the central treaty between the British Crown and the Mi'kmaq nation by many commentators. Instead, the Treaty of 1752, also known as the Hopson Treaty, is seen to be more significant (Tanner and Henderson 1992, 132–33). Unfortunately for the Mi'kmaq nation, the Treaty of Boston permitted the unabated continuation of the English view and stereotype of the Mi'kmaq people as "savages" who thus must be exterminated as soon as possible.

## At War with the British Empire

By the 1740s the Mi'kmaq nation had made an impact upon the French Empire and on France. Far from the British perception of the Mi'kmaq as "savages" and mercenaries, the French also viewed the Mi'kmaq citizens in a plethora of ways, including "noble savages." Miquelon observed that a "modest stream of travel books continued to tease Frenchmen with notions of the exotic. . . . The Canadian Indian, however, did not lose his fascination, and the Baron de Lahontan's *Mémoires de l'Amérique septrionale*, published in 1703, transmuted him into the Noble Savage and secured him a place in the world of French letters" (Miquelon 1987, 262–63). The brief respite brought about by the Treaty of Boston of 1725 did not result in a long-term peace between the Mi'kmaq nation and the British forces. If there was not war in North America between the Mi'kmaq nation and the British Empire, there were always wars ongoing in Europe. For example, the War of the Austrian Succession in the 1740s was followed in the 1750s and 1760s by the Seven Years' War (Stanley 1968, 1–2).

In each of these European wars, the American theater of operations saw the Mi'kmaq nation continuing its relationship with its French allies. But French power in North America was gradually waning. The French navy, in spite of the horrendous cost of the building and maintenance of Louisburg, was no match for the British naval forces. In fact, the Mi'kmaq style of naval warfare, as we have seen, was more effective. Dickason summarized the Mi'kmaq role in these complex military operations: "As the final round of the North American colonial wars got under way, the Mi'kmaq pitched into the fray on land and sea, asserting their right to make war or peace as they willed and reaffirming their sovereignty over Megumaage. Between 1713 and 1760, Louisbourg correspondence refers to well over 100 captures of vessels by Amerindians. The Amerindians liked to cruise in their captured ships before abandoning them, forcing their prisoners to serve as crew. At that time they had no use for ships of that size, just as they had no use for artillery" (2009, 159). In the long term, with little or no assistance from the French navy, the Mi'kmaq nation could not, by itself, match the naval firepower of the British Royal Navy. Louisbourg fell and with it the Mi'kmaq military alliance with the French empire. But the Mi'kmaq nation was never conquered (Brown (1869) 1979, 177). For the Mi'kmaq nation there was no peace at this time.

In 1748, the British began to consolidate their foothold in Mi'kmaq territory by building a naval fortress in Halifax to counterbalance Louisbourg. Building on Mi'kmaq lands evoked a vigorous response from the Mi'kmaq, who, on September 23, 1749, once again declared war on the British Empire (Paul 1993, 107–8). Lord Edward Cornwallis, the British governor, called a meeting of his council on October 1, 1749, and then with its support issued the following proclamation the next day:

> [I] do hereby authorize and command all Officers Civil and Military, *and all His Majesty's Subjects or others to annoy, distress, take or destroy the Savage commonly called Micmac, wherever they are found*, and all

as such as aiding and assisting them, give further by and with the consent and advice of His Majesty's Council, do promise a reward of ten Guineas for every Indian Micmac taken or killed, to be paid upon producing such Savage taken or his scalp (as is the custom in America) if killed to the Officer Commanding at Halifax, Annapolis Royal, or Minas. (emphasis added; PRO, C.O. 217/9/118)

Lord Cornwallis followed this act of attempted extermination of every Mi'kmaq, including those in Newfoundland, by attempting to reaffirm the Treaty of 1725, but this action failed (Paul 1993, 104–6). In response, and somewhat perversely, the French offered Ktaqamkuk (the Foggy Lands), which was still part of Mi'kmaq homeland, as a refuge for the Mi'kmaq from the English bounty hunters (Paul 1993, 112).

### Genocide and the Hopson Treaty of 1752

After becoming governor of Nova Scotia in 1752, Peregrine Thomas Hopson negotiated a treaty with the Mi'kmaq nation in the same year. Immediately before the treaty, in the summer of 1752, Cornwallis's Mi'kmaq scalping proclamation was repealed by the government of Nova Scotia (Paul 1993, 113–14). The Mi'kmaq representative was Jean-Baptist Cope, also known as Major Cope, (?–c. 1758–60), a controversial figure (Johnson 1974, 136–37). According to Mi'kmaq historian Daniel Paul, this treaty was as much an act of desperation by the Mi'kmaq nation as was the one of 1725 (1993, 115–19). The British refused to discuss, acknowledge, or respect Mi'kmaq territory and sovereignty.

The Hopson Treaty of 1752 has been seen as central to Mi'kmaq indigenous title and treaty rights to this day, as it established "a permanent and continuing political relationship with the crown" (Tanner and Henderson 1992, 132–33). This treaty became the framework for the treaty-making process for such subsequent treaties as the Treaty of Saint George's Bay of 1763 and the Royal Proclamation of that same year (Getty and Lussier 1983, 29–37). All of these treaties provide a constitutional foundation and recognition of the Mi'kmaq nation within the Canadian Confederation before and after 1949 (Tanner and Henderson 1992, 132–33).

During the Seven Years' War, deserted by their French allies, the Mi'kmaq nation's resistance continued until the "ammunition ran out" (Paul 1993, 57). With the defeat of the French but not the Mi'kmaq nation in this European war, the Treaty of 1752 was renewed by the Mi'kmaq nation. This would occur at the capitulation of Louisbourg in 1758 and in the treaties of 1761, 1763 and 1767 with the British Crown thereafter. The Treaty of 1752, however, would remain and would become a central tenet in the relationship between the Mi'kmaq nation and the Crown.

The French imperial government before the Seven Years' War had worked, especially in the area of military alliance, in harmony with the Mi'kmaq nation. Its power was maritime-based, as was the British, before the mid-nineteenth century. When the power and influence of the French navy in North America declined, so too did the French presence. It evaporated in the Seven Years' War with the fall and then capitulation of Louisbourg (1758), Quebec (1759) and Montreal (1760). The French imperial government in North America had some control over the Gulf of the Saint Lawrence and less over coastal waters, aided as it was by the Mi'kmaq nation's maritime capabilities. It could exert little control over the lands or the waters of the indigenous nations, except in places of fortification or in small pockets of coastal settlements.

The British Empire defeated the French in the Seven Years' War (1755–63). The outcome was momentous for the French empire, which had once loomed extremely large on the North American continent. The Treaty of Paris of 1763 ended the French influence, except for the two tiny colonies of Saint Pierre and Miquelon in the Gulf of the Saint Lawrence. In addition, the French rights to the fishery on the French shore in Newfoundland, confirmed by the Treaty of Utrecht in 1713, would continue for another hundred years. It was now certain that the island of Newfoundland would remain a colony of the British Empire. It remained so until 1949.

## British Imperial Recognition of Independence and Sovereignty

The Treaty of Paris of 1763 was another European treaty to end another European war. For their part the indigenous nations, including the Mi'kmaq nation, who were independent and sovereign allies of the French Crown, continued to occupy their territories and to exercise their sovereignty (Brown (1869) 1979, 297). The British Crown immediately began the treaty-making process with the Mi'kmaq nation in 1760. Captain John Knox and Governor James Murray recorded these events in March 1760. Knox reported that "we are informed that M. Bois Hibert is arrived in this country from Nova Scotia, and has brought the greatest part of the Natives to reinforce the French army; it must be through this channel that we have received intelligence of the different tribes of Indians in that province, and its dependencies, having buried the hatchet, and concluded a peace with Governor Lawrence" (Doughty 1914–16, 366–67). These articles were repeated by Article XL in September 1760, which stated that "the Savages, or Indian allies of his Most Christian Majesty, shall be maintained in the Lands they inhabit; if they chose to remain there, they shall not be molested on any pretence whatsoever, for having carried arms, and served his most Christian Majesty; they shall have, as well as the French, liberty of religion, and shall keep their missionaries" (Morantz 1992, 103).

The 1760 Articles of Capitulation were significant. By them the British government guaranteed the rights of the Mi'kmaq nation throughout the north Atlantic area, including Newfoundland. This effectively reaffirmed the earlier treaties between the British imperial government and the Mi'kmaq nation. This action, epitomizing the policy of the Crown, was further cemented by the continuance of the king's bounty. The Mi'kmaq nation, unlike the French empire, was not conquered in the Seven Years' War. This was accepted as a fact by the British government in the 1760 Articles of Capitulation and confirmed by the Peace of Paris and Royal Proclamation in 1763.

## The Mi'kmaq Treaty of Halifax of 1761

One year after the capitulation of New France, the British government reaffirmed the treaties of 1725 and 1752 with a burying-of-the-hatchet ceremony held at a public council at Governor Jonathan Belcher's farm in Halifax. This Treaty of Halifax of 1761 was again in the form, style, and substance of the Covenant Chain of Silver. The document recorded that "the Commander in Chief, having finished his speech, proceeded with the Chiefs to the Pillar, where the Treaties were Subscribed and Sealed" (Provincial Archives of Nova Scotia, 1, 162–65). It is difficult to overstate its significance, since it reaffirmed all the treaty promises the Crown had made in 1701, 1725–28, 1752, and 1760. It was the linchpin of the "consensual Treaty order" under the Covenant Chain of Silver (Dickason 2009, 161–62). It paved the way for the specific adhesions to it by the Mi'kmaq nation in the years that immediately followed.

After the capitulation of New France, the British government began to develop and apply new rules and issue new instructions for the treatment of the indigenous nations. For example, on December 9, 1761, King George III issued royal instructions to all the governors of the English North American colonies. These instructions reaffirmed the Covenant Chain of Silver and the treaties made with the First Nations. Yet as Dickason has observed, the Mi'kmaq resistance to the British Empire continued unabated after 1761 (Dickason 1984, 61–54).

Retrospect

In this history of the Mi'kmaq, it is instructive to ask, who were the "savages"? The Mi'kmaq had always been independent and sovereign human beings. They treated their European visitors as equals and as allies, sharing with the visitors the bounty of their economies. They used their resources seasonally and resided throughout their territories. They used their homeland to their own advantage. Attempts at colonization were not new. Dickason concluded her survey of the Mi'kmaq nation by reporting that in the late eighteenth century "this once assertive, far-ranging people on sea and land now had to take what they could get, and that was not very much; in fact, the process was in reverse, as lands were taken from them as settlers began streaming into the homelands they had fought so hard to protect" (Dickason 2009, 162).

Yet, in the years that followed, the Mi'kmaq people would continue to be treated by the British and then the Canadian and Newfoundland governments as "savages," or as the "others" in their own land (McNab 1996, 1–2). Despite all of these treaties and the European legal instruments, including the Royal Proclamation, the Mi'kmaq nation survived as a sovereign and independent entity, until Canada had its first written constitution in 1982. After 1982 they were recognized by the Canadian government as equal, independent, and sovereign people. The Mi'kmaq nation owes its very survival today to its innovation of a constructive treaty-making process and its resistance to European and Canadian attempts at genocide and colonization.

## Notes

1. This chapter was originally part of my expert witness historical report, "Fragments of Time: The Mi'kmaq Nation and Ktaqamkuk, the Foggy Lands," Federation of Newfoundland Indians, August 6, 1996. It is still confidential to the Federation of Newfoundland Indians.

2. It is instructive that, when I first met citizens of the Mi'kmaq nation at Conne River in April 1978, one of their number who was involved in their historical research and who then resided on Cape Breton Island was Willie Basque. This last name was one indication of their relationship with the Spanish Basques since at least the fifteenth century.

3. Dickason (1920–2011) was Métis.

4. See Truth and Reconciliation Commission, 2015, *Canada's Residential Schools: The History, Part 1, Origins to 1939*, (Montreal: McGill-Queen's University Press), 1–6.

## Bibliography

Bakker, Peter. 1989. "'The Language of the Coast Tribes is Half Basque': A Basque-American Indian Pidgin in Use between Europeans and Native Americans in North America, ca. 1540–ca. 1640." *Anthropological Linguistics* 31, nos. 3–4: 117–47.

———. 1991a. "A Basque Etymology for the Amerindian Tribal Name *Iroquois*." *Anejos de ASJU* 14: 1119–24.

———. 1991b. "The Mysterious Link between Basque and Micmac Art." *Native American Studies* 5, no. 1: 21–24.

———. 1991c. "Trade Languages in the Strait of Belle Isle." *Journal of the Atlantic Provinces Linguistic Association* 13: 1–19.

———. 1996. "Language Contact and Pidginization in Davis Strait, Hudson Strait and the Gulf of the St. Lawrence (North East Canada)." In *Language Contact in the Arctic: Northern Pidgins and Contact Languages*, edited by Ingvild Broch and Ernst Hakon Jahr, 261–310. Berlin: Mouton de Gruyter.

Bakker, Peter, with Lynn Drapeau. 1994. "Adventures with the Beothuks in 1787: A Testimony from Jean Conan's Autobiography." *Papers of the 25th Algonquian Conference*. Ottawa. 1–21.

Bartels, Dennis. 1987. "Ktaqamkuk Ilnui Saqimawoutie: Indigenous Rights and the Myth of Micmac Mercenaries in Newfoundland." In *Native Peoples, Native Lands: Canadian Indians, Inuit, and Métis*, edited by Bruce Alden Cox, 32–36. Ottawa: Carleton University Press.

————. 1989. "Micmac Migration to Western Newfoundland." Unpublished Manuscript.

————. 1991. "Newfoundland Micmac Claims to Land and 'Status.'" *Native Studies Review* 7, no. 2: 43–51.

Bartels, Dennis, and Olaf Uwe Janzen. 1990. "Micmac Migration to Western New-foundland." *Canadian Journal of Native Studies* 10, no. 1: 71–96.

Brereton, John. (1906) 1934. "Briefe and True Relation of the Discoverie of the North Part of Virginia, 1602." In *Early English and French Voyages: Chiefly from Hakluyt, 1534–1608*, edited by H. S. Burrage, 325–40. New York: Barnes and Noble.

Brown, Richard. (1869) 1979. *A History of the Island of Cape Breton with some account of the Discovery and Settlement of Canada, Nova Scotia, and Newfoundland*. Belleville, Ontario: Mika Publishing.

Colin G. Calloway. 1987. *Crown and Calumet: British-Indian Relations, 1783–1815*. Norman: University of Oklahoma Press.

————. 1995. *The American Revolution in Indian Country: Crisis and Diversity in Native American Communities*. Cambridge: Cambridge University Press.

Canadian Government. *Indian Treaties and Surrenders*, vol. 2. (1891) 1992. Saskatoon: Fifth House Publishers.

Chabot, Marie-Emmanuel. 1966. "Marie Guyart (Marie de l'Incarnation)." *Dictionary of Canadian Biography*, vol. 1, *1000–1700*, 351–59. Toronto: University of Toronto Press.

Champlain, Samuel de. (1922) 1971. *The Works of Samuel de Champlain, in Six Volumes*. Edited by Henry Percival Biggar. Vol. 1, 1599–1607. Translated and edited by Hugh Hornby Langton and William Francis Ganong. Toronto: University of Toronto Press.

Cook, Ramsay. 1993. *The Voyages of Jacques Cartier*. Toronto: University of Toronto Press.

Davis, Natalie Zemon. 1997. *Women on the Margins: Three Seventeenth-Century Lives*. Cambridge MA: Belknap Press.

Delage, Denys. (1985) 1993. *Bitter Feast: Amerindians and Europeans in Northeastern North America, 1600–64*. Translated from the French by Jane Brierley. Vancouver: University of British Columbia Press.

Denys, Nicolas. 1908. *The Description and Natural History of the Coasts of North America (Acadia)*. Translated and edited by William F. Ganong. Toronto: The Champlain Society.

Dickason, Olive Patricia. 1984. *The Myth of the Savage and the Beginnings of French Colonialism in the Americas*. Edmonton: University of Alberta Press.

Dickason, Olive Patricia, with David T. McNab. 2009. *Canada's First Nations: A History of Founding Peoples from Earliest Times*. 4th ed. Toronto: Oxford University Press.

Doughty, A. G., ed. 1914–1916. *An Historical Journal of the Campaigns in North America For the Years 1757, 1758, 1759, and 1760 by Captain John Knox*, vol. 2. Toronto: The Champlain Society.

Eccles, W. J. 1964. *Canada under Louis XIV, 1663–1701*. Toronto: McClelland and Stewart.

Getty, Ian A. L., and Lussier, Antoine S., eds. 1983. *As Long as the Sun Shines and the Water Flows: A Reader in Canadian Native Studies*. Vancouver: University of British Columbia Press.

Gwyn, Julian. 1979. "Sir William Johnson." *Dictionary of Canadian Biography*, vol. 4, 394–98. Toronto: University of Toronto Press.

Hart, Simon. 1959. *The Prehistory of the New Netherland Company: Amsterdam Notarial Records of the First Dutch Voyages to the Hudson*. Amsterdam: City of Amsterdam Press.

Howley, James P. (1915) 1974. *The Beothucks or Red Indians: The Indigenous Inhabitants of Newfoundland*. Toronto: Coles Publishing.

Innis, Harold Adams. (1930) 1970. *The Fur Trade in Canada: An Introduction to Canadian Economic History*. Revised ed. Toronto: University of Toronto Press.

———. (1940) 1978. *The Cod Fisheries: The History of an International Economy*. Revised ed. Toronto: University of Toronto Press.

Jaenen, Cornelius. 1976. *Friend and Foe: Aspects of French-Amerindian Cultural Contact in the Sixteenth and Seventeenth Centuries*. Toronto: McClelland and Stewart.

———. 1991. "Miscegenation in Eighteenth-Century New France." In *New Dimensions in Ethnohistory: Papers of the Second Laurier Conference on Ethnohistory and Ethnology*, edited by Barry Gough and Laird Christie, 79–116. Ottawa: Canadian Museum of Civilization.

Jennings, Francis, ed. 1985. *The History and Culture of Iroquois Diplomacy: An Interdisciplinary Guide to the Treaties of the Six Nations and their League*. Syracuse: Syracuse University Press.

Johnson, Micheline D. 1974. "Jean-Baptist Cope." *Dictionary of Canadian Biography*, vol. 3, 136–37. Toronto: University of Toronto Press.

Johnson, William. 1953. *The Papers of Sir William Johnson*. Prepared for publication by Milton W. Hamilton. Albany: The University of the State of New York.

Johnston, Basil. 1982. *Ojibwa Ceremonies*. Toronto: McClelland and Stewart.

Lahontan, Baron de. (1703) 1905. *New Voyages to North America*. Chicago: A. C. McClurg.

Lescarbot, Marc. (1618) 1968. *The History of New France*, vol. 1. 3rd ed. English translation, notes, and appendices by W. L. Grant and an introduction by H. P. Biggar. New York: Greenwood Press.

MacBeath, George. 1966. "Nicolas Denys." *Dictionary of Canadian Biography*, vol. 1, *1000–1700*, 256–59. Toronto: University of Toronto Press.

MacKenzie, John M. 1984. *Propaganda and Empire: The Manipulation of British Public Opinion 1880–1960*. Manchester: Manchester University Press.

Marshall, P. J., ed. 1996. *The Cambridge Illustrated History of the British Empire*. Cambridge: Cambridge University Press.

McNab, David T. 1992. "Making a Circle of Time: The Treaty-Making Process and Indigenous Land Rights in Ontario." In *Co-existence? Studies in Ontario-First Nation Relations*, 27–49. Peterborough: The Frost Centre for Canadian Heritage and Development Studies, Trent University.

———. 1996. Expert Witness Historical Report: "Fragments of Time: The Mi'kmaq Nation and Ktaqamkuk, the Foggy Lands." Federation of Newfoundland Indians, August 6. Unpublished.

———. 1999. *Circles of Time: Aboriginal Land Rights and Resistance in Ontario*. Waterloo: Wilfred Laurier University Press.

——. 2001. "The Perfect Disguise: Frank Speck's Pilgrimage to Ktaqamkuk—the Place of Fog—in 1914." *The American Review of Canadian Studies* 31, nos. 1–2 (Spring–Summer): 85–104.

——. 2006. "Following Up on Delgamuukw: Mi'kmaq Oral Traditions and Nicolas Denys (1598–1688)." In *Aboriginal Connections to Race, Environment and Traditions*, edited by Rick Riewe and Jill Oakes, 47–56. Winnipeg: Aboriginal Issues Press, University of Manitoba.

——. 2009. *No Place for Fairness: Indigenous Land Rights and Policy in the Bear Island Case and Beyond.* Montreal: McGill-Queen's University Press.

Miquelon, Dale. 1987. *New France, 1701–1744: A Supplement to Europe.* Toronto: McClelland and Stewart.

Morantz, Toby E. 1992. "Aboriginal Land Claims in Quebec." In *Aboriginal Land Claims in Canada: A Regional Perspective*, edited by Ken Coates, 101–30. Toronto: Copp Clark Pitman.

O'Callaghan, E. B., ed. 1856. *Documents Relative to the Colonial History of the State of New York*, vol. 7. Albany: Weed, Parsons.

Oleson, Tryggvi J. 1963. *Early Voyages and Northern Approaches, 1000–1632.* Toronto: McClelland and Stewart.

Palairet, Jean. 1756. *Description abrégée des Possessions angloises et Françoises du continent septentrional de l'Amérique.* London: Chastell.

Paul, Daniel N. 1993. *We Were Not the Savages; A Micmac Perspective on the Collision of European and Indigenous Civilizations.* Halifax: Nimbus Publishing.

Provincial Archives of Nova Scotia, Halifax. Record Group 1, vol. 165, 162–65; vol. 30, No. 58.

Public Record Office (PRO), Colonial Office records. C.O. 217/9/118. Kew Gardens, London.

Speck, Frank. (1922) 1981. *Beothuk and Micmac.* Edited by F. W. Hodge. New York: AMS Press.

Stanley, G. F. G. 1968. *New France: The Last Phase, 1744–1760.* Toronto: McClelland and Stewart.

Steele, Ian K. 1994. *Warpaths: Invasions of North America.* New York: Oxford University Press.

Tanner, Adrian, and Henderson, Sakej. 1992. "Indigenous Land Claims in the Atlantic Provinces." In *Indigenous Land Claims in Canada: A Regional Perspective*, edited by Ken Coates, 131–65. Toronto: Copp Clark Pitman.

Trudel, Marcel. 1973. *The Beginnings of New France, 1524–1663.* Translated by Patricia Claxton. Toronto: McClelland and Stewart.

Truth and Reconciliation Commission. 2015. *Canada's Residential Schools: The History, Part 1: Origins to 1939.* Montreal: McGill-Queen's University Press.

Walker, James W. St. G. 1983. "The Indian in Canadian Historical Writing, 1971–1981." In *As Long as the Sun Shines and the Water Flows: A Reader in Canadian Native Studies*, edited by Ian A. L. Getty and Antoine S. Lussier, 340–57. Vancouver: University of British Columbia Press.

Warkentin Germaine, ed. 1993. *Canadian Exploration Literature: An Anthology*. Toronto: Oxford University Press.

Whitehead, Ruth Holmes. 1991. *The Old Man Told Us: Excerpts from Micmac History, 1500–1950*. Halifax: Nimbus Publishing.

Wicken, William. 1992. "The Seasonal Migrations of Antoine Tecouenenac in Early 18th Century Mi'Kma'kik." Paper presented at the Conference on Native Peoples in New France, 1663–1763. McGill University, February 15.

Williams, Paul. 1982. "The Covenant Chain." LLM thesis. Osgoode Hall Law School.

# 2

Indigenous Survival and Selfhood
in the Long Nineteenth Century

# 4

# Everything Must Change so that Everything Can Stay the Same

## *Miscegenation, Racialization, and Culture in Modern Mesoamerica*

LUIS FERNANDO GRANADOS

Once upon a time, in old Sicily, there was a nobleman, a scion of the island's ruling elite. He was a little overwhelmed by the emergence of the world of republicanism and pan-Italianism yet not so overwhelmed that he lost sight of the things that mattered. Hence the sentence that—slightly altered—serves as this essay's title: "If we want everything to stay as it is, everything must change," said nephew Tancredi to Prince Fabrizio Salina.[1] We ought to support the revolt against the king of the Two Sicilies in order to avoid the establishment of Giuseppe Garibaldi's republican dream. He might as well have said: we ought to become revolutionary in order to avoid the demise of the old regime. Although these lines come from the Italian author Giuseppe di Lampedusa's *Il Gattopardo* (1958), the same thing can be said of how indigenous peoples were categorized in Mesoamerica during the long nineteenth century. The way to keep things the same is to go with the changes, but in the end the Indians continued to subsist, though perhaps recognizable only in different forms.

Thus *gattopardismo*—a term of choice for anyone wanting to denounce the travesties of liberal modernization and nationalist "populism"–was born. Needless to say, the sentence's point was to cast doubt on the social meaning of *change*, to delineate the limits of true change in a world that continued to be defined by inequality and coercion. I certainly admire its political sense, if only because there are few notions more abused than modern, revolutionary change—particularly in Latin America. And yet it seems to me that stressing the term's moral connotation—politicians are all liars, social justice tends to be a mirage—misses the opportunity to read Tancredi's remark as a reflection on the complex relationship between *continuity* and *transformation* in the making of the modern. Trapped as we are by an understanding of time that privileges its *sequentiality* (over, say, its rhythmic or spatial qualities), it has always been difficult to see the ways in which the old and the new articulate. Insofar as it is a paradox, however, Tancredi's line cannot be subject to these logical and temporal rules; it is rather free to roam, challenging in so doing the very idea of linear progress and thus allowing us to consider a more complex interplay between the emerging and declining aspects that coexist in any historical process—something that could help us to better understand the fate of Mesoamerican peoples in the modern world.

I am more interested in working with the paradoxical mutations alluded to by the expression of gattopardismo than in unmasking the hypocrisy of Latin American politics and politicians. On the one hand, there is the seemingly oxymoronic process that has made, unmade, and made again the peoples of Mesoamerica in the last couple of centuries; on the other, we have the analytic conundrum such a dynamic poses to anyone seeking to weave a history of Mesoamerican peoples without resorting to essentialist, nonhistorical notions of indigeneity. The point of view adopted in these pages, then, implies taking both clauses of Tancredi's sentence seriously: namely, to acknowledge that change has indeed taken place even if the outcome does not look like a change at all and also to argue that indigenous peoples' cultural and political "survival," as well as the persistence of their domination, has been possible not despite but precisely because of the huge transformations experienced by Mesoamerica from the late colonial period through the mid-twentieth century.[2]

In other words, I consider changing in order to stay the same a tool for shedding light on the character of modern Mesoamerican indigenous peoples: on the set of historical processes that have shaped their very existence as *peoples* or collective social actors. For this reason, thinking about change and continuity in modern Mesoamerica is above all a question of public epistemologies: of the way knowledge is socially constructed and deployed, and also of the "identity" of those individuals, communities, polities, and peoples categorized at some point or another as indios or indígenas.[3] Rather than presuming the existence of Indians, Natives, or indigenous peoples—without italics or quotation marks—my goal here is to question the premise that for a long time has shaped the scholarly gaze on things "indigenous": namely, the axiom that proclaims the *identity*, the deep historical connection, between those who built Palenque around the fifth century CE and the Ejército Zapatista de Liberación Nacional (that emerged publicly on the first day of 1994), the conventional wisdom that in December 2012 allowed thousands of Maya priests to celebrate in Tikal (now in Guatemala's department of Petén) the completion of a calendric cycle, known as the Maya long count, with which the people of Tres Zapotes (now in Mexico's state of Tabasco) were organizing their lives by the first century BCE.

I seek to outline a nonlinear historical framework to make sense of the unexpected and contradictory transformations experienced by the peoples of New Spain, Yucatán, and Guatemala, roughly from the time of the Enlightenment to the collapse of (liberal) civilization in the 1930s. That is why this chapter could be seen as an attempt to follow up on the problem posed by Watanabe (1990) in his study on the indigenous communities of Guatemala's western highlands—"ineffable yet enduring," he calls them—while keeping in mind a platitude brilliantly stated by Bloch (1949, 8): "to the great chagrin of historians, men are not in the habit, every time they change their customs, of changing their vocabulary as well."

## An Epistemological Genocide

The problem this chapter seeks to understand is when and how a predominantly indigenous region, home of some of the New World's most celebrated civilizations, became the "racially mixed" countries of today, dominated linguistically by an Iberian dialect and religiously by Christianity. (Despite their unmistakable indigenous flavor, there is no doubt that all countries and societies currently in place within the limits of the cultural area defined by Kirchoff [1943] are as much "indigenous" as they are "Western," at least in broad comparative terms.)

In principle, no one can really be surprised by such a story. It has been many years now since Cook, Simpson, and Borah confirmed that within a century or so after "contact," most people whose ancestors had known the land without Europeans had vanished. It was a reduction of catastrophic dimensions, they argued: between the late fifteenth century and the mid-seventeenth century, the region's population was cut at least by half, perhaps even a decline of about 80 percent (Cook and Simpson 1948; Cook and Borah 1960; Borah and Cook 1960; Cook and Borah 1968; Cook and Borah 1971–79). Even those who question their methods or their conclusions tend to agree with its basic plotline: the European irruption, or rather the microorganisms brought in by peoples and animals born and raised in Eurasia (N. Cook 1998), triggered the biggest human tragedy in the history of the Americas—a tragedy, furthermore, without which the implant of European "civilization" on this side of the Atlantic would have been unimaginable.

It is often forgotten, however, that the magnitude of the collapse notwithstanding, the same or very similar peoples—baptized as indios in the early 1500s—were and continued to represent the majority of the population in the viceroyalty of New Spain, the general captaincy of Yucatán, and the kingdom of Guatemala throughout the colonial period. Smallpox or not, the point to keep in mind is that, before circa 1850, the vast majority of the region's population— just as in the rest of the continent—could not, and most likely did not want to, locate its biological and cultural origins beyond the Atlantic and the Pacific oceans. Admittedly, estimating population sizes before the 1900s is at best a difficult endeavor. But that does not mean that demographic figures cannot shed some light over the realities on the ground.[4]

Based on the extant data from New Spain's first general census of 1790, it could be said that some twenty years before the demise of the Spanish empire, more than two-thirds of New Spain's inhabitants were indios. In the twelve provinces for which the full regional receipts are available (corresponding to roughly half of the viceroyalty's territory), the percentage was 69.24, and it climbs to 75.33 if only the Mesoamerican jurisdictions are considered (Castro Aranda 1977, 140–47; Aguirre Beltrán 1946, 230, table XV).[5] A century later, when the first Mexican national census was conducted (1895), it turned out that only 16.26 percent of those living in the country could be referred to as Indians because their "habitual language" was not Spanish (Dirección General de Estadística 1899, 462–80, 502).[6] And by the end of the twentieth century, in 2000, that figure had declined further, to 7.13 percent of the population (Inegi 2000). All this, moreover, occurred in a context of significant population growth, which was relatively modest in the nineteenth century but spectacular in the twentieth century. (One of the reasons for this decline could be attributed to the northward shifting of the Mexican population, since the main event in nineteenth-century Mexican demographic history was the colonization of the non-Mesoamerican half of the country—see McCaa 1993.)

Guatemala's demographic history is perhaps less dramatic, but even there it is possible to observe a similar trend. Limiting the gaze to the provinces that would come to be the republic of Guatemala, it has been estimated that in 1778, when the kingdom's first census was conducted, something between 69.86 and 90.25 percent of the population was Indian (McCreery 1994, 346; Arias 1976, 12). In 1893, at the time of the second—and first complete—Guatemalan census, the percentage had shrunk to 64.68 (Dirección General de Estadística 1894, 6 and 189).[7] In 2002, finally, only 41.03 percent of Guatemalans considered themselves indígenas, of which the overwhelming majority, 95.70 percent, identified as Maya (Instituto Nacional de Estadística 2003, 30–31). As in Mexico, one likely reason for such decline was the development of regions that in colonial and early national times had been underpopulated—broadly speaking the lowlands, from Petén to the northeast to the Pacific coast (for an overview, see Lovell and Lutz 1991–92).

The point to notice, of course, is that the indigenous decline has been proportionally more pronounced in the last two centuries than during the three slow ones during which the region was under Spanish rule; that is, that it proceeded much more rapidly between the nineteenth century and the late twentieth century than in any other period in history—and with the sharpest decline taking place in nineteenth-century Mexico. Of course, all this implies that the Spanish colonial regime cannot be held responsible for the virtual obliteration of indigenous peoples in that part of the New World. It must have been the nation-states that replaced Carlos V's "universal monarchy"; more importantly, it would seem that both scholars and the public have missed the real and greatest genocide ever to take place in the history of Mesoamerica.

Yet it is impossible to find in the nineteenth and twentieth centuries anything remotely comparable to the images conjured by Bartolomé de las Casas (1552) to denounce the Spanish enterprise in the Americas. Not even the terrifying accounts of the Mexican *reconquista* of Yucatán in the 1840s and 1850s (Reed 1964) or of the gruesome, massive Guatemalan genocide of the 1980s (Rothenberg 2012)—which happened too late in the century to be deemed responsible for such a secular trend anyway—come close to the famous descriptions of Natives being chased down by dogs and worked to death in the Caribbean, the destruction of Mexico-Tenochtitlan in the early 1520s, or the series of cataclysmic epidemics that ravaged the region during the sixteenth century. How could this happen?

I would argue that the only genocide that took place in the long nineteenth century was an epistemological one—or rather that the declining demographic curve is an optical illusion. That does not mean, of course, that the emerging nation-states were not oppressive and exploitative entities, that the indigenous demographic decline could be attributed to "natural evolution," or that state policy in both Mexico and Guatemala had not encouraged the undercounting— the *invisibilization*—of Mesoamerican indigenous peoples. Far from it. All I mean is that the fall of the indigenous population had more to do with certain ways of knowing, and thus of construing, the *india*, rather than with the rise of liberalism or the development of capitalism—even if the nineteenth- and twentieth-century epistemological transformations did shatter the historical experience of Mesoamerican indigenous peoples, leaving them more exposed to pay the price of "development."

It is impossible to read the demographic figures above as a linear historical sequence, much less as an outline of an indigenous demographic history, for a simple reason: because the numbers *do not* refer to the same people. The linguistic convention (the word *indio*) may be the same, but the referred set of human beings is radically different, inasmuch as the underlying definition arises in each case from a different notion of indigeneity. If we were to proceed in strict logical or lexicographical terms, we should stop talking about the *indio* and even about *indias* in the plural—to say nothing of Indians, Native Americans, or First Nations—and start employing superscript numbers to refer to the various historical sets of indigenous peoples that have been defined and existed in the past half millennium.

## Three Different "Indians"

Roughly speaking, three of these notions of indigeneity have been the most influential in defining indigenous identities in modern Mesoamerica. Because of their pervasiveness, they constitute the three main stations within the social history of Mesoamerican indigeneity I am interested in outlining. To be sure, each notion is no more than a cluster of disparate ideas that nonetheless got crystallized, mainly by state action, as principles of social organization and became the effective everyday framework that rendered social life intelligible. This last aspect is important, for I am not trying to rewrite the history of the idea of the indio in nineteenth-century Latin America (Villoro 1950 and Earle 2007 have already done this) but instead to observe the social life of knowledge, that is, the ways in which epistemological considerations have existed beyond the realm of knowing.

I hope non-Mexicanists will forgive me for naming these stations in my own tongue: from past to present, a *colonial*, a *liberal*, and a *revolutionary* indigeneity. After all, each one of them had its greatest influence more or less at the time of these three crucial moments in Mexican history. Nevertheless, in order to think of them more seriously, I also consider three analytical descriptors that might render their meaning more explicit: *political*, *racialist*, and *anthropological*. Each station, in turn, corresponds to a different mode in the nature of both the state and civil society, and thus to the type of relationship that they established with one another. (For somewhat different treatments of the subject, which nonetheless helped me a great deal to think about this problem, see Valdés

1995, Lovell and Lutz 1996, Navarrete 2004, Viqueira 2010, Pla Brugat 2011, and Loveman 2014.)

*Colonial Indigeneity*

The colonial notion of indigeneity must be described as *political* notwithstanding the fact that it sprouted from two earlier distinctions that might be termed *civilizational* and *religious* (*naturales* and *gente de razón* on the one hand; *cristianos* and *neófitos* on the other), and despite the absence of political life as we understand the term today. This is so because the relationship between the Spanish Crown and the "conquered" peoples in the Americas was phrased in feudal-like terms—the old "pact" between protection and acquiescence—and thus it implied constant negotiation in a public sphere, mostly created and sustained by the justice apparatus (Owensby 2008). In part because that was the only form the early modern state could adopt but also because it rearticulated the hegemonic understanding of politics in pre-Hispanic Mesoamerica (Lockhart 1992), this made for a surprisingly thin structure of rule: as it happened, *dominion* rather than *conquest*, subordination rather than obliteration, were the main mechanisms of subjugation in Mesoamerica. As a result, people could only be considered properly *india* insofar as they were constituted in those indigenous polities known as republics—membership to which took the form of a fee known as the tribute, which was paid in cash beginning in the late sixteenth century (Miranda [1952] 2005; see also Granados 2008, chapter 2).

Ethnicity is so often taken for granted—deemed to be obvious—that it is still easy to forget that for most of human history it has not been a stable, holistic reality but rather an accidental and unstable artifact, a linguistic convention useful to tell stories but frequently incapable of fostering analysis per se (but see Kellogg's chapter in this volume). The fact is that both españoles and indios had to learn to be so in the course of the sixteenth century: for example, it took a long time for Tlaxcalan and Kaqchikel nobles to realize that their status as Spanish "allies" would not translate into co-rulership over their former enemies, the Aztecs and the K'iches (see Cuadriello 2004; Restall and Asselbergs 2007). More telling in a sense is that the decision to ban indigenous priesthood happened only toward the end of the sixteenth century (Lunberg 2008) after decades of cultural compromising had produced a Spanish-speaking, horse-riding, power-holding indigenous nobility—that is, a ruling elite at once subaltern and hegemonic that proved indispensable for the establishment of the new kingdoms (Haskett 1991, see also Castañeda de la Paz 2011). Having no priests of Mesoamerican descent would have a significant impact in the future of Guatemala, Yucatán, and New Spain; in the short run, though, it did not preclude the consolidation of a privileged kind of *indios*.[8]

To be sure, the triple effect of long-lasting colonialism, the erosion of pre-Hispanic political institutions, and the demographic crisis helped to deepen the differences between the two realms in which New Spain, Yucatán, and Guatemala—just like most of Spanish America—were divided. In particular the parallel indigenous society—made up of courts, hospitals, autonomous municipalities, collective ownership of farming land, parishes manned by the mendicant orders, and so on—effectively produced an experience increasingly separated from that of españoles, mestizos, and castas, who conversely paid all the same taxes, dealt with the same secular priests, and were governed by municipal corporations where the sale of offices was customary. But that does not mean that the borders between any of these sociocultural groups were as rigid and permanent as the words used to describe them may suggest. It has been seventy years since Aguirre Beltrán (1946) showed that the demographic marginality of people of African descent in late colonial New Spain—in the sixteenth century the destination of most African slaves within the Spanish empire—was not the result of an act of magic but of the collective "rebranding" of most *negros* as indios, mestizos, and españoles. More recently, the work of Tadashi Obara-Saeki on Chiapas (2010) and José González Flores on Michoacán (2013) have confirmed—and deepened our understanding—of the fabulous elasticity of all such "ethnic" labels.

Unsurprisingly, running away from one's tribute obligations—either to the cities or to the frontier, the lowlands in northeastern Guatemala, the plateau north of Querétaro in New Spain—became the most important mechanism for "losing" one's indigenous ethnicity. But this was not because moving into mostly Spanish eco-systems necessarily had a deleterious effect on the migrants' culture or physiognomy (which anyway were almost impossible to hide). Once widely used in the literature, *acculturation* is a term that fails to convey a process at once more complex than the "acquisition" of a new culture and much simpler than an ontological metamorpho-sis. If "passing" as *pardos* (those who had some mixture of African ancestry), mestizos, or españoles was possible for a number of indios, it was simply because, in most rural estates, mining towns, and cit-ies, it was nearly impossible (for anyone in a position of power) to set apart two or three groups of peoples that shared phenotype as much as they shared culture; to put it coarsely, it was simply because most *pardos*, mestizos, and españoles were as dark-skinned, maize-eating, court-seeking, and saint-praying as the fugitive indios. All this, of course, means that mestizaje in early modern Mesoamerica was not primarily the result of actual biological mixing nor of cho-reographed cultural hybridization but a function of shifting social roles and performances—not unlike what countless peasants every-where have done since time immemorial.

Colonial domination in Mesoamerica was often construed as the recognition of a covenant accorded in the past—say between Hernán Cortés and Moctezuma, or between Pedro de Alvarado and the Kaqchikel "nation"—rather than as a *natural* condition in and of itself.[9] Hence the salience of festivals such as Saint Hippolytus's in Mexico City: every year in mid-August, the *urbs* remembered the capture of the last Mexica *hueytlatoani* with a procession that lined up the aldermen of the Spanish city council with the gover-nors of indigenous San Juan Tenochtitlan and Santiago Tlatelolco (Curcio-Nagy 2004). Tradition instead of natural law seemed to reg-ulate the relationship between the Spanish Crown and the indige-nous peoples of Mesoamerica much in the same way superstition regulated the spiritual life of Catholics on both sides of the Atlan-tic, all the while common law—meaning different laws for different groups—controlled the domains of labor and property.

To simplify a little, the golden age of this porous system of "racial" classification—and the *plural society* it fostered, according to Kel-logg (this volume)—lasted less than two centuries: forged at the end of the sixteenth century, by the early eighteenth century it had been undermined by the combined effect of demographic recovery and the expansion of the European-dominated world economy, which produced both incredible wealth and mounting inequality. Increasing competition over cultural and material resources meant in turn that philosophical rationalism and Linnaean taxonomy in particular could be seen not just as fashionable intellectual movements: as the history of the genre of casta painting shows (Katzew 2004), hierarchical, periodic table-looking schemes for understanding New Spain's "racial" diversity would soon be considered the final solution to early colonial confusion.

### Liberal Indigeneity

Ostensibly antihistorical in their opinions, the advocates of reason sought to eradicate the alluvial and the heterogeneous by casting the multitude of historical experiences into one "natural," single mold. Liberating as it might have been, the light shed by the Enlightenment was also freezing: one law for everybody, and a single set of principles of justice deduced by reason rather than being the result of experience. Not for nothing, the French republic would define itself as polity *un et indivisible*—one and indivisible. It was just a matter of time before the emerging ontology of the Enlightenment, the geographic determinism of rationalist intellectuals such as William Robertson and Cornelius de Pauw (Gerbi [1955] 1960), the high profitability of the slave trade, and (paradoxically) a drop or two of Johann Gottfried Herder's reaction to rational universalism, would come together to invent one of the flimsiest, most grotesque, and yet most appealing ideas ever: the modern idea of race.

Outside of the United States and, to a lesser degree, the United Kingdom and its former colonies, the type of holistic, organic categorization of the notion of race has proven to be at once bad science, reductionist epistemology, and very, very bad politics. Nevertheless, I think it is worth doing in this context, for race is no less historical a concept and experience (time- and place-specific, that is) than the political notion of indigeneity developed and cultivated by the Spanish empire in the New World.[10]

Like most social concepts, race has a long history that would be pointless trying to summarize here.[11] Suffice it to say that at the beginning of the nineteenth century, the ideas about "identity" and belonging that would eventually come together to form the notion of race were still dismissed—and not by romantic revolutionaries—as simple, simplistic *physiognomy*, that is, as the tricky, unreliable art of assessing (human) nature by its appearance. As a colonial bureaucrat from Mexico City put it—in an argument ultimately validated by King Carlos IV himself—no dark skin or curly hair could reveal the true nature, the political condition, of any given individual. Skin color was a mask that even people of Mediterranean descent could and would use; skin color and other physical features could not reveal their actual *calidad* (kind).[12] The very notion of kind was—and is—all about the inner self of people; not about their façades (Martínez 2008).

It was perhaps because of the uncertainty of establishing identities solely on the basis of skin color and other phenotypic traits that, almost from its beginning, race tended to be paired with features most modern observers might describe as "cultural." Although language was certainly one of them, *rurality* and clothing emerged as preferred comarkers of ethnicity, particularly in the highlands of Chiapas and Guatemala, where by the end of the nineteenth century a rather complex system of classification developed based on the two most external and thus most public layers of one's personhood (phenotype and dress), closely followed by place of residence and occupation (García de León 1985, Taracena 2002). Thus began to arise the canonical image of the modern indigenous person: the dark-skinned peasant dressed in "traditional" garments, living on the edge of civilization. Thus it began to be impossible to see (or to think of) urban indigenous peoples as well as indios dressed *a la española*: indigenous merchants, indigenous politicians, indigenous landowners, and so forth. In the new world of racialism, indeed, *indigenous rulers* were beginning to be something of an oxymoronic relic.

Paradoxically, the racialization of indigenous politics and culture was a coping mechanism, an epistemological and political strategy intended to fill the void left by the destruction, early in the nineteenth century, of the colonial notion of indigeneity and the institutions and practices that had rendered it concrete. The collapse was truly spectacular—just as the scholarly silence about it has been. In 1810 the Spanish regency abolished tribute in New Spain; a year later the Spanish Cortes extended the decree's application as to include the whole of the empire, and in 1812 the first-ever imperial constitution suppressed the indigenous republican system and elevated all indios and some castas—those deemed not to have African blood—to the "dignity" of Spanish nationals and citizens.[13] Whether these decisions were the result of a short-term tactic to undermine New Spain's popular insurgency or an excess of enthusiasm on the part of the Spanish legislators, the fact is that on the eve of independence, two of the pillars of the colonial edifice (tribute and the republics) were removed . . . by the very institutions that were trying to keep the empire together.[14]

Unsurprisingly, the 1810s and 1820s were a crucial period for the restructuring of the system of ethnic classification in Mesoamerica. Since tribute could not be effectively reinstituted, either because the colonial bureaucracy after 1814 found itself lacking the means to do so or because, as in Totonicapán in 1820, the indios themselves contested the regime's intentions arms in hand (Pollack 2008), certain provinces such as Yucatán and Oaxaca moved toward creating a head tax that took away the constitutional component of the tribute but kept its fiscal component intact (Guardino 2005, Cobá Noh 2009). In Chiapas the state government also passed a law against "vagrancy" that threatened both the economic independence of highland Indians and their political institutions—heralding in this way the infamous regulations implemented in Guatemala in the last third of the nineteenth century (Torres Freyermuth 2010). And throughout New Spain the massive transformation of indigenous republics into "liberal" municipalities in 1814 and again in 1820 (Guarisco 2003) prompted most Mexican state legislatures after independence to pass legislation making such an evolution impossible: and so out of more than four thousand indigenous republics standing in New Spain (plus Chiapas) around 1800, early twenty-first-century Mexico ended up having only some 2,500 municipalities—and those include formerly Spanish cities and towns (Tanck de Estrada 2005). Nevertheless, as any municipal map could show, Mexican municipalities tend to cluster in regions that, up to the 1810s, were particularly rich in indigenous republics: Peter Guardino (2005) has even shown how the survival of indigenous republics in Oaxaca was made possible by the creation of a two-tier municipal system that preserved the name *república* for the indigenous governmental bodies.

Only in Guatemala, after Rafael Carrera's "conservative" regime reestablished the republican system in the 1830s, could it be said that racialization developed within the contours of colonial indigeneity (Woodward 1993; see also Taracena 1999). That may help explain why nineteenth-century Guatemala witnessed a faster and deeper polarization of Indians and ladinos—a term formerly reserved for Spanish-speaking people, though increasingly conterminous with *nonindigenous*—whereas nineteenth-century Mexico seemed to have experienced a massive if regionally uneven process of miscegenation. (That, and the fact that the Guatemalan frontier toward Petén was more impregnable than northern Mexico, where a vibrant and whiter society consolidated after independence.) The "liberal" laws of the 1870s, which regulated the movement of highlanders back and forth to the coffee-growing areas on the Pacific piedmont, only exacerbated the country's spatial and social polarization (McCreery 1994, Reeves 2006). That is why turn-of-the-century Guatemala looks sometimes as if the colonial system had survived intact, more or less as in sisal-making Yucatán. Make no mistake, though: Guatemala's— just as Yucatán's—harsh racial order was essentially a liberal, postindependence creature (see Taracena 2002). And yet, paradoxically, the strengthening of the "ethnic" divide also enabled some indigenous elites—Quetzaltenango's being the prime example—to rearticulate their regional hegemony without challenging the ascendance of the ladino (i.e., white) oligarchy at the national level (Grandin 2000).

More or less at the same time, another development in indigenous culture was taking place: the emergence of a politicoreligious ruling structure in a number of indigenous communities—a perfect example of an "invented tradition"—known as the dual cargo system. According to Chance and Taylor (1985), the cargo system was a response of sorts to the collapse of colonial institutions and practices that had allowed for cultural self-reproduction in the past (but see Carmagnani 1988).

Overall, the invention of race in nineteenth-century Mesoamerica implied both the narrowing down of the notion of indio inherited from the colonial period and the finer articulation—at once more precise and more rigid—of the features that the new concept contained. From a taxonomical perspective, race-as-culture was both more restricted and more consistent a concept. It defined indigenous peoples in ways colonial indigeneity could not have ever considered and, more important, in ways that were harder for individuals to escape from. By the time the first national censuses were conducted—Guatemala's in 1880, Mexico's in 1895—a new borderline had already split the former indigenous realm into two different, increasingly isolated societies: a core of racialized indigenous peoples, poorer, more marginal, largely disenfranchised, and more organically related to their primeval "culture," and a larger, vaguer set of mestizos and ladinos, much more integrated into the political and symbolic economies of the nation-states, no matter if they tended to share eating habits, religious customs, political marginalization, and phenotypical features with the indígenas.

Exemplary of this development was the Guatemalan census of 1880. It is telling that Guatemala outpaced Mexico in conducting a national census by more than a decade, for it confirms that the government of Justo Rufino Barrios faced fewer structural and political obstacles than either Benito Juárez or the young Porfirio Díaz in modernizing Mesoamerica. What makes the census truly revealing is that on the one hand, it enshrined the Indian-ladino divide, raising it up from the domain of folk epistemology, and, on the other, that it used the category of race to do so—and with an illuminating contradiction. Although the taxonomical principle was unmistakably racial (the label reads indeed *raza*), both the questionnaire and the instructions to the census-takers made clear that ladinos could be of *any* race, but not the *indígenas del país*, local Indians (Dirección General de Estadística 1881, XIX)—revealing in this fashion the double standard implicit in the definition.

By the time the next census was conducted in 1893, it was just "normal" that both races could be described as follows: "The Ladinos and Indians are two distinct classes; the former march ahead with hope and energy through the paths that have been laid out by

progress; the latter, immovable, do not take any part in the political and intellectual life, adhering tenaciously to their old habits
and customs. The Indians do not cooperate actively in the progress of civilization, [yet] neither do they resist it. Notwithstanding,
they furnish all the necessary work to make the soil productive,
and this alone creates the national wealth" (Dirección General de
Estadística 1894, 40).[15]

### Revolutionary Indigeneity

Modernity has never been a straightforward condition or a process. Contrary to Guatemala, where race was the master category
for construing the Indian between 1880 and 1950, in Mexico the
path away from colonial indigeneity to turn-of-the-century racialism and eventually the current anthropological understanding of
ethnicity meandered here and there, revealing the contradictions of
the liberal-racialist project but also the ways in which "revolutionary" indigeneity is a legitimate child of the liberal cosmology far
more than its opponent. Discarding race as a notion in the twentieth century, in other words, would come in Mexico and in Guatemala not so much as a result of a rejection of the concept but rather
as the organic development of so "scientific" an idea.

In the beginning, language—the most social-science-sensitive
category employed to construct the indios in Mesoamerica and
ostensibly the least racist and colonialist—was in fact a racialist
device, a tool in the hands of the romantics as they tried, both in
Europe and in North America, to invent the *nation*. The rise of linguistic nationalism—or, perhaps more accurately, of a nationalist
understanding of language—is of course a well-known phenomenon: thinking of language as an avatar of the nation became one
of the few "objective" mechanisms with which to set apart peoples who otherwise lived together and participated, no matter how
unevenly and unequally, in the same culture. But even in countries
like France, whose linguistic nationalism was firmly established
already at the beginning of the nineteenth century (de Certeau,
Julia, and Revel 1975), the ideologues of the nation felt compelled
to praise only one of the many language spoken in the country as
one of the true markers of Frenchness; thus Ernest Renan (1882),

early in his best-known conference, would describe the process of nation building in medieval Gaul in part as a result of the creation of a lingua franca within the Capetian realm.

Renan, of course, was among the founders of the modern discipline of linguistics; thirty-something years before "Qu'est-ce qu'une nation?" he had published *De l'origine du langage* (1848), a widely read essay that argued for a historical understanding of language formation—a historical as opposed to, in his own words, "theological" thesis, which saw language as a divine gift that had appeared in human history fully formed and remained unchanged ever since. That is probably why his notion of nationalism emphasized the emotional willingness to belong to the nation rather than certain deterministic features such as race or a common past. Yet the point remains that, for him as well as for some of his readers, language was one of the main ingredients—a foundation, if you will—of nationalism's intoxicating cocktail.

One of those readers was Francisco Pimentel, a nobleman, a scion of New Spain's ruling elite, who—just like Prince Fabrizio Salina— was a little overwhelmed by the emergence of the world of republicanism and nationalism, yet not overwhelmed enough as to lose sight of the things that matter. In his case, however, politics mattered less than knowledge (though in his only political adventure he was to serve the government of Maximilian von Hapsburg). Nowadays, perhaps as a result of Semo's interest in his work (Pimentel 2005), Pimentel is best known for a tract on the political economy of Mexican indigenous peoples, but in the early 1860s he was regarded mostly as a linguist—indeed as one of the discipline's local founders (Guzmán Betancourt 1994). His *Cuadro comparativo de las lenguas indígenas de México* (Pimentel 1862), a painstaking "chart" describing the grammatical and lexical features of more than one hundred indigenous languages still spoken in nineteenth-century Mexico, is perhaps the first systematic attempt to understand the country's linguistic diversity—casting them in nineteen families that, mutatis mutandis, continues to inform Central and North American linguistics to this day.

Pimentel, of course, was not working in isolation—nor was he by any means marching into uncharted territory. In those same years, other conservative intellectuals such as Joaquín García Icazbalceta and Manuel Orozco y Berra were also adding to a rather venerable domain of inquiry, the study of indigenous languages, cultivated by mendicant friars since the middle of the sixteenth century and later on by secular savants in the 1600s and 1700s. As in the rest of the social sciences, though, the country's political divide was almost imperceptible. In the next couple of decades, an emerging community of "liberal" scholars expanded and deepened their work, clustered mainly around the National Museum of History, Archaeology, and Ethnography and its flagship publication, the *Anales del Museo Nacional* (1877) but also around the Department of Development's statistics office—headed since its creation in 1882 by Antonio Peñafiel.

A medical doctor who had fought the French in the 1860s, Peñafiel edited in the 1880s a number of works devoted to the study of indigenous languages—Diego Baselenque's *Arte de la lengua tarasca* ([1714] 1886) and an anonymous *Gramática de la lengua zapoteca* (1887), among others. Such a background helps to explain why his statistics office chose language rather than race as the criterion for identifying the indigenous population in the census it organized in the mid-1890s. Another explanation was the consciousness that language, ethnicity, and history were all linked—for if something characterizes most nineteenth-century scholars it was their omnivorous reach, a way of understanding knowledge we might now call multidisciplinary.[16]

The endeavors of Peñafiel and his friends had a clear and powerful nationalist bent, which is partially responsible for the ontological ambivalence that has distinguished Mexican anthropology ever since, that is, the paradox of a discipline (a set of disciplines) elsewhere devoted to the invention and the study of the "other," interested above all in discerning the character of the "Mexican self." In ways reminiscent of Spanish colonialism when it tried to incorporate the indigenous populations into the monarchy's body politic, in effect, made-in-Mexico social sciences have grappled from their inception with two contradictory impulses resulting from their epistemic and political ambitions: on the one hand, the goal to discipline "primitive" knowledge and peoples, and on the other, the desire to vindicate and appropriate for the nation the very same "primitive" knowledge and peoples (but see Warman et al. 1970).

By employing language as the main marker of ethnicity, both Mexican anthropology and the state found one of the earliest solutions to the problem posed by liberal nationalism (of the kind embraced by the Mexican founding fathers: the exclusionary inclusion or inclusionary exclusion of the former indios). It was also one of the most enduring, for only in 1921 did the Mexican census (partially) adopt the racialist standard Guatemala had been using since 1880—and the United States since 1790. Not even at that time did the Mexican nation-state entirely renounce the linguistic tool, though: the census *asked* citizens about their sense of racial belonging rather than ascribing it from without. Probably because the experiment resulted in 29.16 percent of the population declaring themselves to be raza indígena when only 14.61 percent could be described as indígenas by virtue of the language they spoke (Pla Brugat 2005, 73, table 3), nine years later Mexico dropped the race question and resumed the exclusive use of language as a maker of indigeneity.

The irony, of course, is that—as the gap between racialized Indians and linguistic indios poignantly illustrates—focusing on language as the most "objective" and stable ethnic feature implied narrowing the scope of the category down once again, and this time to its minimal expression. Born as a proxy for a nation, *language* had experienced a conceptual transformation around the turn of the century that made it more useful as a social tool and, at the same time, less sharp analytically. By the early twentieth century it would have been impossible to keep the concept's original function intact. On the one hand, this was because the Mexican Revolution (1910–40) restored the legitimacy of some key features of colonial indigeneity: the centrality of municipalities within the architecture of the state (considered to be quasi-sovereign since 1915) and more famously the possibility of communal land ownership, which would become the cornerstone of the postliberal state project. On the other, more perversely, this was because relying on language to define membership in the indigenous population allowed the postrevolutionary regime to *nationalize* some of the Mesoamerican features it wanted to ascribe to the Mexican nation: the revamped nation-state was thus able to locate its origins in the pre-Hispanic past, to plant the economic-technological-culinary complex of maize at the center of Mexican (agri)culture (see for example Esteva, Marielle, and Kurlat 2003), and, well, to enshrine the mestiza ideal-typical skin color as the "national" phenotype—the "cosmic race," in the words of one its propagandists (Vasconcelos 1925).

The postrevolutionary consensus on things indigenous only deepened this course of action, as the idealization of the Indian and the pre-Hispanic past effectively allowed most Mexicans to claim as *theirs* almost all indigenous features—all but the dozens of indigenous languages that came to epitomize the Mexican anthropologically informed notion of indigeneity. Even more than in the nineteenth century, when the ascent of racialism had limited the social and political opportunities to be Indian and encouraged the use of a racist language to describe the plight of indigenous communities and peoples, the discursive and political space for being Indian became increasingly narrowed by the social nationalism espoused by the government and its organic intellectuals (Stern 2003). No wonder official discourse has tended to represent Emiliano Zapata's forces, ever since their demise in the late 1910s, as a *peasant* army and the earliest champion of the revolution's agrarian reform (Brunk 2008), notwithstanding their white-cotton trousers, their "copper"-like skin, their religious banners, their proclivity to speak Nahuatl, and the fact that the postrevolutionary *ejido* had little to do with the institutions—*ejidos* and *tierras de común repartimiento* (communal village lands)—most Zapatistas rose in arms to protect.[17]

More significant, at any rate, is that the state policy toward indigenous peoples in the decades following the revolution's "institutionalization" proceeded as though inspired by Aguirre Beltrán's idea that the *most* indigenous areas of Mexico ought to be understood as "refuge zones" (Aguirre Beltrán 1967), that is, presuming that only in the most isolated corners of the country, either symbolically or in deed, would it be possible to find "truly" indigenous peoples to integrate into the modernizing nation. In the early 1950s, soon after its creation, the Instituto Nacional Indigenista began establishing regional offices with the purpose of "coordinating" the actions of government agencies tasked with the country's modernization (paving roads, building hospitals, electrifying settlements, and so on) with the scholarly and political activities of anthropologists and other social scientists interested in documenting and transforming indigenous peoples' lives (Korsbaek and Sámano 2003; Fenner and Palomo 2008).[18] As it happens, the first region chosen to practice Mexican "applied anthropology" was the highlands of Chiapas, home of numerous indigenous groups which dozens of scholars—Vogt (1970) being perhaps the most notorious—have described as possessing an essentially unchanged Maya worldview and social organization, an area, moreover, that in certain circles has come to epitomize the very idea of the resilient, or enduring, or pristine, or backward, or stubborn, or primitive, of fossilized Mesoamerican indigenous world.

### Race versus History

By outlining the intellectual and political foundations of census-making since the late eighteenth century, my goal has been to argue that census figures are noncommensurable because they are based on at least three distinct notions of indigeneity employed by the state and to some extent by society as well: 1) the politicolegal notion of colonial times, 2) the racialist notion of the liberal republics, and 3) the "anthropological" notion the postrevolutionary state of Mexico has been using since 1895 (with a hiatus in 1921) and Guatemala since 1950. I have tried to suggest that each notion construed "the Indian" in different, increasingly narrow, and almost contradictory terms. Projecting any of these indigeneities back or forth in time—to build a consistent demographic trend or, more significantly, the outline of the history of a people—is therefore impossible. What use then could these numbers have? Is there a way to rely on them without presuming the sameness of the peoples they supposedly refer to? Perhaps the only merit of trying something like this is that it might show certain absurdities proper of each type of indigeneity and also—paradoxically—because it might help us think of the indigenous peoples of Mesoamerica in more accurate terms.

If the census figures provided at the beginning of this chapter cannot convey the "real" demographic history of Mesoamerican indigenous peoples, one is then forced to come up with a weird conclusion: either most people in the viceroyalty of New Spain and the kingdom of Guatemala were no longer "true" Indians at end of the eighteenth century, or else most people labeled as non-indigenous (even the *blancos* and mestizos from the Mexican census of 1921 and of course Guatemala's ladinos throughout the last century) were actually of indigenous "stock"—and continue to be so. The social, political, and epistemological implications of any of these explanations are obviously huge: in one scenario, it would mean that no one could really make any claim about original ownership of the continent; in the other, that the very notion of mestizaje, so cherished by Mexican ideologues and such a dominant trope in the Mexican imagination for most of the twentieth century, is not just a "myth" but a lie pure and simple (Bonfil Batalla 1987, but see Bartra 1987). Adopting any of these perspectives, furthermore, could seem to vindicate some of the most vicious political and academic positions: either that indigenous Mesoamerica is a populist fiction, and so everything worthy of note in the region is the result of European colonialism (as the old *hispanistas* would say: language, religion, and civilization), or else that race is indeed a biological or biocultural fact—that races do exist as stable, transhistorical entities, after all—and thus that racial prejudice, discrimination, and segregation are just "natural," commonsense responses arising from the desire to stick to, and protect, one's kind.

For a long time, focusing on language—and more generally on *culture* or *ethnicity*—has seemed to be the best way to navigate these turbulent waters of identity and belonging. Indeed, language appears to provide an "objective" *and* an emic way to locate, both geographically and epistemologically, a single current of indigeneity linking the springs of the most distant past to the fluid, uncertain present. One's language is one's home, as the philosopher used to say. But since anchoring indigeneity in language presupposes that bilingual speakers are somehow not as "pure" as monolingual ones, it should follow that the colonial indigenous elites who spoke Spanish and cultivated classical Nahuatl ought to be considered a little *less* Indian, and thus less representative of the indigenous world, than the *macehualtin* who barely spoke Spanish as late as in the nineteenth century.

Unfortunately, broadening the category's scope as to include other cultural features such as dress, type of dwelling, spirituality, or "custom" does not quite do the trick, for indigenous peoples have been doing "un-Indian" things—like raising chickens, weaving wool, and praying to the Christian god—since the sixteenth century, just as mestizos and ladinos have kept doing rather "Indian" things— such as growing maize in *milpas* and employing noun diminutives to address people worthy of respect—for as long as there have been Europeans in the Americas. Even Alfonso Caso (1948), in the heyday of Mexican indigenismo, was able to perceive it: neither the (palm) hat nor the (cotton) trousers make an Indian.

To be sure, part of the problem is that until recently anthropology seemed to have worked under the assumption that *culture* could be itemized, that is, as though presuming that meaning resides within the artifacts, stories, and practices employed by human groups to make sense of the world, rather than on the networks and contexts—in short, the historical experience—in which those things were deployed, actualized, and exchanged. Reduced to a list of traits, *culture*—any culture—is but a caricature of the conversations, agreements, and misunderstandings that help render intelligible the dynamics of human interaction. It is telling in this regard that one of the reasons Guatemala had for replacing *race* by *ethnicity* in 1950 was that the local ways to define who was an indio and who a ladino were so numerous and so contradictory that the limpid trade of the demographer had become unfeasible (Arias 1976).

Back in the 1970s and 1980s, a number of ethnohistorians—some of them trained in France such as Jean Piel (1989) and Juan Pedro Viqueira (2002), some locally grown like Severo Martínez Peláez ([1970] 1998)—made a series of arguments not dissimilar (though far more sophisticated) to the one I have been trying to outline here. Speaking mainly about the original "invention" of *the* Indian, they argued that between the (glorious) pre-Hispanic era and the colonial period there was an unbridgeable historical and analytical gap that made it impossible to link both epochs and the peoples that inhabited them. In the words of Martínez Peláez, "*there is no Indian per se;* that is an ahistorical abstraction. . . . There are indios because of colonialism and because the colonial structure has transformed itself very slowly. And just as there were no indios before the colonialism shaped them, it must be supposed that there will be none when the development of Guatemalan society has erased all the surviving structures of the colonial period" ([1970] 1998, 508–9).[19] During and after the 1990s, as a new brand of indigenous movements took the fore—the Mexican Congreso Nacional Indígena and, above all, the Guatemalan Indianistas—the argument came to be labeled as "ethnocentric" and their advocates dismissed as heirs of the anthropologists and politicians who had tried to *integrate* the indigenous populations into the nation-state during the twentieth century (Warren 1998, Pérez Ruiz 2005).[20] Breaking the historical continuity between the most distant past and the present looked indeed like an attempt to take away the "historical rights" of late twentieth-century Chiapas's and Guatemala's Mayas. (Nevertheless, it is worth noting that Mexican indigenous organizations tended to establish less extended temporal links: generally speaking, the connection was made between the indigenous polities and peoples "conquered" by the Spanish in the sixteenth century and the indigenous peoples of the late twentieth and early twenty-first centuries [Benjamin 2000]. If the span of indigenous historicization is wider in Guatemala—as illustrated by the Maya religious ceremony of 2012—that is surely the result of the peculiar re-racialization experienced there in the 1980s and the 1990s.)

The irony is that the argument in favor of such rights follows rather closely the modern obsession with historical origins. By reclaiming their "history," the new indigenous movements seem to have forgotten that such a teleological, reductionist, state-sponsored narrative has been instrumental to their own symbolic oppression, that the problem was not their "lack" of history but the fact that it was *that kind* of history. Nationalist history is no doubt a form of history, but as the endeavors of many feminist, postmodern, environmentalist, anticolonial, and "from-below" historians attest, it is far from being the only epistemological alternative available to those seeking to build a better future. Stressing the unity of Mesoamerican indigenous peoples' history—which is to say, considering their multiple pasts as a single narrative stretching from the pre-Hispanic period all the way to the present, affirming their *identity* as "peoples" in the modern Western sense of the term—tends furthermore to distract scholars and activists alike from the various rationales underpinning the indio category and, more important, from the social function of the label at various points in time. Just as (liberal) multiculturalism has been described as a theoretical position that downplays the domination and exploitation experienced by indigenous peoples (Schneider 2013) or as a discursive strategy to keep Guatemala's "racial formation" in place (Hale 2006), I would argue that focusing on the continuity of indigenous historical identity minimizes the actual persistence of indigenous peoples' domination and exploitation. The actions of their oppressors and exploiters could, and indeed tend to, appear as the variable element of their relationship, as the aspect that has changed over time. On the contrary, it seems to me that *domination* and *exploitation* ought to be considered the stable clause—the recurring phenomenon—whereas the "identity" of those dominated and exploited should be construed as the equation's variable. If something has continued to exist, it has been the desire to keep large human groups marginalized and exploited; the different tags employed to identify them—as *indios* and *castas* in colonial times, as *indígenas* and *ladinos* in the nineteenth century, and as *indígenas*, *mestizos*, and *ladinos* in the twentieth century—have been just politicocultural tools that help achieve that goal. And that is just gattopardismo, is it not?

Be it as it may, the one thing we could realize from looking at the different incarnations of the terms *indio* and *indígena*, and the arithmetical pyrotechnics the words have produced, is that turning back to *race* to construe indigeneity makes no sense whatsoever. Race, even when paired with culture, is flimsy science and bad morals and invites the development of nonhistorical narratives. (Besides, racism does not need races to exist—just as nationalists have rarely needed an actual nation to play their tune.)[21] That is what happened in the 1800s, when in the absence of the legal-political framework from colonial times both society and the state turned to more rigid notions of cultural and political identification. That might be happening nowadays as well, as the new science of genomics—and the term's entrenched social meaning in the United States—seems to be on the verge of restoring the legitimacy of that particular way of

knowing and classifying individuals, peoples, cultures, and histories. Noticing identities and continuities in the long run would make
sense only if they were based on something more solid than phe-
notypes, cultural features as they appear within an itemized understanding of culture, or a narrative of the past based not only on the
doings of the state. In the absence of anything solid, of any indigenous "essence," it is perhaps better to underscore the ruptures, the
differences in the ways indigenous peoples have been defined and
perceived—by others and by themselves—over time. And let the
advocates of purity agonize about their *mongrelosity*.

## Notes

In memory of Dolores Pla Brugat (1954–2014)

1. My translation. Rather disappointingly, the canonical English version reads, "If
we want things to stay as they are, things will have to change" (Lampedusa 2007, 28).

2. If this essay does not use *Zapata and the Mexican Revolution*'s memorable opening as its analytical touchstone-"This is a book about country people who did not
want to move and therefore got into a revolution" (Womack 1968, VII)—it is not just
because I would like to avoid the insinuation that Mesoamerican peasants were clumsy
if not outright stupid but also because I think John Womack's book is actually not at
all about "reactionary" peasants.

3. I use quotation marks around *identity* because, following Brubaker and Cooper
(2000), I am more than ready to throw such a sacrosanct term to the social sciences'
garbage bin—and instead think of "identities" as volatile, contingent, and political ges-
tures of *identification*. I am incredibly grateful to Adam Rothman for having introduced me to this article.

4. On the history of population counts in Mexico, see Inegi 1996; for Guatemala,
see Arias 1976, 10–15.

5. Since these percentages are higher than the canonical figures, which tend to
follow Humboldt (1811, vol. 1, 369), who estimated the indigenous population represented 40 percent of New Spain's—yet climbing up to 61.81 percent in the provinces
of Guanajuato, Oaxaca, Puebla, and Valladolid—it is worth mentioning that I relied
on the tables composed by Castro Aranda (Castro Aranda 1977, 140–47) for the provinces of Alta California, Baja California, Guanajuato, Mérida, Mexico, New Mexico, Oaxaca, Sinaloa, Sonora, and Tlaxcala—based in turn on Archivo General de la
Nación (hereafter, AGN), Historia, vol. 522, ff. 246, 267, 274, and 276, and vol. 523, ff.
9, 88, 94, 113, and 145, plus one on Puebla based on *Relaciones estadísticas de Nueva
España* (1944, 51–69); the data for Tabasco comes from Aguirre Beltrán (1946), after
which I also corrected the figures for Mexico (adding some three thousand clergy not
included in the other count). I take Mérida, México, Oaxaca, Puebla, Tabasco, and
Tlaxcala to be Mesoamerican.

6. Unsurprisingly, the southern half of the country was disproportionately "indige-

nous." Although only in two states the majority of the population did not speak Spanish regularly (Yucatán, with 70.37 percent, and Oaxaca, with 53.15 percent), out of the remaining ten states where non-Spanish speakers represented over 10 percent of the population, only one (Sonora, 15.18 percent) was not within the limits of Mesoamerica: Campeche (44.77 percent), Chiapas (37.70 percent), Puebla (31.88 percent), Hidalgo (30.47 percent), Tlaxcala (23.04 percent), Guerrero (22.03 percent), Veracruz (20.73 percent), Mexico (18.88 percent), and Morelos (17.83 percent).

7. Incredibly, the figure given in the text—as opposed to the tables—was ten points lower: 54.6 percent; see Dirección General de Estadística (1894, 6).

8. See also Restall 1998 and Matthew and Oudijk 2007; for a different approach, see also Clendinnen 1987, a superb analysis of the cultural and political conflict between Indians and Spaniards in Yucatán.

9. On the once-famous medieval document that "granted" the church the right to rule over the Roman Empire, later shown—by Lorenzo Valla in the fifteenth century—to be a forgery, see Grafton 1995, 73–74.

10. At any rate, I hope U.S. readers will understand that I am not trying to ignore the concrete and rather brutal social life the "idea" has in the United States. As a former dweller of Washington DC and Chicago's South Side and also as an enthusiastic reader of Loïc Wacquant (2008), I am fully aware that reducing race as a "notion" or a "social construct" could sometimes appear insulting to those on the receiving end of the practice of *race*—people of color, of course.

11. For a superb study of one of the most significant "races," and yet one largely ignored, see Painter 2010.

12. Beltrán to the Contaduría Mayor, Tribunal de Cuentas, Mexico City, August 1, 1800, AGN, Tributos, vol. 55, exp. 12, ff. 11v–17 (341v–347).

13. "Bando del virrey, publicando el de la Regencia de la isla de León, libertando del tributo a los indios," Mexico, October 5, 1810, in *Colección de documentos para la historia* (1878, vol. 2, doc. 70); decreto XLII, March 13, 1811, in *Colección de los decretos y órdenes* (1811, 89–90). Article 5 of the Spanish constitution reads thus: "Son españoles . . . Todos los hombres libres nacidos y avecindados en los dominios de las Españas, y los hijos de éstos" (Spaniards are . . . all free men born and living in the Spanish dominions, and their children). Article 18 defined citizenship as follows: "Son ciudadanos aquellos españoles que por ambas líneas tracen su origen de los dominios españoles de ambos hemisferios, y estén avecindados en cualquier pueblo de los mismos dominios" (Citizens are those Spaniards whose both lineages go back to the Spanish dominions in either hemisphere, and live in any town of said dominions). Articles 309 to 311, in turn, set up the rules for a single system of municipal government, suppressing in this manner the double system of Spanish and Indian local government. See *Constitución política de la monarquía* 1812, 2, 5, and 78–79.

14. I have noticed elsewhere (Granados 2010) that the Spanish regency had no way to know in May 1810 that the largest popular insurrection in New Spain's history would begin four months later in the province with the highest number of *indios laboríos*, the only ones who could not benefit from the corporate protection of the system of indigenous republics.

15. The Spanish version, likely the original, reads even more emphatically: "Son, en realidad, ladinos e indígenas, dos sociedades distintas en el mismo país: la una marcha con la esperanza y el trabajo, por los senderos que el progreso aconseja e impone: la otra está inmovilizada, fuera de la atmósfera intelectual y política, sosteniéndose con testarudez en sus costumbres y hábitos antiguos. Los indígenas no cooperan a la civilización, pero tampoco la entorpecen con otras resistencias que las resistencias de la pasividad. No obstante, a pesar de su indolencia, proporcionan la suma de trabajo que hace producir al suelo y crea la riqueza nacional, en falta de otro concurso y de otras fuerzas" (Dirección General de Estadística 1894, 16).

16. Peñafiel's oeuvre is a case in point, as he authored books as diverse as *Memoria sobre las aguas potables de la capital de México* (1884), *Monumentos del arte mexicano antiguo* (1890), *Nomenclatura geográfica de México* (1897), and *Teotihuacán: Estudio histórico y arqueológico* (1900), and all the while he kept managing the statistics office, organized the first three Mexican censuses, and even found time to design the Mexican pavilion for the Parisian Exhibition Universelle of 1889 (Tenorio Trillo 1996, 73–80).

17. That happened even *chez* Sotelo Inclán (1943), who emphasized the tectonic history of Anenecuilco and portrayed Zapata as a *calpuque* or elected official of his (indigenous) community.

18. For a study of Instituto Nacional Indigenista's policy and practice in other Mexican region, see Schwartz 2016.

19. "*No hay indio en sí*; ésa es una abstracción antihistórica. . . . Hay indios porque hubo coloniaje y porque la estructura colonial se ha ido transformando con gran lentitud. Y así como no hubo indios antes de que la colonia los formara, debe suponerse que dejará de haberlos cuando el desarrollo de la sociedad guatemalteca haya borrado todas las supervivencias estructurales de la colonia." At any rate, see also Guzmán Böckler and Herbert (1970), who in those very years were producing a far more "ethnic" interpretation of Guatemala's history.

20. That is why Lovell and Lutz (2009) could write an apologetic introduction to *La patria del criollo*'s English edition—apologetic and patronizing, which is worse, for they tend to refer to Martínez Peláez as "Severo."

21. Since I take racism to be an *ideology*—that is, a political discourse embedded in social practices, policies, and institutions—I see no reason to consider any of its tenets as an analytical tool, much less as a descriptor of what is going on in the world; hence my disagreement with such scholars as Hale (2006, chapter 7) who have argued that the endurance of racism in Latin America requires bringing race back into the analysis of the region's structural inequality. A good example of the perils of taking his advice too seriously is Telles 2014—a book so simplistic in its perspective, so blindly racist in its argument, that is embarrassing to read.

## Bibliography

Aguirre Beltrán, Gonzalo. 1946. *La población negra de México, 1519–1810: Estudio etnohistórico*. Mexico: Fuente Cultural.

———. 1967. *Regiones de refugio: El desarrollo de la comunidad y el proceso dominical en Mestizo América*. Mexico: Instituto Indigenista Interamericano.

Arias B., Jorge. 1976. *La población de Guatemala*. Guatemala, CICRED.

Bartra, Roger. 1987. *La jaula de la melancolía: Identidad y metamorfosis del mexicano*. Mexico: Grijalbo.

Baselenque, Diego. (1714) 1886. *Arte de la lengua tarasca*. Edited by Antonio Peñafiel. Mexico: Secretaría de Fomento.

Benjamin, Thomas. 2000. "A Time of Reconquest: History, the Maya Revival, and the Zapatista Rebellion in Chiapas." *American Historical Review* 105, no. 2: 417–50.

Bloch, March. 1949. *Apologie pour l'histoire, ou Métier d'historien*. Paris: Armand Colin.

Bonfil Batalla, Guillermo. 1987. *México profundo: Una civilización negada*. Mexico: Centro de Investigaciones y Estudios Superiores en Antropología Social.

Borah, Woodrow, and Sherburne F. Cook. 1960. *The Population of Central Mexico in 1548: An Analysis of the "Suma de visitas de pueblos."* Berkeley: University of California Press.

Brubaker, Rogers, and Frederick Cooper. 2000. "Beyond 'Identity.'" *Theory and Practice* 29, no.1: 1–47.

Brunk, Samuel. 2008. *The Posthumous Career of Emiliano Zapata: Myth, Memory, and Mexico's Twentieth Century*. Austin: University of Texas Press.

Carmagnani, Marcello. 1988. *El regreso de los dioses: El proceso de reconstitución de la identidad étnica en Oaxaca, siglos xvii y xviii*. Mexico: Fondo de Cultura Económica.

———. (2003) 2011. *The Other West: Latin America from Invasion to Globalization*. Translated by Rosanna M. Giammanco Frongia. Berkeley: University of California Press.

Casas, Bartolomé de las. 1552. *Breve relación de la destrucción de las Indias Occidentales: Presentada a Felipe II[,] siendo principe de Asturias*. Schulze y Dean.

Caso, Alfonso. 1948. "Definición del indio y de lo indio." *America Indígena* Vol. 8: 145–81.

Castañeda de la Paz, María. "Historia de una casa real: Origen y ocaso del linaje gobernante en México-Tenochtitlan." 2011. *Nuevo Mundo Mundos Nuevos*. Available at http://nuevomundo.revues.org/60624.

[Castro Aranda, Hugo]. 1977. *Primer censo de población de la Nueva España, 1790: Censo de Revillagigedo, "un censo censurado."* Mexico: Secretaría de Programación y Presupuesto (Dirección General de Estadística).

Chance, John K., and William B. Taylor. 1985. "Cofradías and Cargos: An Historical Perspective on the Mesoamerican Civil-Religious Hierarchy." *American Ethnologist* 12, no.1: 1–26.

Choderlos de Laclos, Pierre-Ambroise-François. (1782) 1995. *Les liaisons dangereuses*. Edited by Yves Le Hir. Paris: Garnier.

Clendinnen, Inga. 1987. *Ambivalent Conquests: Maya and Spaniard in Yucatán, 1517–1570*. Cambridge: Cambridge University Press.

Cobá Noh, Lorgio. 2009. *El indio ciudadano: La tributación y la contribución personal directa en Yucatán, 1786–1825*. Mexico-Mérida: Instituto de Investigaciones Dr. José María Luis Mora—Universidad Autónoma de Yucatán.

*Colección de los decretos y órdenes que han expedido las Cortes Generales y Extraordinarias desde su instalación en 24 de septiembre de 1810 hasta igual fecha de 1811*. 1811. Cadiz: Imprenta Real.

*Constitución política de la monarquía española, promulgada en Cádiz a 19 de marzo de 1812.* 1812. Cadiz: Imprenta Real.

Cook, Noble David. 1998. *Born to Die: Disease and New World Conquest, 1492–1650.* Cambridge: Cambridge University Press.

Cook, Sherburne F., and Lesley Byrd Simpson. 1948. *The Population of Central Mexico in the Sixteenth Century.* Berkeley: University of California Press.

Cook, Sherburne F., and Woodrow Borah. 1960. *The Indian Population of Central Mexico, 1531–1610.* Berkeley: University of California Press.

———. 1968. *The Population of the Mixteca Alta, 1520–1960.* Berkeley: University of California Press.

———. 1971–79. *Essays in Population History: Mexico and the Caribbean.* 3 vols. Berkeley: University of California Press.

Cuadriello, Jaime. 2004. *Las glorias de la república de Tlaxcala: O la conciencia como imagen sublime.* Mexico: Universidad Nacional Autónoma de México (Instituto de Investigaciones Estéticas).

Curcio-Nagy, Linda A. 2004. *The Great Festivals of Colonial Mexico City: Performing Power and Identity.* Albuquerque: University of New Mexico Press.

de Certeau, Michel, Dominique Julia, and Jacques Revel. 1975. *Une politique de la langue: La révolution française et les patois: L'enquête de Grégoire.* Paris: Gallimard.

Dirección General de Estadística. 1881. *Censo general de la República de Guatemala, levantado [en] el año de 1880.* Guatemala: Establecimiento Tipográfico de El Progreso.

Dirección General de Estadística. 1894. *Censo general de la República de Guatemala.* Guatemala: Tipografía y Encuadernación Nacional.

Dirección General de Estadística. 1899. *Censo general de la República mexicana, verificado el 20 de octubre de 1895.* Mexico: Secretaría de Fomento.

Earle, Rebecca. 2007. *The Return of the Native: Indians and Myth-Making in Spanish America, 1810–1930.* Durham: Duke University Press.

Esteva, Gustavo, Catherine Marielle, and Mariana Kurlat. *Sin maíz no hay país: Páginas de una exposición.* 2003. Mexico: Consejo Nacional para la Cultura y las Artes (Museo Nacional de Culturas Populares).

Fenner, Justus, and Dolores Palomo Infante. 2008. "El archivo histórico del Centro Coordinador Tzeltal-Tzotzil de Chiapas: Memoria del laboratorio del indigenismo en México." *Desacatos* 26: 75–86.

Fredrickson, George M. 2002. *Racism: A Short History.* Princeton: Princeton University Press.

García de León, Antonio. 1985. *Resistencia y utopía: Memorial de agravios y crónicas de revueltas y profecías acaecidas en la provincia de Chiapas durante los últimos quinientos años de su historia.* Mexico: Ediciones Era.

Gerbi, Antonello. (1955) 1960. *La disputa del nuevo mundo: Historia de una polémica, 1750–1900.* Translated by Antonio Alatorre. Mexico: Fondo de Cultura Económica.

González Flores, José Gustavo. 2013. "Mestizaje de papel: Dinámica demográfica y familias de calidad múltiple en Taximaroa (1667–1826)." PhD diss., El Colegio de Michoacán.

Grafton, Anthony. 1997. *The Footnote: A Curious History*. Cambridge: Harvard University Press.

Granados, Luis Fernando. 2008. "Cosmopolitan Indians and Mesoamerican Barrios in Bourbon Mexico City: Tribute, Community, Family and Work in 1800." PhD diss., Georgetown University.

———. 2010. "Huérfanos, solteros, súbditos neoclásicos: Microhistoria de la abolición del tributo en el imperio español." In *1750–1850: La independencia de México a la luz de cien años: Problemáticas y desenlaces de una larga transición*, edited by Brian Connaughton, 283–326. Mexico: Universidad Autónoma Metropolitana (Iztapalapa)—Ediciones del Lirio.

Grandin, Greg. 2000. *The Blood of Guatemala: A History of Race and Nation*. Durham: Duke University Press.

Groeber, Valentin. 2007. *Who are You?: Identification, Deception and Surveillance in Early Modern Europe*. Translated by Mark Kyburz and John Peck. New York: Zone.

Guardino, Peter. 2005. *The Time of Liberty: Popular Political Culture in Oaxaca, 1750–1850*. Durham: Duke University Press.

Guarisco, Claudia. 2003. *Los indios del valle de México y la construcción de una nueva sociabilidad política, 1770–1835*. Zicacantepec: El Colegio Mexiquense.

Guzmán Betancourt, Ignacio. 1994. "Para una historia de la historiografía lingüística mexicana: Desde sus orígenes hasta el siglo XIX." *Dimensión Antropológica* 2: 95–130.

Guzmán Böckler, Carlos, and Jean Loup Herbert. 1970. *Guatemala: Una interpretación histórico-social*. Mexico: Siglo Veintiuno.

Hale, Charles R. 2006. *Más que un indio—More than an Indian: Racial Ambivalence and Neoliberal Multiculturalism in Guatemala*. Santa Fe: School of American Research.

Hannaford, Ivan. 1996. *Race: The History of an Idea in the West*. Washington DC and Baltimore: Woodrow Wilson Center Press and Johns Hopkins University Press.

Haskett, Robert Stephen. 1991. *Indigenous Rulers: An Ethnohistory of Town Government in Colonial Cuernavaca*. Albuquerque: University of New Mexico Press.

Hernández y Dávalos, J. E., ed. (1878) 1968. *Colección de documentos para la historia de la guerra de independencia de México, 1808–1821*. 6 vols. Nendeln: Kraus-Thomson Organization.

Hobsbawm, Eric J. 1994. *The Age of Extremes: A History of the World, 1914–1991*. New York: Pantheon.

Humboldt, Alexander von. 1811. *Essai politique sur le royaume de la Nouvelle-Espagne*. Paris: F. Schoell.

Inegi (Instituto Nacional de Estadística, Geografía e Informática). 1996. *Estados Unidos Mexicanos: Cien años de censos de población*. Mexico: Instituto Nacional de Estadística, Geografía e Informática.

Inegi (Instituto Nacional de Geografía y Estadística). 2000. *XII Censo general de población y vivienda*. Mexico: Instituto Nacional de Geografía y Estadística.

Instituto Nacional de Estadística. 2003. *Censos nacionales XI de población y VI de habitación: Características de la población y de los locales de habitación censados*. Guatemala: Instituto Nacional de Estadística.

Katzew, Ilona. 2004. *Casta Painting: Images of Race in Eighteenth-Century Mexico*. New Haven: Yale University Press.

Kirchoff, Paul. 1943. "Mesoamérica." *Dimensión Antropológica* 19: 15–32. Available at www.dimensionantropologica.inah.gob.mx/?p=1031/.

Korsbaek, Leif, and Miguel Ángel Sámano Rentería. 2003. "El indigenismo en México: Antecedentes y actualidad." *Ra Ximhai* 3, no.1: 195–224.

Jones, Tobias. (2003) 2005. *The Dark Heart of Italy*. New York: North Point Press.

Lampedusa, Giuseppe di. 1958. *Il Gattopardo*. Milan: Feltrinelli.

———. 2007. *The Leopard: A Novel*. Translated by Archibald Colquhoun. New York: Pantheon.

León-Portilla, Miguel. 1956. *La filosofía náhuatl estudiada en sus fuentes*. Mexico: Ediciones Especiales del Instituto Indigenista Interamericano.

Lockhart, James. 1992. *The Nahuas after the Conquest: A Social and Cultural History of the Indians of Central Mexico, Sixteenth Through Eighteenth Centuries*. Stanford: Stanford University Press.

Lovell, W. George, and Christopher H. Lutz. 1991–92. "The Historical Demography of Colonial Central America." *Yearbook, Conference of Latin Americanist Geographers* 17–18: 127–38.

———. 1996. "'A Dark Obverse': Maya Survival in Guatemala, 1520–1994." *Geographical Review* 86, no. 3: 398–407.

———. 2009. Introduction. In *La patria del criollo: An Interpretation of Colonial Guatemala*, by Severo Martínez Peláez, edited by Christopher H. Lutz, translated by Susan M. Neve and W. George Lovell, xiii–xlv. Durham: Duke University Press.

Loveman, Mara. 2014. *National Colors: Racial Classification and the State in Latin America*. New York: Oxford University Press.

Lucente, Gregory L. 1984. "*Scrivere o fare . . . o altro*: Social Commitment and Ideologies of Representation in the Debates over Lampedusa's *Il Gattopardo* and Morante's *La Storia*." *Italica* 61, no. 3: 220–51.

Lunberg, Magnus. 2008. "El clero indígena en Hispanoamérica: De la legislación a la implementación y práctica eclesiástica." *Estudios de Historia Náhuatl* 38: 39–62.

Markoff, John. 1996. *The Abolition of Feudalism: Peasants, Lords, and Legislators in the French Revolution*. University Park: Pennsylvania State University Press.

Martínez, María Elena. 2008. *Genealogical Fictions: Pureza de Sangre, Religion, and Gender in Colonial Mexico*. Stanford: Stanford University Press.

Martínez Peláez, Severo. (1970) 1998. *La patria del criollo: Ensayo de interpretación de la realidad colonial guatemalteca*. Mexico: Fondo de Cultura Económica.

Matthew, Laura E., and Michel R. Oudijk, eds. 2007. *Indian Conquistadors: Indigenous Allies in the Conquest of Mesoamerica*. Norman: University of Oklahoma Press.

McCaa, Robert. 1993. "El poblamiento del México decimonónico: Escrutinio crítico de un siglo censurado." In *El poblamiento de México: Una visión histórica-demográfica*, vol. 3, *México en el siglo XIX*, 90–113. Mexico: Consejo Nacional de Población.

McCreery, David. 1994. *Rural Guatemala, 1760–1940*. Stanford: Stanford University Press.

Miranda, José. (1952) 2005. *El tributo indígena en la Nueva España durante el siglo*

*XVI. Prólogo de Andrés Lira*. México: El Colegio de México (Centro de Estudios Históricos).

Navarrete, Federico. 2004. *Las relaciones interétnicas de México*. Mexico: Universidad Nacional Autónoma de México.

Obara-Saeki, Tadashi. 2010. *Ladinización sin mestizaje: Historia demográfica del área chiapaneca, 1748–1813*. Tuxtla Gutiérrez: Consejo Estatal para la Cultura y las Artes de Chiapas.

Owensby, Brian P. 2008. *Empire of Law and Indian Justice in Colonial Mexico*. Stanford: Stanford University Press.

Painter, Nell Irvin. 2010. *The History of White People*. New York: W. W. Norton.

Patriarca, Silvana. 2001. "National Identity or National Character?: New Vocabularies and Old Paradigms." In *Making and Remaking Italy: The Cultivation of National Identity Around the Risorgimento*, edited by Albert Russell Ascoli and Krystyna von Henneberg, 299–320. New York: Berg.

Peñafiel, Antonio. 1884. *Memoria sobre las aguas potables de la capital de México*. With the help of Lamberto Asiain. Mexico: Secretaría de Fomento.

———. 1890. *Monumentos del arte mexicano antiguo: Ornamentación, mitología, tributos y monumentos*. Berlin: A. Asher.

———. 1897. *Nomenclatura geográfica de México: Etimologías de los nombres de lugar correspondientes a los principales idiomas que se hablan en la república*. Mexico: Secretaría de Fomento.

———. 1900. *Teotihuacán: Estudio histórico y arqueológico*. French version by Auguste Genin, English version by Carlos Fernández Galán. Mexico: Secretaría de Fomento.

Peñafiel, Antonio, ed. 1887. *Gramática de la lengua zapoteca*. Mexico: Secretaría de Fomento.

Pérez Ruiz, Maya Lorena. 2005. *¡Todos somos zapatistas! Alianzas y rupturas entre el EZLN y las organizaciones indígenas de México*. Mexico: Instituto Nacional de Antropología e Historia.

Piel, Jean. 1989. *Sajcabajá: Muerte y resurrección de un pueblo de Guatemala, 1500–1970*. Translated by Eliana Castro Ponlsen. Mexico and Guatemala: Centre d'Études Mexicaines et Centraméricaines and Seminario de Integración Social.

Pimentel, Francisco. (1862) 1903. *Cuadro comparativo de las lenguas indígenas de México*. Vols. 1–2 of *Obras completas de Francisco Pimentel*, edited by Jacinto Pimentel y Fernando Pimentel. Mexico: Tipografía Económica.

———. 2005. *Dos obras de Francisco Pimentel: "Memoria sobre las causas que han originado la situación actual de la raza indígena de México y medios para remediarla" [y] "La economía política aplicada a la propiedad territorial en México."* Enrique Semo, introduction. Mexico: Consejo Nacional para la Cultura y las Artes.

Pla Brugat, Dolores. 2005. "'Indígenas, mezclados y blancos' según el Censo General de Habitantes de 1921." *Historias* 61: 67–83.

———. 2011. "Más desindianización que mestizaje: Una relectura de los censos generales de población." *Dimensión Antropológica* 53: 69–91.

Pollack, Aaron. 2008. *Levantamiento k'iche' en Totonicapán, 1820: Los lugares de las políticas subalternas*. Guatemala: Asociación para el Avance de las Ciencias Sociales en Guatemala.

Rabell Romero, Cecilia. 1993. "El descenso de la población indígena durante el siglo XVI y las cuentas del gran capitán." In *El poblamiento de México: Una visión histórica-demográfica*, vol. 2, *El México colonial*, 18–35. Mexico: Consejo Nacional de Población.

Reed, Nelson A. (1964) 2001. *The Caste War of Yucatán*. Stanford: Stanford University Press.

Reeves, René. 2006. *Ladinos with Ladinos, Indians with Indians: Land, Labor, and Regional Ethnic Conflict in the Making of Guatemala*. Stanford: Stanford University Press.

*Relaciones estadísticas de Nueva España a principios del siglo XIX*. 1944. Mexico: Secretaría de Hacienda.

Renan, Ernest. (1848) 1858. *De l'origine du langage*. 2nd ed. Paris: Michel Lévy Frères.

———. 1882. "Qu'est-ce qu'une nation?" Available at http://classiques.uqac.ca/classiques/renan_ernest/qu_est_ce_une_nation/qu_est_ce_une_nation_texte.html/.

Restall, Matthew. 1998. *Maya Conquistador*. Boston: Beacon Press.

———. 2003. "A History of the New Philology and the New Philology in History." *Latin American Research Review* 38, no. 1: 113–34.

Restall, Matthew, and Florine Asselbergs, eds. 2007. *Invading Guatemala: Spanish, Nahua, and Maya Accounts of the Conquest Wars*. University Park: Pennsylvania State University Press.

Riva Palacio, Vicente, ed. 1887–89. *México a través de los siglos*. 5 vols. Mexico-Barcelona: Ballescá-Espasa.

Rothenberg, Daniel, ed. 2012. *Memory of Silence: The Guatemalan Truth Commission Report*. New York: Palgrave Macmillan.

Rozat, Guy. 1993. *Indios imaginarios e indios reales en los relatos de la conquista de México*. Xalapa: Universidad Veracruzana.

Schneider Glantz, Renata. 2013. "Aproximaciones conceptuales al fenómeno de la diversidad cultural: Multiculturalismo, justicia social e interculturalidad." Master's thesis, Universidad Nacional Autónónoma de México.

Schwartz, Diana L. 2016. "Transforming the Tropics: Development, Displacement, and Anthropology in the Papaloapan, Mexico, 1940s–1960s." PhD diss., University of Chicago.

Sotelo Inclán, Jesús. 1943. *Raíz y razón de Zapata: Anenecuilco, investigación histórica*. Mexico: Étnos.

Stern, Alexandra Minna. 2003. "From Mestizophilia to Biotypology: Racialization and Science in Mexico, 1920–1960." In *Race and Nation in Modern Latin America*, edited by Nancy P. Appelbaum, Anne S. Macpherson, and Karin Alejandra Rosemblatt, 187–210. Chapel Hill: University of North Carolina Press.

Tanck de Estrada, Dorothy. 2005. *Atlas ilustrado de los pueblos de indios: Nueva España, 1800*. Mexico: El Colegio de México, Comisión Nacional para el Desarrollo de los Pueblos Indígenas, El Colegio Mexiquense, Fomento Cultural Banamex.

Taracena Arriola, Arturo. 1999. *Invención criolla, sueño ladino, pesadilla indígena: Los*

*Altos de Guatemala, de región a estado, 1740–1871.* Antigua Guatemala: Centro de Investigaciones Regionales de Mesoamérica.

———. 2002. *Etnicidad, estado y nación en Guatemala, 1808–1944.* Guatemala: Nawal Wuj.

Telles, Edward, and the Project on Ethnicity and Race in Latin America. 2014. *Pigmentocracies: Ethnicity, Race, and Color in Latin America.* Chapel Hill: University of North Carolina Press.

Tenorio Trillo, Mauricio. 1996. *Mexico at the World's Fairs: Crafting a Modern Nation.* Berkeley: University of California Press.

Torres Freyermuth, Amanda Úrsula. 2010. "Tutelaje indígena: Ideas, discursos y prácticas en torno al indio chiapaneco en el tránsito de la colonia a la primera república." Master's thesis, Instituto de Investigaciones Dr. José María Luis Mora.

Valdés, Luz María. 1995. *Los indios en los censos de población.* Mexico: Universidad Nacional Autónoma de México (Coordinación de Humanidades).

Vasconcelos, José. 1925. *La raza cósmica: Misión de la raza iberoamericana: Notas de viajes a la América del Sur.* Paris: Agencia Mundial de Libreria.

Villoro, Luis. 1950. *Los grandes momentos del indigenismo en México.* Mexico: El Colegio de México, El Colegio Nacional, Fondo de Cultura Económica.

Viqueira, Juan Pedro. 2002. *Encrucijadas chiapanecas: Economía, religión e identidades.* Mexico: El Colegio de México-Tusquets.

———. 2010. "Reflexiones contra la noción histórica de mestizaje." *Nexos.* Available at www.nexos.com.mx/?p=13750.

Vogt, Evon Z. 1970. *The Zinacantecos of Mexico: A Modern Maya Way of Life.* New York: Holt, Rinehart and Winston.

Wacquant, Loïc. 2008. *Urban Outcasts: A Comparative Sociology of Advanced Marginality.* Cambridge: Polity.

Warman, Arturo, Guillermo Bonfil, Margarita Nolasco, Mercedes Olivera, and Enrique Valencia. 1970. *De eso que llaman antropología mexicana.* Mexico: Nuestro Tiempo.

Warren, Kay B. 1998. *Indigenous Movements and Their Critics.* Princeton: Princeton University Press.

Watanabe, John M. 1990. "Enduring yet Ineffable Community in the Western Periphery of Guatemala." In *Guatemalan Indians and the State: 1540 to 1988.* Edited by Carol A. Smith with Marilyn M. Moors, 183–204. Austin: University of Texas Press.

Woodward, Ralph Lee, Jr. 1993. *Rafael Carrera and the Emergence of the Republic of Guatemala, 1821–1871.* Athens: University of Georgia Press.

Womack, John, Jr. 1968. *Zapata and the Mexican Revolution.* New York: Knopf.

# 5

# From Prosperity to Poverty

*Andeans in the Nineteenth Century*

ERICK D. LANGER

Today, the indigenous peoples of the Andes are seen as inherently poor and marginalized from economic modernity (Hall and Patrinos 2006). This is the image that economists and other social scientists in the World Bank and elsewhere have propagated. They assume that indigenous peoples have been inherently poor because of their marginal status in the power structures since the Spanish conquest. The purpose of this chapter is to clear up the misconceptions of indigenous prosperity by showing how integral the indigenous were in commerce and mining during a significant portion of the nineteenth century.

The abundant literature on the Andean peoples for the colonial period certainly seems to bear out the storyline of impoverished Indians; nevertheless, historians have over the past few decades or so found much more agency among indigenous peoples—especially those in the sixteenth century. However, the vast majority of the literature on the colonial period describes the oppressions under which the indigenous population labored, even though within the colonial structures the Natives ameliorated their situations as best they could. Thus, Andeans were forced to move into new villages during the reducción imposed by Viceroy Francisco de Toledo at the end of the sixteenth century, suffered from waves of epidemics that caused catastrophic demographic decline, and were forced to provide mine laborers for forced labor, the *mita*, in Potosí and Huancavelica.[1] In the eighteenth century, colonial officials squeezed out even more surplus from Andean peoples through the *reparto de mercancías*, in which community members were forced to purchase goods from local officials who were supposed to protect them. Only the Great Rebellion (1780–84), in which such indigenous leaders as Túpac Amaru, Tomás Katari, and Túpac Katari mobilized the masses against the colonial regime, led to the abolition of the *reparto*. Nevertheless, other forms of exploitation continued, and the indigenous communities remained the main source of revenue for the Crown (and other Spaniards) for the rest of the colonial period. Silver mining competed with tribute in terms of royal revenue; both were predicated on the exploitation of the indigenous communities, the former on the virtually free labor of the *mitayos* (a proportion of tributaries from each community who were forced to work in the silver mines) and the latter on an ethnically based tax.

The situation changed dramatically after the independence from the Iberian power of Spanish America, which in the Andes occurred between 1822 and 1825. I have argued in another essay that the decades after the independence wars (1810–25) were a time when indigenous peoples in the Andes enjoyed a de facto independence in political and economic terms (2016). The evidence is clear; the Andean states were uniformly weak and did not have the capability to extend the state into the countryside, much less the indigenous communities. Armies were tiny and used mostly to defend against other elite interlopers (with uneven success) or against the small armies of neighboring countries. The new republics had so few resources that their bureaucratic apparatus paled compared to that of the late colonial period. Indirect rule through local indigenous officials to collect tribute was the best that these states could muster. And tribute exactions remained at the same levels as in the colonial period, making them less onerous as time went on. Despite the demographic increase of community members in the first part of the nineteenth century, a smaller proportion of indigenous community members paid tribute, and the state was unable to force them to do so. The payment of tribute, based on the idea that the indigenous population, though vassals of the Crown, had to pay taxes as a conquered people, had been an important source of revenue for the colonial regime. Andeans paid tribute every semester, an amount that varied according to the access to land that community members maintained. In the Cuzco department and Azángaro province in Peru, they paid less because the state had inaccurate counts of the indigenous Andean population; in Bolivia the percentage of tribute collection went down significantly after the mid-nineteenth century.[2]

Tribute was an important part of indigenous community identity in the postcolonial Andes because it defined the position of the community member and his or her access to land, but this was only one facet of how urban political elites conceived of indigenous peasants in the midst of the body politic of the new nations. Were Indians true citizens? How did the state define its indigenous population, especially in the first generation after independence, a time when most governments consisted of people imbued by liberal ideas? The matter was complicated, for liberals in theory thought of all being equal, though the matter of land ownership—which begs the question of whether Indians who were part of a communal land tenure system were really land owners—was important. According to liberal doctrine, only people who owned their own land could truly think independently, and for this reason community members did not fit into liberal schemas. Although Argentine general José de San Martin declared that all Peruvians, including Andean community members, be considered Peruanos, the liberal elites from coastal Lima—who considered themselves of European descent—did not accept this promiscuous granting of equality to the Indian masses of the Andean interior. Ironically, the name of *Peruano* stuck only for the indigenous peasant population; Peruvian Creoles and mestizos called themselves *ciudadanos* (citizens) instead. This was similar in Bolivia, where members of indigenous communities appeared as *indígena, indígena contribuyente,* or *indígena originario* and those who considered themselves of European extraction as ciudadanos (Barragan, 1999; Langer 2009).[3] Ecuador was similar. Although President Vicente Rocafuerte decreed in 1835 that all Ecuadorians were to enjoy the same rights, this was not the case, as Aleezé Sattar has shown. As Sattar asserts and as was the case in Bolivia and Peru, Indians "were indigenous and not ciudadanos." (2007, 30). In other words, legal discrimination continued, even with government documents, despite the fiction that indigenous members were to participate in the new Andean countries. It created republics in which a small minority justified their rule over the majority, since during the nineteenth century in Peru, Ecuador, and Bolivia, indigenous peasants were the majority of the population. However, as this chapter shows, this indigenous majority was crucial to the economic prosperity of the region.

The debate over indigenous citizenship and its tentative nature related directly to the discussion over the land tenure rights of indigenous communities. For liberals, communal property was anathema because it restricted land markets. In highland Peru and Bolivia, much of the land was indeed in the hands of communities. In Ecuador, in turn, haciendas dominated the landscape, and most of the indigenous village members had to work on the estates of the people who considered themselves *español americanos*, consciously different from the Indians.[4] The problem such systems posed was how to transform communal lands into private property that could be bought and sold.

Different countries tried different solutions. In Ecuador this was not a major problem, since the haciendas already controlled the dependent communities, aided by the state through a practice called *concertaje* (Guerrero 1991).[5] In Peru the advent of guano production and the flood of money to the state put indigenous issues in the highlands on the back burner. The coastal Peruvian elites left the highlands alone to stew while they developed the coast and its plantations (Piel 1975). In Bolivia it was not as simple. Without a coastal population—Antofagasta province on the Pacific was sparsely populated, with mostly Chilean and Peruvian citizens—the center of political and economic gravity remained in the altiplano and the valleys to the east, where the indigenous communities thrived. Recurrent debates broke out about how to transform the communities, pitting those who wanted to follow the Ecuadorian example of taking the land and turning the Andeans into hacienda peons against those who thought the best way to create agrarian development was to give each community member their own parcel and thus turn them into yeoman farmers. The debate did not come to a head until the 1860s with the land reforms under President Mariano Melgarejo; only in 1874 did the yeoman model, which followed the classic Jeffersonian liberal model, win out in Bolivia (Langer 1988; Lofstrom 2013).

MAP 2. The Andean countries, circa 1850. Cartography by Bill Nelson.

In Peru the issue of land tenure and if the state should recognize the indigenous communities was resolved much later, after many communities had lost their lands. The yeoman model finally also prevailed, though late for many communities. Under pressure of the *indigenistas*, in the late nineteenth and early twentieth centuries, the second Augusto Leguía regime (1919–30) finally legally recognized Andean indigenous communities in 1921.[6] Indigenistas were members of the elite who wanted to redeem the Andean indigenous peoples through reforms and education. Given the lack of political and economic importance of the highlands where the vast majority of the indigenous population lived, the state began to recognize communities in the early twentieth century under the Leguía administration in return for community members' obligatory labor on the roads (Davies 1974, de la Cadena 2000).

In other words, Andean peoples were seen as second-class citizens despite the initial attempt by the Gran Colombians (Bolívar and his lieutenants) to destroy the indigenous communities and presumably make everyone equal. The differentiation came about because of the inertia of the colonial system—Andean indigenous peoples saw advantages in their status as forming part of the república de indios—and also because they had always done it this way, and their communities and social structures had been built around semiautonomous settlements. The república de indios was a legal concept that the Spaniards had introduced to distinguish the Indians from the Spaniards, who had their own república de españoles. Under these categories, the Indians had their own legal system and separate land rights that maintained their possessions as a community. In turn, the español americanos could not conceive of making indios equal to them politically and indeed had different systems, embedded in municipal governments, than the communal structures of the Andean villages. These ways of dealing with day-to-day governance reasserted themselves after the Colombians left Peru, Bolivia, and Ecuador in the late 1820s. Indeed, it was the español americanos who had to adjust to a new system under independence more than did the indigenous communities, which could revert to their then centuries-old amalgamation of pre-Columbian and colonial practices.

## Andeans as Economic Actors

The equivocal nature of indigenous citizenship and the concomitant debate about indigenous communities reflected a great ambivalence by the political elites in Peru and Bolivia about how to deal with a Native population that they saw as ethnically different and had, according to the these elites, a different mentality and forms of living from the minority descendants of the Europeans and those who defined themselves as mestizo. The elites struggled with how to deal with the legacy of the colonial period because of the large numbers of peoples they considered ethnically different from themselves and because of the relative weakness of the state to effect any changes upon the majority Natives.

Despite the dithering about the political place of Andeans in the new nation-states, the economic role of community members was clear. They were by far the most important economic actors in the highlands of Peru and Bolivia. They dominated the transport sector, supplied most of the coca leaf, produced and sold most of the food in the urban centers of the highlands, and kept the mining centers supplied with workers and most other inputs needed for mining. However, other than in the mining centers, Andeans consumed relatively few goods that they themselves did not produce. Also, they tended to behave as peasants; that is, they left work in the mines and urban centers when they needed to return to their community plots to sow or harvest their crops. The European-derived liberal conception of the ideal *homo economicus* was that of people fully integrated into markets, which meant that indigenous community members did not fit that model.[7]

The reason indigenous peasants dominated the transport sector was that they owned most of the pack animals. In the altiplano the communities in La Paz, Oruro, and Potosí contained hundreds of thousands of llamas, the "trucks" of the Andean highlands. José María Dalence ([1851] 1975) estimated that the provinces of La Paz, Oruro, and Potosí contained 794,682 llamas in 1848, which represented 95 percent of all of these animals in the country. For example, the rural inhabitants of the region around the city of Oruro, according to Dalence, "do not dedicate themselves to agriculture, contenting themselves with raising llamas and pigs, for which they gain lots of advantages through commerce; the llamas are generally the biggest and most robust compared to those of the other provinces [within Bolivia], selling some as pack animals" ([1851] 1975, 163, 244).[8] The owners of the pack animals were essentially all members of indigenous communities, as haciendas were rare on the altiplano before the late nineteenth century.[9] The number of mules and donkeys was small at midcentury, and many were imported from Argentina. According to Dalence, there were only 54,084 horses, 13,311 mules and 47,383 donkeys in Bolivia in the mid-nineteenth century, dwarfed by the numbers of llamas ([1851] 1975, 246).

It is likely to have been similar in the southern Peruvian highlands, but data are lacking for that region.[10] We know much more about the mule trade, animals indigenous communities tended not to purchase. Arequipa, the other great transportation hub of the southern highlands in Peru, relied heavily on mules brought from Salta, Argentina. Many of the mules were purchased at the fair in Vilque, Peru, where Argentine traders took their mules and donkeys (Jacobsen 1993, 182; Conti and Sica 2011).[11]

The control of the llama herds by the indigenous communities in the central core of the Andes meant that most merchants and miners had to rely on Andeans for their transport needs. It is difficult to prove the ethnic composition of the teamsters who hauled the ore from the mine heads to the refineries, the minerals to the coast, and the imports from the Pacific coast to the interior. We know from the correspondence of import-export merchants that they developed a close relationship with their teamsters, but we can only guess at how many were Andean community members rather than mestizos. The teamsters carried items of great value and even large sums of cash across long distances, requiring a high level of trust and accountability. What we do know is that the teamsters the urban merchants worked with largely followed agrarian rhythms, disappearing at certain times of the year to engage in agricultural activities. In other words, the teamsters remained peasants at heart and made sure to keep up their agrarian base. Even those who came from areas so high up that there was little agriculture remained ensconced in the seasonal community migrations in which members herded their llamas loaded with salt and other altiplano products to the valleys to trade for food-stuffs such as potatoes, maize, and other like products (Platt 1995).

Similarly, miners extensively used the llama herds from the communities. Llamas tended to be less expensive than mules and much more available, even later in the century. From Colquechaca and Huanchaca, two of the most important mining centers in Bolivia, virtually all of the minerals were transported by llamas rather than other pack animals ("Cartas 1888–1889," Libro No. 1, Fondo Vacaflores, Archivo de La Sociedad Agrícola, Ganadera é Industrial de Cinti, La Paz, Bolivia).[12] Mines tended to be located in the middle of territories dominated by Indian communities, and it was logical that the miners would use local labor and resources for their enterprises.[13]

Much of the commerce and mining in the nineteenth century in the highland Andes was intimately linked to smuggling. This is an issue that has not been explored for Peru but does merit discussion for Bolivia. As I have shown based on merchant records, smuggling of silver and of imported goods was a major activity by import-export merchants who did not have to worry about a strong state with the ability to check their activities. Thus, Gregorio Pacheco, the most important merchant in Tupiza, Bolivia (close to the border with Argentina), singlehandedly smuggled out of the country perhaps a third of all of silver production of southern Potosí (Chichas and Lípez provinces) from the 1840s through the 1860s. He also frequently paid a 15 percent duty on imported goods rather than higher rates, as he claimed that his imports were destined for Argentina rather than for sale in the various mining centers of Potosí Department, where he actually sold them.[14] The border with Argentina remained extremely porous, as did the border with Peru; the weakness of the state was unable to prevent massive contraband. Smugglers engaged the help of the llama herders of the indigenous communities. At times, indigenous teamsters went to jail for silver smuggling, but this was rare.[15] Community members whose territories were along the border of the altiplano knew the border regions well and the poorly guarded mountain passes that went through their communities' territories. The close relationship between merchants and indigenous teamsters made the smuggling possible.

Indigenous men and women provided much of the foodstuffs to

the towns of the altiplano and to the mining centers. Since most of this commerce was not taxed, it is difficult to get a handle on its magnitude or the participation of indigenous community members. A fragment of a notebook that a commander of an army post kept in Paria province (Oruro) indicates the importance of indigenous participation in commerce of foodstuffs. From July 24 to July 31, 1837, of the 51 travelers who passed the outpost, 22 individuals were transporting such food as wheat flour, olives and spices, avocados, potatoes, and *chuño*; 19 were transporting coca leaf; and 3 were carrying wool.[16] Although ethnic origin was not given, the names and home towns of the travelers indicate that probably 36 of the 51 were indigenous community members.[17]

In Oruro, one of the major cities on the Bolivian altiplano and an important mining center, for example, the city police records for January 1838 list the taxes on the wheat flour imported into the city. All but one of the purveyors of the 402 *fanegas* of wheat flour were Andeans from indigenous communities.[18] The lone nonindigenous purveyor, Fernando Camacho from Tarata, Cochabamba, only brought two fanegas of flour, a mere 1/2 percent of the total for that month. (See table 2.) Since municipal authorities did not tax other foodstuffs, we do not have information on the total quantities of food brought into Oruro, but likely it was mostly community members who supplied the city as well.

Table 2. Origins of wheat flour for Oruro, 1838

| Location | Number of purveyors | Weight (in fanegas) |
| --- | --- | --- |
| Tangatanga | 10 | 91 |
| Quirquiavi, Cochabamba | 7 | 62 |
| Sacaca, Potosí | 7 | 55 |
| Sora Sora | 4 | 46 |
| Cala Cala | 5 | 42 |
| Various Communities | 12 | 104 |
| Tarata | 1 | 2 |

*Source:* "Planilla del numero de fanegas de arina de trigo qᵉ se han espendido para la rama de panaderías y del medio real qᵉ pagan los internantes de Canchajes qᵉ el Administrador de la Casa de Abasto ha cobrado en el mes dela fha," Año de 1838: Documentos originales de la Policía de Oruro, Tribunal Nacional de Cuentas 10408, Archivo y Biblioteca Nacionales de Bolivia, fs. 2–2v.

One of the most important products that indigenous community members controlled was the coca trade. Community Indians from the altiplano around Oruro, especially those who lived close to Challapata to the south, specialized in the transporting and selling these valuable leaves. They went to *tambos*, way stations where they could sleep and keep their llamas in corrals, in La Paz, where they would negotiate with the wholesalers who brought the coca leaf up from the Yungas valleys to the east of the city. From there, they transported the *cestos* of coca throughout the altiplano and then sold the leaf to the towns and mining centers in the highlands.[19] The coca trade enriched a number of community members, making it possible for some to accumulate haciendas outside of the communities, stores in various villages, and even money to lend to non-Indians in the cities (Langer 2002).

The earnings from these activities, however, in most cases did not go toward individual accumulation. Instead, most community members dispersed at least part of their resources to relatives within the community and others with whom they had social relationships. The probate records of the Indians who had sufficient wealth attest to this dispersal. I have discussed this for one coca trader, Antonia Lojo (Langer 2002). She was one among many such community members. Another coca trader was Roque Titu, who lived in Challapata and was a member of the Quillacas major ayllu. In 1852 he left a testament in which he claimed that nine people owed him 324 pesos, most for coca leaf that he had lent them (probably so that they might sell the coca for him). They appeared all to have been indigenous, as we can glean from their residences and last names; they were probably from the same ayllu. Significantly, his major debtor was his *comadre* from Salinas who owed him 89 pesos worth of coca. He also owed smaller amounts of money (109 pesos 4 reales), among which the largest amount was 50 pesos to a *compadre*.[20] He was relatively prosperous, owning 8 cestos of coca worth 272 pesos, 400 pesos in cash, and various houses and shops in Challapata "in the Quillacas part," as well as 200 sheep, 2 mules, 5 donkeys, a sheep pasture in Parupasto, and some other goods.[21] Testaments and probate records for other community members reveal similar arrangements. In other words, indigenous community members dispersed their wealth and provided others with whom they had close ties with the opportunity to gain through commercial activities.

The kinds of activities and their importance were largely invisible to those who ruled the country and who fancied themselves español americanos. The vast majority saw the community Indians as inefficient producers and as even worse consumers. This was especially the case for the main rubric of imports in the nineteenth century, textiles. The political elites did not see that indigenous community members were engaged in the trade, though they were. Community members were essential in bringing cotton up to coast from the valleys around Tacna, Peru, to sell the product to textile factory owners in the fairs of Paria in the 1830s. When that trade declined, other indigenous community members dedicated themselves to bring textiles from the *obrajes* (textile factories) in Peru. One such community member, Rafael Ignacio of Qullia ayllu, brought blankets and rough textiles from Puno, Peru, to sell in Potosí and Sucre with his peons, also community members, in 1850.[22] However, most indigenous community members manufactured their own clothing, making imported textiles marketable only in the urban centers, mines, or along the eastern frontiers in the jungled foothills of the Andes, traded for access to resources to indigenous groups independent of the national governments (Langer 1997).

Urban dwellers (most of whom did not define themselves as indigenous) tended to be the owners of the silver mines, the main export product of the Andes. Although there is some documentation that there were more indigenous mine owners than previously thought and that many community members engaged in small-scale mining to gain access to cash, the vast majority of mines were in the hands of español americanos and mestizos.[23]

In addition to mining, people outside of indigenous communities owned large swaths of territory, either as haciendas or as smallholdings. Haciendas tended to predominate in the intermontane valleys to the east, below the altiplano. Along the eastern foothills of the Andes, mestizo smallholders who did not have communal social structures or economies eked out a living on their holdings. This was most marked in northern Peru and in Bolivia in the valleys of Cochabamba, but all along the eastern escarpment of the Andes mestizo communities predominated in the area between the highland Andeans and the independent indigenous groups to the east, beyond state control. Other than in Cochabamba and in northern Peru, it is likely that the mestizo smallholders often engaged less in the market than did the Andeans in the indigenous communities because they were far from the mines and the cities and did not have to get cash to pay tribute; the Andean states charged the head tax exclusively of Andean community members and some hacienda peons in regions where indigenous communities existed.[24]

To summarize, political citizenship in the Andes was contested for people who lived in indigenous communities. Español americanos distinguished themselves from community members by appropriating for themselves the term *citizens*, whereas indigenous peoples remained *indígenas* and other permutations of the word. We have evidence that some Andean peoples contested this distinction and their second-class political status. However, the three-century colonial history of separate republics that began with the conquest made most indigenous peoples accept their status in the new republics. They literally knew nothing else; it is unclear whether during the independence wars Andeans imbibed liberal ideas as did the prominent leaders for independence such as Simón Bolívar or, most notably, Antonio José de Sucre.[25] Indigenous members made use of the concept of the república de indios to maintain state protection for communal lands.

Despite the legal inferiority in which the español americanos placed the indigenous peoples, the latter dominated the regional economy. Mining and textile imports were in the hands of the español americanos. The transport sector, the lucrative coca trade, and provisions of foodstuffs and other goods to highland cities, towns, and mining centers were largely in the hands of the indigenous majority. Only in Ecuador did this not matter much, as español americanos and haciendas were able to dominate the indigenous communities in the highlands through a state that became powerful in the countryside under the aegis of President Gabriel García Moreno (1860–65, 1869–75;Williams 2005). In Ecuador the "Indian problem," as it was known throughout the Andes, loomed much less since the indigenous population did not have the political and economic autonomy that Andean peoples had in Peru and Bolivia. The liberal elites from coastal Guayaquil, when they took over in the early twentieth century in Ecuador, began to deal with emancipating the indigenous majority of the highlands but mainly as a way to cut the support for the conservative highland elites.

## Making Indians Poor

During the second half of the nineteenth century, Andeans who had been relatively economically dynamic second-class citizens who utilized their legal separateness and the communal aspects of their communities to prosper became impoverished and economically subordinate Indians who had to be forced into modernity by the Andean state. The image of the Andean Indian as inherently poor thus originates in the late nineteenth and early twentieth centuries, in a double-edged economic and ideological process. The state run by the español americanos, responding to pressures generated by the north Atlantic economies, deliberately marginalized the indigenous peoples of the Andean highlands.

These pressures came from the expanding economies of the north Atlantic and their voracious appetites for Latin American commodities. The industrial revolution had progressed to the point that, to keep the industrial countries' economies expanding, it needed the commodities that such regions as Latin America could supply. These included new industrial minerals such as tin and copper but also foodstuffs that Europe could not produce or new goods that it was wealthy enough to acquire. Combined with the new demand for goods was a revolution in technology, railroads, the telegraph, and steamships that increased the speed of transportation and communication. Military technology improved mightily with the advent of the revolver, the rifle, and the machine gun. Suddenly a small group of men with technologically advanced weapons could dominate the large numbers of people who lacked these weapons. This led to a renewed European (and then U.S.) imperialism, providing access, by force if necessary, to the commodities that the north Atlantic countries wanted.

In Latin America and the Andes, the region was sucked into the vortex of north Atlantic economies, undergoing many of the same processes that had occurred earlier in the industrialized countries of Europe and North America. Latin American elites saw the advantages of the commodities boom and began to promote trade with the more industrialized countries. The new resources that they received as a result of this trade made it possible for Latin American states (including Ecuador, Peru, and Bolivia) to create state structures that permitted them to dominate their own spaces and populations. Bureaucracies expanded. The amount of paper generated by states, one indication of state hegemony, began to increase exponentially. Andean states invested in new machinery for mining but also in new weaponry, which made it possible to suppress peasant rebellions quickly.

In addition to the economic and technological facets, the ideology that justified rule over non-European populations deepened its racist cast. The rise of positivism, and with it social Darwinism, created a new way of looking at indigenous populations. During the colonial period, the Spanish state saw indios as vassals who had to be protected from rapacious Spaniards because they had child-like characteristics.[26] The Spaniards created a bifurcated colonial legal system in which the Indians utilized separate courts set up for them and had officials assigned to them to protect their legal rights. In contrast, the Argentine and the Colombian patriot leaders saw the Indians as potential equals, though the fiscal realities of the needs for tribute to finance the state, the centuries-long prejudices of those who considered themselves español americanos, and the advantages that the indigenous community members saw in maintaining a separate status meant that Andeans were not fully enfranchised. However, as the nineteenth century wore on, elite attitudes toward the communities worsened. Positivism, gleaned from Auguste Comte and other European sources, swept through the universities and elite *tertulias*—social and intellectual gatherings—in Latin America. Eager to distinguish themselves from the indigenous peoples whom the Europeans saw as inferior, the español americanos adopted the racialist views of Herbert Spencer and others. After all, the Latin American elites wanted to be part of the modern world, not a part of what the Europeans claimed were the inferior peoples outside of Europe. The first wave of this racialist thinking came to the Andes in the 1870s and was elaborated upon up to the 1920s.[27]

The permutations of liberal thinking also began to penetrate certain countries. This was most evident in Bolivia, where President Mariano Melgarejo decreed in 1864 and 1867 that all indigenous community land belonged to the state and that the Indians had to purchase their land or forfeit it to public auction. Although the motivation for the land sales was Melgarejo's inefficient administration and his constant need to pay the soldiers who helped him suppress revolts against his authoritarian and illegitimate rule, the intellectual authors of these decrees based themselves on modern liberal ideas.[28] The decrees were overturned in 1871 by a cowed constituent assembly after an Aymara revolt combined with opposition figures exiled the dictator Melgarejo from Bolivia. Despite the repudiation of the liberal land legislation under Melgarejo because of pressure from indigenous rebel allies, in 1874 the Bolivian congress passed another liberal land law that granted each Indian his or her own parcel, though the state did not have the power to implement the law.

Be that as it may, much damage had been done by the Melgarejo-era auctions. The Aymaras of the altiplano in La Paz largely recouped their lands by retaking their lands from the erstwhile hacienda owners, but farther south the prosperous communities around Lake Poopó, which specialized in hauling merchandise and trading coca with their llamas, had actually purchased their lands during the Melgarejo reforms. These communities did not get their money back when they overthrew the dictator. This meant that much of the mercantile capital that the Indians had used for their circuits had disappeared into the coffers of the Bolivian state, severely diminishing their capacity to purchase goods for their traditional mercantile activities. In the southern part of the country, the Indians did not rise up, and the well-connected purchasers of community lands simply kept them (Langer 1991; Langer 2009). This led to indigenous movements in the twentieth century, such as the ones that Waskar Ari-Chachaki discusses in chapter 8 of this volume.

In Bolivia and Peru the loss of the War of the Pacific (1879–84) to Chile brought about a rethinking of the role of the Indian in the respective countries. The defeat and the loss of territory were blamed on the poor integration of the Indian as useful citizens. In Peru Manuel González Prada vituperated against the elites but also ranted about the oppressed Indians, debased by the unholy trinity of the priest, the landlord, and the petty local official (Tauzin 2006; Kristal 1987). The process of hacienda expansion begun in the 1860s accelerated as the Peruvian elites felt that the Indians had to be "civilized" and torn from their communal structures. The Peruvian congress did not pass any specific legislation abolishing the communities but did not foster them either. As the wool export economy accelerated in the southern highlands in the aftermath of the War of the Pacific, community members lost their lands through debt and other means to *gamonales*, petty landlords and merchants who accumulated properties and forced community members to become hacienda peons. Since Indian tribute had been officially abolished in 1854 with income rolling in from the guano boom, the Peruvian national state cared little about the preservation of the communities. However, it did reestablish tribute in other ways, such as a "personal contribution" and a road labor corvée, but that included all Indians, regardless of their communal status.[29]

In Bolivia, which lost its coast to Chile during the war, there was less handwringing and more direct state action. The revulsion at the loss led to the installation of civilian-led governments of and by the silver oligarchs from the southwestern part of the country. Imbued by liberal ideas, they felt that land reform—the creation of a land market in which communal properties were to be eliminated—was essential to the country's development. Thus, even as Bolivia was still technically at war with Chile, in 1880 the new administration urged congress to pass laws that implemented the 1874 legislation abolishing indigenous communities after distributing the land to their members (Cabrera 1880). From 1880 onward, the Bolivian state sent commissions throughout the highlands, dividing community lands into individual holdings and attempting to destroy the communal system. In most areas, community members resisted; the government felt that this was mainly because the Indians did not want to pay the cost of the official stamps and the surveys. Indeed, in most areas, these surveys were never finished (Platt 1982). Nevertheless, in the southern parts of the highlands the slow process of land purchases severely weakened and even destroyed many communities and their communal social and economic structures (Langer 1989, 65–73).

A number of other economic forces weakened even the relatively strong communities in the northern part of the country and around the silver mining regions in the center of the highlands. First of all, in 1872 the Bolivian state decreed the free export of silver mineral, without the obligation of having it coined in the state mining banks. This meant that the most important smuggling, that of silver *pastas*, as it was called, became legal, and the premium that the merchant smugglers had paid to the mainly indigenous llama herders to take the silver across the border disappeared. In another blow to the indigenous communities, in the aftermath of the War of the Pacific, the Chileans built a railroad from the coast into the Bolivian altiplano. Not only did the business of taking goods up and down the mountains disappear for the llama herding communities of the highlands south of Oruro, but the Chileans imported wheat flour into the heartland of Bolivia, displacing demand for the wheat grown mainly by community members in northern Potosí.[30]

Likewise, the advent of the railroad elsewhere in the Andes displaced the indigenous llama teamster from long-distance hauling. This was the case in southern and central Peru as well, as José Deustua has documented, though he asserts correctly that at least initially muleteers and llama herders had more business, since the railroads could handle much more cargo, and transport to and from the railheads by animal increased substantially. However, this involved shorter distances, and eventually the railroads and their side tracks reached the mines in central Peru (as they did the mines on the Bolivian altiplano), taking away the most lucrative business from the Indians and other muleteers (Deustua 2000, 104–73). Indigenous community members slowly but surely lost their predominant position in the commercial transport sector. Instead, as community members became hacienda peons, they took their owners' (and perhaps some of their own) produce to town. This was nothing compared to previous generations, when community members had forged alliances with mine owners to take their minerals to the Pacific coast or worked with import-export merchants to transport (and also smuggle) goods up and down the mountains from the coast. Thus, the merchants and miners, who had liberal tendencies but had held the line on the usurpation of indigenous lands since they had needed the indigenous teamsters, now had no economic incentive to back the communities.

The miners had other reasons not to fear the Indians as much. Most of the mines in nineteenth-century Bolivia were located deep in the Andes in tiny mining towns, surrounded by Indian communities. This was unlike the colonial period, when the major mines turned into the large urban centers of Potosí and Oruro—indeed, Potosí formed the largest city in the Americas in the sixteenth and seventeenth centuries. In contrast, during the nineteenth century, towns that grew up around most of the mines remained relatively small. The most important mines in the nineteenth century, such as Pulacayo, Colquechaca, Portugalete, and San Cristóbal, were small mining settlements surrounded by indigenous communities. Because of the rural nature of most nineteenth-century mines, in the debates up until 1880 mine owners had invariably cautioned against the wholesale usurpation of Indian lands, since revolts could easily destroy their mining concerns. However, after the military modernized its weaponry in the aftermath of the War of the Pacific, the mine owners' fear about the inability to defend against the communities diminished considerably. Also, the peasant population attracted to the mines by the late nineteenth century had slowly turned into a proletariat. As a result, the mine owners were less dependent upon the surrounding peasants to supplement their mine workers. Indeed, in the late nineteenth century, in part because of the expansion of the haciendas onto communal lands, the phenomenon of the mine-hacienda complex emerged in the southern highlands, where the mine owners obligated the community members turned to peons as seasonal mine laborers and transporters of the minerals to the local refinery.[31] The mine owners were thus able to capture the value of the peasant transport sector in ways not possible earlier in the nineteenth century. Similar processes occurred in central Peru, though slightly later. As various scholars have documented for the beginning of the twentieth century, the Cerro de Pasco Mining Company in 1902 combined mines with haciendas to supply rural workers to the mines. In addition to the pull of the mining company, the pollution generated by the smelters in La Oroya poisoned the surrounding countryside, making the rural inhabitants even more dependent on the mines (DeWind 1987; Mallon 1983; Dore 1978).

In Peru the late nineteenth century was just a prelude to the insults and injuries of the early twentieth century. As the wool boom continued in southern Peru, hacienda expansion strengthened, with the occasional peasant rebellions brutally suppressed. The government in Lima refused to take the side of the indigenous peasants; on the contrary, the electoral system favored the gamonales, local landlords who made pacts with the national parties to provide them with voters and so remain in power. Wool profits thus increasingly reverted to those who took over indigenous lands rather than those who worked the land (Burga and Reátegui 1981; Jacobsen 1993).

In Ecuador the Liberal Revolution of 1895, in which the Liberal commercial elites from coastal Guayaquil defeated the conservative forces of highland Quito and Cuenca, aided the indigenous population to a large degree. The Liberals wanted to decouple indigenous labor from the highland haciendas under Conservative landowners so that they might migrate to the labor-hungry coast. The new Liberal administration under Eloy Alfaro decreed the end of concertaje, a system of debt peonage that had tied the Indians to the highland haciendas. In addition, Alfaro promoted the building of a railroad from the coast to Quito as a way to link the country but also to enable the migration of highland Indians to the lowlands. In the end, this program was only partially successful. Nevertheless, the members of indigenous communities received a respite, at least in labor prestations, from the hacienda owners (Baud 2007; Clark 2001).

The process of impoverishment and marginalization of Andean peoples in Peru, Bolivia, and Ecuador began in the late nineteenth century but did not end there. In Ecuador the accession of the Liberals in the late nineteenth century temporarily halted the worsening of the indigenous communities' positions. However, the liberal impulse also included indigenismo, which posited that the Indian was inherently inferior and needed to be lifted up, even through coercive policies, from their abject status. In the end, the Liberals were unable to break the pattern of peonage, called *huasipungo* in Ecuador, keeping the haciendas in charge of the highlands. What the coastal elites, the main supporters of the Liberal Party, wanted was to shake loose the Indians from their highland homes and have them serve as cheap labor in the plantations along the Pacific. This did not imply much help in preserving economic autonomy—just the opposite. Even the Liberals' paternalism toward Indians did not help the indigenous peoples; when the railroad between the port of Guayaquil and Quito reached the village of Alausí, for example, the presence of bubonic plague in 1913–14 (probably brought by railway workers from the coast) resulted in the government burning down the peasants' houses to contain the outbreak (Clark 2001, 147–54).

Indigenismo became important in Peru as well; however, the results of concerns for the highland indigenous peoples were mixed at best. On the one hand, as mentioned above, under the Leguía administration (1911–30) indigenous communities received legal status again. On the other hand, conditions worsened on the economic front. At the same time that Augusto Leguía recognized the communities in the highlands, he also required the members of these communities to serve as laborers for the road-building projects. Thus, the state continued to take away resources from the communities, further impoverishing them (Davies 1974).

In the case of Bolivia, the new liberal elites who took power after the 1898–99 civil war, despite their rhetoric to the contrary, further enserfed the indigenous peoples in the highlands. Hacienda expansion accelerated in the early twentieth century, bringing about a huge transfer of resources from indigenous communities to the español americanos. Though following superficially legal norms, non-Indians usurped community land through fraudulent means. As many scholars have documented, Indians lost their lands through debt, outright fraud, or even force of arms. On the Aymara highlands to the north, curacas were often forced to sign away community lands under duress. In 1907 on the peninsula of Taraco by Lake Titicaca, for example, the Bolivian president Ismael Montes sent in troops to take over lands he wanted from the Indians (Mamani Condori 1991, 60–61).[32]

Perhaps more important to the economic fate of the Andean indigenous peoples was their conceptual marginalization . Brooke Larson, in her *Trials of Nation Making* (2004), is most eloquent and expansive on this point. The pervasive influence of social Darwinism among the español americanos, especially in Peru and Bolivia, made the elites rethink the issue of the "Indian problem." Indians were seen as racially inferior, as conquered peoples who had lost whatever greatness they might have had when they had been the protagonists and subjects of the Inca empire. Instead, the unholy highlands trinity of the priest, the gamonal (in Peru), and the local authority, the corregidor, was seen not only as the oppressors but also as the debasers of all Indians. The solution was not the redemption of the Indian as a human being who had been successful during the postindependence period but his disappearance culturally and biologically through race mixture with "superior" races from Europe (Larson 2004). The frustration of the elites was that the European migrants they had hoped for never materialized, instead going to the River Plate region in Argentina or Uruguay or to the United States. Some elites, such as those in Cuzco, tried to resuscitate the Indian under their paternal guidance, without much success (de la Cadena 2000).

Andeans tried through various means to mitigate and fight back against the prejudices of the governing elites and against the systematic usurpation of their resources. The late nineteenth and early twentieth centuries, when the process of economic, political, and social marginalization was at its greatest, was also the period of indigenous uprisings in Peru and Bolivia, as might be expected. Although one cannot create a direct relationship between diminishing opportunities for Indians and rebellions—each revolt had its unique causes—overall, the increase in the extraction of surplus and the continual usurpation of land brought about resistance from the indigenous population. Although he did not capture all of the revolts, John Coatsworth showed in an important essay that the number of what he termed "village riots and uprisings" jumped significantly in Peru and Bolivia from 1880 onward (1988, see especially the chart on 34). Some were relatively effective in stopping the immediate abuses but did not reverse the general trend. Thus, for example, the Atusparia rebellion of 1885 in Huaylas, Peru, brought about the abolition of the double poll tax, the immediate cause of the rebellion, through a strategy of revolt and, in the aftermath of the rebellion, a long-term petition campaign by local indigenous authorities challenging the state about its discriminatory policies. The Chayanta rebellion of 1927 pressured the Bolivian government to effect measures that diminished the taking of community land through fraud. In addition to rebellions, community members also sought redress for their issues through legal means and petitioning government officials.[33]

## Conclusion

The period after independence was a period of relative prosperity for indigenous peoples of the Andean heartland of Ecuador, Peru, and Bolivia. Although this prosperity varied—in Ecuador the hacienda system siphoned off much greater surplus of the peasants than in the countries farther south—generally speaking the Andean communities were able to forge an existence that included more than peasant subsistence. Indeed, the communities were the active protagonists in the economies of the region and were some of the greatest beneficiaries of the early republican economy.

Economic historians have characterized this period as one of economic stagnation, an assessment that is incorrect. This is because economists have largely measured nineteenth-century economic growth in Latin America by measuring export and import statistics, a measure that captures only a tiny fraction of economic activity during this period. The activities in which Andeans were engaged have not been measured by economists because the data is not easy to come by. Seen on another level, this period was one in which the vast majority of inhabitants of the Andes—indigenous peasants—controlled some of the most important sectors of the economy and were relatively well off. They dominated the transport sector, participated in mining and in smuggling, and provided the raw materials for the textile industry. Andeans were full partners with import-export merchants in their endeavors to provide foreign goods to the cities. They provided most foodstuffs to the cities and mining centers. Indigenous peoples also controlled most of the coca trade, perhaps the most lucrative activity in this period, both in Peru and Bolivia. The wealth that these activities generated was mostly dispersed among the villagers as a whole through networks of kinship and village and ayllu reciprocity.

The prosperity that many indigenous communities enjoyed in the early to mid-nineteenth century disappeared by the end of the century. There were many reasons for this. One was structural. The transportation system, dominated by the indigenous muleteer or *llamero*, changed to one in which the railroad forged along principal routes and, in particular in the Andes, connected the coast with the mining centers in the highlands. The most lucrative llama trips, those of taking minerals down to the coast or imports up to the populations centers in the Andes, disappeared to a large degree. But political reasons predominated. The move toward free trade by the end of the century led to the end of large-scale smuggling and obviated the need for trusted Indian *llameros* to take the contraband to the waiting ships on the coast or to urban centers in Argentina. The change in laws that resulted in the taking of indigenous community lands and the expansion of the haciendas, common throughout Latin America by the second half of the nineteenth century, took away the land base for further commercial activity. Hacienda expansion also siphoned the value of indigenous labor in favor of the hacienda owners when community members became hacienda peons.

The worsening of prejudices against Indians during the late nineteenth century also harmed the communities' economies. First of all, policy makers saw the Indians as a problem rather than as a solution. They failed to recognize the vital role that the communities had played in the economy and instead tried to reform the economic system in such a fashion that eliminated the indigenous contribution completely by eliminating the communities and the Indians as a group. Only in Peru did the government resuscitate the community, though only to utilize free indigenous labor. Even Peruvian president Leguía, as did other heads of government in the Andes, actively fostered foreign immigration and policies that were detrimental to cultural, social, and economic systems that had provided indigenous groups with the ability to prosper in a difficult environment.

To return to the ideas evoked in the introduction to this chapter, most development specialists are heirs to this legacy. Projects are created to reduce poverty rather than to provide the opportunity to thrive again. Andean economic and social systems are seen as archaic and the province of anthropologists and ethnohistorians. In many areas, such as in Ecuador and Peru, indigenous communities are shoved aside—sometimes literally by displacing whole villages—for "real" development such as massive mining projects. In most places, individuality is pushed over communal values as the only means to create higher income. All such pushes forget that indigenous communities once prospered in the nineteenth century, during a time when the state was weak and indigenous peoples of the Andean highlands were central to the economic development of the region.

### Notes

1. The literature is copious. Some of the best is Stern 1987 and 1988, Spalding 1984, Bakewell 1984, and Tandeter 1993.

2. For Cuzco see Peralta Ruiz 1991, 97–104; for Azángaro see Jacobsen 1993, 130–34; and Sánchez Albornoz 1978, 198. Also see Grieshaber 1980.

3. These were different names for Indian tribute-payers that the Andean states used.

4. Literally "Spanish Americans." In other words, the people using this terminology were emphasizing the "superior" ethnic heritage over their nationality.

5. Concertaje was a system by which large landlords obligated villagers to work for them on their estates.

6. Indigenistas were people who tried to "improve" the Indians by supporting their causes but also "lifting them up" from their indigenous condition through education and assimilation.

7. Literally "economic man." In other words, those who base their actions completely on economically rational ideas, which of course is rarely the case.

8. According to Dalence, Potosí contained 384,861 llamas, La Paz 236,137, and Oruro 173,684. The number of llamas in the country totaled 836,845 ([1851] 1975, 244).

9. See Grieshaber 1990. Also see Dalence (1851) 1975:241–42. Even after the period of hacienda expansion at the end of the nineteenth century, llamas remained in the hands of the hacienda peons rather than being owned by the *hacendados*.

10. Nils Jacobsen shows that in the early nineteenth century, llamas outnumbered all other livestock other than sheep in Azángaro province, next to Lake Titicaca. Unfortunately, the next data point is 1920, when sheep and cattle outnumber llamas and alpacas, which together share third place. See Jacobsen 1993, 118, 127.

11. Also see Assadourian 1982, 222–76. For a description of the Vilque fair, see Markham 1862, 284–85.

12. See continuous references to *tropas*, which referred to llamas, rather than *rec-*

*uas*, reserved for mules or donkeys. Only certain goods, such as wines and other more fragile and heavy goods were transported by mule.

13. By the late nineteenth century Chilean and Argentine muleteers began to compete with the community members' llama herds. The Argentines and Chileans had been pushed out by the railroad in their respective countries, though llamas generally remained less expensive even than railroads for a while.

14. See Langer n.d. Smuggling was endemic earlier too. See Lofstrom 1982.

15. January 5, 1843, Notary Angel Mno Delgado, Fondo Notarial, Corte Superior de Oruro. For a more elaborate discussion of silver smuggling by community members, see Langer 2009.

16. *Chuño*: freeze-dried potatoes. Coca is part of the *Erythroxylaceae* family that is sold as a dried leaf. It has cocaine alkaloids that make it possible for individuals who "chew" it (actually, the leaf is placed in the cheek and an alkaline component is added, such as quinoa ash or bicarbonate of soda) to feel more energetic, less hungry, or less thirsty. It is an important cash crop that agricultural laborers and miners used since pre-Columbian times.

17. "Parte qe da el Comandte del Destacamnto de Sebada rio el Sor Givr dela Prova de Paria y es como sigue (1837)," 1834–39 Civiles, Archivo Judicial de Poopó.

18. A fanega was approximately 55.5 liters or twelve imperial bushels.

19. Each *cesto* contains about twelve pounds of coca leaf.

20. *Comadre* and *compadre* literally mean "co-mother" and "co-father." This refers to the relationship that godparents have to the parents of their godchildren, a culturally important role in Andean society.

21. "Challapata: Causa civil de Miguel Antonio Mamani apoderado de Ana Manami sobre rendición de cuentas contra Maria Yucra viuda de Juan Zaabedra. Año 1856," 1850–56 Civiles, Archivo Judicial de Poopó.

22. "Causa cibil seguido por Petrona Ancalli contra Mariano Ignacio sobre cantidad de pesos" 1850, 1850–56 Civiles, Archivo Judicial de Poopó. She also noted that "in my *rancho* there are various persons who have this trade circuit [*giro*]" (f. 2).

23. For the classic study of silver mine owners in the nineteenth century, see Mitre 1981 and Deustua 2000. For a suggestive understanding of small-scale mining by indigenous community members in the late twentieth century, see Godoy 1990. For large-scale mining in nineteenth-century Peru, see Contreras 1987.

24. For Cochabamba, see Larson 1998 and Jackson 1994. For the northern Peruvian highlands, see Nugent 1997, Christiansen 2004, Mallon 1995, 220–44.

25. Sucre, as president of Bolivia, imposed a strictly liberal reform agenda on the country (Lofstrom 1987). For Peru, see Gootenberg 1989 and 1993. Ecuador remained much more conservative. See Sattar 2007 and Williams 2007.

26. There is an ever-growing literature on the attitudes toward indigenous peoples in the Spanish empire. See, for example, Pagden 1982. For an overview of attitudes during this period in a larger context, see Schwartz 1994.

27. There are many works on this topic. A summary of the Andes is Larson 2004, especially 59–70.

28. This is a topic that merits more discussion. See Langer 1988; Ovando Sanz 1985, 120–67; Lofstrom 2013.

29. A good summary is Larson 2004, 153–77. The most detailed analysis of this process is Jacobsen 1993, 107–258. Also see Burga and Reátegui 1981.

30. For the effects of the 1872 law, see Langer n.d. The railroad is treated in O'Brien 1980. For the effect of Chilean flour on the northern Potosí wheat trade, see Platt 1986.

31. For an overview of the transformation of mine labor in Bolivia see Rodríguez Ostria 1991. The process of proletarianization is ably covered in Smale 2010. For the appearance of mine-hacienda complexes, see Langer 1997.

32. For an analysis of hacienda expansion in the Aymara highlands, see Grieshaber 1990 and Rivera Cusicanqui 1978. For an overview farther south, see Langer 1989.

33. The literature on indigenous revolts in the republican-era Andes is too large to cite here. For overviews, see Stern 1987. For Peru, see Kapsoli 1987. For Bolivia, see Gotkowitz 2007. On the Atusparia revolt, see Stein 1982 and Thurner 1997. For the Chayanta uprising, see Hylton 2011 and Langer 1990. Also see the chapter by Waskar Ari-Chachaki in this volume.

## Bibliography

Assadourian, Carlos Sempat. 1982. "El sector exportador de una economía regional del interior argentino: Córdoba, 1800–1860." In *El sistema de la economía colonial: Mercado interno, regiones y espacio económico*. Lima: IEP. 222–76.

Bakewell, P. J. 1984. *Miners of the Red Mountain: Indian Labor in Potosí, 1545–1650*. Albuquerque: University of New Mexico Press.

Barragán, Rossana. 1999. *Indios, mujeres y ciudadanos: Legislación y ejercicio de la ciudadanía en Bolivia (siglo XIX)*. La Paz: Diálogo.

Baud, Michel. 2007. "Liberalism, *Indigenismo*, and Social Mobilization in Late Nineteenth-Century Ecuador." In *Highland Indians and the State in Modern Ecuador*, edited by Kim Clark and Marc Becker, 72–88. Pittsburgh: University of Pittsburgh Press.

Burga, Manuel, and Wilson Reátegui. 1981. *Lanas y capital mercantil en el Sur: La Casa Ricketts, 1895–1935*. Lima: Instituto de Estudios Peruanos.

Cabrera, Ladislao. 1880. *Memoria presentada a la Convención Nacional de 1880*. La Paz: Imprenta de la Unión Americana.

Christiansen, Tanja. 2004. *Disobedience, Slander, Seduction, and Assault: Women and Men in Cajamarca, Peru, 1862–1900*. Austin: University of Texas Press.

Clark, Kim A. 2001. *The Redemptive Work: Railway and Nation in Ecuador, 1895–1930*. Wilmington: Scholarly Resources.

Coatsworth, John H. 1988. "Patterns of Rural Rebellion in Latin America: Mexico in Comparative Perspective." In *Riot, Rebellion and Revolution: Rural Social Conflict in Mexico*, edited by Friedrich Katz, 21–64. Princeton: Princeton University Press.

Conti, Viviana, and Gabriela Sica. 2011. "Arrieros andinos de la colonia a la independencia: El negocio de la arriería en Jujuy." In *Participación de indígenas y campesinos en mercados coloniales iberoamericanos, siglos XVII–XIX: Nuevos Mundos/ Mundo Nuevo*. Available at www.nuevomundo.revues.org/60560/.

Contreras, Carlos. 1987. *Mineros y campesinos en los Andes: Mercado laboral y economía campesina en la Sierra Central siglo XIX*. Lima: Instituto de Estudios Peruanos.

Dalence, José María. (1851) 1975. *Bosquejo estadístico de Bolivia*. La Paz: Editorial Universitaria.

Davies, Thomas M. 1974. *Indian Integration in Peru: A Half Century of Experience, 1900–1948*. Lincoln: University of Nebraska Press.

de la Cadena, Marisol. 2000. *Indigenous Mestizos: The Politics of Race and Culture in Cuzco, Peru, 1919–1991*. Durham: Duke University Press.

Deustua, José. 2000. *The Bewitchment of Silver: The Social Economy of Mining in Nineteenth-Century Peru*. Athens: Ohio University Press.

DeWind, Josh. 1987. *Peasants Become Miners: The Evolution of Industrial Mining Systems in Peru, 1902–1974*. New York: Garland.

Dore, Elizabeth. 1978. "Social Relation and the Barriers to Economic Growth: The Case of the Peruvian Mining Industry." *Nova Americana* 1: 245–68.

Godoy, Ricardo A. 1990. *Mining and Agriculture in Highland Bolivia: Ecology, History, and Commerce Among the Jukumanis*. Tucson: University of Arizona Press.

Gootenberg, Paul. 1989. *Between Silver and Guano: Commercial Policy and the State in Postindependence Peru*. Princeton: Princeton University Press.

———. 1993. *Imagining Development: Economic Ideas in Peru's "Fictitious Prosperity" of Guano, 1840–1880*. Berkeley: University of California Press.

Gotkowitz, Laura. 2007. *A Revolution for Our Rights: Indigenous Struggles for Land and Justice in Bolivia, 1880–1952*. Durham: Duke University Press.

Grieshaber, Erwin P. 1980. "Survival of Indian Communities in Nineteenth-Century Bolivia: a Regional Comparison." *Journal of Latin American Studies* 12, no. 2: 223–69.

———. 1990. "La expansión de la hacienda en el departamento de La Paz, Bolivia, 1850–1920: Una versión cuantitativa." *Andes: Antropología e Historia* 2–3: 33–84.

Guerrero, Andrés. 1991. *La semántica de la dominación: El concertaje de indios*. Quito: Ediciones Libri Mundi.

Hall, Gillette, and Harry A. Patrinos. 2006. *Indigenous Peoples, Poverty, and Human Development in Latin America*. New York: Palgrave Macmillan.

Hylton, Forrest. 2011. "'Now is Not Your Time; It's Ours': Insurgent Confederation, 'Race War,' and Liberal State Formation in the Bolivian Federal War of 1899." *South Atlantic Quarterly* 110, no. 2: 487–503.

Jackson, Robert H. 1994. *Regional Markets and Agrarian Transformation in Bolivia: Cochabamba, 1539–1960*. Albuquerque: University of New Mexico Press.

Jacobsen, Nils. 1993. *Mirages of Transition: The Peruvian Altiplano, 1780–1930*. Berkeley: University of California Press.

Kapsoli, E. Wilfredo. 1987. *Los movimientos campesinos en el Perú*. Lima: Ediciones Atusparia.

Kristal, Efraín. 1987. *The Andes Viewed from the City: Literary and Political Discourse on the Indian in Peru, 1848–1930*. New York: P. Lang.

Langer, Erick D. 1988. "El liberalismo y la abolición de la comunidad indígena en Bolivia en el siglo XIX." *Historia y Cultura* 14: 59–95.

———. 1989. *Economic Change and Rural Resistance in Southern Bolivia, 1880–1930*. Stanford: Stanford University Press.

———. 1990. "Rituals of Rebellion: The Chayanta Revolt of 1927." *Ethnohistory* 37, no. 3: 227–53.

———. 1991. "Persistencia y cambio en las comunidades indígenas surbolivianas (siglo XIX)." In *Los Andes en la encrucijada: Indios, comunidades y estado en el siglo XIX*, edited by Heraclio Bonilla, 133–67. Quito: Ediciones Libri Mundi.

———. 1997a. "The Barriers to Proletarianization: Bolivian Mine Labour, 1826–1918." *International Review of Social History Supplement* 4: 25–49.

———. 1997b. "Foreign Cloth in the Lowland Frontier: Commerce and Consumption of Textiles in Bolivia, 1830–1930." In *The Allure of the Foreign: The Role of Imports in Post-Colonial Latin America*, edited by Benjamin S. Orlove, 93–112. Ann Arbor: University of Michigan Press.

———. 2002. "Género y comercio a mediados del siglo XIX en Bolivia: El caso de Antonia Lojo, una acaudalada mujer indígena en Challapata." In *Archivo y Biblioteca Nacionales de Bolivia Anuario 2002*, 107–27. Sucre: Talleres Gráficos "La Gaviota."

———. 2009. "Bringing the Economic Back In: Andean Indians and the Construction of the Nation-State in Nineteenth-Century Bolivia." *Journal of Latin American Studies* 41, no. 3: 527–51.

———. 2016. "Indigenous Independence in the Heartland of South America, 1800–1870." In *New Countries in a Changing World: The Americas, 1750–1870*, edited by John Tutino, 350–75. Durham: Duke University Press.

———. n.d. "Contraband and Credit: Bolivian and Argentine Merchants and Miners in the Silver and Import Trade." Unpublished manuscript.

Larson, Brooke. 1998. *Cochabamba, 1550–1900: Colonialism and Agrarian Transformation in Bolivia*. Durham: Duke University Press.

———. 2004. *Trials of Nation Making: Liberalism, Race, and Ethnicity in the Andes, 1810–1910*. Cambridge: Cambridge University Press.

Lofstrom William H. 1982. *Dámaso de Uriburu un empresario minero de principios del siglo XIX en Bolivia*. Translated by Marta Urioste de Aguirre. La Paz: Biblioteca Minera Boliviana.

———. 1987. *La presidencia de Sucre en Bolivia*. Caracas: Academia Nacional de la Historia.

———. 2013. *Radiografía de una provincia paceña Omasuyos en 1869*. Sucre: Archivo y Biblioteca Nacionales de Bolivia.

Mallon, Florencia. 1983. *The Defense of Community in Peru's Central Highlands: Peasant Struggle and Capitalist Transition, 1860–1940*. Princeton: Princeton University Press.

———. 1995. *Peasant and Nation: The Making of Postcolonial Mexico and Peru*. Berkeley: University of California Press.

Mamani Condori, Carlos B. 1991. *Taraqu, 1866–1935: Masacre, guerra y "Renovación" en la biografía de Eduardo L. Nina Qhispi*. La Paz: Ediciones Aruwiyiri.

Markham, Clements Robert. 1862. *Travels in Peru and India: While Superintending the Collection of Chinchona Plants and Seeds in South America, and their Introduction Into India*. London: John Murray.

Mitre, Antonio. 1981. *Los patriarcas de la plata: Estructura socioeconómica de la minería boliviana en el siglo XIX*. Lima: Instituto de Estudios Peruanos.

Nugent, David. 1997. *Modernity at the Edge of Empire: State, Individual, and Nation in the Northern Peruvian Andes, 1885–1935*. Stanford: Stanford University Press.

O'Brien, Thomas F. 1980. "The Antofagasta Company: A Case Study of Peripheral Capitalism." *The Hispanic American Historical Review* 60, no. 1: 1–31.

Ovando Sanz, Jorge Alejandro. 1985. *El tributo indígena en las finanzas bolivianas del siglo XIX*. La Paz: CEUB.

Pagden, Anthony. 1982. *The Fall of Natural Man: The American Indian and the Origins of Comparative Ethnology*. Cambridge: Cambridge University Press.

Peralta Ruiz, Víctor. 1991. *En pos del tributo: Burocracia estatal, elite regional y comunidades indígenas en el Cusco rural (1826–1854)*. Cuzco: Centro de Estudios Regionales Andinos "Bartolomé de las Casa."

Piel, Jean. 1975. *Capitalisme agraire au Pérou*. Paris: Editions Anthropos.

Platt, Tristan. 1982. *Estado boliviano y ayllu andino: Tierra y tribute en el Norte de Potosí*. Lima: Instituto de Estudios Peruanos.

———. 1986. *Estado tributario y librecambio en Potosí (siglo XIX): Mercado indígena, proyecto proteccionista y lucha de ideologías monetarias*. La Paz: Instituto de Historia Social Boliviana.

———. 1995. "Ethnic Calendars and Market Interventions among the *Ayllus* of Lípez during the Nineteenth Century." In *Ethnicity, Markets, and Migration in the Andes: At the Crossroads of History and Anthropology*, edited by Brooke Larson and Olivia Harris, 259–96. Durham: Duke University Press.

Rivera Cusicanqui, Silvia. 1978. "La expansión del latifundio en el altiplano boliviano: Elementos para la caracterización de una oligarquía regional." *Avances* 2: 95–118.

Rodríguez Ostria, Gustavo. 1991. *El socavón y el sindicato: Ensayos históricos sobre los trabajadores mineros, siglos XIX–XX*. La Paz: Instituto Latinoamericano de Investigaciones Sociales.

Sánchez Albornoz, Nicolás. 1978. *Indios y tributos en el Alto Perú*. Lima: Instituto de Estudios Peruanos.

Sattar, Aleezé. 2007. "¿Indígena o Ciudadano? Republican Laws and Highland Indian Communities in Ecuador, 1820–1857." In *Highland Indians and the State in Modern Ecuador*, edited by Kim Clark and Marc Becker. Pittsburgh: University of Pittsburgh Press.

Schwartz, Stuart B., ed. 1994. *Implicit Understandings: Observing, Reporting, and Reflecting on the Encounters between Europeans and Other Peoples in the Early Modern Era*. Cambridge: Cambridge University Press.

Smale, Robert. 2010. *"I Sweat the Flavor of Tin": Labor Activism in Early Twentieth-Century Bolivia*. Pittsburgh: University of Pittsburgh Press.

Spalding, Karen. 1984. *Huarochirí: An Andean Society under Inca and Spanish Rule*. Stanford: Stanford University Press.

Stein, William W. 1982. *The Limits of Peasant Movements: Leaders, Followers, and Allies in the Atusparia Uprising of 1885, Peru*. Amherst: State University of New York Press.

Stern, Steve J. 1982. *Peru's Indian Peoples and the Challenge of Spanish Conquest: Huamanga to 1640*. Madison: University of Wisconsin Press.

———, ed. 1987. *Resistance, Rebellion, and Consciousness in the Andean Peasant World, 18th to 20th Centuries*. Madison: University of Wisconsin Press.

————. 1988. "Feudalism, Capitalism, and the World-System in the Perspective of Latin America and the Caribbean." *American Historical Review* 93, no. 4: 829–72.

Tandeter, Enrique. 1993. *Coercion and Market: Silver Mining in Colonial Potosí, 1692–1826*. Albuquerque: University of New Mexico Press.

Tauzin, Isabelle, ed. 2006. *Manuel González Prada: Escritor de dos mundos*. Lima: Instituto Frances de Estudios Andinos.

Thurner, Mark. 1997. *From Two Republics to One Divided: Contradictions of Postcolonial Nationmaking in Andean Peru*. Durham: Duke University Press.

Williams, Derek. 2005. "The Making of Ecuador's *Pueblo Católico*, 1861–1875." In *Political Cultures in the Andes, 1750–1950*, edited by Nils Jacobsen and Cristóbal Aljovín de Losada, 207–29. Durham: Duke University Press.

————. 2007. "Administering the Otavalan Indian and Centralizing Governance in Ecuador, 1851–1875." In *Highland Indians and the State in Modern Ecuador*, edited by Kim Clark and Marc Becker, 37–55. Pittsburgh: University of Pittsburgh Press.

# 6

# Nation Making / Nation Breaking

## *"Effective Control" of Aboriginal Lands and Peoples by Settlers in Transition*

KARL S. HELE

As Canada began transitioning from colonial to nation status in the nineteenth century, its relationship with Aboriginal peoples underwent a fundamental shift. In the settlers' minds, Aboriginal peoples transitioned from vaunted allies to burdens and wards of the state in need of civilizing. The conclusion of the War of 1812 marked the beginning of the dual transitioning of Aboriginal-settler relations and of settler-colony to settler-nation. Aboriginal peoples, the original sovereign occupants of the land, became a central, albeit now forgotten, focus of settler policy as these transitions occurred in the post–War of 1812 era. Indigenous peoples facing transition from colonial to national rule were confronted by settlers intent on imposing their Europeanized versions of the state upon the landscape. Throughout the nineteenth century the settlers sought to establish their "effective control" of the Sault region and its peoples as the shift from colony to nation took place through a series of enactments and treaties aimed at Aboriginal peoples.

With the division of their homeland between two colonial states, British North America (BNA) and the United States, the Anishinaabe became a people betwixt and between. As the two colonial states attempted to establish their respective spheres of power upon the peoples and the landscape of the Sault region (see map 3), the Anishinaabe and Métis sought to carve out their own niche in the emergent new world order. As the settler states sought to "become" nations, the Anishinaabe and Métis "became" indigenous while becoming owned or subjects or citizens of the state. The process of becoming indigenous was not straightforward. Instead, the peoples at Sault quickly discovered that the colonial state created and then attempted to enforce arbitrary definitions of identity, which meant that one could "un-become" as quickly as one became indigenous. Moreover, BNA and the United States sought to control and thereby manipulate identity in subtly different ways that allowed someone in BNA to "become" while in the United States that same individual "un-became." All of this is to say that the process of becoming and its corollary un-becoming was a multifaceted process within the Sault borderlands. As such the Sault borderlands provide an excellent example of the abuses and manipulations that informed how indigenous peoples were defined, displaced, and demoralized as the colonial settler state sought effective control.

As part of the state movement toward control, lines were drawn between Indians seen as residents of either state. The idea of residence in a particular state, either BNA or the United States, remained a complicated notion in the Sault borderlands. State actors generally viewed Indians as residents if they spent the majority of their time inhabiting and hunting with colonial state–claimed borders, thereby becoming American or British Indians. As such any Indians residing permanently in BNA were viewed by the settlers and colonial authorities as British Indians. Similarly, U.S. authorities and settlers viewed Indians resident in the United States as American Indians. Such designations of American or British Indians implied ownership and control by, not citizenship in, the colonial state. For the Indians a declaration of or claim to be a British or American Indian was an expression of alliance and support or a method to claim assistance, not a claim of citizenship or recognition of being state subjects. Likewise, the use of *American* and *British Indian* represents state claims of ownership and control over Indians resident within claimed borders when used by or in reference to the colonial states and their subjects and as a form of alliance or claim on the state when used by Indians. Yet, individual Anishinaabe and Métis, by crossing the border for any length of time, could un-become an American or British Indian while becoming an American or British Indian. These designations of American and British Indian were modified toward the end of the nineteenth century as the colonial

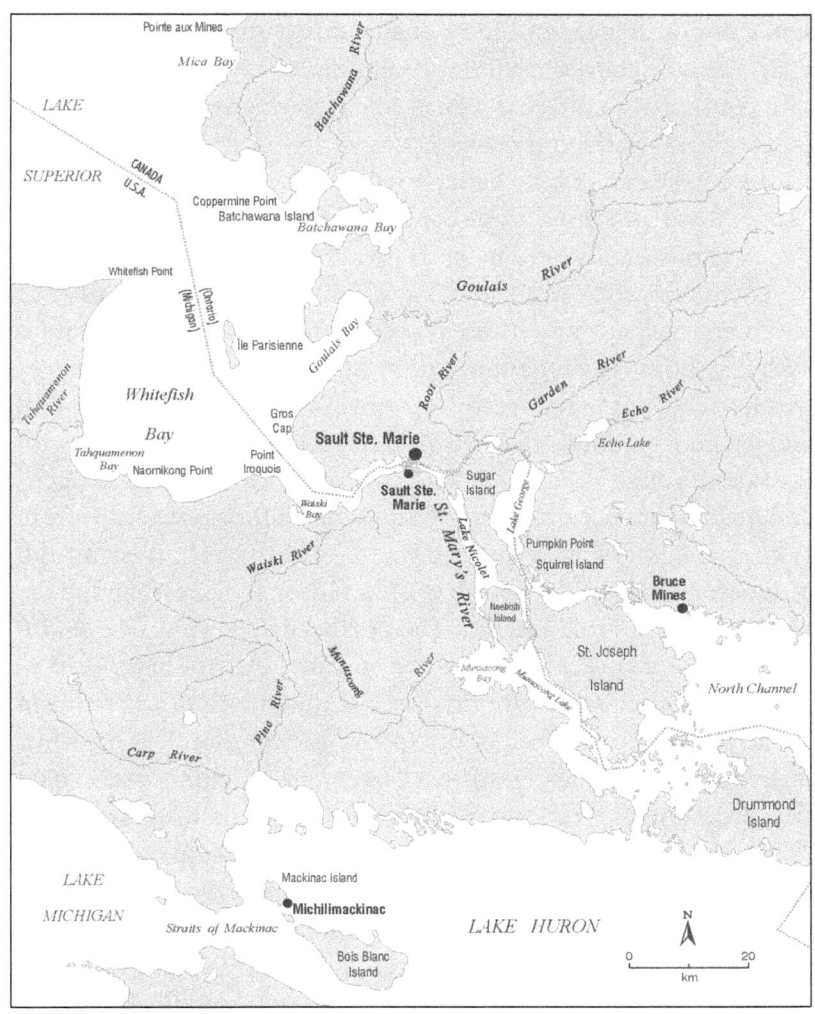

MAP 3. The Sault region. Map courtesy of the author.

states imposed ideas of blood quantum, status, and border controls, yet residency, as well as perceptions of ownership and control, continued to affect Indians seen as permanently residing on U.S.- or BNA-claimed territory.

The Sault Sainte Marie or Sault region is dominated by the Saint Mary's River as it flows from Lake Superior to Lake Huron. While there are not "hard" borders in the Western sense, the Sault region is generally based on the location of hunting territories, alliance and marriage patterns, ethnicity, and definitions of borders found within treaties. The region has both southern and northern edges that have been maintained by the Anishinaabe through their oral and written documents as well as their continued connection with the land, though they did extend their activities beyond the general markers on occasion. Specifically, the southern edge runs from Whitefish Point on Lake Superior in the west to Neebish Island and Munuscong Lake at the mouth of Lake Huron in the east and to the height of land on the interior. The northern edge runs from Coppermine Point and Batchawana Bay on Lake Superior in the west to the Lake George and Pumpkin Point at the mouth of Lake Huron in the east and to the height of land on the interior. It is over this region, as generally described, that two emerging settler states sought to exert influence and control throughout the nineteenth century.

A key indicator of the shifting colony to nation thus rests on the idea of "effective control." When and how did a colony or a nation gain effective control of the Sault region? Adding a layer of complexity to the issue is the international border. While the transitions and their effects around the international border affected the entire region, the gradual establishment of effective control by the state varied slightly. This also complicates the usage of such terms as *nation* and *colony*. First and foremost, the United States became a recognized nation in 1783; while the State of Michigan came into existence in 1837, before that date it was a federal territory. Michigan's Upper Peninsula, where Sault Sainte Marie is located, remained a colony of the Lower Peninsula until the discovery and exploitation of mineral resources as well as the creation of a shipping canal. Second, with the treaty of 1783, British North America became the recognized sovereign power along the Great Lakes northern shores—with Sault Sainte Marie remaining a distant hinterland of Montreal. The Constitution Act of 1791 created Upper Canada, and in 1841 it became Canada West when Britain united it with Lower Canada. While the Sault region remained a hinterland of the fur trade, Upper Canadians saw it as an extension of their southern colony. As such by the 1830s the Sault region had become a colony of a colony. With the creation of the Dominion of Canada in 1867, the Sault region, as part of the newly created province of Ontario, remained a colony of the south until after its industrialization in the latter 1800s—though some settlers in northern Ontario maintain that the region remains a colony of Toronto. Additionally, in the Canadas throughout the nineteenth century, the settlers constructed their sense of nation in terms of loyalty to and citizenship in the British Empire—the transition to Canadian nationhood did little to alter this conceptualization. Nevertheless, British Canadians in Upper Canada/Canada West/Ontario viewed themselves throughout the nineteenth century as British subjects living in a colony-nation that one day would become the heartland of the empire.[1] In short, the terms *nation* and *colony*, used by settlers and within this chapter, reflect the complex interrelationships between the macro and micro as well as between settlers and Aboriginals as the colony (Sault region/northern Michigan/northern Upper Canada/Ontario/BNA) transitioned to nation (BNA-Canada/United States). It is the purpose of this paper to examine the underlying interactions and experiences as well as complexities of the Aboriginal peoples with settlers and the state in and around the Sault region as it transitioned from colonial to national rule.

### Effective Control

A significant contextualizer of the transition of the Sault region from a colony to nation is the issue of effective control. Sault Sainte Marie, as the center of the Upper Lakes region, came to the fore in a 2003 precedent-setting case in the Supreme Court of Canada, that hinged on the concept of effective control. The court ruled that the Métis' right to hunt for subsistence predated European control of the Sault region, which was a modification of the precontact guideline for establishing First Nations' Aboriginal rights (Isaac 2004, 376; *R. v.*

*Van der Peet* [1996] 2 S.C.R. 507). Simply, the court stated that "the constitutionally significant feature of the Métis is their special status as peoples that emerged between first contact and the effective imposition of European control." It further determined that in the case of the Sault Sainte Marie region, the Europeans established control with the signing of the 1850 Robinson-Huron and Superior treaties (*R. v. Powley* [2003] 2 S.C.R. 207). While the date of 1850 may be useful in determining constitutional rights in the modern age, it does not effectively represent the shift to effective control. It speaks to an assumption that a treaty, document, or declaration of jurisdiction moves people into a new realm of legal, cultural, and political influence. This is simply not the case for the Great Lakes borderlands and definitely not the situation for the Sault region. The issue of effective control is a signpost of when the transition from frontier to settlement, from colonial to national control, took place. In other words, the treaty as a signpost of effective control by Europeans forms a key moment in an ongoing process in the transition from colonial to national control. In addition to treaty signing, it took the passage of legislation that governed both the lives and identities of the Aboriginal peoples. It is this challenge that the Aboriginal people in the Sault borderlands faced as their homeland shifted to colonial and national control while the settlers themselves were transitioning from colony to nation.

In 1850 the Ojibwas, Chippewas, or Anishinaabe entered into a treaty with the Crown that surrendered a vast region stretching from approximately Penetanguishene in the east to Thunder Bay in the west and to the height of land in the north (see map 4). The center of this vast region in 1850 was Sault Sainte Marie—it is here that the treaties were eventually negotiated and signed. This region is the homeland to the Anishinaabe and Great Lakes Métis peoples who for generations, despite pretensions of sovereignty by European powers, remained independent Aboriginal nations in full control of their territories. Only a few Europeans, largely traders and missionaries with a few settlers, lived in the region. Nevertheless, the Anishinaabe and Métis knew about and resisted European claims to their homeland. Almost sixty years earlier in 1783, a border dividing their homeland was agreed to by Great Britain and the

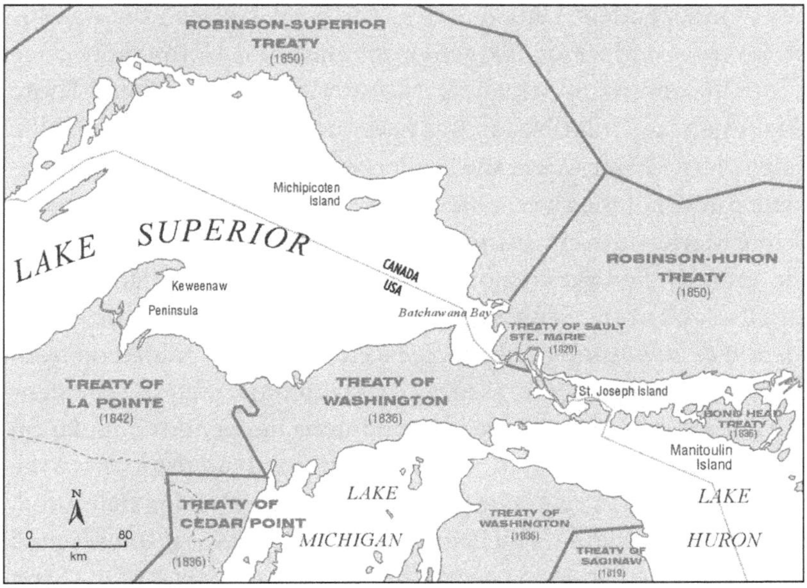
ROBINSON-SUPERIOR
TREATY
(1850)
Michipicoten
Island
LAKE SUPERIOR
CANADA
USA
Keweenaw
Peninsula
Batchawana Bay
ROBINSON-HURON
TREATY
(1850)
TREATY OF SAULT
STE. MARIE
(1820)
TREATY OF
LA POINTE
(1842)
TREATY OF
WASHINGTON
(1836)
St. Joseph Island
BOND HEAD
TREATY
(1836)
Manitoulin
Island
N
0
80
km
TREATY OF
CEDAR POINT
(1836)
LAKE
MICHIGAN
TREATY OF
WASHINGTON
(1836)
TREATY OF
SAGINAW
(1819)
LAKE
HURON

MAP 4. Treaty areas in the Sault region. Map courtesy of the author.

newly independent United States. The border placed the Anishinaabe homeland within two settler colonies—the North Shore came
under the control of British North America while the South Shore
was American. This division was never more evident than along the
Saint Mary's River where the border, which ran down the approximate middle of the river, split the once united community of Sault
Sainte Marie—thereby turning the region into a borderland. While
the entire Great Lakes region can be viewed as a borderland (Bellfy
2011), a look at the Sault Sainte Marie region will focus the examination of how Aboriginal people faced the settlers' transition from
colony to nation. The presence of two colonial states, weak central authority, and a relatively autonomous indigenous population
created and maintained the region as a borderland throughout the
nineteenth century (Adelman and Aron 1999, 815–16; Hele 2008,
65–84). As such, efforts by British North America as it transitioned
from colony to nation to control the Aboriginal peoples of the Sault
Sainte Marie region need to be understood within this context.

In the post–War of 1812 era, both the United States and BNA
attempted to establish control of the Sault region. Before the war the
residents of the region maintained loyalty to Britain and BNA, which
was evident during the conflict—for instance, U.S. troops burned
buildings on both sides of the river. After the war it became essential for both countries to establish or retain allegiances. Nineteenth-
century documents, in a general sense, often refer to the Anishinaabe
people living along both shores as the Saint Mary's River Band or
Sault Band.[2] While generally defined as a single unified band, the
Anishinaabe in the Sault region consisted of several autonomous
communities.[3] In 1848 the Hudson's Bay Company (HBC) post factor
for Sault Sainte Marie, William MacTavish, saw the Anishinaabe in
the region as a semiautonomous community independent of state
or company control (Chute 1998, 124).[4] It was this independence
from state control that needed to be destroyed if the transitioning
governments were to effectively control the region.

To this end the British constructed a post on Drummond Island
and the United States reoccupied the fort on Mackinac Island (see
map 5). These military establishments represented the closest colonial and early national authority from 1815 to 1822. Two U.S. expe-

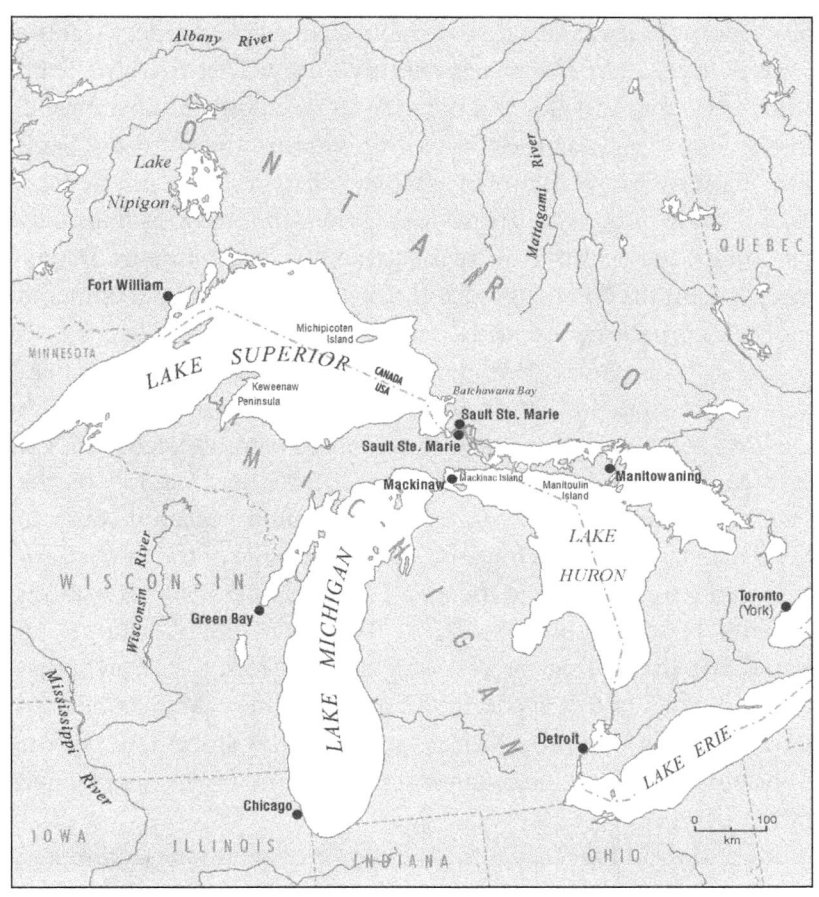

MAP 5. The Great Lakes context. Map courtesy of the author.

ditions sent in 1815 and 1816 to establish American authority at the Sault failed. In 1815 the troops ventured no further than the Sault and departed quickly for fear of being attacked by the Anishinaabe. In the following year the troops who ventured beyond the Sault were fired upon by unknown assailants, forcing the United States to withdraw once again from the region.[5] This obvious failure by the Americans to exert control made the British garrison on Drummond Island the "metropole for the British side of Lake Huron and the St. Mary's River, with the Canadian [and American] Sault . . . as part of its hinterland" (Mount, Abbott, and Mulloy 1995, 9). Inhabitants who wanted to ship and receive goods via BNA traveled to the island to conduct business, ship fur, and communicate with the east (Mount, Abbott, and Mulloy 1995, 9). Rather than rely on the BNA communication routes, inhabitants often ventured south to Mackinac Island in Michigan to take advantage of the larger center's commerce and ties to the east. Large numbers of First Nations gathered at British posts to receive their annual gifts at Drummond Island, Manitowaning, or Penetanguishene from the Crown, distributed by its Indian Department agents.[6] These large gatherings were seen as a threat by American authorities since many of the Aboriginal peoples in attendance resided within territories claimed by the United States.[7]

It was only in the 1820s and 1830s that emergent states attempted to move the region more firmly into their respective realms. First, in 1820 the United States sent an expedition—under the command of the territorial governor of Michigan, General Lewis Cass, along with thirty-four soldiers, a private secretary, an astronomer, a topographer and assistant, a physician, a geologist, an official secretary for the entire expedition, and about thirty voyageurs—to the south side of the Saint Mary's River to establish a fort and sign an Indian Treaty. Cass's desire to seek control of the river and territory from the Anishinaabe while establishing U.S. control almost led to a clash with the local Anishinaabe.[8] After securing the families on the BNA shore, and the timely intervention of calmer heads, the 1820 Treaty of Saint Mary or Treaty with Chippewa, 1820, recognized and affirmed U.S. claims to the area (Bieder 1999, 4). The U.S. government and military hoped this treaty, combined with the eventual construction of a military post, would permanently sever Anishinaabe ties to the British.[9] Nonetheless, the Anishinaabe believed that by allowing the United States to build a fort at the rapids they had not surrendered their sovereignty nor accepted control.

In an effort to bolster U.S. claims and control of the region, 273 officers and enlisted men of the Second U.S. Infantry regiment arrived at the American Sault to erect and maintain a fort in 1822.[10] The first effects of the transitioning of the United States to a nation was felt by all the original inhabitants of the region as the Euro-American settler population jumped from a mere handful to more than four hundred seemingly overnight. Now the U.S. Sault became the hub of the South and North Shore, eventually replacing Mackinac and Drummond Islands. A direct result of this bourgeoning population was the creation of Chippewa County in 1826, which encompassed the entire Upper Peninsula of Michigan from Michilimackinac County. Sault Sainte Marie became the new seat of local and state authority, represented by the building of the Chippewa County courthouse. Additionally, the federal government maintained its presence in the form of military personnel and Indian agents.[11]

The next effect of the increased U.S. presence was the establishment of an Indian agency in 1822 under the direction of Henry R. Schoolcraft. Upon arriving at the village of Sault Sainte Marie with military troops, Schoolcraft informed the assembled Anishinaabe that they must stop visiting British military establishments, accepting their gifts, and listening to their entreaties.[12] From Schoolcraft's perspective, "the establishment of a military post, and Indian Agency, at this place, enables the president to carry into effect, in this remote part of the union, the benevolent views of the American government with respect to the condition and the wants of the Indian tribes; . . . to open a proper intercourse with the most distant bands residing within the northwestern limits of the United States."[13] From 1822 until his departure from the Sault, Schoolcraft worked diligently to establish control over the Anishinaabe, whom he viewed as American Indians.[14]

While the United States was bolstering its control of the region, BNA seemed uninterested or unable to assert its claims. When the international boundary commission awarded Drummond Island to the United States, Britain decided to withdraw its military and Indian agency personnel to Penetanguishene, a two-day journey by schooner, on Lake Huron. From there Britain attempted to maintain its claims on the region (Jameson 1990, 449; Heath 1988, 36–38; Mount, Abbott, and Mulloy 1995, 10–2). It was only with the growing desire among British North Americans to assert themselves that a push was made to establish control with the appointment of a missionary and Indian agent—William McMurray—to the North Shore in 1832.[15]

McMurray's appointment, similar to Schoolcraft's, represented an increased attempt to control and influence the lives of the Anishinaabe at the Sault by transitioning colonial authorities. With McMurray in charge of both the spiritual and temporal welfare of the Anishinaabe deemed to be British Indians, the Upper Canadian government with the support of Lieutenant Governor Sir John Colborne sought to implement a policy of gradual assimilation, while hoping that a civilized village of loyal Anishinaabe on the border, drawn from U.S. and British shores albeit resident in BNA, would help defend the British colony from U.S. aggression, thereby establishing controls in the region. The distant metropole's control over the region proved to be undone by the presence of the international border. McMurray and Schoolcraft became brothers-in-law and often promoted allegiance to their respective governments under the same roof on the South Shore.[16] The cordial relationship enjoyed by the brothers-in-law meant that while undermining national claims of sovereignty, they cooperated in their efforts to assert control over the Aboriginal populations in the region. While cooperation and a blurring of boundaries and controls along the border was the local reality, both men reported to their respective authorities about each other's activities as well as their successes in "controlling" the Indians (Brazer 1993, 294). Thus, through the sharing of kin ties as well as residency in the borderlands, McMurray's and Schoolcraft's, and by extension BNA and American, efforts to exert effective control within their spheres of influence was highly mitigated, leaving the Anishinaabe and Métis to largely continue as they had before the creation of the international border.

While the colonial settler states of BNA and the United States viewed their respective indigenous populations as British or American Indians, the Anishinaabe had yet to become "Indian." The states and their actors saw and treated the Anishinaabe as Indians and as possessed or owned by the state yet not effectively within its control. Simply neither the United States nor BNA could control the movements, alignments, and residency patterns of the Sault Anishinaabe. Yet the mere act of defining the Anishinaabe as American or British Indians made them subject to but not citizens of the state from the perspective of state and its actors. Hence in the 1830s the Anishinaabe were in the process of becoming state-defined and thus legible Indians while un-becoming Anishinaabe. While the Anishinaabe did and continue to see themselves as sovereign and not subject to the border, the assertion of effective control by the United States and BNA gradually eroded the Sault Anishinaabe's ability to maintain effective control of their traditional residency and life patterns in a region that was now bisected by an imposed colonial border. Hence while the Sault region un-became a unified Anishinaabe territory as it became a colonially controlled divided territory, the Anishinaabe can be seen as similarly becoming "possessed" by becoming subject to the controls of colonial states.

Once again the drive in BNA toward nationhood was restrained by a representative of colonial authority. In 1835 Sir Francis Bond Head, the new lieutenant governor of Upper Canada, decided the best option for Indians under his jurisdiction was their removal and centralization.[17] This led to the undermining of McMurray's authority at the Sault and his eventual resignation in 1838. McMurray's resignation only heightened the lack of control by either government in the border region. This lack of control is evident during the rebellion period of 1837–38 in Upper and Lower Canada, as well as the subsequent Patriot War and conflict with the Hunters' Lodges.[18]

When news of the rebellions affecting Lower and southern Upper Canada and subsequent cross-border raids by Patriots and Hunters' Lodges (BNA rebels driven into the United States), reached the Sault in early 1838, rumors and plots began to circulate.[19] For instance, Hudson's Bay Company factor, William Nourse, feared that the Métis planned to capture the post in an act of support for their rebellious French brethren in Lower Canada. To forestall the attack, Nourse asked the U.S. garrison to either arrest or assist in crushing the dissidents should the need arise on either side of the border. The Anishinaabe thought or perhaps hoped that the problems in the south would lead Britain and the United States to war. This interpretation of events led the regional chiefs to make plans to surprise Fort Brady's garrison and drive the Americans from the Upper Lakes. Similarly, BNA's mixed-blood Indian agent at Manitoulin Island, George Ironside, offered to arm the Anishinaabe throughout the lakes and attack Mackinac in a series of engagements reminiscent of events from 1812 (Hele 2005, 171n12). While a direct link between the two proposed schemes has not been established, it is highly likely that Ironside either knew of or encouraged the Sault leadership's endeavors. Nevertheless, George Johnston, a local mixed-blood and U.S. Indian interpreter, claimed that he prevented an Indian war by warning Fort Brady's commander.[20] The HBC also acted to dispel rumors while encouraging the Anishinaabe to remain at peace. Tensions waned until September 1838, when Colonel George Croghan, who was visiting Fort Brady, likely inebriated, and definitely bitter over his defeats in the region during the War of 1812, ordered gunners at Fort Brady to fire on the British Sault. BNA's distant control meant the potential international incident went unreported for some months. When authorities at York finally learned of the incident, it was through a letter from the HBC factor sent via the United States. In the factor's report, he reasoned the incident was harmless since the shot had passed harmlessly into the hillside, and all parties concerned had immediately apologized for the colonel's actions (Mount, Abbott, and Mulloy 1995, 12–15). While the peaceful nature of the cross-border settler community resumed, BNA and the United States were reminded of their overall lack of control by Anishinaabe actions.

The power of the Anishinaabe in the region is seen in a series of letters from U.S. subagent James Ord at Sault Sainte Marie to Henry R. Schoolcraft, the Michigan superintendent of Indian Affairs, from March to May 1838, at the height of tensions in the region. Ord wrote to Schoolcraft, noting "that there is much discontent among the Indians in this subagency" and recommending "efforts to remove it," specifically by sending presents to the Sault for distribution as well as supplying oxen, chain, and a cart.[21] Apparently unimpressed by U.S. gifts, the Indians contacted British agents and had received assurances about the plentiful nature of the queen's bounty. While this correspondence does not indicate whether or not the Americans or the British met each other's standards, a letter written in September 1838 indicates that the Anishinaabe collected numerous gifts from both countries.[22]

Part of the Anishinaabe and Métis hostility toward the U.S. presence in the region was likely linked to the 1836 U.S. treaty negotiations and implementation. The overall collapse of the Michigan economy, a declining fur trade, spread of infectious diseases, and appearance of a severe winter led the Odawa and Chippewas in southern Michigan to request a treaty. More specifically, the Odawa in the Mackinac area sought to surrender their interest in lands in Michigan's Upper Peninsula as well as in Drummond and Manitou Islands—all of which was shared with the Sault Chippewas (Cleland 1992, 225). Lewis Cass, the new secretary of war and de facto head of the Indian Department, and Henry R. Schoolcraft, Michigan superintendent and Mackinac Indian agent, sought to exploit the situation created by the Odawa's entreaties and the poor economy to increase the United States' and Michigan's control over its Aboriginal population (Cleland 2001, 20–21).

The increased power of the United States and its nationhood was evident through Cass and Schoolcraft's machinations. First, both men gathered leaders from the eastern Upper Peninsula, the east coast of Lake Michigan, and Grand River Valley to attend treaty negotiations in Washington DC. By moving the treaty conference to Washington, Cass and Schoolcraft sought to isolate the delegates from the "negative" influences of their tribes. During the negotiations the Indian leadership discovered that the Métis, traders, and government officials were negotiating the treaty among themselves. It was only after cajoling and pressure by Cass and Schoolcraft that the Indian representatives agreed to sign the treaty on March 28, 1836. Under the treaty's terms, the Sault Sainte Marie Anishinaabe representatives—Jawba Wadiek (Waishkey or Waiskey), Waub Ogeeg (Keewyzi), and Maidysage (Maidosagee) representing Kaygayosh—

surrendered all of their claims in the Upper Peninsula east of a line to be drawn between Bay de Noc on Lake Michigan and Marquette, Lake Superior (Cleland 1992, 226–27; Cleland 2001, 21; Treaty with Ottawa, 1836, 450–51, 454).

The next lesson in control came from the U.S. Congress. Under the terms of the American constitution, Congress is required to approve all treaties. During the process of ratification, Congress amended the terms of the treaty proclaimed by the president on May 27, 1836. The new conditions that the Odawa and Chippewa signatories were expected to abide by destroyed land security by placing the reservations in trust for five years, which could only be extended at the pleasure of Congress. To secure consent for the unilaterally amended document, Schoolcraft threatened to and then refused to distribute annuities to anyone who refused to accept the new terms (Treaty with the Ottawa 1836, 451; Cleland 1992, 227–29; Cleland 2001, 21–24).

In an effort to undermine U.S. attempts to control the people, some individuals crossed the river and became British Indians. Leaders of the American Sault's Anishinaabe community strengthened their ties with Britain by visiting its Indian agents and military posts to receive gifts. Others strengthened kin ties to those living along the North Shore in hopes of being able to flee should removal be enforced.[23]

By the end of the 1830s, U.S. and BNA governmental control of the region remained tenuous. The British had attempted twice to impose their presence, only to abandon the region for locales farther east. Laws passed in the south mattered little to northerners, which made York's grasp on the North Shore slippery. The laws and even Upper Canadian authority depended on the HBC for enforcement, and the company remained powerless to press the Anishinaabe on the "niceties" of Upper Canadian laws (Arthur 1988, 132–33; Harring 1998, 109–24, 153–57). Despite the occasional clashes with the missionaries about working on the Sabbath and about the sale of alcohol, the HBC's factors did not interfere with attempts to civilize the Indians at the Sault once Lieutenant Governor Colborne put his support behind the idea of civilization. While the Americans managed to occupy the region militarily and administratively, their authority did not go uncontested. Anishinaabe continued to visit British posts despite American efforts at prevention (Bieder 1999, 11–13). The military never ventured far beyond the limits of Sault Michigan unless they were being transferred to the east or south, leaving the eastern or western fringe of the Sault region American in name only. Although manipulated by U.S. agents, treaty negotiations in 1835 and the Treaty of 1836 did not go uncontested. The Anishinaabe did not feel obliged to follow the agreements when settlers also failed to follow the law. Despite the presence of a courthouse in the Sault, the United States remained reluctant and unable to commit the Anishinaabe to trial. The Chippewa County court did not have the jurisdiction to try Indians since they were a federal responsibility. Additionally, the lack of a suitable jail, large numbers of Anishinaabe and Métis, and movement across the border effectively prevented the arrest and removal of any suspects for trial.[24]

### Resource Extraction and the Need for Effective Control

In the 1840s the need for effective control of the region by the BNA and U.S. governments increased due to the discovery of copper and the resultant rush for mines. Geologist Dougal Houghton's surveys of the southern shores of Lake Superior on behalf of Michigan in 1830, 1837, and 1841, as well as his final report, initiated a rush by speculators and prospectors to stake mineral claims. From 1845 to 1860 116 copper mining companies operated between the Sault and Lake Superior's western end. These discoveries, which were largely impossible without Indian knowledge of mineral locations, their labor as guides and canoeists, and other forms of assistance, led to the negotiation of more treaties with the Anishinaabe in 1837 and 1842 with the United States as well as in 1850 with BNA (Telford 1996, 70–72). While U.S. control over the southern shore increased dramatically with the growing settler population, increased military presence, and construction of canal at the Sault, BNA attempts to exert control remained limited. In fact, until the increase in the settler population in the Canadian Sault at the turn of the twentieth century, BNA benefited from U.S. efforts to control its population and territories.

One such side effect of U.S. activities was the mineral speculation boom along the north shores of Lakes Huron and Superior as well as the 1850 Robinson Treaties.[25] The first response by the newly created United Canadas to the U.S. mineral boom was in 1841, when they asserted legislative control of the northern lands that did not fall under the HBC charter.[26] Essentially, HBC personnel and Anishinaabe living from Sault Sainte Marie to Fort William were now officially under the jurisdiction of the United Provinces of Canada (Chute 1998, 123–24). Two years later in 1843, W. E. Logan, geologist for the United Provinces of Canada, speculated that possibilities for mineral discoveries existed on the British shore. That same year Canada West appointed Joseph Wilson as Crown lands and custom agent. Wilson also served as postmaster, magistrate, Indian agent, fisheries overseer, and in 1849–50 as colonel in the new local militia (Heath 1988, 42). Finally, in 1845 the north began to experience its own mineral boom with the issuing of the first mineral license on the North Shore.

Upon Wilson's arrival at the Sault in 1843, Chief Shingwaukonse contested the efforts by Canada West to control the region by informing the new Crown lands and custom agent about Anishinaabe rights and claims in the area (Capp 1904, 175–76). Despite Shingwaukonse's assertions, Wilson and his masters at York were determined to ignore Anishinaabe rights. Within two years of Wilson's appointment, in 1845, the United Canadas issued the first land lease for mining on Lake Superior's northern shore to John A. Prince, future magistrate of the Algoma District (Wightman and Wightman 1991, 195). The following year, a former and corrupt Indian agent, William Keating, received a 6,400-acre (approximately 2,590 hectares) mineral location known as the Cuthbertson Location near present-day Bruce Mines (Telford 1997, 384). B. H. Lemoine's mineral location granted that same year included the entire Anishinaabe village at Garden River, illustrating Canada West's contempt for Aboriginal rights. By 1846 a further 133 mining applications for Lakes Superior and Huron had been received and granted (Telford 1996, 384).

With a mineral boom underway and the assertion of control in the form of a Crown lands agent, Canada West undertook efforts to survey the region. In 1846 Alexander Vidal arrived in the Sault, assigned with the task to survey and define the town plots within the village of Sault Sainte Marie and the various mineral tracts. Shingwaukonse and his followers confronted Vidal while he attempted to survey near their village at Garden River. Secure in their knowledge that Indian lands could not be infringed without a treaty, the Anishinaabe leadership questioned Vidal's authority to mark their lands and demanded he cease the survey (Chute 1998, 104–5). The assertion of Anishinaabe claims in the face of assumed settler authority was duly reported by Vidal. His report, however, failed to rouse government interest in Anishinaabe claims or the potential trouble that could result should they be ignored.

Shingwaukonse, the British-recognized head chief of Sault Canada, and Nebenagoching, traditional Crane chief in Sault Canada, continued their efforts to enforce Anishinaabe territorial rights, contest assumption of colonial control over land and people, and petition the government for a treaty and protection.[27] For instance, the *Colonial Intelligencer; or, Aborigines Friend* carried the text of an 1849 memorial, the same petition carried in the July 7, 1849 edition of the *Montreal Gazette*, to the governor general. The memorial noted that for three years the Anishinaabe had requested justice and a treaty, but the government refused to negotiate or recognize their title to the land. Furthermore, the petition directly challenged British claims that they treated Indians with greater dignity and justice than the Americans. Based on personal experience, the Anishinaabe, represented by Shingwaukonse and Nebenagoching, informed the governor that the "Long Knives [Americans] . . . have not taken from the Red Skins any lands, unless there was at least some kind of treaty entered into, and a purchase made," whereas the British acted as common thieves.[28]

Despite calls for justice for the Indians by miners, speculators, and missionaries, the government continued to grant mining leases ("Chippewa Indians" 1849, 286–90). In the meantime its supporters began a campaign to deny Anishinaabe claims. For instance, a mineral lessee and "expert on Indians," former Indian agent William Keating, argued in response to the *Montreal Gazette*'s 1849 article that the Anishinaabe along the North Shore, particularly those in the Sault, did not have any legitimate claim to the land or its resources since they were American Indians. Thus, Keating, in an effort to undermine Anishinaabe claims, made American Indians out of British Indians, while knowing that such categories were difficult if not impossible to apply in the Sault borderlands. Likewise a report issued in 1846 by Denis-Benjamin Papineau, commissioner of Crown lands, examined Anishinaabe claims and maintained that they had originated on the Mississippi before violently wresting control of the region from its true inhabitants. The report thus stated that "Indians about Sault Ste. Marie . . . emigrated from the United States" (Keating 1849; Chute 1998, 123). Both Papineau's and Keating's claims negated any Anishinaabe claim based on long-term occupation of the land on the North Shore, thereby justifying BNA's assumption of control as legitimate based on the principle of terra nullius.[29] As such, based upon Anishinaabe claims, as well as contradictory claims represented by Keating's letter and extracts of D. B. Papineau's report, the Crown established a commission to investigate the issue (Chute 1998, 114–15, 138; Montgomerie 1993, 214; Hele 2008).[30]

As part of the effort to secure control of the region, the Anglican Church took up a renewed interest in the local Anishinaabe with the appointment of the Reverend Gustavus Anderson as missionary in 1848. The renewed interest was not entirely based on the church's concern for the spiritual welfare of the Anishinaabe. It is more likely that growing settler interest in the mineral potential on the British shores of Lake Huron and Lake Superior brought about renewed attention. Anderson, like all Anglican missionaries to the Anishinaabe, came armed with government support—financial and familial. His father, Captain Thomas G. Anderson, served as the superintendent of Indian Affairs for Canada West. Reverend Anderson's supporters and father hoped that the minister could influence the Garden River Anishinaabe congregation to support settler usurpation of their lands and rights. His early childhood at his father's stations meant that Reverend Anderson was fluent in Anishinaabemowin. The Garden River congregation, initially reported to be 182 individuals, remained leery of its new minister's motives based on his family ties. This wariness was not misplaced since Captain Anderson requested that his son secure the cooperation of the Anishinaabe in regard to government demands and to report any opinions they might have in the matter directly.[31] In short,

Captain Anderson hoped that Reverend Anderson would encourage the Anishinaabe of the Sault region to sign an unacceptable treaty for their lands (Hele 2003, 213–15). Nevertheless, the more the government refused to recognize Anishinaabe control of their lands, the more unwilling the Reverend Anderson found his congregation to listen to his sermons and councils to heed the queen's laws. Eventually, the missionary found his congregation deaf to his entreaties—he fled the region in 1849 after the fallout from the failed investigation of Anishinaabe claims.

In an effort to demonstrate their control of the region, the Anishinaabe under the guidance of Shingwaukonse issued their own leases. First, to prevent the expropriation of their village, they leased two hundred acres (80.94 hectares) for nine hundred years to the Anglican Church in 1849. This agreement incorporated the Garden River village site and church grounds, while conflicting with a mineral lease issued by the Crown Lands Department the previous year. Next, Chief Shingwaukonse gave several leases to Allan Macdonell, the band's ally and lawyer as well as mineral speculator, including some islands in the Saint Mary's River in 1848–49 (Hele 2008, 79). In spite of these assertions of sovereignty, the two men investigating Anishinaabe claims denied the lease's legitimacy, as did the government after the signing of the 1850 Robinson Treaties (Hele 2011, 40–41).

Nonetheless, the 1849 commission to investigate Anishinaabe claims set out to clarify the situation and reassert Canadian control of the process. The two men in charge of investigating the claims— Alexander Vidal, whom Chief Shingwaukonse had confronted in 1846, and Captain Thomas G. Anderson, superintendent of Indian Affairs and War of 1812 veteran—were both familiar with and well informed of Anishinaabe claims. Throughout their investigative tour of Lakes Superior and Huron, the two commissioners refused to discuss any treaty terms, claiming they had merely been appointed to discuss the specific claims of each band. After a particularly volatile consultation at Garden River, Vidal and Anderson attempted to retain control of the investigation by resorting to threats and storming out of the meeting. The commissioners stated that neither the Métis nor the Anishinaabe would receive compensation for their claims and threatened to strip all the chiefs and their followers of government-granted ranks and presents should they continue their non-compliance with government demands (Telford 1996, 154; *British Colonist* 1849c). After this attempt at control via intimidation, both commissioners left the region and began preparing their self-serving reports. The Anishinaabe, however, faced with settler ignorance and obstinacy, decided to enforce their territorial rights.[32]

On November 1, 1849, Oshawano, Shingwaukonse, Nebenagoching, Allan and Agnus Macdonell, Wharton Metcalfe, and thirty Anishinaabe and Métis drawn from both the United States and BNA boarded a ship and headed for the Quebec and Lake Superior Mining Company's operation at Mica Bay, Lake Superior, where they evicted the trespassing miners and shut down the mine.[33] The contestation of Canadian claims and control of the region was undertaken by both Anishinaabe and Métis who resided in the United States and BNA. Stung by this loss of assumed control and affront to its growing sense of nationhood, BNA soon found itself awash in rumors about the Indian attack. Anishinaabe actions, rumors, and the arrival of "survivors" or "refugees" at Coburg presented Canada West with a justification for asserting control more forcefully (Chute 1998, 135–36). Faced with an apparent rebellion, the government quickly dispatched troops, who eventually reached Sault Sainte Marie on December 1, 1849. Finding the mine site abandoned and securely locked, the soldiers set about arresting the "rebellion's" ring leaders. By December 13 Shingwaukonse, Nebenagoching, and their coconspirators had been arrested and confined to jail for a few days. Interestingly, those arrested did not include the American Indians or Métis. Much to the dismay of authorities, the "rebels" "were released by the Chief Justice, Sir John Beverly Robinson, a relative by marriage of Macdonell [one of the ringleaders]," on the grounds that the group had been illegally arrested (Chute 1998, 136). A direct result of Anishinaabe actions in the Sault was the creation of a rifle company by the Crown lands and custom agent Wilson. The entire intent behind the formation of the militia unit was to aid in the suppression of any future Indian outbreaks. Lastly, the detachment of troops set to liberate the mine remained at the Sault, wintering in the HBC post, also with the intention of preventing further acts of rebellion.[34]

Finally forced to recognize Anishinaabe control of the region, the government of Canada West finally decided to negotiate for a land surrender or treaty. The entire treaty enterprise was one of the colonial government seeking to establish effective control over the region's lands and peoples while the Anishinaabe sought to retain control. Canada West appointed a member of the governing elite and former manager of the Bruce Mines, William B. Robinson, to negotiate and sign a treaty with the Indians of Lakes Huron and Superior. The troops sent to the region in November and December 1849 remained until the conclusion of the negotiations—lending both an air of pageantry and a threat of violence to the treaty process ("Treaty with the Indians" 1850). Robinson also split the negotiating parties into two groups, resulting in two treaties, in an effort to remove those more willing to sign from the more recalcitrant ones. Essentially, the Lake Superior people were more willing to sign based on their relative isolation from settlement and development. Aiding the apparent cooperative stance was the recognition of questionable leadership by Robinson and the failure to bring all the Lake Superior Anishinaabe to the Sault for negotiations (Hansen 1987, 39–60). Once the appointed Lake Superior representatives signed the Robinson-Superior Treaty, Robinson informed the Lake Huron chiefs that he would prepare a treaty for them to sign since the majority appeared to be in agreement. Robinson then threatened Shingwaukonse and other noncompliant chiefs when he stated that those who did not sign would receive nothing (Morris [1880] 1991, 17–21). Faced with Robinson's refusal to bend to higher annuity payments and inclusion of a clause for the Métis, as was the custom in U.S. treaties, Shingwaukonse and other Lake Huron leaders signed the prepared document. Both the Robinson-Superior and Robinson-Huron were signed by individuals resident on either side of the international border but who, for government purposes, were considered British Indians regardless of their actual residency and previous colonial state claims.[35] Interestingly, approximately one month after the signing of the treaty, all charges against the two key leaders of the 1849 "rebellion"—Shingwaukonse and Nebenagoching—were dismissed (Telford 2003, 71–84; Morrison 1996; Hele 2016a; Hele 2016b; Hele 2016c).

Within three years of the signing of the 1850 treaties in the British Sault, the Anishinaabe in the American Sault were once again confronted by a developing state. Due to the mineral boom, settlers began demanding better communication links to the east—more specifically, they demanded a canal be built around the Saint Mary's Rapids. The construction of a shipping canal would allow copper and other resources to be shipped to markets without the need to portage around the rapids. Thus, in 1853 both Congress and Michigan inked deals that saw the construction and completion of a shipping canal and lock system in 1855.

The increased control of lands and people in the Sault region is evident in the process of the canal construction. Ignoring the 1820 treaty, the U.S. government seized various lands, including the Chippewa camping-fishing site, for the purpose of building a canal (Kelton 1889).[36] Charles T. Harvey, who was in charge of the canal construction and had the backing of the state, paid the Anishinaabe $10 to $15 per "cabin" and then ordered all Indians off their fishing sites within twenty-four hours. His action, undertaken with the support of the various levels of government, generated a series of petitions, declarations, requests, and demands from the Chippewas for compensation. These efforts eventually resulted in a treaty, just as the canal officially opened for shipping. The 1855 Treaty with the Chippewa essentially recognized the theft of the 1820 reservation. Under the treaty's terms the Sault Anishinaabe surrendered their campground as well as their right to fish in Saint Mary's Rapids. The government also agreed to appoint a commissioner with the sole ability to determine the amount of compensation due to the Anishinaabe for the loss of buildings, lands, and fishery (Treaties with the Chippewa 1855, 732).

Also within the terms of the U.S. treaty was a clause inserted at the request of the Odawa and Chippewas to terminate the fictional tribal structure created by Schoolcraft and Cass in 1836. In other words, the Odawa and Chippewas wanted an official return to their own national systems of government. The Chippewas and Odawa under this clause were attempting to re-become independent identities. Unfortunately, the state chose to interpret the clause as terminating the tribe and its relationship to the federal government. This state interpretation meant that the Sault Chippewas or Anishinaabe no longer had a special relationship to the federal government and effectively terminated their nationhood in favor of U.S. and state citizenship. In terms of the settler state, the Chippewas or Anishinaabe became individuals with a Chippewa or Anishinaabe and indigenous identity while they had "un-become" a collective identity or nation. This error of interpretation would not be corrected by the United States until the late twentieth century and then only after petitions, claims, and suits brought by the tribes to confront the state's effective control of their nationhood (Cleland 2001: 36–37, 43, 50, 69–70; Hele 2003, 102).[37] Once again the Chippewas and Anishinaabe became a collective identity and nation in the eyes of the settler state. In a manner of writing, the Chippewas and Anishinaabe under the extinguishment interpretation became indigenous, and when the error was corrected they had become Indigenous.

With the signing of the 1855 treaty, termination of tribal government, construction of a shipping canal, development of resources, increased military presence, and further settlement, the transition from colonial to national control in the American Sault was largely completed. This is evident through the U.S. resident Anishinaabe's complete reliance on the state to recognize their entitlements under the 1855 treaty. In terms of land entitlements, the 1855 treaty attempted to resolve, in the United States' favor, issues left outstanding by the treaties signed in the 1830s and 1840s.[38] Specifically, the 1836 treaty left the Ojibwas and Odawa without permanent reservations based on a five-year limitation clause, and since the term expired in 1841, the Anishinaabe occupancy of the lands could be terminated at any time by Congress or the president (Treaty with the Chippewa 1855; Treaty with the Ottawa and Chippewa 1855; Cleland 1992, 236–37). As such, the 1855 treaty reserved blocks of land from which the Indians could select individual plots (Treaty with the Ottawa and Chippewa 1855; Cleland 2001, 26–28). Every Anishinaabe person who was recognized as an Indian (thereby becoming "Indian") by the U.S. federal government under the treaty's terms had the right to select land within the surrendered area reserved for Indians for five years, at which time the remaining reserved blocks would be opened for general sale and settlement. Apparently, a few individual settlers purchased lands in the blocks designated for the Anishinaabe before the declaration of the five-year reservation. Chief Oshawano requested the cancellation of this sale since the two individuals managed to purchase seven of the best sections in the middle of the reservation, effectively rendering Anishinaabe selected lands useless. The cancellation never took place (Cleland 2001, 36).[39] Additionally, delays by the state led to a failure to issue land patents and secure Anishinaabe selections within the five-year grace period (Cleland 2001, 28–29, 34–37). These kinks left the Sault Chippewas in limbo concerning their rights and lands as well as at the mercy of government magnanimity for the rest of the century (Cleland 2001, 237; Reuter 1993, 133).

It was only through an 1860 act of Congress that the U.S. government managed to purchase the Methodist mission grounds at Bay Mills or Gnoozhekaaning, which eventually formed the basis of the Bay Mills Indian Community reservation (Magnaghi 1984, 58; Cleland 2001, 30, 35–39). Regardless of this action, which eventually benefited one of the bands in the American Sault region, land patents continued to be delayed throughout the 1860s, which resulted in Anishinaabe plots being scattered among those purchased by settlers. This led the Bay Mills Anishinaabe to request in 1886 that the Sault, Sugar Island, and Hay Lake Anishinaabe be allowed to reallocate their land allotments or selections to the Bay Mills region where plots were still readily available.[40] One year later, in 1867, Oshawano wrote to the commissioner of Indian Affairs, Nathaniel G. Taylor, wondering when the patents would be issued under the terms of the 1855 treaty.[41] In an effort to find a solution to the patent issue, the Michigan Sault area chiefs proposed to travel to Washington DC and air their grievances directly with the president.[42] Finally, in 1871 the chiefs and their followers received information that their patents would be issued after fifteen years of delays.[43] Despite this information the patents remained unissued in 1875.[44]

The Métis in the American and British Sault fared no better than the Anishinaabe when it came to land rights. Although Anishinaabe chiefs in BNA and the United States had used their authority to grant Métis individuals permission to live on their chosen plots, state governments denied the chiefs authority to grant lands. Instead, both the United States and BNA interpreted Métis land occupancy in terms of squatters' rights. As such, Métis title to their land remained insecure—as squatters they could be evicted by the state or the "legitimate" owners of the land. This left the Métis largely powerless when government officials and other settlers entered the region and began speculating in real estate. In Canada the Métis claim in 1850 was denied by treaty negotiator Robinson. Without security of title, the Métis eventually lost their land claims through fraud, theft, and sale. Construction of a hydroelectric generating station in the 1890s and early 1900s destroyed the community, forcing its members to relocate to both old and new Anishinaabe communities in the Upper Lakes region.[45] In the United States the Métis lost their land through the same means as well as through legal decisions by Congress concerning who owned and did not own property. The U.S. Treaty of 1826 promised a 640-acre (approximately 259 hectares) land for the use of the "half-breeds" along the Saint Mary's River, though it remains unclear how the Métis-held lands were legally alienated during subsequent developments in the Sault region. The U.S. Senate rejected all Métis land grants associated with the treaties. It appears that by 1850 the majority of the Métis in Sault Michigan had relocated outside the boundaries of the settlers' village or migrated to BNA.[46]

Meanwhile, BNA continued its efforts to gain effective control over the Sault Anishinaabe through policy and legislation that began in 1850 and continued beyond the end of the nineteenth century. Hence, as Canada transitioned into nationhood, its efforts to control Aboriginal peoples, lands, waters, and resources across its claimed territory only intensified. The Anishinaabe and Métis people in the Sault region were particularly affected by these state efforts. All British North Americans, as Tina Loo argues about the imposition of British law in British Columbia, hoped to create "rationality" by extending a set of "standardized, rational, and predictable rules [that formed] . . . the basis of the law's authority and, ultimately, . . . liberal order" (1994, 4).[47] The effort to create a liberal order within the 1850 treaties' area began in 1858, when the Sault became the judicial seat for the recently established district of Algoma and Colonel John Prince became its first justice (Chute 1998, 178).

The United Canadas and later Dominion of Canada began creating laws that further restricted Aboriginal peoples' rights and
attempted to define their identities. To prevent Aboriginal protests and further assertions of legal authority over northern Canada West, the government passed a series of legislative acts in the
1850s, such as an Act for the Protection of the Indians of Upper
Canada from Imposition, and the Property Occupied and Enjoyed
by Them from Trespass and Injury (1850) and an Act for the Better
Protection of the Land and Property of the Indians of Lower Canada (1850; Isaac 1993, 40–41, 42–46). Resulting from the 1849 Mica
Bay incident, the 1853 Act to Make Provision for the Administration of Justice in the Unorganized Tracts of Country in Upper Canada was designed to prevent individuals such as Allan Macdonell
from "inciting" the Indians to resist government actions (Act to
Make Provision 1853; Knight and Chute 2006, 97–98; Chute 1998,
156, 181, 237). Basically, encouraging First Peoples to defend their
rights became a jailable offense. Additionally, the act provided for
the establishment of courts and police forces in northern Upper
Canada (essentially within the 1850 Robinson Treaty boundaries).
In 1854 William Rowan, acting governor general, extended by proclamation the 1850 Act for the Protection of the Indians in Upper
Canada to Sault Sainte Marie. This act prevented individuals from
seizing Indian lands or possessions as payment for debt.[48] It also
made "the Commissioners and the different Superintendents of the
Indian Department" by "virtue of their office and appointment . . .
Justices of the Peace within the County, or United Counties, within
which, for the time being, they or any or either of them, may be
resident or employed as such Commissioners or Superintendents,
without any other qualification; any law to the contrary notwithstanding" (Isaac 1993, 42–46). Three years later in 1857, the Gradual
Civilization of the Indian Tribes came into force (Dickason 2002,
228–29; Milloy 1990, 58–60; Surtees 1988, 89). This act created a set
of conditions by which the Indians in Canada West and East could
surrender their status. Before being accepted as citizens of Canada, however, Indians had to meet a strict set of conditions, such
as remaining free of debt for three years (Dickason 2002, 228–29).
With the creation of the Dominion of Canada in 1867, the responsi-

bility for Indian Affairs fell under federal jurisdiction. The first two attempts to legislate for Indians, in 1868 and 1869, generally consolidated previous legislation concerning the protection and management of Indian interests, established measures to implement "self-governing" democratic governments on reserves, as well as "improved" enfranchisement legislation while extending the minister in charge of Indian Affairs' power.[49]

The passage of the Indian Act in 1876 followed by various amendments throughout the period increased the federal ability to administer Indian lands, monies, and people. As a key plank in Canada's national policy—open land for settlement and railway construction—the Indian Acts became more restrictive and increased the Department of Indian Affairs powers to expropriate lands, enfranchise individuals, and impose "democratic" governments.[50]

### Becoming Indigenous: The Power Dynamics of Status Definitions and Names

The second key element in creating a set of rules to effectively govern a population, which signifies its shift from a colonial to a national relationship, is the regulation of identity—or, in another term, the mapping of a population to make it "legible" or "readable" for state policies which are then implemented via legislation (Trouillot 2001, 125–38; Scott 1998; Manzano-Munguía 2011, 404–26). In approximately 1820 the Sault Aboriginal community was self-governing and in full control of its membership. Outsiders generally placed people within a particular category—Métis, Half-breed, Indian, French, or Canadian—based on observation. For instance, individuals would be cast as "Métis" if they spoke French and Anishinaabemowin, had a small garden outside their home, were of a darker complexion, and dressed "in an Indian manner." Individuals were determined to be "French" if they were of a lighter skin, literate, and lived in a floored house. "Canadian" simply referred to Métis or French participants (current or former) in the American fur trade. One was seen as an "Indian" based on skin color, mode of life, lodging, and general inability to speak English or French "properly." While these categories seemed immutable to outsiders, in the reality of everyday life in the Sault region, individuals could and did shift between categories. Essentially, each term was "continually debated by different groups and individuals, [with] each attempting to assert its own understandings, derived from its own assessments of interests" based on previous knowledge and experience. This mutability made it difficult, if not impossible, to enforce state policy and law upon the region's peoples.[51]

An initial attempt to limit the mutability of racial categories took place in the signing of the U.S. Indian treaties. Specifically, the 1836 and 1855 treaties contained "half-breed" provisions. The terms of these provisions specified that to receive compensation for loss of land use, an individual had to reside within the surrendered area and belong to one of three classes of "half-breeds." The first class, or "full half-breeds," had 50 percent Chippewa or Odawa blood combined with either another Indian or non-Indian ethnic group. The second class, or "other half-breeds," had half-white and a quarter Chippewa or Odawa as well as a quarter of another Indian group's blood. The third class, or "quarter-bloods," were simply people who were the relations of the Chippewa or Odawa and had 25 percent Indian blood—essentially, descendants of one of the other categories. According to the sixth article of the 1836 Treaty with the Ottawa, the "three classes of these claimants [existed], the first of which, shall receive one-half more than the second, and the second, double the third" when paid (452). To make the disbursements proceed smoothly, treaty implementation commissioners would interview Indian chiefs, notables from the settler community, and others familiar with the Aboriginal communities covered under the terms of the treaty to determine a person's ethnic or national status. In an effort to speed up the process, individuals were allowed to declare themselves either as an Indian or "half-breed"—suspect cases were duly investigated by the commissioners. Once "paid out" as a "half-breed," you were no longer entitled to any rights or privileges enjoyed by the Indians under the terms of the treaty.

The control of the state and its representatives is evident in the process of implementing the "half-breed" provisions. For instance, a petition dated November 13, 1836, addressed to President Andrew Jackson brought Indian Agent Schoolcraft's manipulation of these provisions to light.[52] The petition alleged that Schoolcraft had paid several people inappropriately and denied others their rights and just compensation based on personal relationships.[53] Similar complaints arose in 1856 against Indian Agent H. Gilbert's implementation of the "half-breed" provisions of the 1855 treaty. George Johnston, mixed-blood interpreter and sometime Indian Department employee, accused Gilbert of failing to ensure the appropriate disbursement of monies and land. According to Johnston, the agent had abused his authority by awarding "favored half-breeds" while rejecting the just claims of others.[54] Approximately six months after Johnston's initial complaint, Captain J. F. Marsac of Michigan informed J. Thompson, secretary of the Interior, that Gilbert refused to distribute treaty money to individuals unless they paid a quarter of it to his business partner G. D. Williams.[55] Although unproven, these accusations forced Gilbert to resign on May 30, 1857.[56] Despite Gilbert's resignation and the appointment of another agent, complaints continued to surface from the late 1850s to the twentieth century concerning various treaty distributions.[57]

During the 1850 negotiations in the British Sault, the Anishinaabe leadership sought the inclusion of the Métis within the treaty. William B. Robinson, however, simply denied their inclusion. The power of the state to determine people's rights was reinforced in 2003 when the Powley decision found that the Métis held Aboriginal rights under the terms of the 1982 Canadian Constitution (Chute 1998, 72–73, 142–43; *Sault Star* 2001).[58] In response to the failed inclusion of the Métis in 1850 negotiations, Shingwaukonse and other chiefs on the North Shore invited trusted Métis to join their communities. BNA negotiator William Robinson was aware of this inclusion when drawing up the treaty lists, as were subsequent Indian agents. Within a decade government representatives sought to strike "Métis" families from the communities based on visual cues (i.e., they looked too white) as well as through the development and application of various laws that defined who was a "treaty" or "status" Indian from 1851 to the modern day.

Such contemporary examples of effective control trace their antecedents to the middle decades of the nineteenth century, when settler definitions of identity increasingly became a means of state control.[59] Before the 1840s, the "Indian" portion of the Aboriginal

population appears to have been less subjected to attempted definition by outsiders. In the nineteenth century, the Sault's Indian population, depending on the observer, was usually referred to as Ojibwa
or Chippewa, Ojibway or Chippeway, and generically as Indian.
Those individuals defined as Indian by settlers generally lived in
wigwams or teepees, followed a seasonal lifestyle, and had a darker
complexion than those defined as Métis. In other words, individuals who fit the "preconceived generic constructions constituted by
Euro-American observers" were considered Indian (Wyss 1999, 63).

While the qualities that made one an Indian were based on observation, the state moved to begin defining and delimiting who its
Indians were. In other words, the state began to differentiate between
those living within its claimed territories and those without. For
instance, British authorities, based on desires to appease American
fears of interference with its Indians as well as the need for fiscal
restraint, restricted "gifts" to those Indians living within BNA borders by 1840 (Clifton 1975, 33–35, 53–54; Nichols 1998, 200; Bellfy
1995, 156–60). To determine eligible recipients, the British government developed three categories of Indians—"visiting," "resident," and "wandering." Individuals or bands classed as "visiting"
or "American" Indians were discouraged from remaining in Canada West and encouraged to return to the United States. "Resident"
or "Canadian" Indians referred to groups or individuals who had a
fixed or identifiable residence within BNA's borders. The people at
Garden River, for instance, qualified as resident Indians since they
had an identifiable village, even though they continued to exploit
the seasonal availability of resources by crossing and recrossing the
international border. Finally, Indians obviously resident in BNA but
who did not have a permanent or readily identifiable abode were
referred to as "wandering" Indians. The state through its agents
sought to settle these groups, thereby turning them into "resident"
Indians (Clifton 1975, 33–35). Likewise, U.S. authorities, at least in
the Sault area, developed British and American Indian classifica-
tions based upon precedents set by the treaties and observable residency patterns (McNab 1990, 92–93; Lovisek 2001, 281–82). This
initial identification, while serving some state purposes, was not
entirely useful when it came to determining who may or may not

have had rights to a particular territory or benefit from a treaty—thus more refined definitions were needed.

Annuities promised with the signing of the 1850 Robinson-Huron and Robinson-Superior treaties forced Canada West to develop a definition of *Indian*. Under the terms of the treaty, the annuity paid to every band member would only decrease should a band's population decline ("No. 61 [Robinson-Huron Treaty]" [1891] 1992, 150). The clause, based upon the premise that the Anishinaabe throughout the treaty area would either assimilate or disappear, appeared to government negotiators as a method to reduce their financial responsibilities in the long term. When it became apparent that the bands were increasing in size, Indian Affairs decided to reduce band numbers. To achieve this end, investigations commenced to determine who did and did not belong on band lists. Many Aboriginal people received the label of "White," "little Indian blood," and "American Indians," which resulted in their exclusion from band rolls.[60] Those deemed American Indians, either by assumed residency in U.S. claimed territory or because they had accepted U.S. treaty annuities, were struck from BNA band lists. Stories circulating within the Garden River community talked of government agents looking for those who appeared white and striking their names off band roles, forcing these newly created "non-Indians" to leave the reserve. Entire families traveled up the Root, Garden, or Echo Rivers to hide until these agents left the community.[61] Despite Anishinaabe protests, government efforts regularly reduced official band population numbers. The various investigations into the status of Garden River Band members resulted in the loss of more than two hundred individuals in the late 1850s, 1860s, and 1870s (Nichols 1998, 175, 190–94; Chute 1998, 177–79).

Specifically, in 1850 the Act for the Better Protection of the Land and Property of the Indians of Lower Canada defined the term *Indian* and membership in a band for the first time. The 1850 definition, considered too broad by British-Canadian authorities, was amended in 1851 to exclude non-Indians living among the Indians and non-Indians married to Indian women that same year. Indian women married to non-Indians retained their status while their offspring were declared non-Indian. The amendment also created the concepts of "status Indians," those officially registered with the government, and "non-status Indians," those not registered. Descent under the 1851 act would be determined through the male line only.[62] Both Canada West's Gradual Enfranchisement Act of 1857 and the newly created Dominion of Canada's 1869 Act of the Gradual Enfranchisement of Indians continued to tinker with the definition of *Indian*. With the passage of the Indian Act in 1876, the definition of *Indian* and *band membership* focused on blood quantum and the male line, both of which remained in place until 1951 and 1985 respectively.[63] Interestingly, by basing Indian status on blood quantum, the Canadian government made an assumption that Indians in 1876 were pure bloods, thus ignoring centuries of interactions with fur traders and their employees. Many "Indians" in the Sault region were of mixed ancestry, including the famous Garden River First Nation Chief Shingwaukonse. Hence, applying blood quantum to "Indians" in 1876 was based on assumptions as well as visual cues by outside observers.

From 1884 to the 1970s the minister of Indian Affairs had the power to forcibly enfranchise individuals who appeared "white"– some of the markers included such mutables as skin color, education levels, or "acting like a Canadian" by serving in the military or purchasing land in fee simple. While the 1985 amendments to the Indian Act claimed to make the passing of Indian status gender neutral, the new laws continued to discriminate against those who married out as well as those who voluntarily or involuntarily enfranchised (Sprague 1995; Grammond 2009). Simply, the descendants of those who were enfranchised under the pre-1985 Indian Act's rules were given a lesser status than those who had not been enfranchised. As such, the discrimination was merely moved a generation forward. Changes to the Indian Act in 2012 allowed the descendants of women who lost their status at the time of marriage to be registered at a higher status, thereby leaving voluntary and involuntary enfranchisees' descendants with a lesser status (INAC 2016). The alterations of 2012 are unlikely to be the last changes to Indian status, as the Liberal government under the leadership of Prime Minister Justin Trudeau has hinted at making overarching changes to the Canadian-Indian relationship, which includes how status is defined (Palmater 2016). The Supreme Court of Canada (SCOC) in 2016 further complicated the issue of status, non-status, and Métis by declaring that for the purposes of the Canadian Constitution under section 91 (24), which grants the federal government legislative powers over Indians, Métis and non-status Indians are or were included when the constitution was originally framed in 1867 (SCOC 2016). While the decision does not alter the Indian Act's definition of *status*, the SCOC as an organ of the state sought to redefine *Indian* in a way that will have repercussions throughout the status Indian community. As such, by making Indians legible to the state, the population could now be effectively administered and assimilated through policy and law (Manzano-Munguía 2011, 404–26). These legislative definitions proved useful in the continual removal of "Métis" or "non-status Indians" from the Garden River and Batchawana band lists into the twenty-first century.

Under government pressure, identities in the borderlands could be difficult to maintain. For example, Piabetassung's and his followers' residency in both Canada and the United States resulted in the band's demise. This band resided on Sugar Island, Michigan, and on the east side of the mouth of Garden River, Canada West. After signing both the 1850 BNA and 1855 U.S. treaties, Piabetassung and his followers accepted annuity payments and government largesse from both states (Cleland 2001, 27, 35–36). Canada West officials declared Piabetassung's band "American Indians," after learning the group had accepted U.S. treaty payments. The United States in turn used the band's acceptance of Canadian annuities to deny them recognition in Michigan. This convergence of U.S. and BNA definitions of *Indian* that did not include dual residency tore the group apart, resulting in former band members blending into the "recognized" groups on both shores or leaving the area (Chute 1998, 171, 177–78).

Identity laws also affected families and individuals. Observers identified Pierre Lavoine (Tegoosh) as Métis due to his adoption of a more sedentary and farming lifestyle, as well as the fact that he resided in a house. After the creation of an annuity list in association with the 1850 Robinson-Huron Treaty, Tegoosh redefined himself and his family as Indian. Despite being Shingwaukonse's son and self-defined as Indian, the Tegoosh family was later removed from the reserve.[64] Finally, the reliance on Indian status as defined by one's connection to an adult male forced dozens of women from the British-Canadian Sault Anishinaabe community when they married non-Indians or American Indians (Hele 2016). Similarly, under the Canadian Indian Act individuals who resided in the United States for five years permanently lost band membership and treaty rights (Venne 1981, 58, 110, 179, 249).[65] Yet if these British or Canadian Indians had 50 percent blood from a single tribal group, they could be recognized as American Indians. The migration of American Indians into Canada saw these individuals "un-become" Indian once in BNA, unless these Indians' parents had been born in Canada, unless they were eligible for or had status, and unless a request was made to and approved by the Indian Department to have the migrants' names added to the band list. The continued effective control of "status" membership by the Canadian government continues. Modifications undertaken to "fix" gender discrimination in regard to status in 1985 and again in 2012, while beneficial to Canada's Indian communities, also serve to highlight government control of community membership, lands, resources, and monies.[66]

## Conclusion

Since it is the purpose of my work to discuss the underlying interactions and experiences occurring around the Sault region as it transitioned from colonial to national rule, the definitions are themselves indicative of the complex fluctuating interrelationships between Anishinaabe, missionaries, and government authorities. Nonetheless, under the terms of the Canadian and American treaties and legislation, identity became an increasingly rigid feature of life in the region. Yet gradual solidification of meaning through Canadian or American legislation did little to freeze community understandings of belonging initially. Issues of membership and self-identification were and remain a highly contested topic within First Nations communities across Canada.[67] Consequently, "kinship and its associated economic responsibilities clashed repeatedly with the Indian agent's [read: state's] determination to delimit cultural identity by blood, residence, and political clout" (Genser 1998, 46). Regardless, it is the willingness and assumed ability of the colonial and then the national authorities to create definitions of legibility that, with the treaty and legislative acts, illustrate the effects on the Aboriginal populations as settler colonies transitioned to settler-nations.

In 2003 the idea of "effective control" entered the vocabulary of the Canadian legal process for determining Métis and Aboriginal rights. This decision, while ignoring the cross-border nature of the Sault Métis, focused on the issue of when exactly the transition to settler control took place. In making the 1850 treaties the signpost of the transition, the Canadian Supreme Court added fuel to the nationalizing myth that all treaties gave settlers and their governments control. The nature, security, and durability of effective control, albeit affected by the international border as well as the subject of Canadian or American nationhood, remain debatable. A determination of effective control, like a line drawn upon the water, ebbs and flows upon closer examination. It is easily erased and rewritten. Simply, effective control remains a contestable feature of life in Canada. Despite the esoteric nature of the debate surrounding concepts of nationhood and effective control, it is obvious that the transitioning states failed to gain effective control of the region until at least the end of the nineteenth century, while the control of the population remained an ongoing challenge well into the twentieth century. And, for Canada at least, the process of nation building is far from complete. Nonetheless, by making the indigenous population legible, both the BNA and Canada and United States were able to exercise policies that gave them the effective control over a region and its people. While these controls have never been complete or uncontested, the ability to determine membership in one's community was and remains a key aspect of state control that continues to divide the Aboriginal community along the borderlands.

## Notes

1. For key works on the Settler shift and their sense of identity and nation, see Berger 1969; Berger 1970; and Greer and Radforth 1992.

2. "[Census of] Sault Ste. Marie Indians, Nos. taken 24 July 1832," RG 10, Vol. 621, 400, Library and Archives Canada (LAC); "Statistical Table of Indian population comprised within the boundaries of the consolidated Agency of Sault Ste. Marie and Michilimackinac in the year 1832 . . ." Sault Ste. Marie Agency, 1824–41, 137, Sault Ste.

Marie Agency Records; American Fur Company Records, Miscellaneous Items, Sault Ste. Marie Collections, Clark Historical Library (CHL), Central Michigan University.

3. Seasonal movements allowed the Anishinaabe to take advantage of fish, maple sugar runs, caribou herds, and many other plant and animal life for centuries. For instance, Sugar Island draws its name from the rich maple groves once found there; Garden River, Pumpkin Point, and Root River refer to planting and trading of pumpkin, cord, and beans; and Whitefish Point alludes to excellent fishing grounds.

4. A factor in the HBC was in charge of a district and its key post. The factors, or chief factors, were entitled to a share in the profits from the district and met in council with the governor of the HBC.

5. George Johnston Memorandum Book, 1817, 1826, Reminiscences by George Johnston, Box 1, George Johnston Papers, 1792–1851, American Fur Company Papers, Sault Ste. Marie Collection, CHL.

6. For more information on the British occupation of Drummond Island, see Cook (1896) 1997; Brumwell 2003.

7. Lewis Cass to H. R. Schoolcraft, April 7, 1822, Sault Ste. Marie Agency Records, Letters Received, Volume 1, April 7, 1822–November 23, 1826, 1–3, Records of the Michigan Superintendency of Indian Affairs, CHL.

8. For information on the 1815 and 1816 incidents, see George Johnston Memorandum Book 1817, 1826, Reminiscences by George Johnston.

9. Cleland 1992, 183–86; Cleland 2001, 16–19; Gutshe, Chisholm, and Floren 1997, 259–61; Lewis (1932) 2000; and Williams 1992, 503.

10. Return from Fort Brady, Michigan, June 1822, Fort Brady, Mich., June 1822–December 1841, Returns from U.S. Military Posts, 1800–1916, U.S. National Archives.

11. Bieder (1999, 4) likewise notes that presence of troops was more than a population boom. Unfortunately, he assumes that the mere stationing of troops in the Sault meant the collapse of Anishinaabe independence.

12. H. R. Schoolcraft to Lewis Cass, 12 July 1822, Sault Ste. Marie Agency Records, Letters Sent, July 12, 1822–May 2, 1833, 1–2, Records of the Michigan Superintendency of Indian Affairs, CHL.

13. Circular, Schoolcraft, Indian Agent, to George Johnston, Elijah B. Allen &c., May 5, 1823, Sault Ste. Marie Agency Records, Letters Sent, July 12, 1822–May 2, 1833, 27–28, CHL.

14. For instance, see H. R. Schoolcraft to Lewis Cass, July 18, 1822, 5–7; Schoolcraft to John H. Paton, Secretary of War, August 7, 1829, Letters Sent, July 12, 1822–May 2, 1833: 246–48, Sault Ste. Marie Agency Records, Volume 1, May 7, 1816–November 1, 1831, Letters received by the Agent at Mackinac, Records of the Michigan Superintendency of Indian Affairs, 1814–1851, CHL.

15. W. McMurray, Sault Ste. Marie, to Colonel James Givens, CSIA, Toronto, January 10, 1837: 62455; McMurray to Col. Givens, February 13, 1837, 62650–3; McMurray to Col. Givens, March 14, 1837, 62828–30, Chief Superintendent's Office, Upper Canada (Col. J. Givens), Correspondence, January 1837–March 31, 1837, RG 10, vol. 64, LAC; F. Audrain to H. R. Schoolcraft, June 21, 1834, Letters Received by the Agent at Macki-

nac, vol. 2, May 1, 1833–December 29, 1834, 364, Records of the Michigan Superintendency of Indian Affairs, 1814–1854, CHL.

16. For instance, see Ruggles 1990, 680–81; Hele 1997, 159; and Hele 2003, 171–286.

17. Sir F. B. Head served as lieutenant governor of Upper Canada from 1835 to 1838. Read 1900, 153–91; Martin 1981a, 3–18; Martin 1981b, 145–70; Wise 1972, 342–45; Nichols 1998, 190–94; Harring 1998, 30–31.

18. For more information, see Greer 1993; Senior 1985; Labelle 2011; Read 1988; Dunning 2009, 129–41.

19. Dunning 1999, 109–21; Barry 1989, 75–89; Mount 1989, 32–36; Duffy and Muller 1974, 153–69.

20. Johnston, Memorandum Book 1817, 1826.

21. J. Ord, subagent, to H. R. Schoolcraft, April 26, 1838; Ord to H. R. Schoolcraft, March 5, 1838, vol. 4, January–June 1838, 253, 137–41, Records of the Michigan Superintendency of Indian Affairs Michigan Superintendent and Mackinac Agent, CHL.

22. J. Ord to H. R. Schoolcraft, September 1, 1838, vol. 5, July–December 1838, 176, Records of the Michigan Superintendency of Indian Affairs Michigan Superintendent and Mackinac Agent, CHL; Hele 2003, 107; Hele 2008, 76–77.

23. For instance, see J. Ord, SSM, to H. R. Schoolcraft, Mackinac, September 1, 1838, 175–77, Letters Received, 1836–51; H. R. Schoolcraft to C. A. Harris, Comm. Ind. Affairs, War Dept, Washington, August 29, 1837, 299–300; H. R. Schoolcraft to C. A. Harris, October 30, 1837, 351–52; H. R. Schoolcraft to Mason, Gov. Michigan, December 26, 1837, 385–87; H. R. Schoolcraft to C. A. Harris, Comm. Ind. Affairs, September 30, 1838, 560–61; H. R. Schoolcraft to C. A. Harris, October 4, 1838, 567–73, Letters Sent, 1836–51, Michigan Superintendent and the Mackinac Agency, CHL. See also Clifton 1979, 3–6, 22, 25.

24. Federal and military court records for this early period remain unexamined simply because they could not be located. County court records, if found, would have been useful in determining local issues surrounding the Métis community. As such, this conclusion is based upon an examination of numerous documents from the U.S. Indian agency as well as missionary reports. The only recorded instance of an Anishinaabeg in a legal case involved Shegud when his fishing boat was stolen in 1837 by soldiers attempting to desert. Additionally, based on the documents it is unclear whether or not Shegud appeared in military court. Once the court records are located, assuming they still exist, these conclusions may change and the unanswered questions answered. For the details of Shegud's case, see James Ord, subagent, to H. R. Schoolcraft, November 16, 1837; oath, Geo. Johnston, to H. R. Schoolcraft (?), November 11, 1837; oath, John M. Hulbert, November 11, 1837, vol. 3: August–December 1837, 487–93; and J. Ord to H. R. Schoolcraft, January 4, 1838, 9; J. Ord to H. R. Schoolcraft, June 5, 1838, 363, vol. 4, January–June 1838, 9, 363, Letters Received, 1836–51, Records of the Michigan Superintendency of Indian Affair Michigan Superintendent and Mackinac Agent, CHL.

25. For more information on mining activities, see Telford 1996; Chute 1998; Murphy (1987) 1990.

26. The colonies of Upper and Lower Canada were bound together in 1841 through the Act of Union. With the creation of the United Canadas, Upper Canada became Can-

ada West and Lower Canada became Canada East. The Act of Union did not contain any sections dealing with the Indians or Métis bounded within its claimed territory.

27. For more information, see Chute 1998, 106–59; Telford 1996, 117–220.

28. "Chippewa Indians" 1849, 287, 286–90; [Shingwaukonse and Nebenagoching's Montreal Statement] 1849; Chute 1998, 122–24.

29. While neither man directly referenced the terra nullius doctrine, their arguments that the Anishinaabe migrated to the region that was "empty" before their arrival implies its application as a justification for Canada West's illegal issuance of mining leases on unsurrendered land.

30. According to Janet Chute in *The Legacy* (1998) there were many more parties, including the *Globe*, who claimed that the Anishinaabe were squatters with no claims and that the Métis were the true agitators. See Montgomerie 1993, 214; "In Council," October 10, 1845, RG 10, vol. 712, 22, LAC; Hele 2008.

31. Drafts of Letters and Reports by Rev. G. Anderson, Sault and Garden River; T. G. Anderson, Coburg, to Son, Gustavus, Sault Ste. Marie, July 24, 1848, T. G. Anderson Papers, Toronto Reference Library; Hele 1994, 47; Telford 1996, 139–43; Chute 1998, 119–21.

32. Alexander Vidal to Catherine Vidal, October 17, 1849, Box 4437, Vidal Family Correspondence, Western University, Ontario.

33. Chute 1998, 132–33, 167; J. Ord to Charles P. Babcock, November 15, 1849, Letters Received by the Superintendent and Indian Agent at Mackinac, 1836–1851, vol. 23: April–December 1849: 359, CHL.

34. For an example of a violent act committed by the troops, see entry January 8, 1850, Journal 5, August 1844–October 1864, Rev. A. Bingham Papers, CHL.

35. Under international law or precedent, a particular state or colony was not supposed to negotiate or sign treaties with Indians not resident within the state or colonial borders. Simply, American Indians were not supposed to participate in BNA treaties nor were British Indians supposed to sign or participate in American Indian treaties. For a larger discussion of the borderland nature of treaties in the Sault and Lake Huron regions, see Hele 2016b and Bellfy 2011.

36. Letter (G145), H. C. Gilbert, Indian Agent for Michigan, Detroit, to G. W. Manypenny, Commissioner of Indian Affairs, July 4, 1853, Folder Mackinac 1853, A169-G173: 66–68, Mackinac Agency, 1828–1880, CHL.

37. The Sault Tribe regained federal recognition in 1972.

38. Jean M. Kelley's presentation, "U.S. Bad Faith: Chippewa Treaty Negotiations; 1855, 1856, and 1889," at the Third International Native American Studies Conference at Lake Superior State University, October 1991, ably illustrated how the American government failed to fulfill its treaty promises in the Upper Lakes region.

39. Letter (G48), H. C. Gilbert, Indian Agent to G. Manypenny, Commissioner of Indian Affairs, March 11, 1856, Folder, Mackinac 1856, A36-G90, 80–81, Mackinac Agency, 1828–1880, CHL.

40. "Report of Special Agent to visit the Indian Reservation with accompanying papers" (A361), H. J. Abrod, Special Agent, to L. V. Bogy, Commissioner of Indian Affairs, November 16, 1866. Folder, Mackinac 1866, A36-L213½, 852–68, Michigan Superintendent and the Mackinac Agency, CHL.

41. Letter (A251), Edward Ashmun, Interpreter, SSM, to N. G. Taylor, Commissioner of Indian Affairs, September 19, 1867, Folder Mackinac 1867, A29-F26, 25–26, Mackinac Agency, 1828–1880, CHL.

42. Letter (S411), Richard M. Smith, Indian Agent, to N. G. Taylor, Commissioner of Indian Affairs, December 2, 1867, Folder Mackinac 1867, S51-W514, 322–28; Letter (S58), Richard M. Smith, Indian Agent, to N. G. Taylor, Commissioner of Indian Affairs, January 16, 1869, Folder Mackinac 1869, M386-W675, 944–47, Mackinac Agency, 1822–1880, CHL.

43. Letter (O49), Chiefs of the Sault Ste. Marie Bands to H. R. Clum, October 12, 1871, Folder Mackinac 1871, L108-O79, Mackinac Agency, 1828–1880, CHL.

44. Letter (O25), Oshawano and others to the Secretary of the Interior, July 5, 1875, Folder Mackinac 1875, I75-W1139, 538–39, Mackinac Agency, 1828–1880, CHL.

45. The establishment of the community appears to date from approximately 1843. Before that the majority of the Métis lived between Ermatinger's estate and the HBC post, which is now downtown Sault Ste. Marie, Ontario. Jameson (1838) 1990, 449; Mount, Abbott, and Mulloy 1995, 12; Heath 1988, 57; and Gutsche, Chisholm, and Floren 1997, 272–73. Also see Powley Case Reports 2013.

46. Overall, the entire question of Métis land loss and theft by settlers needs to be further explored. One article begins the process of untangling the web of ownership for Sault Michigan and legal claims in Sault Ontario promise to add further to the picture of Métis property holdings. See Schenck 2002, 109–20. An exploration of the Ermatinger land claim would be useful in answering this question, for instance see "In Council," June 4, 1847, record by J[?]. Joseph, vol. 710; Joseph Nebenagoching and three other Chiefs of Lake Superior on behalf of the children of Charles O. Ermatinger, January 17, 1851, vol. 119, 728–29; Order-in-Council on the Petition of Charlotte Kattawabide, August 11, 1849, RG 10, vol. 119. 705–6; and Power of Attorney, October 11, 1856, Barbeau Letters, 1855–1858, Box 2, Peter B. Barbeau Papers, American Fur Company Papers, Sault Ste. Marie Collection, CHL.

47. Tina Loo's *Making Law, Order, and Authority* (1994) discusses how various legislative acts, orders, and the creation of an "unbiased" judiciary were developed to ensure orderly development of the colony. While her study is far removed from the Sault, the context of the arguments and observations about the imposition of "White Man's Law" remain valid. For a study of the imposition of law in Ontario, see Harring 1998.

48. See paragraphs III and V of an Act for the Protection of the Indians in Upper Canada (1850); Hele 2011, 19–20; Murphy and Manore n.d., 16–17; and Surtees 1988, 81–95.

49. For the various amendments to the Indian Act since 1876, see Venne 1981.

50. An Act to Further Amend the "Indian Act, 1880," SC 1882, c.30 (45Vict); and the Indian Advancement Act, 1884, SC 1884, c.28 (47 Vict), in Venne 1988, 91–101, 102–6.

51. Genser 1998, 35; White 1997, 405, 418; Kupperman 1997, 193. See also Stone and Chaput 1978, 608; Brown 1975, 217; Mumford 1999, 15–16; Mumford 2000, 38–45.

52. The usage of the term *parole* reflects a sixteenth- and seventeenth-century ritual originating from France's presence in the region. The 1836 document, while retaining the name *parole*, is a complaint with an attached list of signatures and hence closer to the modern conception of a petition.

53. "Parole" from ssm Chippewa (carried by P. Cadotte) to Andrew Jackson, November 13, 1836, regarding March 28, 1836, treaty payments, Letters Received, Office of Indian Affairs, Sault Ste. Marie Subagency, 1824–41, 185–86, Michigan Superintendency Records, CHL; George Ermatinger, ssm to James Ermatinger, October 5, 1836, Ermatinger Family Papers; George Johnston, ssm, to Schoolcraft, sia, Detroit, March 28, 1837, PR Mss Indian Mss no. 3 MU 4642, Archives of Ontario; Charlotte McMurray to Jane Schoolcraft, June 3, 1836, r24, c41, prt1, 14291; Power of Attorney, September 7, 1836, r25, c41, prt 2, 14554, Schoolcraft Papers; Schoolcraft to C. A. Harris, Comm. Ind. Affairs, October 30, 1837, Michigan Superintendent and Mackinac Agent, Letters Sent, 1836–51, vol. 1, July 18, 1836–June 26, 1839, 351–52; Kewenzy Shawwana, Chief of the Sault, to Schoolcraft, October 11, 1836, Michigan Superintendent and the Mackinac Agency, Letters Received, 1836–1851, vol. 1: July–December 1836, 338; Letter (C224) Major W. V. Cobbs, Subagent and Fort Commander, ssm, to C. A. Harris, Commissioner of Indian Affairs, Washington, February 13, 1837; Letter (C244), Major Cobbs to C. A. Harris, March 26, 1837, Folder 1837, A36-G129, 424–28, 431–45; Letter (S430) Schoolcraft to C. A. Harris, Comm. of Ind. Affairs, War Department, July 24, 1837, Folder 1837, S200-S553, 701–11, Michigan Superintendency, 1824–1831, Letters Received by the Office of Indian Affairs, 1824–1881, CHL; and Brazer 1993, 267. Mumford (1999, 14–15) refers to how Schoolcraft hid grants of land on Sugar Island to his wife and child by using their Anishinaabe names. The U.S. Senate eventually rejected the allocation of lands to all mixed-bloods.

54. Letter (J320), G. Johnston to Robert McClelland, Secretary of the Interior, September 17, 1856, Folder Mackinac 1856, G114-L191, 270–73, Mackinac Agency, 1828–1880, CHL.

55. Letter (T533), Isaac D. Toll, Apt. Exe. Patents, to J. Thompson, Secretary of the Interior, April 9, 1857, Folder Mackinac 1857, G260-W413, 722–24, Mackinac Agency, 1828–1880, CHL.

56. Letter (J533), J. (?), secretary to J. W. Denver, Commissioner of Indian Affairs, May 11, 1857, Folder Mackinac 1857, G260-W413, 707–23, Mackinac Agency, 1828–1880, CHL.

57. Letter (J646), W. M. Johnston, Michilimackinac, to G. Manypenny, Commissioner of Indian Affairs, August 27 1857; Letter (W282), S. P. Wright to Robert McClelland, Secretary of the Interior, February 5, 1857, Folder Mackinac 1857, G260-W413, 730–33, 782–801; Letter (F363), A. Fetch, Indian Agent, to J. W. Denver, Commissioner of Indian Affairs, January 26, 1856, Folder Mackinac 1859, B787-F443, 304–5, Mackinac Agency, 1828–1880, CHL; and Cleland 1992, 236–37.

58. In 2016 the Supreme Court of Canada ruled that the Métis population of Canada, while not Indians, fall under the exclusive federal power to legislate for Indians under section 91(24) of the Canadian constitution. This ruling does not place the Métis under the Indian Act, nor does it give or recognize any existing Aboriginal or Treaty rights for the Métis. *Daniels v. Canada* (Indian Affairs and Northern Development), 2016 SCC 12, accessed January 14, 2018, https://scc-csc.lexum.com/scc-csc/scc-csc/en/item/15858/index.do.

59. For a greater discussion of Indian policy for both BNA and United States, see McNab 1983, 85–103; Milloy 1990, 39–55; Tobias 1990, 29–38; Chute 1998; Dippie 1982;

Prucha 1996; Neumeyer 1968; Nichols 1998, 174–205; Dickason 2002, 209–15; Cleland 1992, 164–263; Surtees 1988, 81–95.

60. See "Names of heads of families excluded by the Garden River Band in 1858, the majority of them being considered American Indians," Indian File, Blanchard Papers, Archives of Ontario. According to oral tradition, the exclusions were undertaken by government agents against band wishes.

61. For instance, see Indian File, Blanchard Papers, which contains lists compiled by George Ironside, SIA, in 1859 and 1860. These lists detail who was Indian and Métis as well as who belonged to the Garden River and Sault Ste. Marie Bands.

62. An Act to Repeal in Part and to Amend an Act 1851; Dickason 2002, 228–33; Milloy 1990, 62–63; Surtees 1988, 89–91.

63. See Dickason 2002, 263–65, 313–14; also, see the various Indian acts and amendments in Venne 1981; and Isaac 1993.

64. Sault Ste. Marie—Correspondence regarding Inspector A. Dingman's inquiry relative to a land dispute between the Garden River Band and the Tegosh family, 1892, RG10, box 2649, file 131,221. *Tegosh* or *Tegoosh* is also a short form of *Wametegooshe* or *Frenchman*. Wilson (1874) 1975, 240.

65. For instance, see Garden River Agency—Correspondence regarding the proposed admission of certain families to the Garden River Band, RG10, vol. 2208, file 41, 992, LAC; and Sault Ste. Marie—Garden River Reserve—William Van Abbott reports his payment of annuities to the children of Indian women married out of the band, RG10, vol. 1992, file 6808, LAC.

66. For a discussion concerning state control of identity, see Grammond 2009. Whether one has "status" or not is determined under the definitions of *Indian* under the terms of the Indian Act and affects community membership, access to lands, resources, and monies.

67. These categories, since the creation of "racial" legislation in the United States and Canada that defined who is and is not an Indian, are still debated within the local Métis, Anishinaabe, and settler communities. In the Michigan Sault, settlers regularly complain that the Indians are more French than Indian. In the Ontario Sault, settlers regularly comment that Indians from the Batchawana and Garden River Bands are not really true Indians because they have married or have had children with settlers. In the Canadian Indian community, families are sometimes divided over the issue of Bill C-31 and Bill C-3 amendments to status definitions. Essentially, some argue that women who married out are not really Indian, while others maintain that this categorization of ins and outs is based on settler society's colonial desire to destroy the Indian and usurp the land. In the United States, debates surround who is in and out based on whether or not an individual is related to the charter group. The charter group comprises individuals listed under the 1820, 1826, 1838, and 1855 Indian treaties. Nonetheless, individuals' and families' lives in Aboriginal communities are not affected on a daily basis by questions of membership. These questions only flare into the open during periods of stress. Many settlers, however, see this as an ongoing issue and regularly contest the use of status cards and other visible signs of Indianness.

# Bibliography

Adelman, Jeremy, and Stephen Aron. 1999. "From Borderlands to Borders: Empires, Nation-States, and the Peoples In Between in North American History." *American Historical Review* 104, no. 3: 815–16.

An Act for the Better Protection of the Lands and Property of the Indians in Lower Canada, S. Prov. C. 1850, c.42. 1993. In *Pre-1868 Legislation Concerning Indians: A Selected and Indexed Collection*, edited by Thomas Isaac, 40–41. Saskatoon: Native Law Centre, University of Saskatchewan.

An Act for the protection of the Indians in Upper Canada from imposition, and the property occupied or enjoyed by them from trespass and injury, S. Prov. C. 1850, c.74. 1993. In *Pre-1868 Legislation Concerning Indians: A Selected and Indexed Collection*, edited by Thomas Isaac, 42–46. Saskatoon: Native Law Centre, University of Saskatchewan.

An Act to repeal in part and to amend an Act, entitled "An Act for the 'Better Protection of the Lands and Property of the Indians in Lower Canada.'" 1851. 14 and 15 Vic., no. 268. Toronto: Lovell and Gibson.

Arthur, Elizabeth. 1988. "Beyond Superior: Ontario's New-Found Land." In *Patterns of the Past: Interpreting Ontario's History*, edited by Roger Hall, William Westfall, and Laurel S. MacDowell, 130–49. Toronto: Oxford University Press.

Barry, James P. 1989. "U.S.-Canadian Frictions along the Great Lakes–St. Lawrence Border." *Inland Seas* 45, no. 2: 75–89.

Bellfy, Philip C. 1995. *Division and Unity, Dispersal and Permanence: The Anishinabeg of the Lake Huron Borderlands*. PhD diss., Michigan State University.

———. 2011. *Three Fires Unity: The Anishinaabeg of the Lake Huron Borderlands*. Lincoln: University of Nebraska Press.

Berger, Carl, ed. 1969. *Imperialism and Nationalism, 1884–1914: A Conflict in Canadian Thought*. Toronto: Copp Clark.

———. 1970. *The Sense of Power: Studies in the Ideas of Canadian Imperialism, 1867–1914*. Toronto: University of Toronto Press.

Bieder, Robert E. 1999. "Sault Ste. Marie and the War of 1812: A World Turned Upside Down in the Old Northwest." *Indiana Magazine of History* 95 (March): 1–13.

Brazer, Marjorie Cahn. 1993. *Harps upon the Willows: The Johnston Family of the Old Northwest*. Ann Arbor: Historical Society of Michigan.

Brown, Jennifer. 1975. "Fur Traders, Racial Categories, and Kinship Networks." In *Papers of the Sixth Algonquian Conference*, edited by William Cowan, 209–22. Ottawa: National Museum of Man.

Brumwell, Jill Lowe. 2003. *Drummond Island: History, Folklore, and Early People*. Saginaw: Black Bear Press.

Capp, Edward H. 1904. *The Annals of Sault Sainte Marie*. Sault Ste. Marie: Sault Star Presses.

"The Chippewa Indians and the Huron Lake Mining Companies." 1849. *The Colonial Intelligencer; or, Aborigines Friend* 18 and 19 (October/November): 286–90.

Chute, Janet. 1998. *The Legacy of Shingwaukonse: A Century of Native Leadership*. Toronto: University of Toronto Press.

Cleland, Charles E. 1992. *Rites of Conquest: The History and Culture of Michigan's Native Americans*. Ann Arbor: University of Michigan Press.

———. 2001. *The Place of the Pike (Gnoozhekaaning): A History of the Bay Mills Indian Community*. Ann Arbor: University of Michigan Press.

Clifton, James A. 1975. *A Place of Refuge for all Time: Migration of the American Potawatomi into Upper Canada 1830 to 1850*. Ottawa: National Museum of Man.

———. 1979. "'Visiting Indians' in Canada." Manuscript for a booklet to be issued by Fort Malden National Historical Park, Parks Canada.

Cook, Samuel F. (1896) 1997. *Drummond Island: The Story of the British Occupation, 1815–1828*. UMI Books on Demand.

"Court of Appeal Upholds Landmark Ruling on Rights of Métis." 2014. *CBC News: Aboriginal*. www.cbc.ca/news/aboriginal/court-of-appeal-upholds-landmark -ruling-on-rights-of-m%C 3%a9tis-1.2613834, accessed May 8, 2014.

Dickason, Olive Patricia. 2002. *Canada's First Nations: A History of Founding Peoples from Earliest Times*. 3rd ed. Toronto: Oxford University Press.

Dippie, Brian W. 1982. *The Vanishing American: White Attitudes and U.S. Indian Policy*. Lawrence: University of Kansas Press.

Duffy, John, and H. Nicholas Muller. 1974. "The Great Wolf Hunt: The Popular Response in Vermont to the *Patriote* Uprising of 1837." *Journal of American Studies* 8, no. 2: 153–69.

Dunning, Thomas P. 2009. "The Canadian Rebellions of 1837 and 1838 as a Borderland War: A Retrospective." *Ontario History* 101, no. 2: 129–41.

———. 1999. "The Adventures of Patriot Hunters: Danger, Memory, Place, and Virtue at the Windmill." *Canadian Review of American Studies* 29, no. 1: 109–21.

Genser, Wallace. 1998. "'Habitants,' 'Half-Breeds,' and Homeless Children: Transformation in Métis and Yankee-Yorker Relations in Early Michigan." *Michigan Historical Review* 24, no. 1: 23–47.

Grammond, Sébastien. 2009. *Identity Captured by Law: Membership in Canada's Indigenous Peoples and Linguistic Minorities*. Montreal: McGill-Queen's University Press.

Greer, Allan. 1993. *The Patriots and the People: The Rebellion of 1837 in Rural Lower Canada*. Toronto: University of Toronto Press.

Greer, Allan, and Ian Radforth, eds. 1992. *Colonial Leviathan: State Formation in Mid-Nineteenth-Century Canada*. Toronto: University of Toronto Press.

Gutsche, Andrea, Barbara Chisholm, and Russel Floren. 1997. *The North Channel and St. Mary's River*. Toronto: Lynx Images.

Hansen, Lise C. 1987. "Chiefs and Principle Men: A Question of Leadership in Treaty Negotiations." *Anthropologica* 29: 39–60.

Harring, Sidney. 1998. *White Man's Law: Native People in Nineteenth-Century Canadian Jurisprudence*. Toronto: University of Toronto Press.

Heath, Frances M. 1988. *Sault Ste. Marie: City by the Rapids*. Windsor: Windsor Publications.

Hele, Karl S. 1994. "'Only Calculated to Captivate the Senses': Protestant Missionary Experience of Garden River First Nation." Master's thesis, University of Toronto.

———. 1997. "'How to Win Friends and Influence People': Missions to Bawating, 1830–

1840." In *Historical Papers 1996: Canadian Society of Church History*, edited by Bruce L. Guenther, 155–76. Canadian Society of Church History.

———. 2003. "'By the Rapids': The Anishinabeg-Missionary Encounter at Bawating (Sault Ste. Marie), c. 1821–1871." PhD diss., McGill University.

———. 2005. "The Whirlwind of History: Parallel Nineteenth-Century Perspectives on 'Are They Savage.'" In *Walking a Tightrope: Aboriginal Perspectives and Their Representations*, edited by Ute Lischke and David T. McNab, 149–88. Waterloo: Wilfrid Laurier University Press.

———. 2008. "The Anishinabeg and Métis in the Sault Ste. Marie Borderlands: Confronting a Line Drawn upon the Water." In *Lines Drawn upon the Water: First Nations and the Great Lakes Borders and Borderlands*, edited by Karl S. Hele, 65–84. Waterloo: Wilfrid Laurier University Press.

———. 2011. *An Overview of Garden River First Nation's Lands*. Sault Ste. Marie: Cliffe Printing for the Garden River First Nation Community Trust.

———. 2016a. Introduction. In *This Is Indian Land: The 1850 Robinson Treaties*, edited by Karl S. Hele, vii–xxii. Winnipeg: Aboriginal Issues Press.

———. 2016b. "'Is It Marked in the Bible, that the English and American Should Draw a Line and Do What So He Pleases with the Natives?': The 1850 Treaty as an International Document." In *This Is Indian Land: The 1850 Robinson Treaties*, edited by Karl S. Hele, 93–138. Winnipeg: Aboriginal Issues Press.

———. 2016c. "One of the Dangers in Moving and Marrying into the United States." *Garden River Community Newsletter*.

———. 2016d. "The Robinson Treaties: A Brief Contextualization." In *This Is Indian Land: The 1850 Robinson Treaties*, edited by Karl S. Hele, 1–42. Winnipeg: Aboriginal Issues Press.

"The Indians on Lakes Huron and Superior: Proceedings of the Government Commissioners and the Indians in Councils (From a Correspondent)." 1849. *British Colonist* (Toronto). November 16.

Indigenous and Northern Affairs Canada. 2016. "McIvor v. Canada." Accessed July 4, 2016. www.aadnc-aandc.gc.ca/eng/1100100032433/1100100032434.

Isaac, Thomas, ed. 1993. *Pre-1868 Legislation Concerning Indians: A Selected & Indexed Collection*. Saskatoon: Native Law Centre, University of Saskatchewan.

Isaac, Thomas, ed. 2004. *Aboriginal Law: Commentary, Cases and Materials*. 3rd ed. Saskatoon: Purich Publishing.

Jameson, Anna Brownell. (1838) 1990. *Winter Studies and Summer Rambles in Canada*. Toronto: McClelland and Stewart.

Keating, William. 1849. "To the Editor of the Chatham Chronicle." *Chatham Chronicle*. August 15.

Kelly, Jean M. 1991. "U.S. Bad Faith: Chippewa Treaty Negotiations; 1855, 1856, and 1889." Manuscript presented at the Third International Native American Studies Conference at Lake Superior State University, October.

Kelton, Dwight H. 1889. *Indian Names and History of the Sault Ste. Marie Canal*. Detroit: Detroit Free Press.

Knight, Alan, and Chute, Janet E. 2006. "A Visionary on the Edge: Allan Macdonell and the Championing of Native Resource Rights." In *With Good Intentions: Euro-Canadian & Aboriginal Relations in Colonial Canada*, edited by Celia Haig-Brown and David A. Nock, 106–31. Vancouver: University of British Columbia Press.

Kupperman, Karen Ordahl. 1997. "Presentment of Civility: English Reading of American Self-Presentation in the Early Years of Colonization." *William and Mary Quarterly* 54, no. 1: 193–228.

Labelle, Marcel. 2011. *L'insurrection des Patriotes à Beauharnois en 1838: Une révolte oubliée*. Québec: Septentrion.

Lewis, Janet. (1932) 2000. *The Invasion*. East Lansing: Michigan State University Press.

Loo, Tina. 1994. *Making Law, Order, and Authority in British Columbia, 1821–1871*. Toronto: University of Toronto Press.

Lovisek, Joan. 2001. "The Ojibway vs. the Gerrymander: The Evolution of the Robinson Huron and William Treaties Boundaries." In *Actes du Trente-Deuxième Congrès des Algonquinistes*, edited by John D. Nichols, 278–303. Winnipeg: University of Manitoba Press.

Magnaghi, Russell. 1984. *A Guide to the Indians of Michigan's Upper Peninsula, 1621–1900*. Marquette: Belle Fontaine Press.

Manzano-Munguía, María Cristina. 2011. "Indian Policy and Legislation: Aboriginal Identity Survival in Canada." *Journal of Studies in Ethnicity and Nationalism* 11, no. 3: 404–2.

Martin, Ged. 1981a. "Self-Defence: Francis Bond Head and Canada, 1841–1870." *Ontario History* 73, no. 1: 3–18.

———. 1981b. "Sir Francis Bond Head: The Private Side of a Lieutenant Governor." *Ontario History* 73, no. 3: 145–70.

McNab, David T. 1983. "Herman Merivale and Colonial Office Indian Policy in the Mid-Nineteenth Century." In *As Long as the Sun Shines and Water Flows: A Reader in Canadian Native Studies*, edited by Ian A. L. Getty and Antoine S. Lussier, 85–103. Vancouver: University of British Columbia Press.

"Métis, non-status Indian ruling to be appealed: Higher judicial authority needed before major change, minister says." 2013. CBC.CA. February 6. Accessed February 18, 2013. www.cbc.ca/news/canada/story/2013/02/06/pol-metis-ruling-appeal.html.

"Métis handed 'massive victory': MNO." 2001. *Sault Star*. February 24. www.metisnation.org/pow/powsaultfeb1.html.

*The Métis Hunt for Justice: A Plainspeak of the Powley Decision*. 2000. Vancouver: Pape and Salter.

Milloy, John. 1990. "The Early Indian Acts: Developmental Strategy and Constitutional Change." In *As Long as the Sun Shines and Water Flows: A Reader in Canadian Native Studies*, edited by Ian A. L. Getty and Antoine S. Lussier, 39–55. Vancouver: University of British Columbia Press.

Montgomerie, Deborah Anne. 1993. "Coming to Terms: Ngai Tahu, Robeson County Indians and the Garden River Band of Ojibwa, 1840–1940: Three Studies of Colonialism in Action." PhD diss., Duke University.

Morris, Alexander. (1880) 1991. "Robinson Treaties [William B. Robinson's Report,

September 24, 1850]." In *The Treaties of Canada with the Indians of Manitoba and the North-West Territories including the Negotiations on which they were based, 1880*, 17–21. Saskatoon: Fifth House Publishing.

Morrison, James. 1996. *The Robinson Treaties of 1850: A Case Study*. Prepared for the Royal Commission on Aboriginal Peoples. Treaty and Land Research Section. Final Draft. August 31.

Mount, Graeme S. 1989. "Drums along the St. Mary's: Tensions on the International Border at Sault Ste. Marie." *Michigan History* 73, no. 4: 32–36.

Mount, Graeme S., John Abbott, and Michael J. Mulloy. 1995. *The Border at Sault Ste. Marie*. Toronto: Dundurn Press.

Mumford, Jeremy. 1999. "Mixed-Race Identity in a Nineteenth-Century Family: The Schoolcrafts of Sault Ste. Marie, 1824–27." *Michigan Historical Review* 25, no. 1: 1–23.

———. 2000. "Métis and the Vote in Nineteenth-Century America." *Journal of the West* 39, no. 3: 38–45.

Murphy, Mary-Lynn. (1987) 1990. Draft Research Report: "The Mining Locations of the Garden River Indian Reserve #14." Toronto: Ontario Native Affairs Secretariat, January 1987; revised by Jean Manore, May 1990.

Murphy, Mary-Lynn, and Manore, Jean. n.d. Draft Research Report: "Location of the External Boundaries of Garden River Indian Reserve #14." Toronto: Ontario Native Affairs Directorate.

Neumeyer, Elizabeth E. 1968. "Indian Removal in Michigan, 1833–1855." Master's thesis, Central Michigan University.

Nichols, Roger L. 1998. *Indians in the United States and Canada: A Comparative History*. Lincoln: University of Nebraska Press.

"No. 61. [Robinson-Huron Treaty (1850)]." (1891) 1992. *Canada: Indian Treaties and Surrenders*, vol. 1: *Treaties 1–138*, 149–52. Saskatoon: Fifth House Publishers.

Palmater, Pamela. 2016. "Trudeau's promises of 'renewed relationship' with First Nations evaporated with Liberal budget." *Rabble.ca Blogs*. March 23. Accessed July 4, 2016. http://rabble.ca/blogs/bloggers/pamela-palmater/2016/03/trudeaus-promises -renewed-relationship-first-nations-evaporat.

Phelan, Judge Michael J. [Ruling]. 2013. Federal Court of Canada, January 8, Docket T217299, Citation 2013 FC 6. (The case known as *Harry Daniels, Gabriel Daniels, Leah Gardner, Terry Joudrey and the Congress of Aboriginal Peoples v. Her Majesty the Queen*.)

Powley Case Reports. 2013. *Historic Research, Métis Nation of Ontario*. Accessed January 20, 2013. www.metisnation.org/registry/resources-for-applicants/historicresources.

Prucha, Francis Paul. 1996. *The Great Father: The United States Government and the American Indians*. Abridged ed. Lincoln: University of Nebraska Press.

*R. v. Powley*. [2003]. 2 S.C.R. 207, SCC 43. Judgements of the Supreme Court of Canada. Accessed February 18, 2013. http://scc.lexum.org/decisia-scc-csc/scc-csc/scc -csc/en/item/2076/index.do?r=aaaaaqagcg93bgv5aaaaaaaaaq.

*R. v. Van der Peet*. [1996]. 2 S.C.R. 507. In *Aboriginal Law: Commentary, Cases and Materials*. 3rd ed., edited by Thomas Isaac. Saskatoon: Purich Publishing. 404–22.

*R. v. Harry Daniels, Gabriel Daniels, Leah Gardner, Terry Joudrey and The Congress of Aboriginal Peoples.* 2014. Federal Court of Appeal [Canada]. Docket: A-49-13. 2014 FCA 101.

Read, Colin. 1988. *The Rebellion of 1837 in Upper Canada.* Ottawa: Canadian Historical Association.

Read, D. B. 1990. "Sir Francis Bond Head, Baronet, Lieutenant Governor." In *Lieutenant-Governors of Upper Canada and Ontario, 1792–1899,* 153–91. Toronto: William Briggs.

Reuter, Dorothy. 1993. *Reuter, Methodist Indian Ministries in Michigan, 1830–1990.* Grand Rapids: A Project of the Michigan Area United Methodist Historical Society.

Ruggles, Richard E. 1990. "McMurray, William." In *Dictionary of Canadian Biography,* vol. 12, *1891–1900,* edited by Frances G. Halpenny and Jean Hamelin, 680–81. Toronto: University of Toronto Press.

Schenck, Theresa. 2002. "Who Owns Sault Ste. Marie?" *Michigan Historical Review* 28, no. 1: 109–20.

Scott, James. 1998. *Seeing Like a State: How Certain Schemes to Improve the Human Condition Have Failed.* New Haven: Yale University Press.

Senior, Elinor Kyte. 1985. *Redcoats and Patriotes: The Rebellions in Lower Canada, 1837–38.* Stittsville, Ont.: Canada's Wings in collaboration with the Canadian War Museum, National Museum of Man, National Museums of Canada.

[Shingwaukonse and Nebenagoching's Montreal Statement]. 1849. *Montreal Gazette.* July 7.

Sprague, D. N. 1995. "The New Math of the 'New Indian Act': 6(2)+6(2)=6(1)." *Native Studies Review* 10, no. 1: 47–60.

Stone, Lyle, and Chaput, Donald. 1978. "History of the Upper Great Lakes Area." In *Handbook of the North American Indians,* vol. 15, *Northeast,* edited by Bruce G. Trigger, 602–9. Washington: Smithsonian Institution.

Surtees, Robert J. 1988. "Canadian Indian Policies." In *Handbook of North American Indians: Volume 4, History of Indian-White Relations,* edited by Wilcomb E. Washburn, 81–95. Washington: Smithsonian Institution.

Supreme Court of Canada. 2016. *Daniels v. Canada* (Indian Affairs and Northern Development). 2016 SCC 12.

Telford, Rhonda Mae. 1996. "'The Sound of the Rustling of the Gold Is under My Feet Where I Stand; We Have a Rich Country': A History of Aboriginal Mineral Resources in Ontario." PhD diss., University of Toronto.

———. 1997. "The Nefarious and Far-Ranging Interests of Indian Agent and Surveyor John William Keating, 1837 to 1869." In *Papers of the Twenty-Eighth Algonquian Conference,* edited by David H. Pentland, 372–402. Winnipeg: University of Manitoba.

———. 2003. "Aboriginal Resistance in the Mid-Nineteenth Century: The Anishinabe, Their Allies, and the Closing of the Mining Operations at Mica Bay and Michipicoten Island." In *Blockades and Resistance: Studies in the Actions of Peace and the Temagami Blockades of 1988–89,* edited by Bruce W. Hodgins, Ute Lischke, and David T. McNab, 71–84. Waterloo: Wilfrid Laurier University Press.

Tobias, John L. 1990. "Protection, Civilization, Assimilation: An Outline History of

Canada's Indian Policy." In *As Long as the Sun Shines and Water Flows: A Reader in Canadian Native Studies*, edited by Ian L. Getty and Antoine S. Lussier, 39–64. Vancouver: University of British Columbia Press.

Treaties with the Chippewa of Sault Ste. Marie. (1855) 1904. In *Indian Affairs. Laws and Treaties: Volume II (Treaties)*, edited by Charles J. Kappler, 725–31. Washington DC: U.S. Government Printing Office.

"Treaty with the Indians." 1850. *Lake Superior Journal*. September 4.

Treaty with the Ottawa, etc. (1836) 1904. In *Indian Affairs. Laws and Treaties: Vol. II (Treaties)*, edited by Charles J. Kappler, 450–56. Washington DC: U.S. Government Printing Office.

Trouillot, Michel-Rolph. 2001. "The Anthropology of the State in the Age of Globalization: Close Encounters of the Deceptive Kind." *Current Anthropology* 42, no. 1: 125–38.

Venne, Sharon Helen, ed. 1981. *Indian Acts and Amendments, 1868–1975: An Indexed Collection*. Saskatchewan: Native Law Centre, University of Saskatchewan.

White, Richard. 1997. "'Although I Am Dead, I Am Not Entirely Dead. I Have Left a Second of Myself': Constructing Self and Persons on the Middle Ground of Early America." In *Through a Glass Darkly: Reflections on Personal Identity in Early America*, edited by Ronald Hoffman, Mechal Sobel, and Fredrika J. Tuete, 404–18. Chapel Hill: University of North Carolina Press.

Wightman, Nancy M., and W. Robert Wightman. 1991. "The Mica Bay Affair: Conflict on the Upper-Lakes Mining Frontier, 1840–1850." *Ontario History* 83, no. 3: 193–208.

Williams, Mentor L., ed. 1992. *Schoolcraft's Narrative Journal of Travels*. East Lansing: Michigan State University Press.

Wilson, Rev. Edward F. (1874) 1975. *The Ojebway Language: A Manual for Missionaries and Others Employed among the Ojebway Indians*. Toronto: Rowsell and Hutchison.

Wise, S. F. 1972. "Sir Francis Bond Head." In *Dictionary of Canadian Biography*, vol. 10, *1871–1880*, edited by Marc La Terreur, 342–45. Toronto: University of Toronto Press.

Wyss, Hilary E. 1999. "Captivity and Conversion: William Apess, Mary Jemison, and Narratives of Racial Identity." *American Indian Quarterly* 23, no. 3–4: 63–82.

# 3

## Asserting Indigeneity in the Contemporary Era

# 7

# Asserting Indigeneity in Contemporary Mexico and Central America

## Autonomy, Rights, and Confronting Nation-States

LYNN STEPHEN

On October 12, 1992, thousands of people from the 500 Years of Indigenous, Black, and Popular Resistance in Chiapas and the organization known as ANCIEZ (Alianza Campesina Independiente "Emiliano Zapata"—a precursor to the Ejercito Zapatista de Liberación Nacional [Zapatista Army of National Liberation or EZLN])—participated in a march in San Cristóbal de las Casas. The marchers halted in front of the statue of conquistador Diego de Mazariegos, fastened ropes around his neck, and smashed at the pedestal with sledgehammers. Within a short period of time, the statue of Mazariegos was pulled to the ground. This action was a part of a coordinated set of activities in the Americas marking the 500 Years of Indian Resistance that Native peoples were carrying out in protest of the quincentenary of the "discovery" of the Americas by Columbus (South and Meso American Indian Rights Center [SAIIC 1990]). That same year Rigoberta Menchú Tum was awarded the Nobel Peace Prize "in recognition of her work for social justice and ethno-cultural reconciliation based on respect for the rights of indigenous peoples" (Nobel Foundation 2012).

In the watershed year of 1992, indigenous peoples throughout the Americas engaged in coordinated activities and built long-lasting political networks that have been crucial over the past twenty years to assertions of indigenous autonomy. In this chapter I argue that the concept of indigenous autonomy, understood as the recognition and legitimation of indigenous self-determination through forms of governance, justice, policing, control and defense of territory, and media (particularly radio and video), has been at the heart of asserting indigeneity in Mesoamerica over the past two decades. Establishing autonomy has involved a complex and uneven process involving first the articulation of a series of rights, then uneven attempts to legislate those rights within the frameworks of national and state constitutions, and finally the assertion of these rights through putting them into practice—often without state approval or through using international governance bodies such as the Inter-American Court of Human Rights to pressure states to obey their own legal codes.

After engaging in a theoretical discussion of the concept of indigenous autonomy" as variably understood in contemporary Mesoamerica, I will operationalize the different components of what autonomy means through exploring a series of case studies. Note that in Canada discussion of indigenous rights is often framed in terms of sovereignty among Canada's 650 First Nations (see McNab in this volume). Here, I will first explore the meaning of autonomy in indigenous governance by exploring the system of *caracoles* (regional governments) and *juntas de buen gobierno* (good governance councils), which is a part of the governance structure of Zapatista communities in Chiapas. I will then move to a discussion of indigenous forms of justice and community policing through exploring the work of the Policía Comunitaria and the Coordinadora Regional de Autoridades Comunitarias (CRAC, Regional Council of Community Authorities) in Guerrero. I then explore the importance of indigenous autonomy as maintained through media by exploring struggles for indigenous radio in Oaxaca, Mexico, and in Guatemala. I will close with a discussion of defense of territory by exploring the cases of Awas Tingni and the Miskitu of Tuara, Nicaragua, who have both been engaged in processes of defense of territory through ethnomapping and mobilizing the Inter-American Court to pressure the state of Nicaragua to recognize their ancestral lands.

## On Indigenous Autonomy

The Mexican and Guatemalan governments both signed significant documents advancing indigenous rights and autonomy in the 1990s. I highlight below the parts of each that are most significant to my discussion on autonomy.

From Article II, San Andrés Accords on Indigenous Rights and Culture (1996):

Agreement negotiated between the Mexican government and the EZLN at San Andres in 1996 which the Mexican government refused to implement. Translation by Rosalva Bermudez-Ballin.

1.-The creation of a judicial framework that establishes a new relationship between indigenous peoples and the State, based on the recognition of their right to self-determination and the judicial, political, social, economic and cultural rights that obtain from it. The new constitutional dispositions must include a framework of autonomy. . . .

Autonomy is the concrete expression of the exercise of the right to self-determination, within the framework of membership in the National State. The indigenous peoples shall be able, consequently, to decide their own form of internal government as well as decide their way of organizing themselves politically, socially, economically and culturally. Within the new constitutional framework of autonomy, the exercise of self-determination of indigenous peoples shall be respected in each of the domains and levels in which they are asserted, being able to encompass one or more indigenous groups, according to particular and specific circumstances in each federal entity. The exercise of autonomy of indigenous people will contribute to the unity and democratization of national life and will strengthen national sovereignty.

From the Agreement on the Identity and Rights of Indigenous Peoples (AIDPI), Signed March 31, 1995 by the government of the republic of Guatemala and the General command of the Guatemalan National Revolutionary Unity (Unidad Revolucionaria Nacional Guatemalteca, URNG):

IV. CIVIL, POLITICAL, SOCIAL AND ECONOMIC RIGHTS

A. Constitutional framework

The Government of Guatemala undertakes to promote a reform of the Constitution in order to define and characterize the Guatemalan nation as being of national unity, multi-ethnic, multicultural and multilingual.

B. Local indigenous communities and authorities

1. Recognition is accorded to the importance the Maya and other indigenous communities have had and continue to have in the political, economic, social, cultural and spiritual spheres. Their cohesion and dynamism have enabled the Maya, Garifuna and Xinca peoples to preserve and develop their culture and way of life, despite the discrimination to which they have been subjected.

2. Bearing in mind the constitutional commitment of the State to recognize, respect and promote these forms of organization which are peculiar to the indigenous communities, recognition is accorded to the role of the community authorities that were constituted in accordance with the customary norms of the communities, in the management of their affairs.

Within eleven months of one another, two historic documents on indigenous rights were signed in Mesoamerica. In March of 1995, the Agreement on the Identity and Rights of Indigenous Peoples (AIDPI) was signed in Mexico City by the Government of the Republic of Guatemala, the General Command of the Unidad Revolucionaria Nacional Guatemalteca, representatives of the United Nations and others. In February of 1996, the San Andrés Accords on Indigenous Rights and Culture was signed in San Andrés Larráinzar by the EZLN and Mexican president Ernesto Zedillo. Both of these documents contain language that has been fundamental to the way that indigenous autonomy has been interpreted and practiced by indigenous peoples in Mesoamerica. AIDPI in Guatemala first recognizes the multiethnic, culturally plural and multilingual nature of Guatemala and then specifies the collective rights of indigenous Guatemalans, particularly political, social, and economic rights (Armon, Seider, and Wilson 1997, 66). AIDPI also recognizes cultural rights relating to language; names, surnames and place-names; spirituality; temples ceremonial centers and holy places; indigenous dress; science and technology, education reform, and indigenous mass media (AIDPI 1995).

The San Andrés Accords on Indigenous Rights and Culture laid the groundwork for significant changes in the areas of indigenous rights, political participation, and cultural autonomy in Mexico. Most importantly, they recognize the existence of political subjects called pueblos indios (indigenous peoples, towns, or communities) and gave conceptual validation to the terms "self-determination" and "autonomy" by using them in the signed accords. The accords emphasize that the Mexican government takes responsibility not only for reinforcing the political representation of indigenous peoples and their participation in legislatures but also for guaranteeing the validity of internal forms of indigenous government. They further note that the government promises to create national legislation guaranteeing indigenous communities the right to 1) freely associate themselves with municipalities that are primarily indigenous in population, 2) form associations between communities, and 3) coordinate their actions as indigenous peoples (see Aubry 2003).

In addition, the accords state that it is up to the legislatures of individual states to determine what the best criteria are for self-determination and autonomy. These criteria should accurately represent the diverse aspirations and distinctions of indigenous peoples. It is important to note that the accords do not deal with the key issues of land redistribution and agrarian policy, notably the revision of Article 27 of the Mexican Constitution in 1992 that ended land reform and encouraged privatization of communally held land.

According to the terms of the 1996 Guatemalan peace accords, AIDPI and other constitutional reforms had to be ratified in a popular referendum (*consulta popular*) to become law. A national referendum on indigenous rights and three other questions in May of 1999 was defeated 53 percent to 47 percent, although only 19 percent of the country voted and 81 percent abstained (Warren 2003, 149–50; see also Hale 2006b, chapter 2, on the bumpy path of neoliberal multiculturalism in Guatemala). Thus the reforms that would have recognized indigenous peoples' rights to use their customary forms of law (among other rights specified in AIDPI) were not ratified nor officially recognized. Later proposals to create new referendums for some of the rights contained in the original AIDPI accords also found little formal political traction. According to Rachel Seider, however, "different forms of community-based conflict resolution were increasingly promoted within indigenous areas of the country as part of overall efforts to reform the justice system" (Seider 2008, 77). Seider suggests that by promoting alternative forms of community-based forms of conflict resolution that would strengthen community authorities in their exercise of Mayan law, indigenous rights activists had some impact in furthering indigenous rights at the local level in postwar Guatemala. Such advances, however, were also offset by a weak Guatemalan state colonized by criminal groups (Seider 2008, 85). Mexican drug trafficking organizations such as the Zetas and the Sinaloa cartel as well as domestic organized crime groups, transnational gangs or *maras*, such as Mara Salvatrucha (MS-13) and the Eighteenth Street Gang (M-18) have had a strong presence in Guatemala and have operated with impunity. In 2007 the United Nations created the International Commission against Impunity in Guatemala (CICIG) to investigate and prosecute criminal groups believed to have infiltrated state institutions. The CICIG arrested the chief of police and his top antinarcotics intelligence officer, both accused of being on the payroll of the powerful Mexico-based Zetas cartel, in 2010 (Panner and Beltrán 2010). In September of 2015, Otto Pérez Molina resigned as the president of Guatemala, as did his vice president, after the Public Ministry formally charged him with "being part of a criminal organization, with the purpose of defrauding the state" (Dada 2015). In June of 2016, new charges were filed against Pérez Molina by Guatemala's Attorney General that included charges for illicit campaign finance, illegal association, passive bribery, and money laundering.

The San Andrés Accords were never legislated in Mexico. Instead, constitutional amendments for Articles 1, 2, 3, 18, and 115 were implemented by the Mexican senate in a legislative package officially known as La Reforma Constitucional sobre Derechos y Cultura Indígena but as "San Andrés lite" by indigenous leaders and activists. The package fell far short of much of what was proposed in the San Andrés Accords.[1] Since these reforms in 2001, Article 1 of the Mexican constitution now prohibits all kinds of discrimination, including racial and ethnic discrimination, and Article 2 now includes a specific definition of *pueblo* that follows that outlined in International Labour Organization convention 169: "The Nation is one and indivisible. The Nation has a pluricultural composition based originally upon its indigenous peoples [*pueblos*], who are those descended from the population living within the present territory of the country at the beginning of colonization, and who conserve their own social, economic, cultural and political institutions, or at least a part of them. The consciousness of their indigenous identity has to be a fundamental criterion to determine to whom the dispositions for indigenous peoples are applicable" (translation from de la Peña 2006, 291–92).

The 2001 reforms granted states the right to limit indigenous rights proposals, confined "indigenous autonomy to communities within single municipalities, denied constitutional recognition of indigenous peoples as subjects with the right to decide upon their own forms of governance and development, and maintained a paternalistic relation in which the federal government would provide social services to indigenous communities" (Harvey 2001, 1048). Most importantly, the fact that formal recognition of indigenous peoples and communities was left up to the legislatures of individual states resulted in extremely uneven implementation of the constitutional reforms across Mexico and also resulted in significant interlegalities with conflicts between what many state laws mandate and what is in the Mexican constitution. For example, indigenous claims to local governmental and legal autonomy through customary indigenous law were codified into Oaxaca state law and official election procedures in the 1990s. These legislative changes allowed municipal-level and lower authorities to be selected through traditional electoral systems—usually in open meetings known as *asambleas* and also legalized customary indigenous law and justice systems. Oaxaca's laws are the most progressive in Mexico regarding issues of indigenous autonomy and in many ways match up well with the proposals in the San Andrés Accords of 1996. The state of Guerrero, however, has never reformed its laws to recognize indigenous rights. There, the community police forces and the community justice system run by the Regional Coordinating Committee of Communitarian Authorities, which joins together more than one hundred communities, is essentially illegal (Sierra 2010, 35).

While both the San Andrés Accords and the AIDPI fell short in terms of their legislation and implementation at the federal level and within the different states of Guatemala and Mexico, I begin my discussion of autonomy here because of their political importance as references within indigenous movements. As becomes evident in my discussion of case studies, the fact that neither the Mexican nor Guatemalan state has formally implemented these agreements has not stopped some of their central ideas from being implemented in practice. In some cases this implementation has had partial approval or at least a lack of intervention from states. In other cases it has had active resistance from states and other organizations, most prominently military forces and drug cartels in the context of both nations.

In practice, indigenous autonomy is centered to a large degree on recognition of collective (versus individual) rights, customary law and traditions (*usos y costumbres*) linked to consensus decision-making practices, local administration of justice, and election of authorities through traditional means without the intervention of political parties. In most instances this means the creation and maintenance of decision-making spaces that focus on horizontal and participatory processes (see Olivera Bustamante 2004; Baronnet, Mora Bayo, and Stahler Sholk 2011, 29–30; Speed 2008). As Walter Mignolo argues in his discussion of the Zapatistas' theoretical revolution, ideas such as "the return to human dignity," "the right to be different because we are all equals," "a world composed of multiple worlds," and "to rule and obey at the same time" are fundamental precepts to autonomy (Mignolo 2011, 239, 234–35).

Contemporary states in Mesoamerica have usually not legislated international or national agreements concerning indigenous autonomy that they have signed. If they have passed legislation on indigenous autonomy, such legislation is often not enforced. Constitutions and legislation become empty signifiers. In the experiences of many contemporary indigenous communities and movements, legal processes are void of justice and inadequate for the resolution of conflict, and the political and economic structures that represent "the rule of law"(including laws that are supposed to promote indigenous autonomy and rights) remain out of reach. Because of the Zapatista movement's political and cultural importance in demonstrating the meaning of indigenous autonomy, their shift from trying to engage the state through the signing of accords to pursuing their own model of autonomy unilaterally in 2003 set an important precedent in Mexico and other countries in Mesoamerica. As noted by Shannon Speed and Alvaro Reyes, "by unilaterally pursuing their autonomy projects, people in Zapatista base areas made a fundamental discursive shift: indigenous peoples' right to self-determination was being asserted as prior to, and regardless of, their establishment in the legal regimes of the state" (2009, 288).

This pivot illustrates the distinction that philosopher Cornelius Castoriadis makes between autonomy as *auto-nomos*, or the making or giving of one's own laws in a deliberate and reflective manner, and heteronomy, or the submission to the laws of another. Castoriadis further discusses autonomy in terms of its collective political implications: "we want everyone to be autonomous, that is to say, we want all people to learn to govern themselves, individually and collectively: and one is able to develop one's capacity to govern oneself only by participating on an equal footing, in an equal manner, in the governance of common business, of common affairs" (Castoriadis 1991, 164).

As discussed by Granados in chapter 4 of this volume, this move by the EZLN signals, in part, an escape from certain ways of knowing and construing indigenous peoples as seen from the optic of the state. At the same time, however, it also mobilizes anthropological logics and notions of indigeneity found in postrevolutionary Mexico that suggest a primordial indigenous essence. By calling for the reinstatement of indigenous rights and partially following a modern narrative of origins, the EZLN may have fallen partially into state logic—at least in terms of their narrative. Although the EZLN is mobilizing what might be seen by some as an essentialist construction of indigeneity, it is using this narrative strategically to build concrete political, economic, and social relations of autonomy and sovereignty, not a politics of assimilation. This has been called strategic essentialism by indigenous activists and their allies as it takes advantage of preestablished narrative categories and uses them to move forward a specific political agenda. In the United States, narratives of strategic essentialism are constantly deployed by Native peoples as they push for tribal recognition, land and mineral rights, treaty recognition, and more.

For Speed and Reyes, the indigenous rights claims pressed for by the Zapatistas through the San Andrés Accords "not only demand that the institutions of sovereignty within a nation recognize indigenous peoples for who they are—human beings with the right to equal treatment—but they also demand that those same institutions not impede the functioning of an existing and parallel power structure (internal indigenous political and judicial mechanisms) to allow the indigenous peoples themselves to decide who they are and who they want to become" (2009, 289). In the case of the Zapatista movement, the Mexican state's failure to fulfill the commitment it made to real constitutional reform recognizing indigenous rights and autonomy had the ultimate effect of giving the Zapatistas and subsequently other indigenous movements and communities the moral high ground in proclaiming their own autonomous communities, municipalities and projects (Speed and Reyes 2009, 287; Hernández Navarro 1998). The declaration of indigenous autonomies is a process which continues to the present in Mexico. The more significant reforms to the constitutions of Colombia (1991), Bolivia (1994), and Ecuador (1998) granted collective rights, languages, and indigenous territorial autonomy for particular regions. In Mexico and Central America the struggle for territorial autonomy is ongoing.

## Case Studies of Autonomy

*1. Juntas de Buen Gobierno, Caracoles, and Community Assemblies in Zapatista Chiapas*

While the full-blown Zapatista autonomy project was unveiled in 2003, indigenous communities in Chiapas began to assert themselves as autonomous regional governments as early as 1995. Pluriethnic autonomous regions (RAP) organized by various groups from within civil society began to establish local and regional councils and a statewide parliament in 1994 and 1995. In 1998 the Zapatistas announced the establishment of Autonomous Zapatista Rebel Municipalities or MAREZ (Municipios Autónomos Rebeldes Zapatistas). By 2003 there were approximately thirty-one MAREZ and seven to eight RAP, though the RAP were distanced from the EZLN (Burguete Cal y Mayor 2003, 192).[2]

Regional autonomy as framed within the MAREZ involves the demarcation of territory, demarcation of jurisdictional authority, the construction and acceptance of a normative framework regulating members of the region, election and establishment of parallel authorities and government organs, the creation of governmental organizations, and infrastructure (Burguete Cal y Mayor 2003, 195). It also involves rejection of official government authorities, resources, and institutions and the creation of real alternatives for people. The EZLN justified the establishment of the MAREZ by reference to the recognition of municipal autonomy in article 15 of the Mexican constitution and the rights of indigenous peoples to live according to their customs and practices as outlined in Convention 169 of the International Labour Organization, which was signed by Mexico (Barmeyer 2009, 61). The MAREZ were divided into five zones in eastern Chiapas: Altos, Norte, Altamirano, Selva Tzeltal, and Selva Tojolabal. Each of these regions had a cultural and political center associated with a civilian guerilla base known as an Aguascalientes. They included facilities for large meetings, "assembly halls, sleeping quarters, and also a number of workshops and machines, such as tractors or coffee roasters, used by all Zapatista communities pertaining to the respective region" (Barmeyer 2009, 61).

As suggested by a number of authors (Mattiace 2003a; Mattiace 2003b; Barmeyer 2009; Harvey 1998; Leyva Solano and Ascencio Franco 1996), the structure upon which Zapatista models of autonomy were built reflects the historical importance in many Zapatista communities of ejidos. Many of the communities that today are solidly Zapatista were founded from the 1950s to the 1970s as ejidos (see Stephen 2002, 91–133; Cerda García 2011). An ejido is a communal form of land tenure in which members have use rights. Ejidos were created after the Mexican Revolution to satisfy the demands of landless peasants who had seen their communal lands usurped by large agricultural estates or who served as laborers on those estates. *Ejido* refers to a specific area of land, often understood as a territory. Those who are members of the ejido are referred to as *ejidatarios* and they elect authorities who are responsible for the administration of the land and its resources to the collective of individuals who share use rights. Ejido decision making is centered in an open public assembly that holds ultimate authority over elected officials. The *comisariado ejidal* (ejidal commissariat), the *consejo de vigilancia* (vigilance committee that controls boundaries and access to the ejidio territory), the *agencia* (local governance structure with elected officials lead by the *agente*), a deacon linked to local catechists and the Catholic Church, and a series of elected committees were found in many Zapatista communities before the formal emergence of the EZLN. They continued to function under the Zapatistas, but were integrated initially with the EZLN's military command structure known as the Comité Clandestino Revolucionario Indígena (see Stephen 2002, 124–25, 141–44; Leyva Solano 1995, 382; Barmeyer 2009, 89).

Zapatista communities that were not ejidos and held communal land were administered by civil-religious cargo systems and assemblies of *comuneros* (communal land holders), similar to what I have written about in Oaxacan indigenous communities. These communities are located in the Los Altos region of Chiapas and have much longer histories of settlement and continuous presence. They are primarily Tzotzil and Tzeltal communities in places such as San Andrés Larráinzar and Teopisca.[3]

In indigenous communities where customary law is practiced, citizenship consists of a collective set of rights and responsibilities that guide the governance of the community in its many locations spread out in Mexico and the United States (Stephen 2005a). These responsibilities usually include:

1. Participation of primarily adult men, and increasingly some women, in the local system of civil cargos or civil offices arranged in hierarchy to execute the tasks necessary to run local governments. This is a local system of governance in which community members perform governmental duties without pay. Tasks can be divided among dozens of positions, or cargos, that range from mayor, judge, and police officer to school and irrigation committee member.

2. Participation of adult men and women in the religious cargo system (set of religious positions organized into a hierarchy to fulfill the tasks of local Catholic churches, particularly of the cult

celebrations of saints believed to care for communities or inter-cede in specific areas such as rainfall). These cargos are integrated with in the practice of *mayordomías*, in which community mem-bers sponsor the celebrations of the feast days of saints vener-ated in the local Catholic church. Religious sponsorship of saints requires significant expenditures on feasting, music, and ritual activities (see Stephen 2005b, 230–81).

3. Participation of adult men and women in *tequio* or commu-nal labor.

4. Payment by adult men and women of specific *quotas* or amounts of money for community projects or celebrations, known as *cooperación*.

Citizenship rights include:

1. Access to communal land for farming or house construction;

2. Access to community forests, water, sand, minerals, plants, and wild game;

3. The right to burial in the community cemetery;

4. The right to express opinions and vote in the decision-making process that takes place in community assemblies.

Citizenship is thus commonly understood as constituted by the responsibilities and rights outlined above, most of them collective responsibilities. This is a general description that may have differ-ences from one region to another in Chiapas and Oaxaca. The power of community assemblies in decision making is at the center of the administrative structures of ejidos, *comunales* (communal lands), and civil-religious cargo structures of governance.

In August of 2003, the Zapatistas announced the creation of five regional caracoles (literally meaning "snail shells" but also meaning houses; also a Mayan symbol that represents the "opening to the heart") that are the seats for five juntas de buen gobierno (Castro Soto and Hidalgo 2003). For the EZLN, this announcement also marked the transfer of power from military to civilian authorities in each of its five regions (Speed 2007, 185). Each caracol brings together the MAREZ in each of the five Zapatista regions mentioned above. The former Aguascalientes sites that had held countless large meetings between the EZLN and civil society as well as councils, workshops, celebrations, basketball tournaments, dances, and more were thus redesigned as caracoles. Each of the five juntas de buen gobierno housed in a caracol includes one to three delegates from each of the existing Autonomous Councils in each zone who rotate on a weekly or biweekly basis.

According to Speed this means that for "each Junta, there are between 28 and 60 people participating in the decisions for their regions" in addition to *suplentes* or alternates who are also present and actively engaged (Speed 2007, 185). The rotating structure of the groups ensures that leadership and authority are diffused and not concentrated in a small group of people. The people elected to serve as *consejos* or delegates were chosen because of their experience holding an ejidal of municipal office or perhaps because of military experience in the EZLN, according to Barmeyer (2009, 92). The system of rotating the delegates out every fifteen days permitted them to work in their fields, tend to other projects, and have time with their families. Ethnographers working in Zapatista communities after the caracoles were formed to house the juntas de buen gobierno reported that the functions of the juntas include: monitoring projects and community works in MAREZ; monitoring the implementation of laws that function within the jurisdiction of the MAREZ; care for Zapatista territory in rebellion that it manages, and overseeing education and health programs (Barmeyer 2009; Forbis 2006; Speed 2008).

At the local level, assemblies of different kinds are involved in decision making that pertain to all issues of community political life, land, education, and health. Community assemblies drawn from ejidos, communal lands, and catechists are involved in electing local representatives and naming committees. Neil Harvey summarizes some of the aspects of autonomy described by more than two hundred indigenous participants in 2007 at a large gathering known as the Segundo Encuentro de los Pueblos Zapatistas con los Pueblos del Mundo (the Second Encounter of the Zapatista Peoples with the Peoples of the World). He writes that municipal agentes named by assemblies are supposed to apply local justice and watch over the rivers and forests that pertain to their territory; autonomous judges named by the municipal assembly are supposed to attend to local problems that are severe and cannot be resolved by other authorities or committees; and Zapatista communities also name local health and education committees (Harvey 2011, 180–84).

Other anthropologists have conducted local fieldwork in specific communities or municipalities that are part of the Zapatista autonomy project. Alejandro Cerda García conducted his PhD dissertation work on health and education in the autonomous municipality of Vicente Guerrero, which incorporates seventeen ejidos. He describes the way that autonomy works at the local level through education and health programs in specific communities (Cerda García 2011). Within the autonomous municipality of Vicente Guerrero there are bilingual Tojolabal-Spanish primary schools in four ejidos. Each community has a local parents' group and elected educational delegates who interface with parents, give classes, coordinates events, and take care of school infrastructure. At the level of the autonomous municipality, there is an education commission that works with the delegates from each location and also coordinates education in the municipality above the primary level. The municipal education commission also coordinates its work with the zone-level educational commission (Cerda García 2011, 214). The educational content in the local autonomous schools includes political education, discussions of what autonomy means and how it is represented in school. Curriculum also emphasizes the importance of language and culture, intercultural values, learning methods based in theory and practice, and methods geared toward learning technical skills and careers that can serve local communities (Cerda García 2011, 223–27). Others who have conducted ethnographic studies of autonomous education in communities that are a part of the Zapatista autonomy project include Bruno Baronnet (2009), Raúl Gutiérrez Narváez (2005), and Kathia Núñez Patiño (2005).

The structure for health programs mirrors that of schools, with local, municipal, and regional committees working with local health promoters and health commissioners. The Zapatista autonomous health program emphasizes the use of traditional medicinal knowledge, practices, and materials (see Cerda García 2011, 252–70; Forbis 2006). In her description of autonomous health programs in Zapatista communities, Melissa Forbis notes that naming women as health promoters was a way to increase women's participation in the governance systems of local communities and autonomous municipalities. Being named as a health promoter is one of the cargos that form a part of local systems of governance and was one avenue for women to gain experience and then be promoted to positions of higher responsibility within the Zapatista structures of governance. "Becoming a promotora is a way for women to organize and contest gender hierarchies publically—by demanding their right to work for the good of the community through health, just as men have done" (Forbis 2006, 189).

The Zapatista model of indigenous autonomy is the most developed and extensive in Mexico and has served as a touchstone for other regions that have announced themselves as autonomous municipalities. Other recently declared autonomous municipalities include San Juan Copala (Triqui) in 2007 and San Francisco Tlapancingo (Mixteco) in 2011 in Oaxaca, Huamuxtitlán (Nahuatl, Tlapaneco, Mixteco) in Guerrero in 2012, and Cherán in Michoacán (Purépecha) in 2012, among others.

*2. Indigenous Forms of Justice and Community*
*Policing: The Policía Comunitaria de Guerrero*

In Mexico and elsewhere in Mesoamerica where militarization and narco-violence have become the norm, indigenous communities have demonstrated remarkable creativity and organizational potential in putting forward their own systems of security and justice in the hopes of securing social order and peace. They rely on different models of justice and policing that have in some instances been much more successful in achieving their aims than security and justice operations run by the state. In this section I discuss the Policía Comunitaria de Guerrero (Communal Police of Guerrero) and the Coordinadora Regional de Autoridades Comunitarias, which together integrate the Sistema de Seguridad, Justicia y Reeducación Comunitario (Community System of Security, Justice, and Reeducation) in the Costa Chica–Montaña region of the state of Guerrero, Mexico.

Serving seventy-two communities in eighteen municipalities that include na'savi (Mixteco), me'phaa (Tlapanecas), mestizos, and Afro-mestizos in a multiethnic part of Mexico, these integrated institutions work together to maintain security, detain people who have committed crimes, try them in community courts, and mete out punishment with the goal of reincorporating offenders back into society. Born in a region of Mexico that is well known for its wide range of social movements (indigenous movements, teachers' movements, the Guerrero Council of 500 Years of Indigenous, Black and Popular Resistance, among others), as well as armed guerilla groups active in the 1970s and more recently through the emergence of the Popular Revolutionary Army and the Revolutionary Army of the Insurgent People, the CRAC and Policía Comunitaria came out of a context where robberies, homicides, and rape, along with more minor crimes like cattle theft, were running rampant. State security and police forces were not stopping the wave of crime, and the state legal system was not prosecuting criminals. With the encouragement of nonprofits, human rights, and other supporting organizations, people in one municipality decided to take action (Sierra 2013, 191).

The Policía Comunitaria (hereafter known as the Comunitaria) was founded in 1995 in Santa Cruz del Rincón in the municipality of Malinaltepec. Three years later in 1998, the Coordinadora Regional de Autoridades Indígenas (later renamed the Coordinadora Regional de Autoridades Comunitarias or CRAC when they incorporated mestizo and Afro-mestizo communities) was formed in the community of Potrerillo Cuapinole in the municipio of San Luis Acatlán. The organization was born in a regional assembly when citizens decided that in addition to taking control of their own security, they also needed to take on the task of administering justice to those who were found guilty of crimes. While the community police were working day and night to detain and stop criminals, they found that once they turned them over to the authorities of the state judicial system, that they were being freed for a supposed "lack of evidence" (Sierra 2013, 197). Many were freed simply through paying off justice officials.

The challenge of organizing a justice system that worked in parallel with the structure of community policing required a system of punishment and readaptation. Unlike some other nonstate justice systems that may use corporal punishment, the CRAC does not. Inspired by community models of reconciliation and agreement through long processes of discussion and mediation, the CRAC decided that it needed to emphasize collective work for the community, or *faena*, as the basis for punishment and social reintegration. They called this community reeducation (*reeducación comunitaria*). Here is how the Policía Comunitaria explains its system of justice and law on its website: "The search for reconciliation, free access to justice, the possibility of speaking in our own languages, these are the characteristics of the new law we are constructing as indigenous peoples. This is a different sense of law than the law that the state imposes on us and which has not helped us to resolve the problems we have to face. Because of this we are required to construct a system of justice and law which reclaims what our peoples did before but adjusts it to current conditions" (Policía Comunitaria 2012a, my translation).

The process of reeducation through collective labor that benefits the community is supposed to "'generate consciousness' in the lawbreakers about their errors and restore the damage they have caused in communities" (Sierra 2013, 197). After they are judged guilty of a particular crime and sentenced to community labor, lawbreakers spend fifteen days in one community where townspeople watch over them with the support of community police while they labor. They are then transferred to another town where they work again. This fifteen-day rotation continues for as long as the term of their sentence. They may be employed in manual labor, construction, digging for roads and drainage, or a variety of other tasks. Sentences can range from a few weeks to up to eight years of community labor for crimes ranging from simple theft to murder.

At the end of 2012, the Policía Comunitaria had approximately 877 community policemen who served 77 communities in 12 municipalities with more than 100,000 total inhabitants. In the Costa Chica region these municipalities include San Luis Acatlán and Marquelia. In the Montaña region these include Malinaltepec, Iliatenco, Metlatónoc, Atlamajalcingo del Monte, Cochoapa el Grande,

Copanatoyac, Xalpatlahuac, Tlapa de Comonfort, Xochistlahuaca, and Acatepec. They identify four ethnic groups they serve: Tlapanecos, Mixtecos, mestizos, and Amuzgos (Policía Comunitaria 2012b). About 85 percent of the population served by the Comunitaria and the CRAC are indigenous, and about 15 percent are mestizo and Afro-mestizo (LeGrand 2012). In addition, they have three courts or Casas de Justicia and dozens of elected officials who participate in the system (Sierra 2013).

The Comunitaria is armed with low-caliber rifles registered with the military. María Teresa Sierra reports that "this measure was taken when the organization was founded and has allowed the Comunitaria to avoid being harassed or disarmed by the army" (Sierra 2010, 36). The region where the Comunitaria patrols is notorious for military incursions, illegal detention, torture, rape, and even assassinations. Because the Comunitaria exists to defend indigenous territory and not to confront the state (unlike the Popular Revolutionary Army and Revolutionary Army of the Insurgent People guerilla forces, which also have a presence in the region), they struggle to walk the fine line between protecting their territory and citizens inside the law while also maintaining cordial relationships with the military (Sierra 2010, 36). This has proven increasingly difficult as drug cartels moved into Guerrero and disputed the territory in a wave of violence. In one weekend in Guerrero in 2010, a dispute between a cartel known as La Familia and another known as the Beltrán Leyva resulted in more than forty executions (Castillo García 2010). Rumors of army collaboration with cartels complicate all relationships with the armed forces.

The decision to keep the security operations of the Policía Comunitaria separate from the justice system has been an important one. The CRAC, whose members are elected in regional assemblies, is in charge of the enforcement and administration of justice. It is also in charge of coordinating sentences of community labor and reeducation. As described above, community labor and reeducation processes take place in communities for fifteen days at a time. Prisoners work for a fifteen-day period in one community and are fed by community members, educated by community elders, and watched over by local community police. Reeducation involves intensive discussions with community elders and authorities. They work with prisoners to help them examine their conduct (Policía Comunitaria 2012b).

The justice system is guided by a local legal code (*reglamento interno*) developed by consensus in community assemblies and textualized emphasizing justice norms and community rights. As noted by Sierra, this legal code is subject to constant modification in relation to new legal situations and practices that surface. In 2009, for example, the code was modified to include such new rights for women as the right to participate in regional assemblies, to put forward their own proposals, and to guarantee their equal rights as women with men (Sierra 2013, 199). Sierra notes that the legal code is hybrid, based on a mixture of regional cultural ideas, collective rights, and human rights (Sierra 2013, 198).

The structure of the CRAC is linked to the administrative systems of municipalities as specified in Mexican law. The first place where legal cases land in CRAC territory is before the municipal commissioner (*comisariado municipal*), community authorities recognized by the state who are charged with administering local laws, licensing, sanitation, and other matters of public concern in communities. At the local level, CRAC has elected authorities chosen in community assemblies who will listen to a case in a community assembly if the municipal commissioner cannot resolve it. CRAC authorities work with townspeople in a public assembly to carry on an open public trial. For example, in April of 2010, community members of Potrerillo del Rincón in the Tlapa region of Guerrero, along with their Policía Comunitaria, detained a group of people accused of killing two people and of growing and selling marijuana. The accused were community members. Sierra describes the trial presided over by CRAC officials in this way:

> The detained were presented before the community assembly in the presence of CRAC authorities, where they had their first trial. Given the seriousness of the events, the people in the community were extremely tense, and voices were heard asking for their lynching, something that hasn't been heard in the region since the entrance of the communitarian police force. These voices though were on the fringe, but gave a

new and concerning context. After a long collective trial, in the presence of family, community members, and the accused, authorities of the CRAC emphasized the importance of rehabilitation for the guilty parties. In the last regional assembly . . . when the case was discussed, it was decided that they would perform eight years of community service, enough time to determine whether they had been rehabilitated. (Sierra 2010, 37)

The majority of cases that come to CRAC for trials include fraud, lack of payment, debt, beatings, domestic violence, intent to rape, rape, homicide, robberies, insults and defamations, family conflicts, and land conflict (Sierra 2013, 202).

If community CRAC officials and assemblies cannot resolve a case, then it will be heard in a regional assembly whose purpose is to support the CRAC. The regional assembly includes elected regional coordinators and counselors who are past CRAC authorities of prestige who monitor the CRAC and can intervene in conflictive and serious cases. The regional assembly is the highest level in the community justice system. Sierra describes a regional assembly she attended in 2010 that included the presence of regional authorities, citizens of the communities from the three different headquarters of the CRAC, new municipal commissioners, and others. "It involved three complex cases presented by the CRAC for consideration and discussion. . . . One involved fraudulent activity on the part of a group of people against their community, one was homicide . . . and the other was for diseases and accusations of witchcraft" (Sierra 2013, 215).

While Sierra does not discuss the outcome of the cases, she signals that the more important result was the legitimacy of the agreements reached in the regional assembly and the way in which normative ideas and discourses were developed. Finally, she underlines the continued pressure that the regional assemblies feel to respond to the state legal system, particularly when people who are accused under the CRAC system of justice also go outside of it to engage with official legal authorities and procedures (Sierra 2013, 216).

Much attention has been paid to the claims of the Policía Comunitaria and the CRAC that their Community System of Security,

Justice, and Reeducation has reduced the crime rate in their area of influence by 95 percent since they began (Policía Comunitaria 2012b). Researchers who have worked in the region note the exceptional confidence that men and women who live there feel to move about without fear, in contrast to most other parts of the state (Sierra 2005, 59). While more recent conflict in the area involving the military and drug cartels has complicated the ability of the CRAC and Comunitaria to guarantee security, the region is nonetheless deemed safer than some other parts of Mexico.

At a larger level, the security and justice program of the CRAC and Policía Comunitaria, which exists in a legal limbo in relation to the Mexican state, illustrates the importance of lived autonomy through practice—similar to the experience of the caracoles and juntas de buen gobierno in Chiapas, Mexico. The histories of both of these autonomy projects reflect the fragility of this legal limbo in Mexico, as both the CRAC and the EZLN have had ongoing struggles with intervention by paramilitaries and state and national officials who are constantly trying to stop their autonomy projects from advancing. In the meantime, while both the CRAC and the EZLN continue their practices at local and regional levels, more and more indigenous people grow up with the knowledge and experience they are gaining in these parallel systems of governance, security, and justice. This no doubt has an influence in the socialization of future generations.

### 3. Autonomy through the Right to Indigenous Media

In addition to governance and justice, one of the most important themes discussed in the San Andrés Accords in Mexico and the AIDP in Guatemala concerns the rights of indigenous peoples to produce and disseminate their own media.[4] Historically, indigenous radio in Mexico had been initiated and managed by the National Indigenist Institute or INI since 1979 when they open the first station in Tlapa, Guerrero. By 1994, the year that the Zapatista rebellion broke out in Chiapas, INI was managing fifteen radio stations. The challenge to INI's right to manage indigenous radio stations came from the Zapatistas, as well as from other indigenous organizations and leaders.

Part of the Zapatistas' agenda was to establish indigenous community radio as a collective right of indigenous communities, which could use the power of radio to fortify indigenous autonomy through the arena of cultural rights. While I do not discuss them here, Zapatista communities have also participated in a revolutionary indigenous video production project known as Promedios in Mexico and the Chiapas Media Project in the United States (see Wortham 2013, 177–206).The San Andrés Accords on Indigenous Rights and Cultures included a section that dealt specifically with communications media. The document made explicit reference to turning over control of state-run radio stations, which were administered by the INI, to indigenous communities. The accords also laid out further specifics for empowering indigenous communities with rights within the area of communications. In Document 2 of the accords, section III, item 8, titled Communications Media, states:

> Therefore, it will be proposed to the respective national authorities that they prepare a new communications law that will allow the pueblos indígenas to acquire, operate, and administer their own communications medias.
>
> The federal and state governments will encourage the conversion of the National Indigenous Institute's communications media into indigenous communications media. . . . The Federal government will recommend to the respective authorities that the seventeen INI (National Indigenous Institute) radio stations be turned over to the indigenous communities in their respective regions with the transfer of permits, infrastructure, and resources.
>
> . . . It is necessary to create a new legal framework in the area of communications that may consider the following aspects: the nation's multiculturalism; the right to use indigenous languages in the media; the right to rebuttal; guarantees to rights of expression, information, and communication; and the democratic participation of the pueblos indígenas and communities in relation to the authorities who decide on matters of communication. (San Andrés Accords on Indigenous Rights and Culture 1996)

Following the signing of the San Andrés Accords, six new INI radio stations were created between 1995 and 1999 in the states of

Campeche, Sonora, Chiapas, Michoacán, Hidalgo, and Quintana Roo. None of the new stations came under the independent control of indigenous organizations and communities.

While the EZLN and other indigenous organizations struggled to get the San Andrés Accords that President Zedillo had signed legislated, INI was one of the few doors open for the creation of licensed stations. But INI administrators began to decrease the autonomy of the network of indigenous radio stations, severely undercutting the ability of operators to program and operate their stations independently. Wortham reports that by the end of 1994, "INI installed cut-off boxes at all its stations allowing the signals to be cut remotely from INI's office in Mexico City" (2013, 101).

In Guelatão, Oaxaca, and elsewhere, radio operators sympathized with the Zapatista movement and pushed to have their radio stations transferred to indigenous control. XEGLO in Guelatão was taken off air numerous times through the INI cut-off box. XEGLO's Zapotec director, Aldo Gonzalez, was eventually forced to resign after he became an advisor to the EZLN (Wortham 2013, 101). Jaime Martínez Luna, who was set to step into the radio director position at XEGLO, was passed over and subsequently left the radio station, a pattern repeated elsewhere. In 1997 Mixe leader Adelfo Regino Montes worked with XEGLO operators to get INI to transfer the station over to local indigenous control, but their efforts were briskly dismissed. According to Regino, INI Director Carlos Tello stated to him that "radio stations were a matter of national security and could not be in the hands of the pueblos" (Wortham 2013, 104). Such experiences led to the proliferation of independent media projects in indigenous communities in Oaxaca and elsewhere.

In Chiapas as elsewhere, indigenous radio, video, and now multiplatform projects are often used to document and raise awareness of legal conflicts, struggles over territory, and legal recognition. In this way indigenous radio has a kinship with earlier work done by Native crews such as on *You Are on Indian Land*, directed by Mort Ransen. This film documents "the conflict between the St. Regis Mohawk community of Cornwall Island (now called Akwesasne) and the local and federal authorities, over Natives' right to bring goods over the Canada-U.S. border without paying duty (as per the Jay Treaty of

1794, passed by the U.S. government but not Canada)" (see Santoro, chapter 9, page 330 in this volume). Such early work and later documentary work such as Alanis Obomsawin's *Incident at Restigouche*, which deals with infringement upon Native sovereignty by government authorities in Quebec, find echoes in the struggles for autonomy and control of territory in Mesoamerica. The concept of visual sovereignty supported by a *prise de parole* and "an emphasis on the right to speak and the duty of the spectator to listen" discussed by Miléna Santoro (page 329 in this volume), is closely connected with the right to speak and be heard that is expressed in indigenous and community radio elsewhere (Stephen 2013, 122–23). The concept of visual sovereignty was first coined by Michelle Raheja (2010) and is expanded to the category of representational sovereignty by Laura Graham (2016).

While the national legislation on indigenous rights passed in 2001 in Mexico states that it aims "to establish conditions for villages and indigenous communities to acquire, operate, and administer mass media," indigenous access to media was to be granted "in accordance with existing laws" (McElmurry 2009, 4). The limitations inherent in this phrase prohibited significant reforms that would give better access and control of media to indigenous communities. This became particularly evident in 2006, when Mexico's congress passed a modification to the Mexican Federal Telecommunications Law and Federal Radio and Television Law that clearly favored corporate media and severely disadvantaged community radio and other forms of grassroots media. The law established that radio and television enterprises that hoped to gain access to new parts of the TV and radio spectrum would be granted licenses through a process of competitive public bidding. While this process was supposed to facilitate much-needed transparency in granting media licenses, it placed poorer community radio stations at a clear disadvantage. Since the bidding process contains no consideration of social or cultural reasons for granting licenses, few indigenous radio stations outside of the INI-controlled network of stations currently have licenses. Operating without a license makes them illegal.

Eugenio Bermejillo, coordinator for Boca de Polena—a network-building organization that supports community radio stations—estimates that there are 150 to 200 community radio stations in

Mexico and that only 15 to 20 percent of them are licensed by the Mexican government (McElmurry 2009, 4). The majority of community stations are unlicensed "pirate" radio stations, seen by the Mexican government as operating outside of the law. This makes them vulnerable to equipment seizures under the General Law of National Goods, which defines radio-phonic space as a public good possessed by the nation, something that cannot be used without legal permission (Prieto Beguiristáin 2009, 2).

The emergence of community radio networks has indelibly shaped political participation in indigenous communities. Community radio stations provide important roles in communication, community-building, and the promotion of local cultural forms. These roles include hosting a call-in show that indigenous migrants in the United States can use to communicate with their relatives; broadcasting local dance or music performances; and airing programs to discuss health, education, and human rights. Community radios are often considered to be sources of cultural revitalization. Here are several examples from Oaxaca (see also Wortham 2013, 142–48).

### RADIO JËN POJ, TLAHUITOLTEPEC, OAXACA

Radio Comunitaria Jën Poj ("energy of the wind" in the Ayuujk or Mixe language), was formed in August 2001. In 2004 Radio Jën Poj received a license, making it one of the first indigenous community stations in the state to operate legally. The website for Radio Jën Poj states the following on the radio station's history:

> Radio Jën Poj was born in August 2001 in the heart of the Mixe community—Ayuujk in our language—Tlahuitoltepec, Oaxaca, when Mixe students, professionals, and community members came together to build a radio transmitter. Now it is a space where collective thought is transformed into winds of words that for a long time had been held back and restricted and today can be heard by men and women throughout the region.
>
> We want to contribute to the development of the community through communication spaces and media that lead to the participation of its inhabitants and responds to their needs and expectations in a non-profit relationship and with a cultural linguistic perspective. (Jën Poj 2013)

Radio Jën Poj is run primarily by students from the community but includes many other people in an open-mic program where anyone can come to speak. The community authorities ask the radio station to cover local cultural events and to provide a public forum for discussion of issues such as the lack of water. Through their coverage of events and their open-mic forum, the core group of young people that runs the station also interviews and brings in the perspectives of many others. As a result, many people in the community are tuned into the station on a daily basis, according to Roberto Olivares of Ojo de Agua Comunicación, who regularly visits the community.

RADIO TOTOPO, TEHUANTEPEC, OAXACA

In the Zapotec Isthmus of Tehuantepec, where there are more than twenty radio stations, Radio Totopo (meaning "baked corn tortilla"—a hallmark of the Isthmus Zapotec food culture) broadcasts in Zapotec. First on the airwaves in 2005, Radio Totopo is located in a neighborhood known as the Barrio del Pescador (fisherman's neighborhood), one of the oldest and most marginal neighborhoods of Juchitán. Local residents who volunteer there receive support from others in the form of food and small donations. The station includes musical programming from a group of young people, Alcoholics Anonymous programs in Zapotec, the promotion of local events, and also an ongoing project to use Zapotec words that people have forgotten and replaced with Spanish.

RADIO DIDHZA KIERU, TALEA DE CASTRO, OAXACA

Further north, in the community of Talea de Castro, a collective of six women and five men run an indigenous community station called Didhza Kieru, Zapotec for "our words," that transmits in Zapotec fifteen hours per day. This collective is recognized and supported by the local authorities in the municipality and by the assembly of communal landholders (see Ojo de Agua Comunicación 2009). The station is acknowledged as part of the structure of local governance and recognized within the same political and cultural structure that houses community assemblies. The radio station exists in parallel with the assembly, and working in the station is recognized as a form of contributing service to the community as part of a civil cargo or volunteer community governance position. In the fall of 2013, Talea de Castro expanded its control over communications by beginning its own cell phone network. It installed an antenna on a special pole and have widespread coverage which has cut the cost of calls to the United States and elsewhere by up to 90 percent (BBC 2013).

The perseverance and proliferation of community radio—particularly in indigenous communities—illuminates the changing political cultures and spaces of participatory democracy in Oaxaca. Meanwhile, these same two traits of community-based radio have provoked ongoing efforts by the government to control and eliminate it in Mexico, and as we will see below, also in Guatemala. In 2008 the Asamblea de Radios Comunitarios y Libres de Oaxaca (Assembly of Free and Community Radio Stations) was formed in response to repression aimed at indigenous stations, such as the attempted shooting of two Zaachila radio station operators in 2008. Comprised of twenty-two Oaxacan community radio stations, along with three international stations, representatives from eight universities, and a wide range of NGOs, this assembly was formed just one day after federal and local police sacked the community radio station known as La Rabiosa, a Mixtec radio station based in the town of Huahuapan de León. Despite a concerted effort by the regional government to raid radio stations and harass its practitioners, community radio in Oaxaca continues to grow.

INDIGENOUS RADIO IN GUATEMALA

The 1996 Peace Accords in Guatemala promised indigenous peoples the right to broadcast on local radio frequencies. Specifically the accords state that measures that the government is required to adopt include:

a. Create opportunities in the official media for the dissemination of expressions of indigenous culture and promote a similar opening in the private media;

b. Promote, in the Guatemalan Congress, the reforms of the existing Act on radio communications that are required in order to make frequencies available for indigenous projects and to ensure respect for the principle of non-discrimination in the use of the communications media. Furthermore, promote the abolition of any provision in the national legislation which is an obstacle to the right of indigenous peoples to have their own communications media for the development of their identity; and

c. Regulate and support a system of informational, scientific, artistic and educational programmes on indigenous cultures in their languages, through the national radio, television and the written media. (Canton 2000)

While a special rapporteur for freedom of expression of the Organization of American States filed a report in 2000 (Canton 2000) encouraging the Guatemalan government to implement the above measures, they were never legislated. Nevertheless, since the accords were signed, hundreds of pirate indigenous radio stations have proliferated, broadcasting in twenty-three indigenous languages. Some sources estimate that more than two hundred Mayan stations are operating without licenses and sponsor shows that include news stories, educational content, health information and Mayan music. As in Mexico, there has been strong opposition by the national government and licensed commercial radio stations to indigenous radios stations operating without a commercial license, which is most of them. Like stations described above in Oaxaca, they not only provide important services such as alcoholism counseling and children's programming but they are also an important source of music and information in local political processes.

For example, Radio Ixchel located in Suponga in the central Guatemalan highlands broadcasts sixteen hours a day in Kaqchikel to between five thousand and seven thousand listeners, is staffed by volunteers, and runs on a budget of about $250 per month (Boals 2011). The station offers cultural programming, health and nutrition information and has also helped local police track down criminals. As in Mexico, Guatemalan community and indigenous radio stations have formed federations. The Association of Community Radios (Asociacíon de Radios Comunitarios) has brought together community radio stations for the past thirteen years (AMARCG 2013).[5]

In 2009 a broad group of community and indigenous radio stations in Guatemala pushed for legislation of the Community Media Bill (Ley de Medios de Comunicación Comunitaria), which would recognize nonprofit community media as a new category distinct from the current legal recognition of commercial, public, and ham radio designations. The bill also called for each of Guatemala's thirty-three municipalities to have its own radio station (Frederick 2012). The Community Media Bill was presented to the Guatemalan congress on August 3, 2009. Despite several years of lobbying by a wide range of Guatemalan organizations and by Cultural Survival (which has staff in the United States, Canada, Guatemala, Nicaragua, South Africa, Kenya, and Nepal), the law has been indefinitely shelved. It is one of ten different bills dealing with indigenous rights that has been accepted by the Guatemalan congress but then indefinitely tabled (Frederick 2012). In a decision in 2012, the Constitutional Court of Guatemala urged congress to reform the current laws to in favor of indigenous peoples access to radio. The congress has not responded to the court's recommendation (Cultural Survival 2012).

In August of 2012, Bill 4479 was introduced by the right-wing Renewed Democratic Freedom (Libertad Democrática Renovada) Party in congress. This bill proposed a reform to the criminal code that would sanction the imprisonment of individual actors and representatives of radio stations that do not have legal authority to broadcast. Indigenous and community radio stations have existed in legal limbo as they are not covered by current law, but there are no laws penalizing their operation. While this has provided some security, some stations have been raided by police and charged with criminal activity. In 2006 Radio Ixchel in Sumpongo, Sacatepequez, was raided, its director facing possible imprisonment. But founder Anselmo Xunic appeared before a judge and was able to fight charges against his station that broadcasting without a legally authorized frequency was a crime (Frederick 2012).

While the proposed legislation against community radio stations was circulating in the Guatemalan congress, Cultural Survival in conjunction with community radio activists submitted a petition to the Inter-American Court of Human Rights to put pressure on the Guatemalan government to change the communications law in favor of legalizing indigenous and community radio stations in accordance with the ruling of the Constitutional Court of Guatemala. "'The state of Guatemala would advance a great deal if it would promote reforms to the current Telecommunications Law that would recognize community radio as a fundamental tool for the development of Indigenous Peoples, their culture, and the protection of Mayan languages,' declared Anselmo Xunic (Kachiquel), manager of Sobrevivencia Cultural in Guatemala" and founder of Radio Ixchel (Cultural Survival 2012).

Indigenous and community radio is clearly a leading ground for the defense of indigenous autonomy and rights in Mexico and Central America. The rights to speak and to be heard have emerged as fundamental parts of indigenous struggles throughout the world and are integral parts of the strategies and programs that accompany indigenous struggles for self-determination. The maintenance and proliferation of community-based radio, particularly in indigenous communities, has created fertile ground in which nonmainstream political processes, strategies, and ideas have continued to exist and grow. In many cases the right to access to radio and television frequencies outside of a commercialized spectrum is fundamental to the defense and maintenance of indigenous languages. Like the defense of territory, the right to media access for indigenous peoples often takes them through legal struggles in national congresses and courts and then beyond that to international legal forums and courts.

*4. Defending Indigenous Territory Claims When the State Doesn't Obey Its Own Laws: The Cases of the Mayagna Community of Awas Tingni and the Miskitu Community of Tuara, Nicaragua*

Perhaps the most difficult arena of autonomy for Mesoamerican indigenous communities to defend in relation to nation-states has been territory. Even when constitutions do recognize the existence of communal forms of land ownership of indigenous peoples, that is no guarantee that these peoples will receive legal recognition of their ancestral lands. In this section I discuss two cases from the northern coast of Nicaragua that focus on how indigenous autonomy relates to land rights and territorial control.

When the Sandinistas took power in Nicaragua in 1979, they initially demonstrated sympathy toward indigenous land claims that were cancelled in the 1960s. In 1987 Law 28 of the Autonomy of Indigenous Peoples and Communities of the Atlantic Coast defined the rights and obligations of the regional autonomous governments of the coast that inhabit the Autonomous Region of the North Atlantic (Regiones Autónomas de la Costa Atlántica de Nicaragua). The law also stated that indigenous communal property consists of the "land, water, and forests that have traditionally belonged to the communities of the Atlantic coast" (Estatuto de Autonomía de las Regiones Autónomas de la Costa Atlántica de Nicaragua 1987). This region has special significance as the first area in the Americas with an autonomous indigenous polity. The indigenous autonomy law written into the constitution "granted political autonomy for the entire coastal population, divided into two autonomous regions. In each autonomous region there would be an election to pick a regional assembly that would legislate regional matters" (Diskin 1991, 164–65). In part, the autonomous region was built on Miskitu claims to sovereignty based on the British protectorate of the Miskitu Reserve in 1894.

In the early 1980s, during the Reagan-supported Contra War against the Sandinista government, the Mayangna village of Awas Tingni, along with ninety other Miskitu and Mayangna indigenous communities on the Atlantic coast, were destroyed. Residents of Awas Tingni and other communities lived in refugee camps in Honduras, some perhaps fighting with the Contras (Wainwright and Bryan 2009, 157). Once the Sandinistas were defeated in elections in 1990, the people of Awas Tingni and other indigenous insurgents returned to Nicaragua and began to press land claims. State officials insisted that the area around what had been the community of Awas Tingni were national lands belonging to the state.

According to Wainwright and Bryan, in order to ensure their position within the "territorialization of post-war relations, Awas Tingni residents produced a sketch map of an area that they claimed in 1992" and then used the map to secure "a logging contract with a Nicaraguan company, MADENSA, headed by former Sandinista officials." In 1993 the terms of the contract were modified and with the help of the World Wildlife Federation (WWF) so that what would have been a standard logging contract was transformed into a "model community forestry project that included sustainable timber practices with recognition of indigenous land rights" (Wainwright and Bryan 2009, 157). While officials from the Nicaraguan Ministry of National Resources promised to approve the new community forest project and title and demarcate Awas Tingni's land claim, in practice they did just the opposite. They granted a 63,000-hectare logging concession to a Korean finance company, SOLCARSA, on lands claimed by Awas Tingni.

With the help of lawyers from the WWF, their original map and an additional map buttressed by ethnography carried out by a North American anthropologist, Awas Tingni took the Nicaraguan government to court, claiming the state had violated its rights to property established by their traditional use and occupancy of the area. The Nicaraguan Supreme Court dismissed the case on a technicality, and the community's lawyers brought the case before the Inter-American Court of Human Rights. In 1998 the Inter-American Court released its report directing the Nicaraguan government to negotiate with community and produce a shared resolution. The Nicaraguan government refused to suspend the logging concession with the Korean company and to recognize the land claims of Awas Tingni. After two years of inaction, the commission filed a petition on behalf of the Awas Tingni against the Nicaraguan government in the Inter-American Court, resulting in the first-ever proceeding focused on indigenous land rights.[6] As noted by Charles Hale, "The petition to the court cites violations of three articles of the Inter-American Human Rights convention, the most important of which is Article 21: 'Rights to Private Property.' Here, for the first time in the convention's 30-year history, Article 21 is being applied to property held collectively and validated by traditional occupancy rather than legal title" (Hale 2006a, 96–97).

Ruling in 2001, the court affirmed the Awas Tingni petition and their right to property, as affirmed in the Inter-American Convention on Human Rights, which protects the traditional land tenure of indigenous peoples. The court also concluded that "Nicaragua had violated the rights of the Mayagna community of Awas Tingni by granting a logging concession within the community's traditional territory without obtaining its consent and after ignoring the consistent complaints and requests of Awas Tingni urging demarcation of the territory" (University of Arizona Law and Policy Program n.d.). As a remedy, the court ordered the government of Nicaragua to demarcate and title the community's ancestral lands within a period of fifteen months. In addition, the court mandated that the Nicaraguan government reform its laws and administrative procedure to guarantee the land rights of all indigenous peoples.

In January of 2003, the Law of the Communal Property Regimen of the Lands of Indigenous Peoples and Ethnic communities of the Atlantic Coast of Nicaragua and of the Coco, Bocay, Indio and Maíz Rivers (Law 445) was formalized. While the deadline for the implementation of the Awas Tingni judgment for the government to title the community's territory was at the end of 2002, this was not completed until December of 2008. Despite having won title to their lands after a thirteen-year struggle, according to geographers Wainwright and Bryan, residents of Awas Tingni still feel insecure. Other indigenous communities have continued to challenge Awas Tingni's right to land (Wainwright and Bryan 2009, 168).

The notoriety of the Awas Tingni case and the 2003 Law of the Communal Property Regime provided political impetus for communities like the Miskitu community of Tuara to map, measure, and title their territories.[7] In 2005 community members of Tuara together with representatives of a research team from the University of the Autonomous Regions of the Caribbean Coast of Nicaragua discussed the possibility of mapping and titling Tuara lands. The community of Tuara chose community representatives and discussed the project in a meeting presided over by community authorities, religious leaders, elders, and teachers. They then carried out a series of workshops that revealed, among other things, that many people had no knowledge of the actual physical location or perimeter of Tuara territory. The combined research team of community representatives and university investigators designed a project that included exploring social and environmental relations, legal history, and a cartographic and demographic analysis that would develop information and a collective conceptual basis for defining the territory traditionally occupied by Tuara. This process thus incorporated both oral tradition and written records to document the territory of the Tuaras in preparation for the possibility of petitioning first the Nicaraguan government and, if unsuccessful, the Inter-American Court, following the logic of the Awas Tingni case.

The strategy of using both written and oral history records as carried out by Awas Tingni and Tuara communities in Nicaragua has also been used by Native peoples in the courts of Canada, which recognize both forms of record keeping. In chapter 3 of this volume, David McNab highlights the importance, independence, and sovereignty of oral traditions and the difficulties of juxtaposing oral histories with written records. It is a strategy used by many Native peoples in legal and other claims, but is not always successful in all courts. In this case, more traction was gained in international courts than in Nicaraguan national courts.

Using a process of ethnomapping, the research team took a wide range of information from oral histories, focus groups, historical documents, and socioeconomic and demographic data and generated five kinds of maps. The first described the customs of Tuara in relation to land and its incorporation into their cosmovision. The second is a map of specific land areas claimed. The third is a map of zones of common use for hunting, fishing, and gathering shared with other communities. The fourth map documents the overlaps of Tuara traditional territory with those of other communities. The fifth and last map locates mestizo immigrants and others without titles in the areas claimed by the Tuaras.

The mapping project reveals key differences in the way that Nicaragua national law conceives of territories versus how they have actually been constructed and lived in by the Miskitus of Tuara and other indigenous groups. The land titles call for the resolution of conflicts and absolute boundaries between communities. Traditionally, and even currently, the people of Tuara do not operate with the notion of an "exclusive" territory. Rather, there are overlapping realms of territory used for hunting, fishing, and gathering and other areas of shared resources with other communities. For Tuara community members, territory is not exclusive but shared in different ways with different communities, perhaps varying through

time. The Tuaras are pursuing their land claims through Nicaraguan legal processes. They are no doubt conscious, however, of the
possibility of going above the Nicaraguan government to international bodies such as the Organization of American States if their
request for demarcation and titling is not honored by the Nicaraguan government.

What do these cases tell us about autonomy and territory? The
case of Awas Tingni suggests one of the important strategies used
by indigenous peoples to push states to honor the legislation they
have regarding indigenous autonomy. Many scholars have focused
on the ways that those who are disenfranchised from political participation work through transnational and nonnational political
spaces and strategies (Levitt 2001; Bosniak 2000; Sassen 1999). In
her more recent work, Saskia Sassen has suggested important ways
in which, even inside capitalist democracies, there is "the emergence of a type of political subject that does not quite correspond
to the notion of the formal political subject who is the voting and
jury-serving citizen" (2006, 321). Her argument is that processes of
globalization have produced a growing distance between the state
and the citizen. Some of this distance involves the ways in which
states have accommodated global ideas and institutions, such as
the rule of law and respect for private authority from the inside—
reinscribing the global within the national.

In the case of Awas Tingni, global norms and expectations about
the rights of indigenous peoples forced the Nicaraguan court to
reform national land law and to implement that reformed law. This
paved the way for such groups as the Tuaras to also pursue land
claims. The relative success of this strategy in forcing nation-states
to reform land laws to grant access to indigenous peoples in accordance with existing national constitutional reforms through appealing to such supra-state institutions as the Inter-American Court
of Human Rights has also been used for securing legal access for
indigenous peoples to other rights as well, not only from Central
America, Mexico, and First Nations Canada, but in other regions
as well. At a larger level, the troubling global pattern of large-scale
land grabs and mining concessions granted to companies on territorial lands of indigenous peoples underlines the importance of

controlling territory as a key material base for the sustainability of indigenous autonomy projects (Borras and Franco 2012; Borras et al. 2012; Kerssen 2013). As Karl Hele suggests in chapter 6 of this volume, securing territorial land rights is the basis for achieving sovereignty in other arenas as well.

## Conclusions

The case studies analyzed here suggest that while indigenous autonomy is advancing on many fronts in contemporary Mexico and Central America, such efforts are happening without the cooperation of nation-states and in fact usually in the face of significant resistance by states—even to their own constitutions, signed agreements, and laws. In order to advance their projects of autonomy, indigenous peoples in Mesoamerica have had to go above the nation-state and use international institutions to pressure the nation-states they live in *and* have also had to assert their right to self-determination as legitimate regardless of the establishment of legal regimes by the state. This is similar to strategies used by First Nations in Canada to achieve territorial and political recognition (see chapters by McNab, Hele, and Santoro in this volume) and by other indigenous peoples in the Americas. In the case of the declaration of autonomous municipalities in Mexico, this has involved unilaterally pursuing autonomy projects, first in Chiapas and then elsewhere. In the case of other autonomy projects such as community policing, justice systems, and indigenous media projects, this has often involved existing in legal limbo with de facto recognition by local and some state officials but also the danger of being declared illegal where the projects are not forcibly quashed.

Mexico and Central America are now plagued by a culture of what some have called "neoliberal multicriminalism" (Speed 2016)—referring to political, economic, and legal processes and spaces that have incorporated sophisticated and vast criminal enterprises centered on drugs, human, and gun smuggling, among other things, into some of the pillars of the Mexican, Guatemalan, and other states, including into the armed forces, police forces, justice systems, political parties, and more. The legal limbo of many of the autonomy projects described here exists in an uneasy parallel to these spaces of neoliberal multicriminalism. For indigenous peoples in the region, in order to continue any forward momentum in sustaining autonomy projects of governance, justice, policing, media, and territory, a multipronged strategy is required. This includes working within state systems where possible, as is being done in Guatemala, to reform local legal systems at the municipal level. It also involves continuing to produce self-determination projects and laws in a deliberate and reflective manner and not submitting to national laws that are not enforced, as in the case of the declaration of municipal autonomous regions of good government in Chiapas in 2003. The last strategy is to form alliances with other organizations and to refer indigenous autonomy projects to higher international instances of justice, such as the Inter-American Court of Human Rights, when nation-states refuse to validate their legitimacy. All three of these strategies have proven necessary in any forward movement of indigenous autonomy projects in the region.

While the overall picture of change in relation to the willingness of nation-states in contemporary Mesoamerica to accommodate projects of indigenous autonomy is depressing compared to some Andean counterparts, in fact the level of strength and accomplishment of indigenous movements in this region is encouraging if compared with several decades ago. In the 1970s and 1980s, indigenous movements were localized and regional at best in Mexico and Central America. They are now articulated at a national level and even internationally. It is not unlike the slow and uneven process of granting limited sovereignty to First Nations in Canada. While state intransience is a difficult obstacle to overcome, in some ways it also provides a useful referent for indigenous movements to continue to work against, as their autonomy projects gain traction at local and regional levels. *Todos somos indios*–we are all Indians— was unthinkable as a slogan fifty years ago in Mexico, where anti-indigenous racism prevailed at all levels of society. The fact that more people are recognizing their indigenous ancestry and indigenous movements have moved into the mainstream political arena speaks much about the gains made.

# Notes

1. See Centro de Documentación sobre Zapatismo 2001 for a comparison between the San Andrés Accords and the Constitutional Reform on Indigenous Rights and Culture.

2. In 2001 Zapatistas and participants in the RAP of Tumbalá had engaged in significant friction over conflicting land claims (Hidalgo 2006; Barmeyer 2009, 61).

3. See Rus (1994) and Rus and Collier (2003) for a historical perspective on these communities, which differ significantly from those in the Selva Lacandona.

4. This section draws on ideas I discuss in "Community and Indigenous Radio in Oaxaca: Testimony and Participatory Democracy," in *Radio Fields: The Anthropology of Radio in the 21st Century*, ed. Danny Fischer and Lucas Bessire (New York: New York University Press, 2012), 124–42.

5. AMARCG stations are found in the following locations: AJ TV, Santiago Atitlán, Sololá, Kumol, Nebaj, Quiche; Radio Catarina, San Marcos; Radio Dulzura, Rio Blanco, San Marcos; Radio Kamol'Be, Alta Verapaz; Radio Kastajinel, Balanya, Chimaltenango; Radio La Compañera, Nahualá Sololá; Radio La Niña, Totonicapán; Radio La Unión, Alta Verapaz; Radio La Voz de Catarina, San Marcos; Radio Libertad, CPR Petén; Radio San Pedro, Atitlán, Sololá; Radio Sinakan, Patzún, Chimaltenango; Radio Villa Nueva, San Marcos (AMARCG 2013).

6. Both the Inter-American Commission on Human Rights and the Inter-American Court on Human Rights are under the auspices of the Organization of American States.

7. This section draws on material discussed in Charles Hale and Lynn Stephen, Introduction, in *Otros Saberes: Collaborative Research on Indigenous and Afro-Descendent Cultural Politics* (Santa Fe: School for Advanced Research Press, 2013).

# Bibliography

Agreement on Identity and Rights of Indigenous Peoples (AIDPI). 1995. Available at: http://en.wikisource.org/wiki/Agreement_on_Identity_and_Rights_of_Indigenous _Peoples/.

Alvarado, Leonardo J. 2007. "Prospects and Challenges in the Implementation of Indigenous Peoples' Human Rights in International Law: Lessons from the Case of Awas Tingni vs. Nicaragua." *Arizona Journal of International and Comparative Law* 24, no. 3: 609–43.

AMARCG (Asociación Mundial de Radios comunitarios en Guatemala). 2013. AMARC Guatemala radio. http://amarcguatemala.blogspot.com/.

Armon, Jeremy, Rachel Seider, and Richard Wilson. 1997. "Reframing Citizenship: Indigenous Rights, Local Power, and Peace Process in Guatemala." *Accord*, 66–73. www.c-r.org/sites/c-r.org/files/Accord%2002_6reframing%20citizenship_1997 _eng.pdf/.

Aubry, Andrés. 2003. "Autonomy in the San Andrés Accords: Expression and Fulfillment of a New Federal Pact." In *Mayan Lives, Mayan Utopias: The Indigenous Peoples of Chiapas and the Zapatista Rebellion*, edited by Jan Rus, Rosalva Aída Hernández Castillo, and Shannan Mattiace, 219–42. Lanham: Rowman and Littlefield.

Barmeyer, Niels. 2009. *Developing Zapatista Autonomy: Conflict and NGO Involvement in Rebel Chiapas*. Albuquerque: University of New Mexico Press.

Baronnet, Bruno. 2009. "Autonomía y educación indígena: las escuelas Zapatistas de Las Cañadas de la Selva Lacandona de Chiapas, México." PhD thesis, University of Paris III-Sorbone/El Colegio de México.

Baronnet, Bruno, Mariana Mora Bayo, and Richard Stahler Sholk. 2011. Introducción. In *Luchas "muy otras": Zapatismo y autonomía en las comunidades indígenas de Chiapas*, edited by Bruno Baronnet, Mariana Mora Bayo, and Richard Stahler Sholk, 19–58. Mexico City: Centro de Investigaciones y Estudios Superiores en Antropología Social (CIESAS), Universidad Autónoma Metropolitana, Universidad Autónoma de Chiapas.

BBC News. 2013. "Mobile Phone Network Launched by Remote Town," September 2, 2013. https://www.bbc.com/news/technology-23929009.

Boals, Connor. 2011. "Pirate Radio, Mayan Style: Indigenous Stations Want to Come in from the Cold." *Columbia Journalism Review*, August 24. www.cjr.org/reports /pirate_radio_mayan_style.php?page=1/.

Borras, J. H., and J. Franco. 2012. "A Land Sovereignty Alternative: Towards a Peoples Counter Enclosure." Transnational Institute Agrarian Justice Discussion Paper. www.tni.org/briefing/land-sovereignty-alternative?context=69566/.

Borras, S. M., J. C. Franco, S. Gómez, C. Kay, and M. Spoor. 2012. "Land grabbing in Latin America and the Caribbean." *Journal of Peasant Studies* 39, nos. 3–4: 845–72.

Bosniak, Linda. 2000. "Citizenship Denationalized, Symposium: The State of Citizenship." *Indian Journal of Global Legal Studies* 7, no. 2: 447–510.

Burguete Cal y Mayor, Araceli. 2003. "The de Facto Autonomous Process: New Jurisdictions and Parallel Governments in Rebellion." In *Mayan Lives, Mayan Utopias: The Indigenous Peoples of Chiapas and the Zapatista Rebellion*, edited by Jan Rus, Rosalva Aída Hernández Castillo, and Shannan Mattiace, 191–218. Lanham: Rowman and Littlefield.

Canton, Santiago. 2000. "Preliminary Evaluation of Freedom of Expression in Guatemala." Special Rapporteur for Freedom of Expression. Washington DC: Organization of American States. April 18. www.oas.org/en/iachr/expression/showarticle .asp?artid=30&lid=1/.

Castillo García, Gustavo. 2010. "21 Marzo, 2010. Cárteles de la droga se agrupan en dos bandos para luchar por las regiones." *La Jornada*. www.jornada.unam.mx /2010/03/21/politica/010n1pol/.

Castoriadis, Cornelius. 1987. *The Imaginary Institution of Society*. Cambridge, Mass.: MIT Press.

———. 1991. "Power, Politics, Autonomy." In *Philosophy, Politics, Autonomy*, 143–74. Oxford: Oxford University Press.

Castro Soto, Gustavo, and Onecimo Hidalgo. 2003. "EZLN-Se organizan los Caracoles y las Juntas de Buen Gobierno." San Cristóbal de las Casas, Chiapas: CIEPAC. August 5. www.ecoportal.net/Eco-Noticias/ezln_-_Se_organizan_los_Caracoles _y_las_Juntas_de_Buen_Gobierno/.

Centro de Documentación sobre Zapatismo. 2001. Cuadro comparativo entre los Acuerdos de San Andrés y la reforma constitucional sobre derechos y cultura indígena. www.cedoz.org/site/content.php?doc=720&cat=143/.

Cerda García, Alejandro. 2011. *Imaginando Zapatismo: Multiculturalidad y autonomía indígena en Chiapas desde un municipio autónomo.* México DF: CIESAS/Porrúa.

Chatterton, Paul. 2010. "Autonomy." *Antipode* 42, no. 4: 897–908.

Cultural Survival. 2012. Press Release: "Protecting Indigenous People's Free Speech and Access to Media in Guatemala: Cultural Survival Submits Petition to Inter-American Commission on Human Rights." Cambridge MA. October 1. www.culturalsurvival.org/press/guatemala/press-releases/.

Dada, Carlos. 2015. "Corruption Charges Turn Guatemala Upside Down." *The New Yorker.* September 5. www.newyorker.com/news/news-desk/corruption-charges-turn-guatemala-upside-down.

de la Peña, Guillermo. 2006. "A New Mexican Nationalism?: Indigenous Rights, Constitutional Reform and the Conflicting Meanings of Multiculturalism." *Nations and Nationalism* 12, no. 2: 279–302.

Diskin, Martin. 1991. "Ethnic Discourse and Challenge to Anthropology: The Nicaraguan Case." In *Nation-States and Indians in Latin America,* edited by Greg Urban and Joel Sherzer, 156–80. Austin: University of Texas Press.

Estatuto de Autonomía de las Regiones Autónomas de la Costa Atlántica de Nicaragua. 1987. Asamblea Nacional de la República de Nicaragua División de Informática Legislativa. Publicada en *La Gaceta: Diario Oficial* no. 238, October 30.

Forbis, Melissa. 2006. "Autonomy and a Handful of Herbs." In *Dissident Women: Gender and Cultural Politics in Chiapas,* edited by Shannon Speed, Rosalva Aída Hernández Castillo, and Lynn Stephen, 176–203. Austin: University of Texas Press.

Frederick, James. 2012. "Guatemalan Mayans Take Fight to the Airwaves." *Tico Times.* January 27. www.ticotimes.net/Current-Edition/Top-Story/News/Guatemalan-Mayans-take-fight-to-the-airwaves_Friday-January-27-2012/.

Graham, Laura R. 2016. "Toward Representational Sovereignty: Rewards and Challenges of Indigenous Media in the A'uwē-Xavante Communities of Eténhiritipa-Pimentel Barbosa." *Media and Communication* 4, no. 2: 13–32. http://cogitatiopress.com/ojs/index.php/mediaandcommunication/article/view/438.

Gutiérrez Narváez, Raúl de Jesús. 2005. "Escuela y Zapatismo entre los tsotsiles: entre autónomos." Master's thesis, Centro de Investigaciones e Estudios Superiores en Antropología Social (CIESAS), Sureste.

Hale, Charles R. 2006a. "Activist Research v. Cultural Critique: Indigenous Land Rights and the Contradictions of Politically Engaged Anthropology." *Cultural Anthropology* 21, no. 1: 96–120.

———. 2006b. *Más Que Un Indio: Racial Ambivalence and Neoliberal Multiculturalism in Guatemala.* Santa Fe: School for Advanced Research Press.

Hale, Charles, and Lynn Stephen. 2013. Introduction. In *Otros Saberes: Collaborative Research on Indigenous and Afro-Descendent Cultural Politics,* 1–29. Santa Fe: School for Advanced Research Press.

Harvey, Neil. 1998. *The Chiapas Rebellion: The Struggle for Land and Democracy.* Durham: Duke University Press.

———. 2001. "Globalization and Resistance in Post-Cold War Mexico: Difference, Citizenship, and Biodiversity Conflicts in Chiapas." *Third World Quarterly* 22: 1045–61.

———. 2008. "Beyond Hegemony: Zapatismo, Empire, and Descent." In *Empire and Dissent: the United States and Latin America*, edited by Fred Rosen, 117–36. Durham NC: Duke University Press.

———. 2011. "Más Allá de la Hegemonía: El zapatismo y la otra política." In *Luchas 'muy otras': Zapatismo y autonomía en las comunidades indígenas de Chiapas*, edited by Bruno Baronnet, Mariana Mora Bayo, and Richard Shaler-Sholk, 163–94. México DF: Universidad Autónoma Metropolitana, CIESAS, Universidad Autónoma de Chiapas.

Henderson, Victoria. 2008. "Sound as a Dollar: The Propertization of Spectrum Resources and Implications for Non-Profit Community Radio in Guatemala." Master's thesis, Queen's University.

Hernández Navarro, Luis. 1998. "Ciudadanos iguales, ciudadanos diferentes." In *Los Acuerdos de San Andrés*, edited by Luis Hernández Navarro and Ramón Vera Herrera, 15–22. Mexico City: Ediciones Era.

Hidalgo Domínguez, Onésimo. 2006. "Los Acuerdos de San Andrés a Diez Años Después." Chiapas al Día 494. San Cristóbal de las Casas: CIEPAC. February 15. www.ciepac.org/boletines/chiapasaldia.php/.

Jën Poj. 2013. "Quiénes Somos?" Tlahuitoltepec, Oaxaca: Radio Jën Poj. http://radiojenpoj.info/quienes-somos/.

Kerssen, Tanya M. 2013. *Grabbing Power: The New Struggles for Land, Food, and Democracy in Northern Honduras*. Oakland: Food First.

Legrand, Diego. 2012. "San Luis, México: ¿Cuál es la ley en esta tierra?" *El Puercoespin*. September 11. http://lamanodelfuego.wordpress.com/tag/el-puercoespin/.

Levitt, Peggy. 2001. *The Transnational Villagers*. Berkeley: University of California Press.

Leyva Solano, Xóchitl. 1995. "Catequistas, misioneros, y tradiciones en Las Cañadas." In *Chiapas: Los rumbos de otra historia*, edited by Juan Pedro Viqueria and Mario Humberto Ruz, 375–406. México DF: Universidad Nacional Autónoma de México.

Leyva Solano, Xóchitl, and Gabriel Ascencio Franco. 1996. *Lacandona al filo del agua*. México DF: Centro de Investigaciones y Estudios Superiores en Antropología Social / San Cristóbal de las Casas: Centro de Investigaciones Humanísticas de Mesoamérica y el Estado de Chiapas / Tuxtla Gutiérrez: Universidad de Ciencias y Artes del Estado de Chiapas / México DF: Fondo de Cultura Económica.

Mattiace, Shannan. 2003a. "Regional Renegotiation of Space: Tojolabal Ethnic Identity in Las Margaritas, Chiapas." In *Mayan Lives, Mayan Utopias: The Indigenous Peoples of Chiapas and the Zapatista Rebellion*, edited by Jan Rus, Rosalva Aída Hernández Castillo, and Shannan Mattiace, 109–34. Lanham: Rowman and Littlefield.

———. 2003b. *To See with Two Eyes: Peasant Activism and Indian Autonomy in Chiapas, Mexico*. Albuquerque: University of New Mexico Press.

McElmurry, Sara. 2009. "Indigenous Community Radio in Mexico." Washington: Americas Policy Program. http://americas.irc-online.org/am/5977 (page inactive).

"The Mexico Village That Got Itself Talking." 2013. BBC News. October 14. www.bbc.co.uk/news/world-latin-america-24450542/.

Mignolo, Walter O. 2011. *The Darker Side of Western Modernity: Global Futures, Decolonial Options*. Durham NC: Duke University Press.

Nobel Foundation. 2012. "The Nobel Peace Prize 1992." Press Release. www.nobelprize
.org/nobel_prizes/peace/laureates/1992/press.html/.

Núñez Patiño, Kathia. 2005. "Socialización infantil en dos comunidades choles, rupturas y continuidades: escuela oficial y escuela autónoma." Master's thesis, Centro de Investigaciones e Estudios Superiores en Antropología Social, Sureste.

Ojo de Agua Comunicación. 2009. "Didhza Kieru." Oaxaca: Ojos de Agua Comunicación. www.ojodeaguacomunicacion.org/index.php/videoteca/87-ojo-de
-agua-comunicacion/programas-de-ojo-de-agua/espacios-de-comunicacion
-comunitaria/151-didhza-kieru/.

Olivera Bustamante, Mercedes. 2004. "Sobre las profundidades de mandar obedeci-
endo." In *Tejiendo historias: tierra, género y poder en Chiapas*, edited by Maya
Lorena Pérez Ruiz, 219–47. Mexico: INAH.

Panner, Morris, and Adriana Beltrán. 2010. "Battling Organized Crime in Guatemala." *Americas Quarterly*, November 5. www.americasquarterly.org/node/1899.

Policía Comunitaria. 2012a. "Qué Hacemos?: Somos una organización de los pueblos."
Policía Comunitaria Sistema de Seguridad y Justicia Comunitaria de la Costa Chica
y Montaña de Guerrero. www.policiacomunitaria.org/content/que-hacemos/.

———. 2012b. "Quienes Somos: Datos Generales." Policía Comunitaria: Sistema de
Seguridad y Justicia Comunitaria de la Costa Chica y Montana de Guerrero.
www.policiacomunitaria.org/content/quienes-somos/.

Prieto Beruiristáin, Iñigo. 2009. *Radio Nomndaa: The World of Water*. Washington
DC: American Policy Program. http://americas.inc-online.org/am/6164, accessed
January 20, 2010.

Raheja, Michelle H. 2010. *Reservation Reelism: Redfacing, Visual Sovereignty, and Representations of Native Americans in Film*. Lincoln: University of Nebraska Press.

Rus, Jan. 1994. "The 'Comunidad Revolucionario Institutional': The Subversion of
Native Government in Highland Chiapas, 1946–1968." In *Everyday Forms of State
Formation: Revolution and the Negotiation of Rule in Modern Mexico*, edited by
Gilbert M. Joseph and Daniel Nugent, 265–300. Durham: Duke University Press.

Rus, Jan and George Collier. 2003. "A Generation of Crisis in the Central Highlands
of Chiapas: The Cases of Chamula and Zinacantán, 1974–2000." In *Mayan Lives,
Mayan Utopias: The Indigenous Peoples of Chiapas and the Zapatista Rebellion*,
edited by Jan Rus, Rosalva Aída Hernández Castillo, and Shannan Mattiace, 33–
62. Lanham: Rowman and Littlefield.

San Andrés Accords on Indigenous Rights and Culture. 1996. Translated by Rosalva
Bermudez-Ballin. http://struggle.ws/mexico/ezln/san_andres.html.

Sassen, Saskia. 1991. *The Global City: New York, London, Tokyo*. Princeton: Princeton University Press.

———. 1999. *Globalization and Its Discontents: Essays on the New Mobility of People
and Money*. New York: New Press.

———. 2006. *Territory, Authority, Rights: From Medieval to Global Assemblages*. Princeton: Princeton University Press.

Seider, Rachel. 2008. "Legal Globalization and Human Rights: Constructing the Rule
of Law in Postconflict Guatemala?" In *Human Rights in the Maya Region: Global*

*Politics, Cultural Contentions, and Moral Engagements*, edited by Pedro Pitarch, Shannon Speed, and Xóchitl Leyva Solano, 67–90. Durham: Duke University Press.

Sierra, María Teresa. 2005. "The Revival of Indigenous Justice in Mexico: Challenge for Human Rights and the State." *PoLAR: Political and Legal Anthropology Review* 28, no. 2: 52–72.

———. 2010. "Indigenous Justice Faces the State: The Community Police Force in Guerrero, Mexico." *NACLA* 43, no. 5: 34–38.

———. 2013. "Desafiando al Estado desde los márgenes: justicia y seguridad en la experiencia de la policía comunitaria de Guerrero." In *De las reformas multiculturales al fin del reconocimiento. Justicia, pueblos indígenas y violencia en México y Guatemala*, edited by María Teresa Sierra, R. Aída Hernández and Rachel Sieder, 185–229. México DF: CIESAS-FLACSO.

South and Meso American Indian Rights Center (SAIIC). 1990. "500 Years of Indian Resistance." Call to Action on the First Continental Meeting of Indigenous Peoples (Fall 1989/Winter 1990), 16–18. www.nativeweb.org/papers/statements/quincentennial/firstcont.php/.

Speed, Shannon. 2007. "Exercising Rights and Reconfiguring Resistance in the Zapatista Juntas de Buen Gobierno." In *The Practice of Human Rights: Tracking Law between the Global and the Local*, edited by Sally Engle Merry and Mark Goodale, 163–92. Cambridge: Cambridge University Press.

———. 2008. *Rights in Rebellion: Indigenous Struggle and Human Rights in Chiapas*. Stanford: Stanford University Press.

———. 2016. "States of Violence: Indigenous Women Migrants in the Era of Neoliberal Criminalism." *Critique of Anthropology* 36, no. 3: 1–22.

Speed, Shannon, and Alvaro Reyes. 2009. "'Asumiendo Nuestra Propia Defensa': Resistance and the Red de Defensores Comunitarios in Chiapas." In *Human Rights in the Maya Region: Global Politics, Cultural Contentions, and Moral Engagements*, edited by Pedro Pitarch, Shannon Speed, and Xóchitl Leyva Solano, 279–304. Durham and London: Duke University Press.

Stephen, Lynn. 2002. *Zapata Lives!: Histories and Cultural Politics in Southern Mexico*. Berkeley: University of California Press.

———. 2005a. "Negotiating Global, National, and Local 'Rights' in a Zapotec Community." *Political and Legal Anthropology Review* 28, no. 1: 130–50.

———. 2005b. *Zapotec Women: Gender, Class, and Ethnicity in Globalized Oaxaca*. Durham: Duke University Press.

———. 2012. "Community and Indigenous Radio in Oaxaca: Testimony and Participatory Democracy." In *Radio Fields: The Anthropology of Radio in the 21st Century*, edited by Danny Fischer and Lucas Bessire, 124–42. New York: New York University Press.

———. 2013. *We Are the Face of Oaxaca: Testimony and Social Movements*. Durham: Duke University Press.

Subcomandante Marcos. 2003. "EZLN-Se organizan los Caracoles y las Juntas de Buen Gobierno. Durante la segunda quincena del mes de julio del 2003, el Ejercito Zapatista de Liberación Nacional (EZLN) en voz del Subcomandante Insurgente

'Marcos,' emitió diez comunicados anunciando cambios y nuevas estrategias del EZLN." Ecoportal.

University of Arizona Law and Policy Program. n.d. "Nicaragua Issues Title to Awas Tingni Land." www.law.arizona.edu/depts/iplp/international/pdf/Awas%20tingni.pdf/.

Wainwright, Joel, and Joe Bryan. 2009. "Cartography, Territory, Property: Postcolonial Reflections on Indigenous Counter-Mapping in Nicaragua and Belize." *Cultural Geographies* 16: 153–78.

Warren, Kay. 2003. "Voting against Indigenous Rights in Guatemala: Lessons from the 1999 Referendum." In *Indigenous Movements, Self-Representation, and the State in Latin America*, edited by Kay Warren and Jean Jackson, 149–80. Austin: University of Texas Press.

Wortham, Erica Cusi. 2013. *Indigenous Media in Mexico: Culture, Community, and the State*. Durham: Duke University Press.

# 8

# Against Coloniality

*Andrés Jach'aqullu's Indigenous Movement in the*
*Era of the Bolivian National Revolution of 1952*

WASKAR T. ARI-CHACHAKI

On August 21, 1957, indigenous activist Andrés Jach'aqullu was one of seventeen indigenous people who arrived in Sucre to denounce the state-controlled peasant union in the community of Muxuquya. Jach'aqullu was a member of the Alcaldes Mayores Particulares (AMP), which means "major autonomous mayors," a large network of indigenous activists who promoted the Indian Law. They claimed that union leaders had jailed them for twenty days with little food or water. Zenón Galarza, Rafaelino Montaño, Marcelino Gallo, Severo Navia, and Cecilio Colque said that they had been detained to coerce them into agreeing with peasant union leaders. Andrés Jach'aqullu, a former policeman who was new to indigenous activism, explained that many similar cases had occurred over the past two years. He was concerned that this type of problem was becoming engrained in many parts of the countryside in the late 1950s.[1] These accusations revealed a new face of the Bolivian National Revolution that began in 1952 and that had promised, among other things, radical reform in favor of the indigenous masses. This face was characterized by the repression of and violence against dissident indigenous people who rejected the hegemonic discourse of the 1952 National Revolution.

Andrés Jach'aqullu is a fascinating individual and central to the development of the Bolivian indigenous movement of the second half of the twentieth century. Jach'aqullu represented a different kind of indigenous activist who was not motivated by class concerns but instead wanted to create an ethnic and cultural, even spiritual, revival of Indians. He epitomizes the work of an AMP activist during the time of the National Revolution. Jach'aqullu helped position ethnic politics as central during a period when other organizing movements attempted to erase indigeneity in the interest of class-based politics within the framework of Marxist discourse and concepts. Jach'aqullu lived in a world with such complex and fragile relations of power that he had to change his last name two times, going by Andrés Cerrogrande and Andrés Ticona. He and the other AMPs were the precursors to the ethnic revival of the 1990s and beyond, including the era of Evo Morales and Bolivia as a plurinational state. In this chapter, I argue that Andrés Jach'aqullu used what he called the Indian Law as way to challenge the discursive emphasis on nation making through whitening that was prominent in Bolivia after 1952. As a second-generation AMP leader, Jach'aqullu also adjusted and re-elaborated ideas about the Indian Law. Jach'aqullu and the second generation of the AMP were the bridge that connected the work and ideas of the movement of *apoderados* with the modern indigenous activist movements that emerged in the 1970s.[2] Principal among these movements were the Indianistas, who argued that the Indian agenda should be to fight oppression as a nation, and the Kataristas, who instead insisted that Indian peasants were oppressed as both a class and a nation.

The Indian Law is not Bolivian official legislation. Rather than a single document, it is a political discourse used by Jach'aqullu and the broader AMP movement that combined Aymara religious and political ideas from the first half of the twentieth century with a reinterpretation and re-elaboration of the colonial-era Law of the Indies, which advocated for two separate republics: one Indian, the other white (or Spanish). The Indian Law is an amorphous concept that the AMP invented to incorporate their views of the Pachamama with their ideas about older colonial and republican legislation. It reflected traditional legal concepts related to land, territory, nation, faith, religion, rights, and Indianness. Laura Gotkowitz has already emphasized the importance of legal culture to indigenous movements in mid-twentieth-century Bolivia. She defines *legal culture* as traditional concepts related to communal land ownership and rights that indigenous movements used to reinterpret Bolivian legislation and then act on it (Gotkowitz 2007, 50–130, 192–290).

Using a different framework from Gotkowitz, this chapter draws on oral histories and indigenous families' archives to offer a concrete example of the rich tradition of indigenous legal culture: the Indian Law, as elaborated by the AMP and Jach'aqullu.

## Jach'aqullu and the AMP after the National Revolution

The events denounced by Jach'aqullu described at the outset of this chapter took place in the context of the changes wrought upon the elite sectors of Bolivia by the 1952 Revolution. The *Rosca* mining oligarchy was replaced by an emerging middle class that allied with the labor movement and rural indigenous people to nationalize the mines and institute an agrarian reform. The goal of the agrarian reform was to break up large, unproductive haciendas into individual plots of land in the highland and valley regions of the western side of the country. This revolution represented a rite of passage into the modern era since it profoundly changed the previous racialized social order by incorporating a large part of the Bolivian population from indigenous heritage into a notion of liberal citizenship. It was led by the Movimiento Nacionalista Revolucionario (MNR), a political party that became a crucial actor in the complex and ever-changing alliances between classes and power players in Bolivia. To ensure its power after the revolution, the MNR instituted a one-party system that lasted for more than a decade and organized state-controlled peasant unions in the countryside. These unions existed throughout the national territory and tended to follow three patterns. Some peasant organizations, such as the one in Jach'aqhachi, La Paz, were run primarily by Indians who were able to assimilate this institution to their needs, making these unions work according to the ayllu or community model.[3] In other regions, the unions conformed to the pattern of Ucureña, Cochabamba, becoming associations of ex-hacienda peons. In this second type, class and labor ideas dominated the goals. In other regions, such as northern Potosí and some parts of Chuquisaca, however, the rural middle class appropriated the peasant unions to serve their own needs.[4] This was the case in 1957 when Andrés Jach'aqullu and his group denounced the cholo- and mestizo-run unions (Rivera 1984, 120–70). Jach'aqullu and the AMP found an important audience among people who were being dominated by this third group of unions; their work reinvented the AMP social movement in the era of the National Revolution.

By preventing women's participation within the peasant unions, promoting education only in Spanish, insisting that Indian men not wear traditional clothing, and empowering the mestizo provincial elite in some regions of Bolivia, the National Revolution reintroduced a racial assimilation discourse. The new revolutionary state, with its emphasis on westernization, also considered many of the ayllus' ritual practices to be uncivilized, superstitious, and leading to alcoholism and coca addiction, and it resolved to combat them with what it considered "scientific" education.[5] Furthermore, because of their failure to support the peasant unions that were controlled by the rural middle class, the ex-peons were accused of opposing the modernizing ideas of agrarian reform and the National Revolution. The MNR gradually became a populist party with a middle-class agenda, developing a discourse of mestizaje that purported to end the caste system (Antezana Ergueta and Bedregal Gutiérrez 1992, 1–35). Originally from the colonial era, the term *casta* (caste) persisted in Bolivia even into the twentieth century and was used to refer to racialized hierarchies. Integration interested them as a way to promote their version of Bolivian nationalism; however, their integrationist vision differed from the leftist version that emphasized unions and dreams of a socialist state (Calderón and Dandler 1984, 135–200). In other words, Bolivian nationalism was the nationalism of the new elite, while socialists emphasized international unionization of rural workers and the rights of the working class.

In the Muxuquya case, Sucre's Radio La Plata broadcast a public denunciation of the peasant union leaders' actions, and Attorney General Gerardo Córdoba agreed to hear the case. Andrés Jach'aqullu, whose native languages were Aymara and Quechua but who was also fluent in Spanish, described to the attorney general how the ex-peons from the ex-Hacienda Rodeo Chico in Muxuquya had escaped from captivity by traveling for four days by foot. Jach'aqullu emphasized that the indigenous ex-peons only moved at night because they were afraid of getting caught by the peasant union and jailed again. They wanted the attorney general in Sucre to give them a guarantee of protection from Celedonio Reina and Agapito Peña, the leaders of the Central Agraria of Muxuquya, Chuquisaca. Jach'aqullu argued that since the 1952 National Revolution, a group of mestizos from small towns had organized *centrales agrarias* (peasant unions) and *comandos revolucionarios* (revolutionary committees) that had coopted structures meant to represent the indigenous population, thus suppressing the true indigenous voice. He felt a true indigenous voice would emphasize ethnic concerns from the AMP's perspective and saw the current peasant unions in Chuquisaca as mostly run for mestizo pro–middle class leaders. Indeed, as in other parts of southern Bolivia, these peasant unions forced indigenous peoples to participate in pro-MNR activities. According to the MNR's ideology, ethnicity should be slowly suppressed in favor of a class perspective among indigenous populations. Indeed, the ex-peons, with Jach'aqullu acting as translator, said that they were not followers of the MNR and that they did not want to participate in the union run by the mestizos because it did not represent their concerns. This group of former peons stated that their autonomy and right to practice their Native religion was of utmost importance to them, and they announced that they were part of the group known as Qullasuyus, which belonged to the AMP network and had been confronting peasant unions in various parts of southern Bolivia (Rivera 1984, 5; Arias 1994, 50–120). Here it is important to clarify that peasant unions in Chuquisaca and northern Potosí were a special case. As mentioned earlier, in Jach'aqhachi and Ucureña, the peasant unions had different relationships with ethnicity and thus produced different historical patterns between the left, unions, and ethnicity.

In the August 21 meeting, Jach'aqullu argued that the Qullasuyus, a regional name for the AMP, were not part of the peasant unions, which were supposed to represent indigenous concerns, because these entities would not allow them to argue for autonomy and to "worship their cults," by which he meant perform ceremonies to honor the mother earth and worship their ancestors. During this process, the unions accused the Qullasuyus of not wanting "to be civilized" and instead wanting to "stay as they were in old times." Responding to these accusations, Jach'aqullu said that "Julian Zen-

teno, just as many other *caudillos* [leaders] of the pro-state peasant union and the revolutionary commandos, thought that his job
was to punish the people who disagreed" with the MNR's vision of
modernity and to make sure that people obeyed the dictates of the
1952 National Revolution, using any means possible—including
violence (Rivera 1984, 9–11). Consequently, a critical analysis of the
goals of National Revolution and its ideas about modernity emerged
from these hearings. Former peons rejected state- and middle-class-
controlled unions, and the AMP took the lead in denouncing the
unions' coercive methods and despotic actions.

This type of violent imposition by the state was frequent, especially in southern Bolivia, where the rural middle class successfully
coopted the revolution, and Indians did not directly feel the revolution's effects on their daily lives (Healy 1987, 50–320). Groups of
peasant indigenous intellectuals such as the AMP began to speak out
against revolutionary policies that they deemed abusive. In Tipapampa, Cochabamba, for example, ex-peons complained about how
peasant union leaders from Chinguri and Tinta persecuted those
who did not follow their orders. Common punishments included
jailing, hanging offenders *al chancho* (upside down), and making
them stand *al plantón* (standing upright for a long time); the first
and second were most often applied to men and the latter to women
and older men.[6] In Tipapampa the leadership imposed arbitrary obligations based on personal whims, making ex-peons provide food
for the *sindicatos'* meetings and take care of farm animals belonging to the Central Agraria's leaders.[7]

The unions were an important part of the MNR's modernizing
project, and it is ironic that not all of them were tolerant of the ways
of indigenous people. In Sutalaya, La Paz, the peasant union forced
indigenous men to cut their long braids "as a way to incorporate
them into civilization," and in Tarabuco, Chuquisaca, the peasant
union encouraged people to abandon their indigenous dress in order
to become "civilized."[8] The peasant unions and other revolutionary institutions were part of a new hegemony in the countryside.
Intolerant of dissent, many of them conceptualized civilization and
modernization as a way to "deindianize" and "peasantize" the country. Framing indigenous worldviews as "uncivilized and primitive,"

many encouraged peasants to abandon Indian dress and tradition and commit to revolutionary rhetoric.[9] The worldview underlying these peasant unions' racialized policies toward Indians and their goals for transforming the countryside were still colonial. They favored a class perspective and rejected ethnicity (indigenous languages, religiosity, and worldviews).

The first generations of the AMP, such as Toribio Miranda and Gregorio Titiriku, specifically organized indigenous people against hacienda landowners and the oligarchic state before 1952. They emphasized use of the Indian Law against feudal powers and struggled for the abolition of forms of indentured service and local bossism. They had both political and religious goals and particularly emphasized ethnicity in their agenda. During the 1930s and 1940s, the AMP had built up a network of indigenous activists consisting of about 450 cells distributed throughout haciendas and communities in mostly Aymara and Quechua regions of Bolivia. Today Quechua is the largest indigenous First Nation in Bolivia, followed by the Aymara nation. For centuries, the Aymaras were the most powerful ethnic group, until Quechua speakers arrived in Bolivia with Inca domination in the fifteenth century.

Jach'aqullu's experiences of racialization in his daily life in Wanuni and Oruro, especially in his relationship with working-class miners who mostly spoke Quechua, represented a larger process in which segregationist and assimilationist discourses were simultaneously at play in the years after the 1932–35 Chaco War between Bolivia and Paraguay.[10] In the 1940s the process of nation making also shifted from a society that defined itself by race to one that defined itself by class—a middle ground promoted by many populist groups and parties. This transformation was not only discursive; it left behind people like Jach'aqullu and the AMP who did not have their own peasant unions or fit into the discourse of equality emphasized by the new populist state that emerged after the revolution. Indeed, indigenous peoples in many areas of the Southern Andes still suffered abuse at the hands of the rural middle class—now often represented by peasant unions—and, in this context, they articulated a postrevolutionary AMP program. Jach'aqullu became a spokesperson for the AMP after he reassumed his indigenous identity and embraced the AMP's decolonization project. As the older generation died or retired, Jach'aqullu expanded the AMP's agenda to include new regions such as Wanuni. Jach'aqullu and his generation reworked the agenda of decolonization to fit the new conditions that reigned after 1952, rejecting the liberal policies of land tenure through agrarian reform, contesting power for the rural middle class through peasant unions, and opposing the need for the indigenous population to obtain birth and marriage certificates and national ID cards. In regions such as Icla and Tarwita, Jach'aqullu also supported the resistance to agrarian reform. Since hacienda landowners and many other elites were vehemently opposed to agrarian reform, Jach'aqullu and the AMP's resistance was at risk of being misunderstood. While the dominant class rejected giving up their land claims in favor of indigenous peoples, the AMP rejected the *style* of the agrarian reform. Jach'aqullu and the AMP rejected individual landholding in favor of collective landholding. In an era when Indianness was seen as antiquated and ethnic dress was rejected as backward in the cities, he insisted on wearing AMP ethnic dress. Every part of the AMP ethnic dress was handmade because they wanted to make a symbolic statement about self-sufficiency and reject the dependency embodied in the ways of modernity. Since Jach'aqullu was fluent in Spanish and, in the racialized stereotypes of the time, was considered to have light skin, he broke many stereotypes about Indianness. He clearly understood that class liberation would not work without ethnic reaffirmation in the Andes of his era.

In promoting his agenda of decolonization, Jach'aqullu also took his discourse to an international audience by contacting the International Labour Organization, which worked on the first international legislation for indigenous populations in the late 1950s. Jach'aqullu also associated with the Baha'is and traveled internationally while building indigenous activism in the cities. During this period, many indigenous peoples moved to the cities, where their experiences of rejection and frustration led them to embrace these new movements' ideas. Ethnic pride, appreciation of indigenous faith, and heritage were the main attractions of the AMP's ideology. They also rejected peasantization because of its disconnection from ethnicity and their strategies of self-appreciation and pride.

Jach'aqullu was part of the last generation of the AMP, so this chapter also narrates the fall of the AMP in the early 1970s. Jach'aqullu had to confront the assimilationist or integrationist context that followed the 1952 National Revolution. Jach'aqullu passed through many worlds by the time he joined the AMP. I mostly focus here on the years after the 1952 National Revolution had consolidated its goals, which limited the ways that Jach'aqullu could conduct his struggle and forced him to depend more on kinship ties.

### Racialization in International Mining Zones and Aymara Ayllus

Wilaqullu, a village that belonged to a large Aymara ayllu and in the jurisdiction of the *Corregimiento* of Wanuni, gave birth to a second generation of AMP activists who recreated the discourse of the Indian Law. A singular relationship emerged between the working class and indigenous peoples in Wilaqullu and Wanuni that would shape Andrés Jach'aqullu's life story. Wilaqullu was part of the Aymara Chullpas nation, which was located between southern Oruro and northern Potosí in the area where the most famous Bolivian mines of the twentieth century (Uncía, Q'atawi, Wanuni, Llallawa, and Siglo XX) were located (Aisakayu, "Andrés Jach'aqullu," APAJMC 1984, 4–6). Although these mines produced tin for the international economy, the region was also home to the country's largest ayllus, or indigenous communities, which depended on a long-standing agrarian economy based on exchange-in-kind between ayllus and other regions (Klein 1992). The wealthiest of these mines—Wanuni, Llallawa, and Q'atawi—belonged to Patiño Mines, the largest mining company in Bolivia. Wanuni and Uncía benefited from the mining boom; from the 1920s to the 1940s, Uncía had the best medical specialists in the country, some of whom were North Americans brought in to attend to the company's management. As enclaves of the international economy, Wanuni and Uncía were, for a time, the largest tin producers in the world (Klein 1992).

Andrés Jach'aqullu was born into an Aymara family in 1921. His father, Domingo Jach'aqullu, wanted his children to be educated, so Andrés, the youngest of five, walked five hours from his village to the elementary school in Bombo, which was the main village of the Chullpas ethnic group. On weekends he went with his par-

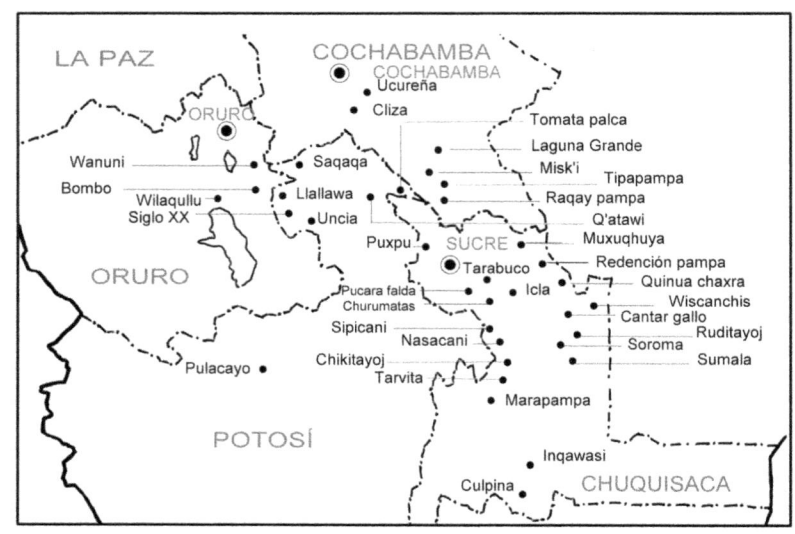

LA PAZ

COCHABAMBA
◉ COCHABAMBA
• Ucureña
• Cliza

ORURO ◉

Wanuni • Tomata palca
Bombo • Saqaqa • Laguna Grande
Wilaqullu • Llallawa • Misk'i
Siglo XX • Uncia • Tipapampa
• Raqay pampa
Puxpu • Q'atawi
SUCRE • Muxuqhuya
ORURO ◉ Tarabuco • Redención pampa
Quinua chaxra
Pucara falda • Icla Wiscanchis
Churumatas Cantar gallo
Sipicani Ruditayoj
Nasacani Soroma
Chikitayoj Sumala
Pulacayo • Tarvita

POTOSÍ

• Marapampa

• Inqawasi
Culpina • CHUQUISACA

MAP 6. Bolivia. Cartography by Walter Murillo.

ents to sell dried potatoes, meat, and corn in the street market of Uncía, where they also bought sugar, bread, canned food, and school supplies. When Jach'aqullu and his mother sold goods in Wanuni, they traded frequently with working-class housewives who wanted to buy Indian goods at low prices, but Jach'aqullu's mother often refused. These women were called *cholas* because they embodied cultural mixing with Western mainstream culture even though they had mostly indigenous backgrounds. Cholas dressed in a modified indigenous style with Western fabrics and lived in urban areas. Cholas of Uncía and Wanuni frequently insulted Jach'aqullu's mother as an "ignorant Indian" since she did not speak Quechua or Spanish. Most cholo/as in Uncía and other mining towns did not speak Aymara during this time and defined themselves as superior to the rural Indians (Aisakayu, "Andrés Jach'aqullu," APAJMC 1984, 13–16). Cholas were originally Quechua speakers from the Cochabamba valleys and were often ex-*piqueras* or formal small land owners from hacienda regions, who had worked in Chilean mines in Antofagasta and Tarapacá in the 1920s before moving to the Bolivian mines (Harris and Albó 1989, 4–6).

Since 1890 Quechua-speaking miners from Cochabamba had migrated to the mining towns of Llallawa, Uncía, Catawi, and Siglo XX for work, but the towns also contained enclaves of Aymara speakers (Rivera Cusicanqui 1984, 19–21).[11] Later, Quechua not only gained full hegemony in the mining towns but also gradually spread into the Aymara ayllus of the entire region. Over the course of several decades, the region's ayllus became bilingual in Aymara and Quechua; in other regions, Quechua became consolidated as a new language in one or two generations. Spanish also became more widely spoken in these regions, complicating language use in ayllus and mining towns.

The miners, defined as cholos in the racialized language of Bolivia, working in Llallawa, Siglo XX, Uncía, and Catawi organized some of the world's most powerful mining labor movements between 1920 and 1940. The labor unions of these centers confronted the mining companies, demanding housing and an eight-hour workday; the unions organized several general strikes in the 1920s despite severe repression. Through the powerful Federación de Trabajadores Mineros de Bolivia (Bolivian Federation of Mine Workers), the working-class people of these towns provided a coherent political agenda for the Bolivian working class. They created the Thesis of Pulacayo in 1946, which advocated for improved labor conditions, promoted the state's takeover of mines, and defined Bolivia as a primitive capitalist country. The document was one of the most radical in Latin America, and its spirit impacted Bolivian politics for many years (Lora 1980, 19–83; Jach'aqullu, "Bayetas," APAJMC 1977, Fondo 17A, 33–45). The Federación de Trabajadores Mineros de Bolivia would later play a key role in creating the Central Obrera Boliviana, an umbrella organization that would become one of the most powerful union confederations in the world. Frequent confrontations between the emerging labor movement and conservative governments resulted in the constant repression of workers between the 1920s and the 1940s (Jach'aqullu, "Phichuwawas," APHOA 1977, Fondo 3, 11–17). Jach'aqullu came of age in this context of strife. His uncle, Zacarías Jach'aqullu, was one of nearly one hundred miners who were killed when the army and police repressed a 1923 strike at Uncía.

Literacy was a long-standing obsession in the Jach'aqullu family. His grandfather was a nephew of Felipe Beltrán, who had promoted education in Aymara and Quechua in the 1870s. Although he had some schooling, Jach'aqullu's father was only partially literate because he did not practice his reading and writing skills, but he wanted his son to be fully literate. In a time when few Indians from the ayllus had access to schooling, this family's focus on formal education was unusual (Aisakayu, "Andrés Jach'aqullu," APAJMC 1984, 13–16). For two years in the early 1930s, Jach'aqullu attended the public school of Uncía, where both the teachers and the students subjected him to jokes about the Aymara language. People in the mining town considered Spanish to be the most cultured language and Quechua to be acceptable, but they had no tolerance for Aymara since it was associated with the indigenous people of the surrounding ayllus. Jach'aqullu's teacher told him that "Aymara is a primitive language," while "Quechua is sweet and the language of the Inkas" (Villka, "Muruhuta," FPAPM 1981, Fondo 1, 5). Quechua was considered the language of the working class who identified themselves with the Inka elite (Villka, "Muruhuta," FPAPM 1981, Fondo

1, 5–9). From Jach'aqullu's perspective, however, these cholos were also Indians; the only difference was that they spoke Spanish and Quechua and lived in mining towns. The cholos, though, considered themselves to be mestizos rather than Indians.

After finishing elementary school in 1932, Jach'aqullu returned to his village of Wilaqullu to farm and accompany his father on trips to trade dry goods for corn and wheat in the lowlands of nearby Misk'i, Cochabamba. In 1940, when he was nineteen, he sought employment with the police department of Uncía. However, when filling out his application at the Police Enrollment Center, he had a challenging decision to make (Jach'aqullu, "Phichuwawas," APHOA 1977, Fondo 3, 21–17). Jach'aqullu gave his real name, but the policeman in charge of IDs encouraged him to change his last name, telling him that since his "skin was too light to be Indian," he did not need to "carry such an Indian last name, which was hard to pronounce." Jach'aqullu thus decided to translate his last name into Spanish; as it meant "high hill," he became Cerrogrande. In 1939 he obtained a national identity card that reflected this new name (Jach'aqullu, "Phichuwawas," APHOA, Fondo 3, 1977, 11–15).

Between 1939 and 1942, he was posted in Uncía, where he learned that a policeman's job frequently involved abusing indigenous community members. In 1942 Cerrogrande was sent to reinforce a police squad that was protecting the Patiño Mining Company from widespread strikes. He saw twenty people killed and one hundred others wounded—an experience that affected him profoundly. He became critical of the white elite's power and requested a transfer to another post. Although he would have preferred to leave his job with the police, he needed the money (Aisakayu, "Andrés Jach'aqullu," APAJMC 1984, 13–16). Late in 1942 he was sent to Wanuni, where he witnessed a woman being gang raped by a group of policemen.[12] At other times he observed police forcing indigenous women to pick up garbage that they had not dropped and accusing them of defecating in the main street of Wanuni. This exposure to the constant humiliation of indigenous peoples and the working class laid bare the deep inequality in Bolivian society, and it slowly changed the way Jach'aqullu saw the world.

During this time he met Matilde Qulqi from the Parapiani community, which was another part of his own ayllu. Matilde shared Jach'aqullu's budding perspectives on indigenous politics and was familiar with local oral history. Her father was an indigenous priest, and she was faithful to the Aymara religion as practiced through highland indigenous spirituality and rites. She attempted to convince Jach'aqullu to leave the police force and return to the community. Although she refused to move with him to Wanuni for this reason, the couple finally married in December 1942 (Qulqi, "Inkawawas," APHOA 1981, Fondo 2, 13–16).

Earlier that year, Jach'aqullu was sent to Oruro, where he was appointed to a police station on Camacho Avenue. It was there that in 1943 he met detainee Toribio Miranda, a founder of the AMP. Miranda's thoughts and political ideas had a transformative effect on Jach'aqullu, convincing him to leave the police in late 1944 and return to his community, where he started to organize for the AMP. To demonstrate that he had adopted a completely different worldview, he not only abandoned his police uniform but also adopted Indian dress as Toribio Miranda required, donning a gray poncho and handmade pants (Jach'aqullu, "Phichuwawas," APHOA 1977, Fondo 3, 21–25; Aisakayu, "Andrés Jach'aqullu," APAJMC 1984, 15–19). In addition, he started to encourage long hair among AMP members and let his own hair grow below his shoulders, according to ancient Aymara customs.[13]

From 1945 to 1957 Jach'aqullu and Matilde Qulqi advocated the ideas of the AMP in the region surrounding Wanuni, building on the work that had already been done by people like José Villka and Eusebio Quyu. In 1952 Miranda and Titiriku suggested to Jach'aqullu that "he should help the activists in those regions" because he was traveling to Chuquisaca and Misk'i. Since these areas were mostly under the hacienda system, Titiriku and Miranda thought that Jach'aqullu's experience in the mines and with the labor movements in Wanuni would help the AMP in Chuquisaca.[14]

With Matilde's support, Jach'aqullu not only organized the AMP among ayllus of northern Potosí and southern Oruro but also worked with the activists of Chuquisaca. His initiative came from living in a region with a powerful labor movement that had taught him the importance of activism. Jach'aqullu had confronted in his own life racial subordination when he had to translate his last name from Aymara to Spanish in order to obtain a working-class job as a policeman. Similarly, he had a long history of having to confront negative reactions to his Aymaraness from the cholo working class, who considered him a "backward Indian." His marriage to Qulqi, who was a devout follower of Aymara religion and his exposure to AMP ideas, shaped the path he would forge in the crucial years of the 1950s.

### De-Indianization and Its Impact on Race and Ethnicity

The emergence in the 1940s of a new generation of ex-Indians and ex-cholos connected to class paradigms rather than the caste system had a profound influence on Jach'aqullu's story. The caste system slowly disintegrated after the Chaco War (1932–35), which had brought Bolivian men of widely disparate backgrounds together for the first time. The concept of de-Indianization became more popular as many cholos adopted a leftist discourse and focused their energies on class struggle. Crucial to de-Indianization, integration started to affect ethnic and racial identities. Influenced by the labor movement, the ethnic category of cholo was abandoned in favor the term *obrero* (worker), which privileged class over ethnic identity for urban male Aymaras. Cholo artisans during the 1940s and 1950s in Jach'aqhachi, La Paz, for example, strongly preferred the designation obreros over cholos (Albó 1979, 16–38).

Some cholos' daughters adopted "full Western dress" and became *birlochas*, which implied that they were of plebeian origin and no longer cholas (Rivera 1996, 17–85, 163–285). Ana Paredes, an accountant and the daughter of a prosperous vendor in the Camacho market, provides a good example of this tendency. Because her family was originally from Oruro, they were acquaintances of Jach'aqullu, who, when he was in La Paz for his work as an indigenous activist, often rented a room in the home of Ana's mother, Mercedes Mamani.[15] He was personally affected when Mercedes Mamani died in 1941. Ana Paredes wanted to sell her mother's market stall, but the other vendors opposed the sale, arguing that it was collective property. The market cholas had a verbal confrontation with Ana and used the fact that she had changed her surname from the Aymara "Colque" to the Spanish "Paredes" to bolster their argument that she was no longer one of them. Ana Paredes took them to court for libel, explaining that one had said: "Birlocha, *refinada* [refined woman]. You have forgotten your mother's *polleras* [indigenous skirt] and now you act like any other white. You are a *refinada* . . . You are Paredes, go to the Paredes. Do not come back here."[16] Ana believed that she should be treated with greater respect because she was a lady and not from the same class as the market vendors. She argued that she only wanted to sell her mother's market stall as soon possible and that she had changed her last name with the permission of both parents. But the street vendors' association prevailed, preventing the sale and assigning her mother's stall to another member. Although Jach'aqullu helped Ana Paredes by serving as witness in the libel case, he did not want Aymaras and other indigenous communities to feel as if they had to take the path of whitening or reject their identity like Ana had, and as he had also done in the 1930s. Cases like Ana's reinforced his commitment to work against whitening by promoting the Indian Law as a project of decolonization.[17] Despite Jach'aqullu's views, this case demonstrates how class identity trumped ethnic identity for a second generation of cholos, like Ana Paredes, in this period (Rivera et al. 1996, 163–285; Stephenson 1999, 1–34). Ethnic rejection also affected other dimensions of social life; most notably, a paternalistic vision of needing to protect Indians reemerged. As a consequence of a 1925 law passed by President Bautista Saavedra (1921–25), Indians' land could only be sold through the prosecutor's office. Saavedra came from the rural elite and had some Aymara heritage. Before his presidency, he had strong links with indigenous activists, but once he became president, he used his knowledge of indigenous activists to better control indigenous movements and maintain the status quo. In the legal terms of the time, Indians were considered minors, which strongly encouraged them to abandon their Indianness (Gómez 1975, 229). Although Saavedra justified this decree by arguing that it would protect Indians from being exploited by lawyers, the measure reinforced the idea of Indians as powerless. As a result, Indians in the 1940s no longer had the freedom to sell or buy land. Jach'aqullu believed that land tenure in Bolivia needed to undergo a major transformation and proposed that the Indian Law structure the system (Jach'aqullu, "Phichuwawas," APHOA 1977, Fondo 3, 11). He argued in favor of collective and ethnic ownership.

Adopting the elite's hegemonic strategies and ideas about race, cholos also assumed a paternalistic attitude toward indigenous peoples in the countryside. They largely internalized their own struggles against the elites and did not recognize the vibrancy and power of ethnic organizations such as the Aymara ayllus nor the way in which the indigenous peoples as a subaltern nation had been systematically attacked by the Bolivian state. Instead, they argued that the struggle against the traditional elite should only be addressed from a working-class perspective, which, they asserted, embodied Indian concerns. By the 1940s cholos and their labor movement had adopted a vision of Indians as a "problem" and, rejecting the term *Indian*, insisted on referring to indigenous peoples as *campesinos* (peasants) (Lehm and Rivera Cusicanqui 1988, 129). Their labor organizations argued that Indians needed to "modernize" their forms of protest, from rebellion to "union organization, hunger strikes and Marxist organization."[18] To this end, they promoted unionization in the Aymara regions from the 1920s to the 1940s, creating the Federación Agraria Departamental de La Paz in 1946. Although at first the Federación counted important Indian leaders, such as Santos Marka T'ula, among its ranks, in its later years, it advocated cholification for Indians (Andrade 1988, 14–17). By this time, the Federación Obrera Local was no longer in the hands of anarchists but was controlled by less radical leftists. Both anarchists and leftists dominated the early labor movement in Bolivia; over time, anarchists slowly lost power to different groups of leftists in the movement. Jach'aqullu emerged from this world of the cholo labor movement, which was influenced by Marxist literature and contemporaneous social movements in Latin America. As a way of advancing their social struggle, this ex-cholo labor movement attempted to re-elaborate the past in terms of class. In other words, liberals and leftists wanted Bolivia to "westernize," while Jach'aqullu and the AMP not only wanted to retain their Indian heritage but also had their own modernization project. Some of their goals were education in Native languages, the renovation of indigenous institutions, and autonomy.

In Bolivia's racialized history of nation making, 1943 to 1945 was a period in which the government emphasized integration. The MNR and its ally, military president Gualberto Villarroel, initiated this process by organizing the first National Indigenous Congress and promoting the incorporation of indigenous people into political parties. The May 1945 congress, which was the first one organized by the Bolivian state in the twentieth century, brought together three thousand indigenous people, mainly Aymaras and Quechuas. Although the congress attracted many grassroots indigenous groups, the government marginalized indigenous radicals by jailing them in the days and months leading up to the event. Despite these circumstances, this was a momentous event in terms of Bolivia's history of racialization; for the first time, a president attended an Indian gathering and addressed them (Antezana and Romero 1979, 101–11). According to the newspaper *La Calle*, "Something extremely unusual happened yesterday[:] . . . the inauguration of the National Indigenous Congress . . . with the assistance of the whole executive branch [of the Bolivian state], . . . the national army, . . . the diplomatic body, . . . all with the highest form of dignity to inaugurate an indigenous gathering. . . . This shows a break from the norm [of the country]."[19] Following the lead of other populists in Latin America, Villarroel signed a decree at the congress that abolished free hacienda labor by peons.[20] The MNR later used this as a means to attract new militants to the party, arguing that an MNR government had made that possible. These actions reflect how the party had begun competing for hegemony among indigenous peoples by incorporating representatives from the Indian world (Jach'aqullu, "Phichuwawas," APHOA 1977, Fondo 3, 11–15).

Augusto Céspedes, who became a key ideologue of Bolivian nationalism in the 1940s and 1950s, emphasized the central role mestizos played in the making of the new Bolivian nationalism. He believed that *el pueblo*—the cholos—and moderates among the elite were mixing to creating a mestizo identity that would become the ruling ethnic and racial category in opposition to Indianness (Céspedes 1956, 35–70). In this context, the cholo started to be absorbed into this new mestizo identity, in which Indians were represented as ancestors rather than as living social and political actors. In other words, mestizaje became a discourse of whitening or de-indianization that became crucial in the era after 1952. This whitening also became central to how colonialism operated in this new era and what an activist like Jach'aqullu had to resist.

During the 1940s and 1950s, the core of the racialized Bolivian caste system was deconstructed and racial ideologies were transformed. Although Indians remained at the bottom of the hierarchical system, they were there for a different reason. This transformation took place in the context of an intense political struggle between the left and right in Bolivia, between groups that wanted to retain colonial privileges and those that wanted a new order. The assimilationist ideas and policies that emerged from this conflict were the dominant force that the AMP would address after the National Revolution.

### Indian Law and the Wak'as versus *MNR* Assimilation Programs and Agrarian Reform

After the 1952 National Revolution, Andrés Jach'aqullu and the leadership of the AMP still promoted the Indian Law, but it was modified by the changes of the revolution, which rejected Indian clothing and insisted that Indians were simply peasants. In response, the AMP reinforced the indigenous dress code as the core of its indigenous identity and argued that wearing Indian clothing symbolized better communication with the mother earth and the *Achachilas*, the spirits of the mountains. Jach'aqullu believed that militant ethnic dress was necessary to differentiate indigenous people from cholos in all spheres of life. To him, cholo or Western dress was evidence of coloniality (Villka, "Muruhuta," FPAPM 1981, Fondo 1, 11–13; Jach'aqullu, "Phichuwawas," APHOA 1977, Fondo 3, 25–30; Aisakayu, "Andrés Jach'aqullu," APAJMC 1984, 19–21). While this emphasis on Indian clothes was obviously not new in the AMP, Jach'aqullu reemphasized and revised the tradition by encouraging people to wear Indian clothes in all colors rather than only gray tones, as Titiriku and Miranda had done (Ramos, "Sutulaya," APHOA 1973, Folio 3, 11–12). Jach'aqullu also placed more emphasis on the Aymara religion and the resumption of widespread and open worship of local deities, or *Wak'as*, in Wanuni, a mining region in Oruro. He described the purpose of this in a letter published by a local newspaper in 1953: "Gaining an understanding of the Qullasuyu heritage, the true link to nature . . . [and] to recuperate, restore, conserve and protect the Wak'as."[21] The AMP and Jach'aqullu earned the nicknames Qullasuyus and *bayeta camisas* (referring to the fabric their clothing was made from) because they promoted Indian dress and talked about the revival of the Qullasuyus; in so doing, they were rejecting the whitening path that Bolivia was following.[22]

Jach'aqullu also began to discourage indigenous people from getting married in the Catholic Church and instead urged them to celebrate their baptisms and death rituals outside of the church.[23] In September 1950 he and his wife Matilde Qulqi performed one of their first marriages, between AMP members Julio Cutrina and Isabel Wari in Wilaqullu, Oruro next to a Wak'a on the top of the hill known as Waraq Achachila.[24] They performed four other weddings from December 1950 to May 1952, and Jach'aqullu became known as the "Indian Priest in Wanuni." As a result, the local Catholic priests and the Corregidor of Bombo accused him of being a "false priest" and argued that "he was working against the government" by promoting an officially unrecognized religion. Church officials in Wanuni argued that he did "not follow the Catholic Religion" and that he wanted to establish schools "to gain influence among the Indians" (Aisakayu, "Andrés Jach'aqullu," APAJMC 1984, 13–16, 9–11). These denunciations landed him in Wanuni's municipal jail in December of 1951, but since his accusers could not prove their case, he was released in February 1952.[25]

In the years to come, Jach'aqullu continued celebrating weddings, death rituals, and baptisms, leading to his jailing in August 1952 and again in April 1953.[26] During his last detention, Jach'aqullu was jailed along with his pregnant wife and four of his children. Matilde Qulqi did not want to leave her husband alone in jail, and since she was herself accused of being a "woman priest," she was imprisoned as well. As the children did not have anyone else to care for them, they were allowed to be with their parents. The mining unions of Wanuni hired a lawyer who helped to end the family's detention, arguing that the children should not be imprisoned (Jach'aqullu, "El Kollasuyu," APAJMC 1984, 33–35; Qulqi "Inkawawas," APHOA 1984,

Fondo 2, 12–14). Although labor and indigenous organizations had moments of collaboration and support, as demonstrated in this case, after the 1952 Revolution they had different agendas. Labor organizations were focused on the needs and concerns of the working class, so whitening was not an issue for them; on the other hand, Indian organizations such as the AMP focused on ethnic and religious components in their AMP agenda of decolonization.

Meanwhile, a new political atmosphere developed throughout the country as a result of the 1952 National Revolution. Peasant unions started to organize in indigenous communities and haciendas. But in such regions as Icla where the AMP was strong, unions were mainly led by mestizos and therefore did not represent indigenous people. In the mid-1950s, requests for Toribio Miranda and Gregorio Titiriku's support increased dramatically in the ex-hacienda regions of Cochabamba, Chuquisaca, and northern Potosí. Peons and ayllu members from Icla, Muxuqhuya, and Misk'i engaged in bitter conflicts with the MNR peasant union, and some AMP members ended up in jail (Jach'aqullu "El Kollasuyu," APAJMC 1984, 23–25). Since Miranda was over eighty years old and ill, he could no longer march on the front lines of activism as he had in the past. Titiriku also needed to stay in La Paz to denounce abuses on the haciendas to newspapers and international organizations. Under these circumstances, Miranda asked Jach'aqullu to tour these regions of conflict and support the AMP cells there (Quevedo, "Su historia," FPTQ 1979, 23–25; Titiriku, "Para recordar," APPM 1977, 13–15).

In August 1956 Jach'aqullu started the long trip from Chuquisaca to Cochabamba, finding conflicts with peasant unions and MNR cells everywhere he went. His clothing marked him as an Indian activist, which helped him gain acceptance in the region quickly. In the Chuquisaca countryside, ethnic fashion was a signifier of Indianness, and Jach'aqullu took advantage of this to promote the AMP's goals (Jach'aqullu, "El indio Uru-Morato," APAJMC 1977, Fondo 3, 3–35; Orieta, "Tata Toribio Miranda," APHONS 1957, 3). In Icla, Mariano Malpartida, a former administrator of the hacienda of Churumatas, had assumed the leadership of a new peasant union, the Central Agraria of Icla. He forced indigenous people to attend demonstrations in support of the MNR cell in Tarabuco.[27] When AMP members Ezequiel Urieta, Francisco Rivera, and Eladio Padilla refused to follow this order, Malpartida jailed thirteen people, saying: "All of them are in a conspiracy against the National Revolution [for] not collaborating in the production of food supplies for the markets in Sucre."[28] Indeed, the national government assigned production quotas to the region of Icla, and the unions were responsible for reaching these goals between 1953 and 1958.[29]

In Muxuqhuya, Chuquisaca, the community's situation was also very difficult in the mid-1950s because of the power of the state-sponsored unions. The mestizos from the town led the Central Agraria of Muxuqhuya and were hungry to exercise their new power over the ayllus of the region. In 1955 Pedro Quispe and Andrés Mayta, both from Qullachiwanway, had a dispute over a piece of land. Mayta did not agree with the results of the mediating ethnic authorities, and his godfather Claudio Peralta, a mestizo from the town of Muxuqhuya, persuaded him to seek "the justice of the peasant unions." The ayllus of the region rejected this recourse and resisted the arrival of Peralta and his people in the village of Qullachiwanway. At the next Muxuqhuya Sunday fair, Peralta attempted to detain all the leaders of the ayllus, many of whom were AMP members. Ultimately, the leaders were all detained and imprisoned in Tarabuco.[30]

In Misk'i, Cochabamba, the unions led by mestizos entered into similar conflicts in 1958. In Quiwinal, Tinta, and Tipapampa, the influence of Zenón Ibañez, a rural teacher and a leader of the Regional Peasant Union that had a vast network stretching from Misk'i to Aiquile, helped expand the renting and sharecropping of ex-piqueros' land, essentially turning landowning ex-peons into landless workers.[31] The unions used this type of arrangement to dominate indigenous people and took on an abusive hacienda-like role. Similar relationships developed in Saqaqa (northern Potosí), where Pedro Qarita, a regional chief of the Central Agraria de Saqaqa expanded his farm holdings in various indigenous communities.[32] Despite their disputes over ethnic ceremonies, the AMP used their connections to the Catholic Church to respond to these tactics. At the AMP's request, in 1962 Cardinal José Clemente Maurer, who was originally from Germany and became the first Bolivian cardinal, wrote a letter to the Indian communities in Sucre urging them to "try to respect each other."[33] This letter stemmed from the good relations that the AMP's Tomas Quevedo from Chuki Chuki, Chuquisaca, had with the church due to his sister's marriage to Elias Sacaca, who was a deacon and became a close assistant of Cardinal Maurer. In the letter of support, the cardinal did not address his differences with indigenous religiosity but instead emphasized his concern regarding the violence that had occurred in Chuquisaca. Frequently, this type of letter was used as protection against the repression of unions and revolutionary orders. Given the hegemonic nature of the MNR in Bolivia during the late 1950s, the church was often the only refuge for dissidents.

In this context, Jach'aqullu intensified his activism and discovered a receptive environment in which to promote his ideas. He visited the Icla region in June of 1957, Muxuquya in December of 1957, and Tipapampa in April of 1958.[34] Throughout this tour he strongly denounced the political situation, arguing that "we should follow the Indian Law [Ley de Indios] and worship for the protection of the Wak'as and Achachilas, spirits of ancestors. We should beg the Pachamama, or mother earth, the lighting and the water [*uma kankaña*] and the Achachilas especially for protection against forced participation in peasant unions."[35] Jach'aqullu believed that a return to Aymara religion would liberate Indians from the suffering that had continued under the peasant unions after the 1952 National Revolution. He argued that these regions were having problems because their regional Wak'as (indigenous deities) were not worshiped as often as the Wak'as in the highlands. He advocated worship on the hills and using appropriate Indian dress as the most effective way to solicit the intervention of the Pachamama and the Wak'as. Jach'aqullu also called on everybody to act as "good children" of the Pachamama and the Achachilas.[36] The Pachamama is the mother earth, the most important goddess in modern Andean indigenous history, and Achachilas are the deities of the hilltops or mountains where it is believed the indigenous ancestors rest.

However, an incident that led to controversial rumors about the AMP marred Jach'aqullu's tour of Chuquisaca in late 1957. Two AMP men from Sipiqani, Claudio Villka and Teodoro Martínez, died in

Pucara Falda, Icla when they fell into a ravine that they did not see while they were climbing the hill on a dark night to worship their local Wak'as, wearing militant ethnic dress and long hair.[37] Emilio Estrada, the Icla corregidor, who was the main authority of the county, charged Jach'aqullu with promoting ideas that "caused death in the region," a charge to which Jach'aqullu never responded.[38] As a result of these events, the rural elite of Icla declared: "Jesus punished the idolatrous worshipers, [and that the] 'Qullasuyus' were the weirdest people [they had] ever seen." They pointed out, for example, that: "the 'Qullasuyus' do not send their children to school, nor do they want to invest time in building public schools."[39]

By contrast, believers in indigenous religions had a different interpretation of the events. According to them, Martínez and Villka had not been truly faithful to the Pachamama and the "rites of Qullasuyu," so the Pachamama and the Achachilas of Pucara Falda had punished them for their lack of faith. These indigenous adherents urged people to worship and devote more energy to the Pachamama, or other punishments might be doled out. Indeed, AMP leaders associated the poor harvest between 1956 and 1958 with the people's lack of faith in the Pachamama and the Indian Law's lack of power in the region. The AMP urged widespread worship in the hills and more prayers to the Pachamama to end the "bad times that the Revolution brought to them" (Orieta, "Tata Toribio Miranda," APHONS 1982, 14).[40] As a result, worship in the name of the Andean gods increased. Cantar Gallo and Nasaqani emerged as new centers of worship in the Icla region. From Icla the worship of Wak'as and the Pachamama expanded to Poxpo, Muxuquya, Poroma, and Inqawasi.[41]

The death of Martínez and Villka fed myths about indigenous peoples, eventually leading to a belief in the existence of a group of Chuquisaca Indians who were *phawayrunas*, or "flying men." According to this myth, these men wore strange clothes that were not proper for the peasants of Chuquisaca, did not send their children to school, and died when they tried to fly. The Chuquisaca media's focus on this and other myths shaped the urban collective imagination about indigenous peoples. For instance, when some AMP leaders converted to the Baha'i faith in the mid-1960s, the Baha'is had to issue a public statement clarifying that the idea of flying men was "misleading" and that the myth predated the Baha'i faith in Chuquisaca. This collective imagination was racialized, with urban denizens ready to believe that Indians could do strange things. Although the media later argued that this was only a fantasy, this perception of differently dressed Indians helps illustrate how people could believe that Indians were able to fly and disliked schools. Indeed, urban Bolivians were ready to accept such myths because they dehumanized Indians and represented them as opposed to modernity.[42] In the context of these racialized myths, the Icla region had a mixed response to the application of the agrarian reform. Since Jach'aqullu kept promoting adherence to the Indian Law, he was accused of opposing the Agrarian Reform of 1953, which had broken up haciendas and given the land to the former hacienda peons. In late 1958, the peasant unions of Muxuqhuya denounced him as having said that the "true law is the Indian Law and that if Indians followed it ex-peons would not need more laws because as 'jallp'a sangres,' or the blood of our lands, we are the true owners of the land."[43] Based on these alleged comments, the peasant unions concluded that Jach'aqullu "encouraged the rejection" of the implementation of the National Commission of Agrarian Reform.[44]

Icla's mestizos were among the strongest supporters of the agrarian reform because it helped them consolidate land acquisitions. Therefore, some indigenous activists organized a boycott of land measurement, a process in which topographers visited every peasant plot and measured the lots in order to distribute private property titles. Francisco Rivera, Agapito Ponce, and Teodoro Cabezas urged the communities on the ex-haciendas of Wisk'anchis, Suruma, and Sumala to reject these measurements because the AMP believed that indigenous persons were already the legitimate owners of the land. Felix Vela Ortiz and Claudio Paye also organized similar protests (Aisakayu, "Andrés Jach'aqullu," APAJMC 1984, 13–16). During one such protest in Marapa, indigenous participants also burned national ID cards, state-issued birth certificates, marriage certificates, and some currency as an expression of their rejection of the modernity arriving in the region based on ideologies of whitening and consumerism (Ponce, "Los poderantes," FPHE 1982, 4–11). As these ideas spread, the topographers encountered resistance and often failed in their efforts to measure boundaries between lots. They reported: "It was only on the third attempt that we could measure the properties of this region . . . but Marapampa could not be done because of the opposition of indigenous peoples. . . . [At] the last moment the indigenous peoples brought a list of people from the region and they requested collective property [instead of individual property]. They do not understand the Agrarian Reform Law."[45] In the villages of Redención Pampa and Quinua Chaxra, the commissioners in charge of the application of agrarian reform encountered similar problems; references to the Indian Law occur frequently in the records of their efforts (Rivera Cusicanqui 1984, 17–78).[46] Peons rejected agrarian reform, arguing that as followers of the Indian Law, they should not follow other laws. They believed that the Indian Law embodied all their rights to land, so they did not need titles from the Bolivian state. This widespread attitude shows how embedded the AMP discourse had become in Icla. The agrarian reform had brought to the region the domination of the cholo peasant unions.

Jach'aqullu's discourse and activism helped to disseminate the notion of the Indian Law in the context of the 1952 National Revolution. His handling of religious rituals such as weddings and his calls for people to worship the Aymara gods confronted the challenges brought by the agrarian reform. As in Miranda and Titiriku's time, the ideas of the Indian Law gained support because they dovetailed with local issues, such as the abuse of state-sponsored unions. Jach'aqullu thus helped to reshape the AMP's Indian Law in the 1960s.

### Speaking Out and Subverting Racial Stereotypes in Postrevolutionary Bolivia

In the mid-1960s a new political context began to emerge in Bolivia. After twelve years of the National Revolution, the MNR disintegrated, and a succession of military regimes governed the country. Some ideas initiated by the revolution, such as private ownership of land, peasant unions, and the right to vote, finally coalesced and were appropriated by the indigenous peasantry in many parts of the country. During the time of Jach'aqullu and the AMP, a new generation of grassroots leaders emerged at the local level of the peasant unions and gradually replaced the mestizo ruling elite at the head of peasant unions in Chuquisaca, northern Potosí, and southern Cochabamba. This new generation was more sympathetic to Jach'aqullu and ideas of the Indian Law. The AMP especially disliked the era of clientelism and paternalism that came with the MNR and the National Revolution. In the countryside, it was hard to separate clientelism from voting rights, universal education from assimilation, and agrarian reform from capitalist land tenure. Thus, by the 1970s, the peasant unions had stopped working against the AMP in Sumala and Cantargallo, Chuquisaca. As had occurred in the Aymara highlands, these regions gradually came under the control of the former hacienda peons. This process started on the most productive ex-haciendas and gradually extended throughout the entire area (Salamanca Trujillo 1978, 10–210). In 1964, the sons of ex-peons in Churumumu took control of Icla's largest peasant union, the Central of Uyuni. By 1967 most of the Central Agraria of Icla was under grassroots control, but the top positions still remained in the hands of mestizos (Antezana and Romero 1979, 35–45; Salamanca 1978, 99–108; Gordillo 2002, 50–125). Confrontation accompanied this process of change elsewhere in the Bolivian countryside. In the valley of Cochabamba, a power struggle emerged between Clisa and Ucureña. However, it was not until the Katarista movement of 1979 that the national leadership of the peasant unions landed in the hands of indigenous persons (Rivera Cusicanqui 1984, 70–125).

After Miranda died in 1959, the AMP went through crucial changes, and Jach'aqullu was asked to remain in La Paz. Although Titiriku was still active during the 1960s, he could not perform many duties, and by the early 1960s, Jach'aqullu had emerged as a central figure in the AMP. Little did he know, but the end of the AMP was drawing near (Jach'aqullu, "El indio Uru-Murato," APAJMC 1977, Fondo 3, 33; Orieta "Tata Toribio Miranda," APHONS 1954, 34; Titiriku, "Para recordar," APPM 1977, 35). Jach'aqullu saw the rural elite, made up mostly of mestizos, as a central problem that would be difficult to confront. Although Jach'aqullu was active in the countryside of Cochabamba and Chuquisaca during the 1950s, he stayed away from the regions of greatest activity in the early 1960s because different MNR cells and centrales agrarias had obtained warrants against him. In 1961 a judge in Icla issued a warrant against him for the accidental deaths of Villka and Martínez in 1957. A judge in Aiquile issued another warrant in 1963 for "cultivating uprisings." And the subprefect of Misk'i province accused him of "giving the wrong ideas to the peasants of Laguna Grande [by] telling them [that] the Revolution was not good for them [and] that they should follow the Indian Law."[47]

Like Miranda and Gallardo who distributed hacienda lands in late 1940s in the name of the Indian Law, Jach'aqullu used the Indian Law to contest the liberal and populist program of the agrarian reform. However, Jach'aqullu and other AMPs were not the only ones in the late 1950s and early 1960s to resist the problems caused by the agrarian reform in the region of Lake Titicaca. Laureano Machaca, who was one of the leaders of the new peasant unions in Escoma, distanced himself from the progovernment peasant unionist agenda and called for regional autonomy and the creation of an Aymara Republic on the shores of Lake Titicaca (Paredes 1980, 10–43). While Machaca's project was an Aymara nationalist one, it was totally secular and centered on creating an Aymara republic run by indigenous peasant unions. In Escoma the mestizos retained the municipality and exercised power from there, while in Icla and Tarvita, Jach'aqullu's hometown, mestizos also ran the peasant unions (Ramos, "Sutulaya," APHOA 1973, Folio 3, 1–15). Machaca and Jach'aqullu were both opposed to way that the National Revolution kept the mestizos in power and perpetuated a racialized hierarchy in the countryside in which Indians were at the bottom. However, Jach'aqullu and the AMP's project emphasized cultural and religious transformation, while Machaca's project lacked these components. Indigenous resistance to the projects of the 1952 Revolution was strongest in areas where mestizos had clearly different priorities and where exclusion and racialization continued long after 1952, such as Icla and Tarvita.

Although Jach'aqullu gained some new followers in Marapampa and Ch'ikitayox, his audience began to decline in southern Bolivia, and he had to find other ways to carry out his political agenda. The city of La Paz was quickly acquiring an Aymara majority; however, most Aymaras were cholos who had adopted Western, working-class dress. Jach'aqullu's handmade woolen clothes and long hair allowed him to represent himself as a "true" Indian in the urban imagination. Because he appeared to be from a remote indigenous community, he shocked people when they learned that he was literate or heard him speak Spanish fluently. For example, Luis Monje, one of the lawyers of the International Labour Organization, wrote in 1967: "We had a labor discussion [meeting] at the University of La Paz and [an] Indian from Oruro, Andrés, came and he, surprisingly, spoke Spanish well and he was literate, he was very smart."[48] During this time, Jach'aqullu broke all the racial stereotypes established after the 1952 National Revolution, contradicting ideas that anyone dressed as an Indian had to be an illiterate person from the country who only spoke Native languages. Due to his command of Spanish, his literacy, and his experience as a policeman, Jach'aqullu would have been considered a cholo in La Paz if not for his clothing.

In 1958 Jach'aqullu focused on defending indigenous rights by requesting the support of Bolivian intellectuals and international organizations based in La Paz, specifically writers such as Juan María Salles, Gabriel Gosalvez, Enrique Baldivieso, José Espada Aguirre, Waldo Belmonte Pool, Juan Cabral García, Fernando Diez de Medina, and Fausto Reinaga. This group of intellectuals frequently wrote in national newspapers about indigenous issues. José Espada helped Jach'aqullu connect with such international organizations as the United Nations. Gabriel Gosalvez wrote frequently in defense of "indigenous culture" (Aisakayu, "Andrés Jach'aqullu," APAJMC 1984, 38–41). Because Jach'aqullu spoke Spanish, could give them first-hand information, and could attend meetings in La Paz, he was a crucial source of information and inspiration about indigenous issues and identity for these intellectuals and international dignitaries. During this time, Jach'aqullu advocated the right to follow Native religions, denounced the abuses of MNR unions, and declared the Indian Law to be the best path for indigenous people to regain their rights. Jach'aqullu's ideas had an especially powerful influence on Fausto Reinaga and Fernando Diez de Medina. In the 1970s Reinaga became the most influential writer on Indian nationalism, and he remained prominent until the end of the twentieth century, inspiring different indigenous movements.

The relationship between the AMP and their audience changed in the new political context that emerged after 1964. As Steven Feierman has asserted, activist intellectuals must perform and speak for a specific audience because their representations are meaningless without such a link (Feierman 1990, 23–50). AMP activist intellectuals advocating subaltern nationalism lost their audience in the 1960s and 1970s because ex-peons and their children were gradually empowered as they gained influence in the peasant unions. These unions ceased to be non-Indian organizations, and indigenous peasants gradually appropriated the revolution's ideas. Activist intellectuals such as Jach'aqullu continued to insist on subaltern nationalism through their mode of dress and their faith in Indian gods, but they became increasingly powerless as their audience diminished.

In a November 1973 radio broadcast in Aymara and Quechua, a man using the name Andrés Tikuna called all Indians to a meeting in Tiwanaku (Aisakayu, "Andrés Jach'aqullu," APAJMC 1984, 12–34). Tikuna was actually Andrés Jach'aqullu; he had taken his mother's maiden name in the early 1970s because his clandestine indigenous activism had become dangerous under the Banzer dictatorship, which persecuted activists of all kinds. Additionally, Tikuna (Jach'aqullu) had become a Baha'i preacher in the mid-1960s, and the Baha'is strictly forbade its members to be politically active. These circumstances forced Jach'aqullu to hide his activism (Qulqi, "Inkawawas," APHOA 1981, Fondo 2, 23–28). Preaching for the Baha'is provided Jach'aqullu with income to support his family and allowed him to travel widely as an international preacher and visit Indian communities throughout the Americas, such as the Mapuches in Chile, the Navajos in the United States, and the Mayas in Mexico. By the late 1960s, he was the most famous Indian in the Baha'i international arena, even visiting the Baha'i World Center in Israel. However, while Jach'aqullu might have developed a hybrid religiosity, there is evidence to indicate that his faith in the Pachamama and the good spirits embodied in the Wak'as remained strong (Jach'aqullu, "El Kollasuyu," APAJMC 1977, 35–39).

The AMP refused to join the leftist parties because they were too secular, rejected Indian nationalism, and condemned the Aymara religion. However, some AMP members decided to become Baha'is because the religion offered them legal protection against the abuses they suffered at the hands of the state-run peasant unions. When the Baha'is focused on Latin America as part of their strategic plan in the early 1960s, the AMP were in desperate need of legal aid. As Andrés Jach'aqullu searched for support, he found the Baha'is, whom he convinced to give legal support to AMP activists. Over the years, Jach'aqullu and other indigenous activists became believers. Several of the AMP activists joined the Baha'is because the religion's syncretic vision did not condemn the Aymara religion as the Catholic and Protestant faiths did. The AMP was naturally attracted to this more open position (Jach'aqullu, "El Kollasuyu," APAJMC 1984, 13–18). Recounting his conversion to that faith in the late 1960s, Teodoro Tellez remembered that Andrés Jach'aqullu had told several AMPs in La Paz, "I met a group of very good people and their religion is good, let us get into this religion, they will help us [with our legal problems], and they will become our allies." The AMPs responded by completely rejecting the idea, saying "our religion is the Wak'as, our path is the Indian Law, and our worship is to the Pachamama. The Baha'i come from the whites and it is for the Spaniards" (Ponce, "Los poderantes," FPHE 1982, 23). When Andrés Jach'aqullu insisted on his proposal and brought the Baha'is to Chuquisaca, several AMPs did enroll, though many others never accepted the new faith. When those who did join asked the Baha'is for their opinion on Aymara religion, their response was, "your religion is good, it is truth." According to Tellez, after that, various AMP groups decided to "get into that religion to get protection against the [peasant] unions that persecuted us" (Ponce, "Los poderantes," FPHE 1982, 23).

Indeed, when the AMP used the phrase "to get into" to refer to conversion, they meant that they were using the organization as a resource to maintain their counterhegemonic views. However, many left Baha'ism after just a few years. The rupture came during a 1974 International Baha'i meeting that was held in Sucre, with more than two hundred AMP members attending from the valleys of Chuquisaca (Orieta, "Tata Toribio Miranda," APHONS 1957, 23–28; Quevedo, "Su historia," FPTQ 1979, 17–21). They all came wearing the AMP dress and congregated at the main cinema of Sucre, where the conference was being held. The AMP was particularly interested in speaking to Hooper Dunbar, one of the Baha'i leaders who had come from the World Center in Israel. Agapito Ponce asked to speak and was turned down, probably because the conference's leaders knew that he would raise controversial topics. Other members also tried unsuccessfully to speak during the first day of the meeting. The second day, Francisco Rivera finally had a chance (Peralta, "Fausto Reinaga," APHOMI 1979, 14–17; Ponce, "Los poderantes," FPHE 1982, 23, 29). He asked if the Indians who had converted to the Baha'i faith should follow the Ley de los Españoles, which meant the current Bolivian law (liberal, conservative, or populist), or if the Baha'i faith would enforce the Indian Law. The response he got from Hooper Dunbar was that the Baha'is should honor the Bolivian law and obey the government, whatever its political affiliation. After his response was translated into Quechua and Spanish, the two hundred AMP members stood up and started speaking loudly in Quechua, then left. That night, this group congregated on the Killa Killa hill and decided to found their own official religion, which would allow them to practice without persecution. This resulted in the founding of the Hermanos Espirituales (Spiritual Brotherhood), which passed bylaws in 1969 and was legally recognized by the government, thus becoming the first institutionalized Native religion in Bolivia (Rivera "Las haciendas," FPHE 1978, 14, 18; Ponce, "Los poderantes," FPHE 1982, 5–7).

Despite this break in 1974, the Baha'i and Protestant churches had shaped the AMP, and the Indian Law had transformed over time. The Hermanos Espirituales remained a branch of the AMP that followed its dress code, created its own Bible narrating the suffering of the indigenous people in hacienda times, and incorporated the AMP's early messages. They remembered Toribio Miranda, Gregorio Titiriku, Feliciano Inka Marasa, and other AMP members from the time of the haciendas as sacred people with a special message from their god. At the beginning they spoke about a god called the sun, but by the 1990s they called that being only God or the angel Gabriel (Loayza "El Congreso de Sucre," APEO 1973, 5–8; Orieta, "Tata Toribio Miranda," APHONS 1957, 21–23). In 1970 the Hermanos Espirituales built a temple with colonial and modern elements in Ruditayox, Tarwita, Chuquisaca. The religion still exists today, albeit in a much reduced form, in the region of Tarwita. Its adherents are still opposed to participation in national elections, unions, development projects, and municipal government. They believe in the Indian Law, but in a millenarian way that contains more Christian elements than before (Arias 1994, 177–78). The Hermanos Espirituales in Cantar Gallo are not the only ones who directly trace their roots to the AMP. There is a small group in Culpina, Chuquisaca, that invented its own language using a system similar to kipus, the ancient Inca and pre-Inca recording devices, and that also practices a form of Native religion. The other Hermanos Espirituales in Tumata Palqa, northern Potosí, emphasize indigenous medicine and religion. Thus, in going from being a political conception of society to a type of religious utopia, the Indian Law lost its power to transform people in the name of the Wak'as, as it had in the 1940s and 1950s, and with this shift, the AMP began its decline.

Despite this, Jach'aqullu's role among the indigenous population, though clandestine and precarious, was quite important and influenced the development of Katarismo in the 1980s. In 1973 different groups of Indian intellectuals, students, and Indian peasant organizations gathered in a meeting called the Congreso de Tiwanaku, in La Paz. Jach'aqullu was one of the main organizers of the meeting, along with Constantino Lima, Jaime Apaza, and Luciano Tapia (Arias 1994, 33; Hurtado 1986, 240–60). There, Jach'aqullu held well-attended discussions about Gregorio Titiriku and Toribio Miranda's work within the AMP. Based on these talks, the congress produced the Tiwanaku Manifesto, a founding statement of Katarismo and one of the most important documents in the history of civil rights in Bolivia. Referring to the relationship between non-Indian Bolivians and indigenous peoples, the manifesto states that "a nation oppressed by another cannot be free."

The congress asked Jach'aqullu to assume a position on the permanent board it created, but Tikuna refused because he would have had to give up his work as a preacher. Instead he proposed placing his son, Rogelio Cerrogrande, on the board of directors (Apaza, "Andrés Ticona," APAJMC 1984, Fondo 5, 11–15; Qulqi, "Inkawawas," APHOA 1981, Fondo 2, 18–22). He followed a similar strategy in 1977, when he helped organize the first indigenous political party in South America, the Movimiento Indio Tupak Katari (MITKA), an Indianist party that advocated power and self-determination for the indigenous peoples of Bolivia. Again, he was asked to serve on the board of directors but could not risk losing his source of income as a preacher, since he had three children in college. This time, Tikuna proposed his wife as a member, so Matilde Qulqi became responsible for MITKA women's affairs (Villka, "Muruhuta," FPMG 1981, 15–18). Qulqi also stood as a MITKA candidate for the Bolivian Chamber of Deputies from the Oruro Department in the 1978 election—the first in Bolivia following military rule. At the time, the idea of Indians running for office and the very notion of an Indian party was considered more fiction than reality. Although Matilde Qulqi did not win the post, she was very involved with the media and with party activities.[49]

Other indigenous activists of the AMP followed similar paths. In the 1960s and 1970s, many AMP members worked silently with Fausto Reinaga and helped form the Partido Indio de Bolivia (Bolivian Indian Party), which disbanded shortly after the 1978 election (Ugarte, "Los antiguos caminantes," APHOMI 1979, 23–28; Orieta, "Tata Toribio Miranda," APHONS 1957, 15). The interrelationship with the AMP helped Reinaga write a large number of books that developed the ideology for the modern phase of the indigenous movement in Latin America. Among the movement's leaders were Julian Ugarte, Agapito Ponce, Celestino Peralta, and Matilde Qulqi, who later were crucial figures in both the AMP movement and later the Indianist and Katarista movement (Ponce, "Los poderantes," FPHE 1982, 23). In the early 1970s, this group of activists even raised money in indigenous communities to publish the first edition of Reinaga's *Revolución India* (Ugarte, "Los antiguos caminantes," APHOMI 1979, 27). Reinaga also installed a facility in his house for indigenous people who came from other parts of the country (Peralta, "Fausto Reinaga," APHOMI 1979, 11). Some of the people who spent time with Reinaga were Baha'is, Methodists, Adventists, or involved in earlier versions of community-based Catholic groups in La Paz, Oruro, and Sucre. In 1970 many of the Indians from Potosí and Chuquisaca who came to La Paz to attend the Baha'i meeting, which paid for their travel expenses, also attended a meeting with Fausto Reinaga to learn about the new ideology called indianismo (Qulqi, "Mi religion," APHOA 1979, 28–32; Titiriku, "Para recordar," APPM 1977, 35–39).

The Katarista movement of the 1980s emerged out of this experience of indianismo. The Katarista and Indianista movements are modern indigenous political parties that sought the advancement of the indigenous peoples of Bolivia during the last third of the twentieth century. Their ideology was in dialogue with the history of liberal, leftist, and populist thought in Bolivia. Because the Indianistas focused on oppression as a nation, they emphasized the racial oppression of indigenous peasants by whites and mestizos. This was too radical for Bolivian politics of 1970s and thus was not accepted into the progressive agendas dominated by the Left. The Kataristas, on the other hand, argued that Indian peasants were oppressed as both a class and a nation; this movement was thus more readily accepted into the political context because of its emphasis on class-based struggle, a legacy of the 1952 Revolution. Thus, in practice and especially in the progressive Bolivian world of the 1970s dominated by unions, the Kataristas were more successful than the Indianistas in gaining political space. Katarista activists used an ethnic discourse that strongly condemned racialization when they spoke to the 1978–79 Confederación Nacional de Trabajadores Campesinos de Bolivia, a national umbrella organization of Bolivian peasants. Katarista ideology also influenced two political parties that had some clout in the late 1980s: the Movimiento Revolucionario Tupak Katari Liberación, a Katarista party, and Movimiento Indio Tupak Katari, an Indianist party. In fact, Víctor Hugo Cárdenas from the Movimiento Revolucionario Tupak Katari Liberación became the first Aymara vice president of Bolivia in 1994. Additionally, Felipe Quispe, an Aymara from La Paz who placed fourth in the 2002 election, brought the notion of two republics to the national arena. Quispe was closely aligned with the last generation of AMP in Chuquisaca and organized the Ayllus Rojos, an armed Indian militia led by the AMP's descendants in the 1980s. While Jach'aqullu and the AMP's notion of two republics was used to express differences between Indians and mestizos following the 1952 Revolution, Quispe used the same idea to express political and ideological differences between the white power structure and the indigenous movement in the Banzer era (1971–78) (Arias 1994, 3). In contemporary Bolivian language, this contradiction is often expressed as mestizos versus originarios (Native peoples).

## Conclusion

Jach'aqullu's history shows how indigenous activism changed in the decades after the consolidation of the 1952 National Revolution, during which the AMP became a dissident voice, as the cases of Icla, Tarwita, and Wilaqullu demonstrate. After the revolution, the vast majority of the population was still in a subaltern position and ruled by a minority of whites and mestizos, who promoted whitening in the national discourse. In this new era, indigenous people still felt the sting of racism after they migrated to urban areas, and this became the context in which the nationalism of *jaqi peoples*, or Indians, reemerged (Rivera 1984, 115–73).

Assimilation discourse promoted a form of de-Indianization during the stage of Bolivian modernization that overlapped with the 1952 National Revolution. Assimilation was the leftists' main goal in the 1940s, and the populists considered it to be their greatest achievement after the 1952 National Revolution. In 1953 Víctor Paz Estenssoro, the leader of the National Revolution and four-time Bolivian president, told an indigenous crowd they were "no longer" Indians but "peasants" (Huizer 1972, 94). Astenio Averanga, an intellectual and policy maker of the Revolution, argued that the National Revolution would essentially repopulate the country by transforming people's premodern Indianness. Paz Estenssoro and Averanga perceived this "transformation" as "profoundly meaningful" because, for them, it meant that Indians could become modern. As state policy after the National Revolution, de-Indianization through the removal of Indian signifiers was an alternative and nonviolent way of practicing ethnic cleansing (Antezana and Romero 1979, 203–64).

After the 1952 Revolution, ex-peons in possession of land in regions like Icla and Tarwita turned to the Indian Law because they were worried that the agrarian reform was empowering the rural mestizos, who controlled state-oriented peasant unions and reinforced racialized practices against Indians. As such, the Indian Law became a way to articulate an agenda of decolonization that spoke to the contradictions created by the National Revolution of 1952. Postrevolution indigenous activists developed their own nationalism based on faith in Wak'as and a narrative of the Aymara past, and they promoted this project through a network of cells in the western part of the country. The enactment of this indigenous network also called on gender relationships in strategic ways. Matilde Qulqi represented Jach'aqullu politically at several points over the years, and she acted as co-priest in various indigenous ceremonies. In both religious and political contexts, Jach'aqullu and Qulqi's relationship fits the Aymara world's notion of gender complementarity and was an essential part of their struggle. The Katarista and Indianista movements still incorporated issues of gender in their work but with less emphasis than the AMP. In the end, from the 1950s through the 1970s, the AMP had a major, though at times indirect, effect on the modern Bolivian political system. It helped not only to invigorate a new type of activism in the late 1970s but also to provide more contemporary indigenous activists with historical context and concepts with which to fight late twentieth-century coloniality (Aisakayu, "Andrés Jach'aqullu," APAJMC 1984, 23–33). One such enduring concept was the idea of two Bolivias, which expresses the contradiction and inequality between indigenous peoples and whites and mestizos.

## Notes

### Abbreviations

| | |
|---|---|
| AJPC | Archivo Judicial de la Provincia Campero |
| AJPD | Archivo Judicial de la Provincia Dalence |
| APAJMC | Archivo Privado de Andrés Jachakollo y Matilde Colque |
| APEO | Archivo Privado de Ezequiel Orieta |
| APHOA | Archivo Privado de Historia Oral Amuyasiñataki |
| APHOMI | Archivo Privado de Historia Oral de Manuel Ilaquita |
| APHONS | Archivo Privado de Historia Oral de Nabil Saavedra |
| APPM | Archivo Privado de Pedro Mamani |
| CDHSFX | Centro Documental é Histórico de San Francisco Xavier |
| FPAPM | Fondo Privado De Agapito Ponce |
| FPFR | Fondo Privado de Francisco Rivera, Sumala |
| FPGTRR | Fondo Privado de Gregorio Titiriku y Rosa Ramos |
| FPHE | Fondo Privado de los Hermanos Espirituales |
| FPMG | Fondo Privado de Melitón Gallardo Saavedra |

FPTQ     Fondo Privado de Tomás Quevedo
SNRA     Servicio Nacional de Reforma Agraria

1. Proceso judicial Vela contra Reina, 1953–56, 7–11, CDHSFX.

2. Since 1874 the term *apoderado* has referred to the legal Indian representative of an Indian community.

3. This means the new peasant unions reproduced and recreated a lot of political and organizational ideas from indigenous peoples' culture.

4. *Vecinos de pueblo*: rural elite, usually racialized as white or mestizo.

5. "Decreto Supremo 3937," *La Gaceta de Bolivia* 2, no. 10, July 3, 1956.

6. "Demanda judicial de Félix Cutrina," April 11, 1958, 2–3, APJC.

7. "Demanda judicial de Félix Cutrina," April 11, 1958, 5–6, APJC.

8. "Carta de Pedro Añawaya dirigida al Corregidor de Janqulaime, Septiembre 15, 1957," 3–5, APHOMI; "Demanda de Filiberto Quispe contra Reynaldo Ramírez, Enero 3, 1958," 6–7, APEO.

9. "Demanda judicial de Félix Cutrina, April, 11, 1958," 3–10, APEO.

10. Bolivians commonly remember this war as pushed by the British and U.S. companies interested in exploring oil reserves. Defeat in the Chaco War made Bolivia's white elite vulnerable.

11. Proceso judicial Vela contra Reina, 1953–56, 7–11, CDHSFX.

12. "Hojas de servicios de Andrés Cerrogrande, 1944," Comando Departamental de la Policía Boliviana, Oruro, 2–4, Fondo 4, APAJMC.

13. "Los hijos del Sol," *Revista del Trabajo* 9 (1956): 22–23, Fondo 7, APAJMC.

14. "Carta de Toribio Miranda a Andrés Jach'aqullu nombrándolo su apoderado," April 11, 1951, Fondo 8, APAJMC.

15. Julio Zalles, "El sufrimiento de los Alcaldes Particulares," (testimony, 1964), 14, 16, Folio 2, FPFR.

16. "Expediente Paredes vs. Iturri, 1928–1932," 7–23, FPGTRR.

17. "Expediente Paredes," 17.

18. "Manifiesto de la Federación Agraria Departamental La Paz, Octubre 1939," 3–5, Fondo Prefectural, 1940, AHLP.

19. "Algo que Pudo Parecer Insólito," *La Calle*, May 11, 1945, 4.

20. Getúlio Vargas, president and dictator of Brazil, was admired by Villarroel and other socialist military officers in Bolivia. Villarroel admired Vargas for fostering "updated" or "modernized" labor relations in Brazil in 1930s. See "Memorias of Raúl Riveros, Villarroel, Vargas y Brazil," La Paz, 1972, APHOA.

21. "El Kollasuyu," *La Patria*, September 2, 1953, 3.

22. "Declaración del diacono Edgar Silva sobre los Kollasuyus de la loma de Huanuni," September 22, 1953, 5–9, Fondo 4, APAJMC.

23. "Sumario judicial que inicia el diacono de Bombo contra falsos sacerdotes," 9–11, Fondo 1945–1958, AJPD.

24. "Certificado de matrimonio bajo la Ley de Indios de Julio Cutrina y Berna Ledesma, September, 21, 1950," 45, Fondo 7, APAJMC.

25. "Acta de libertad del reo Andrés Jach'aqullu," February 28, 1952, Fondo 1, APAJMC.

26. "Acta de libertad," 14–15.

27. "Proceso agrario de la 'hacienda Churumatas,' 1954–1962," 124, Fondo Zudáñez, SNRA.

28. "Informe del jefe del Comando del MNR, Enero 1954," 23–25, Fondo Prefectural, 1950–1955, CDHSFX.

29. "Informe del jefe."

30. "Expediente agrario de Qullachiwanway, 1953," 23–45, 1958, Fondo Zudáñez SNRA.

31. "Demanda contra Zenón Ibáñez por compra fraudulenta de un lote, Enero 1956," 5–7, Fondo 6, APAJMC. Piqueros owned land, either on or off a hacienda. After the agrarian reform piqueros tended to have larger plots of land than ex-colonos; this gave them more influence on the structures of local power.

32. "Felipe Lima, Mallku Mayor del Ayllu Qillu Qullana quejándose contra Qarita por apropiarse tierras del ayllu, 1957," 35, Fondo 2, APPM.

33. "Carta Pastoral del Cardenal Maurer, Julio 6, 1956," Fondo 2, FPTQ.

34. "Carta de Andrés Jach'aqullu a Matilde Qulqi, Mayo 4, 1958," Fondo 7, APAJMC.

35. "Carta de Andrés Jach'aqullu a Fermín Vallejos, Enero 3, 1958," Fondo 3, APPM.

36. "Expedientes agrarios Sumala," 1961, 87; "Soroma, 1959," 53; "Viscanches, 1958," 21; "Jatun Mayo 13, 1961," Fondo Zudáñez, SNRA.

37. "Sumario informativo contra Andrés Jach'aqullu, Francisco Rivera y otros conocidos como hombres voladores, Diciembre, 1957," 7–8, Fondo 1, APTQ.

38. "Sumario informativo," APTQ.

39. "Solicitud de reactivación de proceso contra hombres voladores del Corregidor de Icla, Ángel Estrada, al Juez de Tarabuco, Enero 1959," 5–8, Fondo Prefectural 1950–1959, CDHSFX.

40. "Carta de Francisco Rivera, a Fermín Vallejos, Marzo 3, 1959," 1, Fondo 3, APHE.

41. "Informe del Subprefecto de Azurduy, Julio Maturana, Febrero 1960," 2–3, Fondo Prefectural 1960–1973, CDHSF.

42. "*La Plata*, Abril 1960," 1, Fondo 3, APHE.

43. *Jallp'a sangres*: Term that mixes Quechua and Spanish; used by Melitón Gallardo to inspire racial pride and religious devotion to Indian deities among supporters of the AMP.

44. "Expediente agrario Qullachiwanway, 1959–1966," 67, Fondo Zudáñez, SNRA.

45. "Expediente agrario Marapampa, 1956–1967," 98–103, Fondo Azurduy, SNRA.

46. "Expediente agrarios de Quinua Chacra, 1954–1969," 33–35, Fondo Azurduy; "Redención Pampa, 1956–1964," 51–53, Fondo Zudáñez, SNRA.

47. "Denuncia ante el juzgado penal de Misk'i del Subprefecto de la provincia, Febrero 14, 1964," 3–4, Fondo 1, FPMG.

48. Monje, "El Kollasuyu," *Revista Andina* 9 (1956): 22–33, Fondo 7, APAJMC.

49. "Primeros pobladores," *Presencia*, December 14, 1978: 11–15.

# Bibliography

## Archival Sources

*Chuquisaca*
Archivo Privado de Ezequiel Orieta (APEO), Churumumu

Archivo Privado de Historia Oral de Nabil Saavedra (APHONS), Mesa Verde
Centro Documental é Histórico de San Francisco Xavier (CDHSFX), Sucre
Fondo Privado de Francisco Rivera, Sumala (FPFR)
Fondo Privado de los Hermanos Espirituales (FPHE), Roditoyoj
Fondo Privado de Melitón Gallardo Saavedra (FPMG), Sucre
Fondo Privado de Tomás Quevedo (FPTQ), Guerra Loma
Servicio Nacional de Reforma Agraria (SNRA)

*Cochabamba*
Archivo Judicial de la Provincia Campero (AJPC), Aiquile

*La Paz*
Archivo Privado de Historia Oral Amuyasiñataki (APHOA)
Archivo Privado de Pedro Mamani (APPM), El Alto
Fondo Privado de Gregorio Titiriku y Rosa Ramos (FPGTRR), Chukiawu Marka

*Oruro*
Archivo Judicial de la Provincia Dalence, Huanuni (AJPD)
Archivo Privado de Andrés Jachakollo y Matilde Colque (APAJMC)

*Potosí*
Archivo Privado de Historia Oral de Manuel Ilaquita (APHOMI), Cala Cala

## Published Sources

Albó, Xavier, and Mauricio Mamani. 1979. *Achacachi: Medio siglo de lucha campesina*. La Paz: CIPCA.

Andrade, Claudio. 1989. *José Santos Marka Thola, 1879 a 1939: Cronología del primer "sindicalista" campesino*. Sucre: TIFAP.

Antezana Ergueta, Luis, and Guillermo Bedregal Gutiérrez. 1992. *Origen, fundación y futuro del M.N.R.* La Paz: Ediciones Abril.

Antezana Ergueta, Luis, and Hugo Romero. 1979. *Historia de los sindicatos campesinos: Un proceso de integración nacional en Bolivia*. La Paz: MACA/CNRA, Investigaciones Sociales.

Arias, Juan Félix. 1994. *El tata Fermín. Historia de una esperanza*. La Paz: Aruwiyiri-THOA.

Calderón, Fernando and Jorge Dandler. 1984. *Bolivia, la fuerza histórica del campesinado*. La Paz: CERES, UNRISD.

Céspedes, Augusto. 1956. *Sangre de mestizos*. Santiago: Claridad.

Gómez, Eugenio. 1975. *Bautista Saavedra*. La Paz: Biblioteca del Sesquicentenario.

Gordillo, José M. 1998. *Arando en la historia. La experiencia política campesina en Cochabamba*. La Paz: Plural/CERES/UMSS.

———. 2000. *Los hombres de la revolución: Memorias de un líder campesino, Sinforoso Rivas Antezana*. La Paz: Plural.

———. 2002. *Campesinos revolucionarios en Bolivia. Identidad, territorio y sexualidad en el valle Alto de Cochabamba, 1952-1964*. La Paz: Plural.

Gotkowitz, Laura. 2007. *A Revolution for Our Rights: Indigenous Struggle for Land and Justice in Bolivia, 1880-1952*. Durham: Duke University Press.

Feierman, Steven. 1990. *Peasant Intellectuals: Anthropology and History in Tanzania.* Madison: University of Wisconsin Press.

Harris, Olivia, and Xavier Albó. 1989. *Monteras y guardatojos: Campesinos y mineros en el Norte de Potosí.* La Paz: CIPCA.

Healy, Kevin. 1987. *Caciques y patrones.* Cochabamba: El Buitre.

Huizer, Gerrit. 1972. *The Revolutionary Potential of the Peasant in Latin America.* Lexington: Lexington.

Hurtado, Javier. 1986. *El Katarismo.* La Paz: Hisbol.

Klein, Herbert. 1992. *Bolivia: The Evolution of a Multiethnic Society.* New York: Oxford University Press.

Lehm, Zulema, and Silvia Rivera Cusicanqui. 1988. *Los artesanos libertarios y la ética del trabajo.* La Paz: THOA.

Lora, Guillermo. 1980. *Formación de la clase obrera boliviana.* La Paz: Masas.

Paredes, Alfonsina. 1980. *El indio Machaca y la República Aymara.* La Paz: Producciones Isla.

Rivera Cusicanqui, Silvia. 1984. *Oprimidos pero no vencidos, luchas del campesinado Aymara y Qhechwa de Bolivia 1900–1980.* La Paz: Hisbol.

Rivera Cusicanqui, Silvia, Denise Arnold, Zulema Lehm, Susan Paulson, and Juan de Dios Yapita. 1996. *Ser mujer, indígena: Chola o birlocha en la Bolivia postcolonial de los años 90.* La Paz: Subsecretaría de Asuntos de Género.

Salamanca Trujillo, Daniel. 1978. *Los campesinos en el proceso político boliviano.* Oruro: Quelco.

Stephenson, Marcia. 1999. *Gender and Modernity in Andean Bolivia.* Austin: University of Texas Press.

# 9

# Reel Visions

*Snapshots from a Half Century
of First Nations Cinema*

MILÉNA SANTORO

In her 2010 book, *Reservation Reelism: Redfacing, Visual Sovereignty, and Representations of Native Americans in Film*, Michelle Raheja suggests the term *visual sovereignty* to describe "the space between resistance and compliance wherein indigenous filmmakers and actors revisit, contribute to, borrow from, critique, and reconfigure ethnographic film conventions, while at the same time operating within and stretching the boundaries created by those conventions" (193). While one might take issue with her category of Native "Americans" to describe the culturally diverse and territorially distinct indigenous peoples she discusses, Raheja's conception of visual sovereignty offers a particularly useful framework for describing the development of First Nations filmmaking in Canada since the 1960s, especially given that the self-assertion and self-determination implied by the word *sovereignty* allow us to connect the visual art of filmmaking to the political goals that so many First Nations peoples have pursued over the past fifty years.

Just as in the political arena Natives have encountered significant obstacles to their autonomy and aspirations, so too have indigenous filmmakers had to struggle to find their voices in a cinematic milieu where they have historically been the object of the camera's gaze rather than the ones controlling the image. On this point, Cree filmmaker Neil Diamond's documentary *Reel Injun: On the Trail of the Hollywood Indian*, winner of a prestigious Peabody award for 2010, is an engaging yet profound critique of how, in "over 4000 films about Native people [made] over 100 years," Hollywood has "defin[ed] how Indians are seen by the world." Since the late 1800s, in fact, when some of the earliest films made by Edison and by the Lumière brothers' envoys to Canada recorded Native dances, there has been a fascination for the "disappearing culture" of indigenous peoples. One has only to evoke the landmark film about the Inuit, Robert J. Flaherty's 1922 *Nanook of the North*, to demonstrate both the allure and the condescending objectification of Native peoples as portrayed by a Caucasian camera, even one with essentially ethnographic or documentary intentions. As Diamond's archival research demonstrates, most Hollywood movies of the past century present stereotypes of the "Injun" as "noble," "savage," or "groovy," to name but three of the caricatural cinematic treatments *Reel Injun* highlights. Clearly, such fantasies not only are hard to counter, given the worldwide dominance of Hollywood productions, but also remain destructive influences on contemporary generations of Native peoples who still struggle to have their cultural specificities and dignity affirmed in the public sphere. Indeed, in one of the most eviscerating moments of *Reel Injun*, Diamond silently films the faces of Native children watching Arthur Penn's 1970 western *Little Big Man*, allowing us to see clearly how Hollywood images of Native people, despite sympathetic or revisionist intentions, can create feelings of distress, confusion, and alienation in Native viewers.

Kerstin Knopf, in her volume *Decolonizing the Lens of Power: Indigenous Films in North America*, offers a succinct synopsis of the obstacles to First Nations filmmaking, explaining that "an Indigenous national cinema in North America has not been able to develop, chiefly because Indigenous nations are not politically independent and autonomous nations, and, further, because the 'imperialist center of film production' is situated on the same continent. [North American] indigenous filmmakers, more than any other postcolonial filmmakers, are compelled to create work in relation to Hollywood practice" (2008, 53–54).[1] For his part, Scott MacKenzie speculates as to "whether the category of 'national cinema' can be as easily applied to minor, third, alternative or aboriginal cinemas" (2000, 241), though in "Mimetic Nationhood: Ethnography and the National," he does a convincing job of showing "how colonised or otherwise oppressed groups can adopt through mimesis the trappings of nationhood in a series of both positive and negative ways in order to comment on, reinforce, or critique the (post-) colonial nation-state" (2000, 242). In other words, both MacKenzie and Knopf, among other critics, see indigenous cinema as relationally defined, caught in a pattern of imitation and resistance in the search for a "vision" of Native peoples.

It is my contention here that "trappings of nationhood" that MacKenzie observes in certain ethnographic films are in fact constitutive elements of what Raheja calls visual sovereignty but that such sovereignty is only truly made legible and efficacious in films that Native peoples have made about themselves and their communities. In this, I concur with Knopf in her assertion of the importance of the decolonizing process for Native cinema, when she writes: "For Indigenous filmmakers, decolonization starts when they take their image-making and self-representation into their own hands, creating decolonized cultural, historical, and political discourses, and becoming progressively emancipated from the Hollywood-dominated industry. This decolonizing process works in a twofold manner: first, as a political struggle, through the creation of self-fashioned images and anticolonialist rewriting and filming of history; and, secondly, as an aesthetic struggle, through defiance of and/or negotiation with established conventions of feature and ethnographic film" (2008, 63). While some Native thinkers and writers, such as Thomas King (1990, 11–12), object to the framing of Native cultural productions within and by postcolonial theory, to my mind there is no question that the Native filmmakers who have successfully emerged in Canadian cinema of the past fifty years have both undergone and promoted a "decolonizing process" and thereby have anticipated or created works of visual sovereignty.

This chapter offers a few salient examples of this process in films made by indigenous filmmakers in Canada, as a way to chronicle both the evolution and the achievements of Native cinema since the 1960s. It should be noted here that defining what makes a film indigenous is somewhat controversial. Generally, a film's being directed by a Native person is enough to ensure the film is considered a Native production, while a film made by a non-Native director but using Native actors and themes does not warrant the label.[2] Such is the case with Denis Boivin's 2003 feature *Attache ta tuque!*, which is not recognized as the first Native feature in Quebec even though its protagonist is Native and the film features indigenous actors playing Native roles. By contrast, Yves Sioui Durand's 2011 *Mesnak* has been crowned Quebec's first Native feature film because Durand himself is Huron-Wendat despite the fact the Native protagonist is played by a non-Native actor.[3] Although this restrictive, and some might even say essentialist, definition of what constitutes a Native production means the exclusion of many Canadian and Quebec films that prominently feature Native stories or characters, this strategic demarcation nonetheless has the merit of ensuring that the examples selected are more thoroughly informed by the cultural context being portrayed, and thus more likely to offer examples of visual sovereignty than they would if made by an "outsider."[4] The Native films I highlight as manifestations of visual sovereignty fall into three roughly chronological segments: first, early short films made under the Challenge for Change/Société Nouvelle program, which ran at the National Film Board of Canada (or NFB) from 1969 to 1980; second, documentaries that follow from or illustrate the impact of the NFB's mission and tradition, in particular those made by Alanis Obomsawin from 1984 through the present; and finally, Native experimental narrative films and feature filmmaking, which began to appear in the late 1990s and have become what is arguably the most promising development of the past decade in Canadian cinema.

### The National Film Board's Challenge for Change Program and the First All-Native Film Crew

The National Film Board of Canada was created in 1939 after the pioneering Scottish documentarian John Grierson submitted his report on Canadian government film activities and drafted the language of what would be passed as the National Film Act. Although it functioned primarily as a producer of propaganda during the Second World War, there is no question that in the decades since then the NFB has been an crucial catalyst for the development of what we now call Canadian and Quebec "national cinemas," by fulfilling its founding principle "to make and distribute films . . . designed to help Canadians . . . understand the problems and way of life of Canadians in other parts of the country" (National Film Board of

Canada, 2011). If the NFB has offered a training ground and spring-
board for the careers of many notable directors from across Canada, the relocation of its headquarters to Montreal in 1956 made
it especially important for the development of Quebec's cinematic
voice during the 1960s, and, by the same token, for the rise of Native
filmmaking in the region as well.

In 1967, spurred by the 1966 documentary by Tanya Ballantyne, *The
Things I Cannot Change*, in which the director exposed the depths of
poverty in Canada using the Bailey family as a case study (Zéau 2006,
413–15), the NFB initiated a program called Challenge for Change.
By 1969 this program was merged with its francophone counter-
part, Société Nouvelle, and was consolidated in its mandate and its
funding by Cabinet decree (Zéau 2006, 421). In brief, the objective
of Challenge for Change, or CFC, was "to help Canadians to understand and accept changes affecting their social environment, and to
become active participants" (Zéau 2006, 422, translation mine) in
addressing the issues involved. While initially the films made under
the auspices of the program addressed broad social issues like poverty, the conditions and concerns of Native peoples quickly became
integral to that focus. As explained by Noel Starblanket, in a 1968
article reprinted in the edited volume *Challenge for Change: Activist Documentary at the National Film Board of Canada*:

> Eighteen films have been produced about Indians by the National Film
> Board, and all of them have been made by *outsiders* looking in on the
> situation. Last year the Challenge for Change Program included three
> more films about Indians. These three were not sponsored by any par-
> ticular government department with a specific message. They were
> closer to depicting a truer perspective of the "Indian problem." How-
> ever, these films still lacked a real Indian point of view. A number of
> people felt like the next logical step would be to involve Indians as
> filmmakers. [. . . The resulting NFB-trained] crew felt that this was the
> first time the knowledge, opinions, and feelings of Indians were being
> sought, encouraged, and appreciated by any kind of government agency
> (Starblanket 2010, loc. 1049).

As one of the original cohort of Natives recruited and trained by
the NFB as part of the CFC program, Starblanket clearly understood

what was at stake, and the potential for authentic self-expression and self-assertion that films made by Native crews held.[5]

In this interview Starblanket briefly describes the making of the first two documentary shorts produced by members of that crew, *The Ballad of Crowfoot* and *These Are My People*, released in 1968 and 1969, respectively. These two films constitute the first-ever all-Native projects in Canadian film history, and as such, they perhaps deserve more attention than they have received.[6] In *The Ballad of Crowfoot*, Willie Dunn's montage of archival photos and newspaper clippings, set to a song he wrote and recorded himself, offers a moving and militant portrayal of the suffering and betrayals visited upon Native peoples in the Canadian West, symbolized by the figure of Crowfoot, a Blackfoot leader who lived from 1830 to 1890. This short montage film earned four awards in festivals held in Halifax, Uruguay, and the United States, a testimony to how effectively it tells its story.[7] With no dialogue and virtually no live action (with the exception of some archival clips of buffalo), Dunn uses zooms, pans, close-ups, and, at the end, an accelerated montage—well before Ken Burns famously used such techniques—to bring the archival images alive. His song, both doleful and indignant, underscores how to interpret the montage by posing pointed rhetorical questions, as in the following stanza:

Today the treaty stands on the table . . . ,
It offers food, and protection too.
Do you really think they'll hold true?
It offers a reserve, now isn't that grand?
And in return, you cede all of your land.

Dunn's ten-minute film offers an excellent example of what Knopf terms an "anticolonialist rewriting and filming of history," and as such it develops a visual sovereignty because it both exposes and protests the collective dispossession and degradation of the Plains Indians perpetrated by westward colonial expansion and modernity. While the form of address used by Dunn in his song is "you," his reappropriation of Native history is clearly born of solidarity, conscious of the need to retrieve and rehabilitate such historical figures as a source of pride, but also as manifestations of a shared destiny.

In one of his final stanzas, Dunn at last uses the song's only instance of the pronoun "we" that serves to unite the past with the present, specifically referencing the year 1967. Perhaps coincidentally, this was also the year of Montreal's Universal Exposition, centered on the theme of "Terre des hommes" or "Man and His World," which underscores the bitter irony of Dunn's lyrics: "There's still hypocrisy, and still the hate, / . . . We're all unhappy pawns in the government's game, / and it's always the Indian who gets the blame."

Dunn also collaborated with Mike Mitchell, Starblanket, and two others on the CFC Native crew to film the live action short *These Are My People*, in which the Mohawk of Akwesasne present their Longhouse religious and political traditions. While this film seems less powerful than Dunn's *Ballad*, it does present, through the relatively uninterrupted discourse of Native leaders, a vision of nationhood that counters negative indigenous stereotypes and even points to the Iroquois Confederacy's influence on Canadian and American constitutional governance.[8] As Michelle Stewart underscores, this aesthetic privileging of long speeches "arises from a respect for the significance of oral history within Native traditions" and, in the case of this film, "the effect is to undergird [the] characterization of the Longhouse tradition as an effective contemporary model of peaceful governance for whites and Indians" (2007, 59). It seems to me to be particularly significant, then, that both of the first two films made in Canada by indigenous crews focus on telling a story of (loss of) sovereignty through one or two speakers, or by a singer, in the case of Dunn's *Ballad*. In both cases, the claim for visual sovereignty is thus supported by a *prise de parole* or an emphasis on the right to speak and the duty of the spectator to listen. In this way, these two films can be seen as a documentary extension of the oral tradition so central to Native history and community life because they essentially translate that form of knowledge transmission to the screen, emphasizing how image and word work dialogically (and sometimes ironically) together to convey a memorable message that offers a counternarrative to colonial history.[9] This strategy also characterizes Dunn's later codirected project with Martin Defalco, *The Other Side of the Ledger: An Indian View of the Hudson's Bay Company*, a documentary released in 1972 as a response to the three-hundredth anniversary celebrations of that famous institution of colonial capitalism in Canada.

One final documentary that resulted from the first Native crew's collaboration with the CFC program must be mentioned here, even though its titular director is non-Native, principally because of its high profile and lasting influence. Released in 1969, with Mort Ransen credited as director, *You Are on Indian Land* chronicles the conflict between the Saint Regis Mohawk community of Cornwall Island (now called Akwesasne) and the local and federal authorities, over the Natives' right to bring goods across the Canada-U.S. border without paying duty (as per the Jay Treaty of 1794, passed by the U.S. government but not Canada). According to George Stoney, who was the CFC producer involved at the time, this film was made at the request of Mike Mitchell, a Saint Regis Mohawk who knew of plans to block the international bridge if negotiations between his tribe and the government did not produce positive results (Starblanket 2010, loc. 3569). While the question of the film's authorship has been the subject of some debate, given that Mitchell instigated the project, the fact that Mitchell himself was arrested during the bridge blockade meant that, materially, he could not be behind the camera. This is one reason why Ransen is officially credited, even though the latter has taken pains to recognize the important contributions of the Native crewmembers, particularly Mitchell, in the making and editing of the final product (White 2006, 82).

Notwithstanding such debate over its Native credentials, *You Are on Indian Land* was highly influential in its time, for Mitchell insisted on immediately showing the raw footage to both the Mohawk community and the authorities as a way to promote negotiations, and, subsequently, as Michelle Stewart documents, "the film's reach extended south of the border," where it was even seen by the Native American activists occupying Alcatraz from late 1969 to 1971 (2007, 63).[10] Stewart also succinctly articulates the central thrust of the film and the protest it documents, which is "that sovereignty involves the self-identification and definition of a people and a demarcated territory over which they exercise control" (2007, 61–62). Although the Mohawk shown in the film clearly aspire to that control more than they possess it, the confrontation documented here is emblematic of a series of efforts by Native groups over the past fifty years to assert greater political and territorial sovereignty. Indeed, the fact that the three films made by the first all-Native film crew were released during the same period Prime Minister Trudeau's government was drafting the infamous White Paper—which recommended abolishing the Indian Act as well as land claims, and which was countered in 1970 by an indigenous response nicknamed "The Red Paper"—is a testimony to their status as part of a rising tide of resistance to government policy and of renewed affirmation of First Nations rights and concerns in the 1960s in Canada.[11] In this context, *You Are on Indian Land* clearly foreshadows the efforts of later Native filmmakers including Alanis Obomsawin to document violations of Native rights and territorial control, and as such, while its political impact is undeniable, it is an equally important landmark in the quest for visual sovereignty in indigenous cinema.

Although, as Métis filmmaker Gil Cardinal has noted, the "Indian Film Crew" project was relatively short-lived, it was followed in 1971 by the "Indian Training Program," which set out to initiate a new generation of Natives to the "experience of film production and distribution," in part with assistance from Dunn and Mitchell, who both trained as directors with the first Native crew (Cardinal n.d.). As others have pointed out, however, this second group was "not necessarily assigned to projects treating Native issues" (Stewart 2007, 66), and films about Natives made during this second initiative under the CFC rubric were not necessarily directed by indigenous filmmakers.[12] That said, this early period, which saw Native film crews address shared Native concerns, had considerable influence and political importance. Writing about the lasting legacy of *You Are on Indian Land*, Faye Ginsburg affirms that it "signaled a crucial shift in assumptions about who should be behind the documentary camera," adding that "it is significant that the timing of the film coincided with the first wave of the modern movement for Aboriginal political rights in Canada and clearly helped to make those efforts visible" (1999, 66–67). While one cannot argue with this judgment, I would in fact extend it to include all of the films made by the first indigenous film crew, for they were all a result of that "crucial shift" in thinking supported by the NFB's CFC program, and they collectively show an aspiration to visual sovereignty that accompanies, illustrates, and encourages a discourse of Native self-determination and self-expression that continues to resonate today.[13]

## Alanis Obomsawin and the Native Documentary Tradition at the NFB

In his introduction to the NFB's retrospective playlist "The Aboriginal Voice," Gil Cardinal points out that "the period between the Indian Training Program and the next major initiative in 1991 saw a mini surge in Aboriginal documentary filmmaking. It was during this time that a number of films marked the beginning of the distinguished career of Alanis Obomsawin. In addition, other Aboriginal directors began working with the Board on a freelance basis" (Cardinal, n.d.). If the film crews trained under the auspices of the CFC program constitute a watershed moment in the birth of indigenous cinema in Canada, equally important was the NFB's hiring in 1967 of Alanis Obomsawin, an American-born Abenaki singer and storyteller raised in Quebec, whose subsequent career as a documentary filmmaker has garnered her many well-deserved honors and awards. If there is a First Nations cinema today, it is in no small measure due to pioneers and engaged artists like Obomsawin, who has continued to work at the NFB since the 1960s, arguably creating the single most important body of films on indigenous peoples and their concerns in North America, with over twenty titles to her credit to date.

Obomsawin's films tend to focus on local experiences and representative individuals that reflect the broader context of indigenous struggles. In Jerry White's article "Alanis Obomsawin, Documentary Form, and the Canadian Nation(s)," he underscores her role as a visionary "social filmmaker" by pointing to how her films are always "working towards cohesive First Nations" (White 2002, 364, 371). Quoting Benedict Anderson's *Imagined Communities*, which proposes this eponymous notion as one way to define a nation, White asserts: "this image of imagining tells us a great deal about the way Obomsawin constructs her Native community. Her films contribute, in a way that very few other films have, to an *image* of

FIG. 5. Alanis Obomsawin. Photo used by permission of Alanis Obomsawin and the National Film Board of Canada.

'a deep, horizontal comradeship,'" adding: "because they deal with situations that centralize the experience of a specific group of people (whose similarities may or may not be imagined, *pace* Anderson), Obomsawin's films have the thematic consistency of a national cinema. . . . Through a set of common signs and situations, Obomsawin makes it clear . . . she is speaking about . . . Natives' place in North America" (White 2002, 371, 372).[14] Although I continue to have reservations about applying the term *national* to indigenous cinema, especially on the basis of the work of a single auteur even as influential and prolific as Obomsawin, I concur with White in his recognition of the intent of her work, which is to show the shared nature of the Native sociopolitical struggles and of the cultural values she documents.

If Obomsawin established her credentials as a Native filmmaker beginning with her earliest projects in the seventies, it is not until 1984, with *Incident at Restigouche*, that she produced a film that deals directly with an infringement upon Native sovereignty by governmental authorities.[15] Ostensibly provoked by salmon overfishing on the Mi'gmaq reservation, the 1981 raids by Quebec Provincial Police documented by Obomsawin offer her an opportunity, as Christopher Gittings puts it, to "dispel the myth of Canada as a postcolonial nation that embraces difference and human rights by locating the ugly and violent colonial reality confronting First Nations firmly in the Canadian nation's present" (2002, 217).[16] Obomsawin's understanding of the broader stakes of the local issue of sovereign fishing rights is made famously clear by her interview with the Quebec minister of fisheries, in which she initially includes her presence in countershots, then shares the frame with her subject, visually emphasizing their equal footing. The official policy and discourse of the Quebec government representative inspires such resistance and ire that Obomsawin confronts him directly with her own counternarrative, exposing and returning "the colonial gaze that would structure Micmacs as nationless, cultureless, subjects of the Québec state" (Gittings 2002, 218), and would thus justify their mistreatment at the hands of a hypocritical Quebec government that itself insists on the province's "national" identity even as it denies the same status to Native groups living within its territory. In this exchange, with the camera positioned somewhat more on Obomsawin's side of the room, thus directing our gaze toward her adversary, we instinctively empathize with her anticolonialist discourse that seeks to rectify the misunderstanding of the francophone majority about their precedence in the territory now called Quebec, but which the Natives inhabited for millennia before colonization. This is clearly an important instance of the decolonization process in Native film, which serves the double purpose of articulating and legitimizing Native visions of history and of affording them visual sovereignty through the control, framing, and thus "angle" of film images and the story they tell.

In *Incident at Restigouche*, then, we witness Obomsawin "creating decolonized cultural, historical, and political discourses" (Knopf 2008, 63) even as she develops an aesthetic style that inflects traditional conventions of NFB documentary with distinctly Native forms of self-expression or storytelling strategies. Jerry White has convincingly argued that Obomsawin simultaneously continues and contests the Griersonian vision of documentary as an educational and nation-building tool, ideas upon which the NFB was founded (see White 2002). Although he does mention *Incident* along with Obomsawin's 1993 masterwork, *Kanehsatake: 270 Years of Resistance*, as both offering "radical critiques of the way nationhood has been constructed by Canadian and Québec society" (White 2002, 371), like many other critics, White tends to privilege the later, more famous film in his discussion of Obomsawin's formal aesthetics.[17] Because *Incident* documents a similar kind of conflict between government forces and a Native community and because it precedes *Kanehsatake* by almost a decade yet utilizes many of the same narrative strategies that the later film is famous for, I will focus on the earlier film here as an indicator of how Obomsawin finds her voice and develops a cinematic vocabulary to promote her vision of Native nationhood.

If critics like White have readily recognized the "oddly pared-down form" of Obomsawin's "non-narrative, elliptical documentary" (White 2002, 366, 370) style, it is in part because she has consistently cultivated this aesthetic, of which *Incident at Restigouche* presents an early iteration. Despite using title cards to underscore the chronology of the two police raids that resulted in the trial of two tribe members, Obomsawin actually presents the elements of her narrative in a nonlinear fashion, interweaving segments of postconflict interviews with Mi'gmaq and government representatives with found footage, photographs, and archival images, as well as contemporary sequences illustrating the natural world and everyday activities of the Native community. Indeed, even before the title of the film appears, Obomsawin presents a complex, chronologically nonlinear sequence composed of stills of the police cohort, overlaid with the sounds of marching boots, then a clip of a tribal elder recounting in Mi'gmaq his stand against them, followed by a postconflict segment of an interview with the fisheries minister, and finally a presentation of the Native perspective on colonial history, illustrated by maps of North America, with Obomsawin herself providing the voiceover. Such voiceover historical contextualizations also appear in later films, including *Kanehsatake*, causing White to observe that while Obomsawin's narrations "may echo the conventions of documentary form, . . . their effects are the exact opposite: they assert a specific cultural identity rather than hide behind a faceless false objectivity" (2002, 367). In both *Incident* and *Kanehsatake*, it is Obomsawin's own voiceover narration that situates the action and affords the viewers a greater contextual understanding. While her inclusion of historical segments is a strategy clearly designed to educate a white audience rather than her Native interlocutors, it serves, much as in Dunn's *Ballad*, as an anticolonialist positioning of the story being told, highlighting the importance of the Native perspective and the Native storytelling style to the issues at stake.

Indeed, subjectivity is central to Obomsawin's aesthetic, be it her own point of view or that of her Native interlocutors, whom she often films speaking at length and uninterrupted. I would argue that this strategic deployment of narrative—either historical or personal—is one way that she recalls the importance of orality and storytelling to indigenous cultural identity. As critic Zuzana Pick puts it: "the narrative elements of documentary (voiceover narration, interviews, observational shots, and found footage) are needed to articulate a worldview based on interdependence and reciprocity. . . . On the other hand, this operation involves a nonlinear patterning of narrative elements to reinvoke the poetry of oral traditions" (2003, 183–84). White refers to this poetic component of Obomsawin's films as a manifestation of "a pronounced lyrical sensibility that is at odds with a strictly pedagogical function and is closer to developments in recent experimental documentary" (2002, 369). For my part, I would contend that the lyrical element, far from being "at odds" with the documentary form, in fact constitutes an essential strategy in Obomsawin's creation of a visual sovereignty that results in both individual and collective self-assertion.

Nowhere is this more evident than in Obomsawin's most personal film about First Nations' struggles, *Waban-Aki: People from Where the Sun Rises*, which won the Best Documentary Award at the ImagineNATIVE Film + Media Arts Festival in 2006. Somewhat surprisingly, this is the first film in which Obomsawin directly presents her own people, the Abenaki, and so it seems fitting that she begins her film with her own voice, in a sequence showing a younger version of herself, singing a traditional song in her own language, intercut with images of the land's natural beauty. As in her earlier films, Obomsawin includes a map-based presentation of the history of her people, decimated by conflict, disease, and displacement in the colonial period, and by the continued pressures of assimilation and blood quantum definitions of belonging in the contemporary context. The most powerful symbol Obomsawin uses for both the threat of loss and the continuing work of cultural survival of her people, however, is the image of a drum strewn with pine needles that frames her film. The circular form of the drum is of course echoed by the film's circling back to this symbol, but, more importantly, Obomsawin's narration explains that when the drum is sounded, the pine needles begin by moving away from the center only to be drawn back to it if the vibrations continue.

In *Waban-Aki*, the drum as a metaphorical representation of the scattering and reuniting of the Wabanaki peoples is supported by equally exquisite images of the natural beauty of the territories they call home, a connection to the geographical rootedness of these people's identities and lives, which have been and continue to be threatened by the borders and the laws that cut ties and sever peoples from their lands and history. Indeed, although in the course of

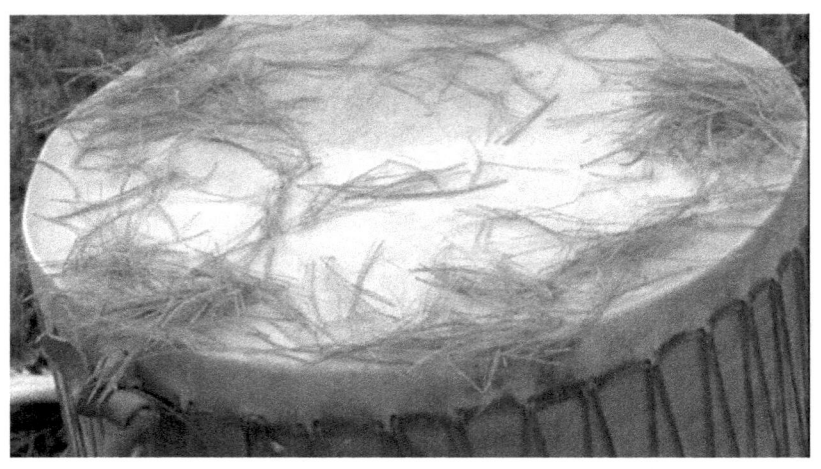

FIG. 6. The drumhead from *Waban-Aki*. Film still used by permission of Alanis Obomsawin and the National Film Board of Canada.

this film we learn that Vermont passed legislation that would ultimately lead in 2010 to state recognition for some Abenaki tribes
(Bill S. 222), the bill explicitly excluded land claims.[18] In this sense,
Obomsawin's film beats a literal and figurative cinematic drum to
draw the scattered tribes back to a common cause, a cultural center based on a relation to territory that persists despite national
and provincial borderlines and legal obstacles. That the drum is
a highly symbolic instrument shared by so many Native peoples
also speaks to Obomsawin's broader aspiration to appeal and give
voice to all those whose experience of dispossession and dispersion
resonates with her own. In this sense, it is both an oral and aural
element (repeatedly emphasized by the soundtrack) that is inseparable from the film's more traditional documentary presentation
of Wabanaki political self-assertion, offering a clear example of
Raheja's visual sovereignty, to recall the passage quoted earlier, as
that "space between resistance and compliance wherein Indigenous
filmmakers . . . reconfigure ethnographic film conventions, while at
the same time . . . stretching the boundaries created by those conventions" (2010, 193).

## The Rise of First Nations Fiction Films

Although Obomsawin's central place in the tradition of First Nations
documentary beginning in the 1980s does not entirely overshadow
the work of her contemporaries like Mosha Michael, and later, Gil
Cardinal and Loretta Todd, her influence and presence are undeni-
ably dominant.[19] Indeed, one can trace direct effects of her work not
only on such contemporary Native documentaries as those of Tracey
Deer, Reaghan Tarbell, and Sonia Bonspille Boileau, who explore
Mohawk women's history as well as the blood quantum and identity issues first documented by Obomsawin, but also on the emergence of fiction filmmakers like Jeff Barnaby, who has cited *Incident
at Restigouche* as a formative influence on his Mi'gmaq consciousness and cinematic vocation (Krupa 2011).[20] At the NFB the Oka
crisis and Obomsawin's presentation of it in *Kanehsatake* have been
seen as precipitating the 1991 creation of Studio One, headquartered
in Edmonton and devoted to indigenous filmmaker training and
productions, which was succeeded by the Aboriginal Filmmaking

Program in 1996 (Cardinal n.d.).[21] The most recent iterations of such support for indigenous film initiated during the past decade at the NFB include programs like First Stories, Second Stories, the Nunavut Animation Lab, and the Wapikoni Mobile (National Film Board of Canada 2011).

The NFB's largely documentary vocation has also been complemented in the past twenty years by several other important media developments, such as the founding of the first Inuit production company, Igloolik Isuma Productions, by Zacharias Kunuk and Norman Cohn in 1990, and the creation of the Aboriginal Peoples Television Network, originally incorporated in 1992 as Television Northern Canada, headquartered in Manitoba and broadcasting nationally at the time of this writing. The crowning achievement of the 1990s is undoubtedly the release of Atanarjuat / The Fast Runner in 2000, Kunuk's masterwork and "the first Inuit-produced, Inuktitut language, feature-length dramatic film" (White 2006, 225), which garnered critical and popular favor, winning nearly twenty prizes nationally and internationally, including the coveted 2001 Caméra d'Or in Cannes. This is the film that nearly brings Ojibway critic Jesse Wente to tears in Diamond's Reel Injun (2009) and causes the venerable André Dudemaine, one of the founders of Terres en Vues / Land InSights, which has sponsored the annual Montreal First Peoples Festival for over twenty years, to rhapsodize about a renaissance of indigenous filmmaking and culture.[22]

While I will not repeat what others have said about this extraordinarily important expression of Inuit visual and linguistic self-affirmation and sovereignty, Kunuk's landmark work, set entirely in the Inuit community's storytelling history and language, undoubtedly inaugurated the contemporary upsurge of First Nations narrative filmmaking that has seen a number of directors releasing their first features.[23] Shortly after Atanarjuat, Shirley Cheechoo came out with Bearwalker (2002) "the first fiction feature to be written and directed by a Native woman" (White 2006, 235). Although Shelley Niro made several quirky and experimental short and medium-length fictional films in the 1990s, her 2010 Kissed by Lightning is a moving foray into full-length narrative, which I and others have analyzed elsewhere (Santoro 2013). Noteworthy too is Yves Sioui

Durand's 2011 adaptation of his play *Hamlet-le-Malécite* into a feature film called *Mesnak*, which, as stated earlier, has been hailed as the first Native feature film in Quebec cinematic history.[24] Alongside these First Nations productions, since the turn of the millennium there seems to have been a resurgence of non-Native directors making features focused on Native characters as well, including *Ce qu'il faut pour vivre* (Benoît Pilon, 2008), *Uvanga* (Marie-Hélène Cousineau, 2013), *Maïna* (Michel Poulette, 2014), and *3 Histoires d'Indiens* (Robert Morin, 2014), not to mention Canada's first 3D animated feature, *La Légende de Sarila*, by the Quebec producer-director Nancy Florence Savard (2012).

Among the films now testifying to the growing consciousness and creative energy of First Nations peoples, *Rhymes for Young Ghouls*, Mi'gmaq director Jeff Barnaby's first feature film, released in 2013, is a landmark in many respects. Based on a script for which Barnaby won a Tribeca All Access Creative Promise Award in 2012, the film has been shown in over twenty festivals to date, and won the Best Canadian First Feature prize, ex aequo, at the Vancouver International Film Festival. Barnaby was also recognized by the Toronto Film Critics Association and Norman Jewison with the Technicolor Award for creative promise.

Such success stems undoubtedly from Barnaby's ability to make a film that entertains and engages even as it exposes specific instances of the oppression and social injustice that have afflicted generations of Native communities in Canada, in particular the system of residential schools, capriciously and cruelly enforced under Canada's Indian Act by truant officers, whose power Barnaby underscores by quoting from the act to begin his film.[25] *Rhymes for Young Ghouls*, often abbreviated to RFYG, is a title borrowed from a poetry collection Barnaby encountered while writing the script (Adams 2014), and this allusive appropriation is but one of many the film displays. Indeed, the strategies of allusion and destabilizing appropriation also characterize his early short films, which, like RFYG, tend to integrate various cinematic conventions (from horror and science fiction genres, most notably) with other art forms (particularly comic book or graphic novel sequences and graffiti, but also painting, drawing, and music), and incorporate frequent literary

references (such as a poem by Pablo Neruda or allusions to Shake-
speare or classical sources). Principally a tale of revenge gone awry,
RFYG's focus is Aila, a teenage drug dealer whose father has been
in prison and whose uncle trains her in the business and also in
the pragmatics of survival on Red Crow Reserve in the mid-1970s.
Aila and her crew avoid being sent to the residential school by paying a "tax" to Popper, the truant officer or "Indian agent" who also
seems to run the school (a conflation of roles that is more fictional
than factual) and who steals the drug money intended to pay the
tax early on in the film, thus unleashing the revenge plot hatched by
Aila in order to recover their profits. Aila's situation is complicated
by her father Joseph's return home after his release and his desire
that she not be part of the lifestyle his brother Burner so clearly rel-
ishes. There are in fact no model citizens in the "Kingdom of the
Crow" (an alternate title considered for the film; see Adams 2014),
where the three rules of existence Aila expresses in her narrative
voiceover are "never befriend an Indian agent," "stay out of debt,"
and "take care of your family."

Taking care of one's family is easier said than done in this community, however, for in the opening scenes, we learn that Aila's
mother commits suicide after drunkenly running over a boy named
Tyler, with a young Aila on her lap to help her steer straight. This
childhood trauma is compounded for Aila by Joseph's concomitant
arrest, and, in the years that follow, Burner's apparent lack of concern for Aila's moral development. The adolescent Aila we meet as
the film opens is thus seeking solace where she can, sharing dark
humor with her crew, drawing in the sketchbook that her mother
left behind, and sitting at the knee of the tribe's matriarch and green-
house supplier, Ceres, who tells her stories in Mi'gmaq, keeping
Aila connected with their history and language. In one of the surprising formal experiments in this film, Ceres's tale of "The Wolf
and the Mushroom," which resembles a Native myth even though
it is entirely invented by Barnaby, is accompanied by an animated
sequence that shows the predation of an ultimately self-destructive
monster that "devours" Native youths and then itself in a desolate
landscape that foreshadows contemporary urban blight.[26] Given this
grim prospect, coupled with Aila's own recognition that the drug

life is an "art of forgetfulness" that "brings [her] people together" even as it destroys them, the fact that Ceres and Aila speak Mi'gmaq together, remembering their identity and common bond, constitutes an act of resistance both to being "devoured" and to forgetting. Barnaby's film, in an important way, thus also recognizes the forces provoking forgetfulness and loss of identity, but strives to combat them by affirming his people's language and resiliency over time. It bears recalling, as detailed in McNab's contribution to this volume, that the Mi'gmaq have survived and kept their language during the almost five hundred years since Jacques Cartier planted a cross on the Gaspé peninsula, where Barnaby himself grew up on the reserve at Listuguj (formerly spelled *Restigouche*, as seen in Obomsawin's film title).

Emblematic of survival of the Mi'gmaq people despite the sustained influence of colonial rule, Aila is a warrior, or *matnaggewinu* in the Mi'gmaq language, whose strength and ruthlessness comes from remembering her pain, and who will put herself and others at risk to pursue her revenge.[27] Her resiliency despite her losses is emblematic of a community for whom "courage . . . means gritting your teeth, moving forward and not paying attention to the consequences," to borrow the words the Red Crow war veteran Gisigu offers Aila. In this film, Barnaby makes explicit reference to the role of art in helping Native peoples, and more specifically creators like himself, "move forward." Aila's own philosophy, even with respect to rolling joints, is that you can "turn anything into an art form," but it is also clear that the most expressive and enduring creations spring from one's cultural identity and experiences. In support of this authentic self-expression, however, Barnaby borrows from Hollywood horror films, bending the genre to his own purposes. We thus see Aila haunted by zombies and ghosts, but rather than reacting with fear, she seems to see them as a comfort and as guides. The zombies of her mother and Taylor first emerge from their unnamed graves in the woods. When Aila is later stripped, shorn, and thrown into a cell in the school after not being able to pay the truancy tax, Taylor's zombie guides her dreaming self to a mass grave where lie the bodies of so many other Native children, victims of a residential school system whose merciless and oppressive regime evokes wartime atrocities.[28] When Jujijj—Aila's younger protégé whose name means "Bug" in Mi'gmaq (an oblique reference to *The Wire*)–springs Aila from her cell, we see she has left ghostly etchings on the wall, a visual remembrance of those children who were lost to and in the system.[29] Her gang's subsequent raid on Popper's office in the school, however, will create yet more victims, including Ceres, killed vengefully by Popper; Joseph, who will return to prison; and, finally, Popper himself, shot by Jujijj to prevent him from raping Aila.

Part supernatural thriller, part darkly humorous revenge caper, part gritty drama, Barnaby's film appropriates genres and various sources, from Greek myth to the comic novel, to tell a tale of resistance to the oppression and to the loss of identity experienced by many Native groups in Canada and elsewhere. His work displays an uncompromising, often violent incitement to decolonization, which, to recall Knopf, involves "the creation of self-fashioned images and anticolonialist rewriting and filming of history" as well as "an aesthetic struggle, [encompassing] defiance of and/or negotiation with established conventions of . . . film" (Knopf 2008, 63). If RFYG must be seen "in relation to Hollywood practice" (Knopf 2008, 53–54) by Barnaby's own admission with respect to his influences (Barnaby 2013b,), his film nonetheless appropriates and subverts conventions and storylines that would stereotype Natives as losers, victims, savages or "drum-and-feathers" spiritual beings. As much if not principally addressed to a Native audience, scathingly exposing the danger of their willful "forgetfulness" and lack of commitment to their languages and identity, this film also pulls no punches about the abuses they have suffered, and the strength that indigenous peoples have needed to survive them. None of the characters in Barnaby's film are paragons, but it is clear that the real evil devouring "The Kingdom of the Crow" is the power exerted by the colonizer's system that literally beat Native children into submission and forced adults into compromising activities by depriving them of traditional lifestyles and survival practices, including fishing for their subsistence. The price of Aila's revenge in this setting is nonetheless steep, and, while Jujijj points to a future in the film's final line ("What do we do now, boss?"), it is

FIG. 7. Aila (Kawennahere Devery Jacobs), by Jan Thijs, 2012. From the Jeff
Barnaby feature film *Rhymes for Young Ghouls*, courtesy of Prospector Films.

clear that this call to continue the quest for social justice is one that, decades after the time frame of this film, has still not borne the fruit that some Native activists might have wished. Barnaby's obvious commitment to that social justice expresses itself in the visual sovereignty of his film, which focuses on flawed but courageous Native characters and engages Native and non-Native audiences alike through the use of cinematic tropes and narrative structures that appeal to our need for entertainment even as we are offered a story of deep contemporary political and social significance. Barnaby's deft negotiation of Hollywood conventions is coupled with a determination to tell Native stories otherwise by appropriating and repurposing those filmic practices, such that his is now one of the most original and compelling voices leading a new generation of indigenous creative talent.

Clearly, whereas in the sixties, seventies, and even into the eighties, there were relatively few features being made by First Nations filmmakers, the past two decades have seen an unprecedented explosion of creative energies and support opportunities for such projects. Within Quebec itself, arguably the most productive and promising initiative to cultivate Native filmmaking during the past decade is the Wapikoni Mobile, established and led by filmmaker Manon Barbeau, who initially conceived of an itinerant filmmaking training unit housed in an RV that would visit Native communities across Quebec and assist aspiring creators in completing short film projects. In partnership with several First Nations groups as well as the NFB, Barbeau's initiative has since developed into several permanent and mobile studios, which have produced over nine hundred short films in thirty-two Native communities to date (Wapikoni Mobile 2018).[30]

To round out this overview of key moments in the development of visual sovereignty in First Nations cinema in Canada, I wish to highlight but two of the shorts produced by the Wapikoni because they are representative of ways in which this new generation of filmmakers offers both continuations and extensions of the storytelling aesthetics highlighted in the earlier periods of First Nations cinema. The first is by Kevin Papatie, an Anishinaabeg who has made several award-winning short films since 2005 and who has taken on a leadership and training role at the now permanent Wapikoni studio in his community of Kitcisakik. In his 2009 short, *Nous Sommes / We Are*, Papatie describes how a visit to the Zapatistas in Mexico, whom he calls his brothers, "awakened the fighter" in him. Even as this affirmation recalls Obomsawin's intent to cultivate solidarity among different Native peoples, Papatie's film also retains the personal, subjective approach she also privileges. In fact, in this film we see shots of Papatie's son, Drake, and hear drums played by his spouse Louisa Papatie, making this a family story, where the microcosm of those closest to the director stands in for the collectivity, the "we" of the title, who Papatie encourages to "rise" in response to the polluted environment because, as his whispered words in Algonquin (translated by subtitles) tell us: "We are the devastated landscape. We cannot remain still while watching ourselves perish. We are our land." The sober images, deliberate pace, use of drums, and theme of connection to and responsibility for the land in this short film are all features that echo the aesthetic of earlier filmmakers like Obomsawin but with a distinct Papatie inflection, for his whispered Algonquin narrative and his play with depth of focus, close-ups, and strikingly beautiful image composition (even when the shots reveal a devastated landscape) are distinctive characteristics of his work. While clearly inspired by a feeling of solidarity with other Native activists and by an ancestral connection to the land shared by many indigenous peoples, this film has a personal voice and vision and yet also a universal appeal, since Native and non-Native viewers alike understand how the health of the land affects our present and future survival.

Réal Junior Leblanc's *Nanameshkueu/Earthquake*, released in 2010, presents in less than three minutes a spellbinding visual and verbal poem that, like *We Are*, speaks of the past even as it looks to future possibilities for Native self-affirmation. Whereas Papatie adopts a stark and static image-making style, Leblanc's complex and innovative film uses horizontal and vertical split screens, multiple image layers, and constant shifting of frame and focus to create a sense of mystery and movement. Leblanc's poem, read in voiceover during this film, is short enough to allow its presentation in full:

FIG. 8. Film stills from *Nous Sommes / We Are*, by Kevin Papatie. Courtesy of Wapikoni Mobile.

Since the beginning of time, I've been contemplating the moon.

I've yelled many songs at her.

I've always been alone, forgotten by God.

The moon knows my hatred.

The mountains are filled with my tears. Always hunted.

Will I need to hide again among the trees and the fog for the world to
leave me alone?

I only want to hunt and fish, and go back to my forgotten lands.

To the very place where my grandfathers used to live.

My heart beats to the rhythm of the rain.

My soul is healing little by little.

After each wave that dies, a new one is born again, ever stronger.

I am the earthquake. I am the one who will rekindle my people's flame
again.

What makes this film exceptionally powerful, in addition to the history and hope it articulates, is the way in which the split-screen images alternate between land, sky, and human habitations, with images often trading places but seemingly unified by the use of superimpositions, which sometimes overlap both images and which sometimes give way to full screen images, such as of an older man's face during the line about grandfathers, images that are in turn dappled by what looks to be the texture of land formations, rock, or water. Whereas Papatie uses words to convey the unity of Natives with the land, Leblanc uses the visual effect of superimposition to metaphorically make a man's or a child's face (the latter shown when the director speaks of the new "wave" that is "born again, ever stronger") into a landscape. That the narrator, the filmmaker, identifies himself as an earthquake, able to shake things up (like the soft focus, and moving images in the split screens), is yet another metaphor for how an activist Native leader can inspire others to act, thus "rekindling" the spirit of his people.

While one may prefer either the photorealistic or artistically innovative approach, what both of these Native filmmakers show is that they still share the drive to political and visual sovereignty that inspired their predecessors, even as they expand visual, linguistic, and political horizons, either because they find solidarity with

FIG. 9. Film stills from *Nanameshkueu/Earthquake*, by Réal Junior Leblanc. Courtesy of Wapikoni Mobile.

other Native groups beyond their borders or because they utilize the aesthetic possibilities of the film medium to create storytelling possibilities in their native languages, much as Barnaby does, even as they find audiences that were unimaginable or inaccessible in the past by virtue of the technology available to make and disseminate their work. For both these reasons, the productions of the Wapikoni Mobile constitute the most exciting recent development in First Nations cinema, on the cutting edge of what new media theorist Henry Jenkins calls "convergence culture," because they are already readily available on the web, which is, after all, the virtual version of the oral tradition or the "Longhouse" where people of all nations can converge to listen, watch, and share their stories.

Conclusion

Despite "the political economy of cultural production in Canada that privileges white representations of the Native over Aboriginal representations," as Canadian film historian Christopher Gittings so aptly puts it (2002, 215), the past half century has seen the birth and development of Native cinema in Canada, that is, films made by indigenous directors about issues and stories and told from a Native point of view. That said, in their edited collection *Walking a Tightrope: Aboriginal People and Their Representations*, Ute Lischke and David McNab nonetheless feel compelled to observe that "Aboriginal people are still walking a tightrope with the European noose of representation around their necks. Only very slowly has this begun to change in incremental ways" (2005, 4). As I hope to have shown, at least in the last segment of this overview of indigenous filmmaking in Canada, the pace of that change has recently accelerated, in part because of the influence and perseverance of documentarists like Obomsawin, but also because of the directorial achievements and leadership of filmmakers like Jeff Barnaby and the grassroots training and support of a younger generation by programs like the Wapikoni Mobile.

In conclusion, I can only concur with George Melnyk when he suggests that "a renewed affirmation of a historically suppressed nationality, language, or ethnic identity brings forth cinematic innovation. The new voice reinvents its identity from inside, rather than accept an externally imposed identity" (2004, 264–65). This is precisely what is rendered visible by the assertion of visual sovereignty in Native filmmaking, a reappropriation or redefinition of both collective history and cinematic form that, to return to Knopf's trajectory of decolonization, "starts when [indigenous filmmakers] take their image-making and self-representation into their own hands, creating decolonized cultural, historical, and political discourses, and becoming progressively emancipated from the Hollywood-dominated industry" (2008, 63). Given the past and contemporary achievements I have outlined here through a few representative snapshots, one can only anticipate with excitement and even wonder what "reel visions" of Native realities and aspirations the next fifty years of Native filmmaking will offer us.

## Notes

1. It is important to note, in this volume that deals with hemispheric indigenous peoples and their cultural practices, that Central and South American indigenous filmmakers may not be reacting to Hollywood but rather to other, more locally defined mainstream or hegemonic film practices in their work. Such differences are not within the scope of this article.

2. Knopf, for example, defines as Native only those works that are "written, directed, or produced by an Indigenous person" (2008, 30).

3. This recognition appeared in all the major Quebec newspapers at the film's release, including *Le Devoir*, *Le Journal de Montréal*, *La Presse*, and *Voir Montréal*. I am indebted to Denis Boivin for alerting me to this controversy of definition (Boivin, personal email exchange with the author, 2012).

4. Examples of such "outsider" films include *Circle of the Sun* (Colin Low, 1960), *Le Festin des morts* (Fernand Dansereau, 1965), *Red* (Gilles Carle, 1970), *Les Maudits sauvages* (Jean Pierre Lefebvre, 1970), *Cree Hunters of Mistassini* (Tony Ianzelo and Boyce Richardson, 1973), *Our Land is Our Life* (Tony Ianzelo and Boyce Richardson, 1974), *Cold Journey* (Martin Defalco, 1975), *Le Goût de la farine* (Pierre Perrault, 1977), *Le Pays de la terre sans arbre* (Pierre Perrault, 1980), *Mémoire battante* (Arthur Lamothe, 1983), *Visage pâle* (Claude Gagnon, 1985), *La Conquête de l'Amérique* (Arthur Lamothe, 1990 and 1991), *Black Robe* (Bruce Beresford, 1991), *Map of the Human Heart* (Vincent Ward, 1992), *L'Automne sauvage* (Gabriel Pelletier, 1992), *Clearcut* (Richard Bugajski, 1993), *Road to Saddle River* (Francis Damberger, 1993), *Windigo* (Robert Morin, 1994), *Dance Me Outside* (Bruce McDonald, 1995), *Le Silence des fusils* (Arthur Lamothe, 1996), *Kwekànamad: Le Vent tourne* (Carlos Ferrand, 1999), *L'Autre Amérique* (Jean-Pierre Masse, 2002), *The Invisible Nation* (Richard Desjardins and Robert Monderie, 2007), *Americano* (Carlos Ferrand, 2007), *Ce qu'il faut pour vivre/The Necessities of Life* (Benoît Pilon, 2008), and *Avant les rues* (Chloé Leriche, 2016).

Indeed, as such an outsider myself, I am particularly sensitive to the need to consider these films on their own terms and conscious of the limitations of my own knowledge of the Native issues being presented. The intent of this article is thus primarily to encourage increased awareness and understanding of this marginalized and relatively unknown cinematic tradition rather than to offer the kind of in-depth cultural analysis that others have performed admirably elsewhere (see my bibliography).

5. The six Natives recruited and trained were Roy Daniels (Ojibway), Willie Dunn (Mi'kmaq), Mike Mitchell (Mohawk), Tom O'Connor (Anishinaabe), Noel Starblanket (Cree), and Barbara Wilson (Haida).

Starblanket went on to have a career in band politics and governance, as documented in the NFB film *Starblanket* (Brittain 1973).

6. Even in the 2010 anthology on the CFC (cf. Waugh et al.), precious few excerpts deal in any depth with the Indigenous Film Crew and their productions.

7. It won the Award of Excellence at the Atlantic Festival; First Prize, Mention and Best Selection at the SODRE International Festival of Documentary and Experimental Films in Uruguay; the Blue Ribbon Award at the American Film and Video Festival in New York; and the Golden Hugo in the short film category at the Chicago International Film Festival. See http://onf-nfb.gc.ca/en/our-collection/?idfilm=10462. Accessed March 7, 2013. The film can be viewed through the NFB website.

8. See Rabb (2011), who summarizes Native influence on the writing of the U.S. constitution and extends that argument to apply to the Canadian Confederation as well.

9. Graham, among other scholars (Morris, Peterson), has critiqued the privileging of the visual in indigenous films as a reflection of Western analytic and perceptual conventions. Graham argues that Raheja's useful term *visual sovereignty* would be better formulated as *representational sovereignty*, which allows for a focus on the oral (among other components of representation) that is so central to indigenous cultures. While I agree that *representational* is a more encompassing adjective, my primary interest here is in the visual, particularly since the earliest films that were made of indigenous peoples were produced during the silent era. There is much work yet to be done on the more contemporary appropriations and subversions of mainstream dialogic and sound conventions by indigenous filmmakers. In-depth exploration of such "representational sovereignty" is, however, beyond the scope of this chapter.

10. According to Stoney, "[within] two weeks it was screened at least ten times, all around the reservation. This clarified what happened for the Indians" (Starblanket 2010, loc. 3582).

11. For full text of the White Paper (Government of Canada, 1969), see: www.aadnc-aandc.gc.ca/eng/1100100010189/1100100010191/. The "Red Paper" was reprinted in *Aboriginal Policy Studies* under the title "Citizens Plus" signed by the Indian Chiefs of Alberta. Available at www.scribd.com/doc/130005551/citizens-plus-red-paper/.

12. Of *Cree Hunters of Mistassini* and *Our Land is Our Life*, directed in 1973–74 by Tony Ianzelo and Boyce Richardson, Caroline Zéau writes: "ces deux films témoignent donc à la fois des interdits qu'un tel programme rencontre, des transgressions qu'il peut occasionner et de la récupération institutionnelle dont elles font l'objet *a posteriori*" [these two films testify therefore at one and the same time to the taboos that such a

program encounters, to the transgressions it can permit and to the institutional recu-peration of such transgressions after the fact]. She does give the films some credit for being able to "attirer l'attention de l'opinion sur le sort des autochtones" [direct pub-lic attention and opinions on the fate of Natives] (2006, 425).

13. I would be remiss here if I did not draw attention to the 1969 animated short by Duke Redbird, *Charley Squash Goes to Town*. While not a member of the IFC, Red-bird's humorous story of negotiating Native identity and political aspirations in rela-tion to white society is contemporaneous with the work of the Native crew and shares in the same political and social consciousness.

14. White is quoting Anderson here: The nation "is imagined as a *community*, because, regardless of the actual inequality and exploitation that may prevail in each, the nation is always conceived as a deep, horizontal comradeship" (Anderson [1983] 2006, 7).

15. Obomsawin's first Native short was *Christmas at Moose Factory* (1971), followed by two educational filmstrips, *Manawan* (1972) and *L'il'wata* (1975) (both recently released on DVD), and, finally, *Mother of Many Children* (1977).

16. The spelling used even today by the Listuguj community to name its tribal affil-iation is Mi'gmaq (see www.listuguj.ca/migwitetm-commemoration-walk/). This is also the spelling that appeared in early biographies and interviews with filmmaker Jeff Barnaby, who is from Listuguj. However, as David McNab points out in the first chapter in this volume, the communities of indigenous peoples that occupied the ter-ritories of New England, the Maritimes, Newfoundland, and Quebec used various spellings of the ethnonym, depending on their language and geographical location, including *Micmac* (an older term used mostly in English), *Migmaq*, and *Mi'kmaq*, which now seems to be the most widely accepted spelling. I choose to use *Mi'gmaq* in this instance because it is the initial spelling that Jeff Barnaby personally gave me, and because it remains the spelling his community uses to this day.

17. See Gittings 2002; McIlroy 2006; Monk 2001; and Pick 2003, for example.

18. This in fact echoes what occurred in Canada with the Mi'kmaq of Newfound-land, as David McNab narrates in chapter 3, whose demands for status were finally granted in 2011 but whose tribal recognition by the federal government did not include land rights.

19. Mosha Michael's three short films are *Natsik Hunting* (1975), *Asivaqtin/The Hunt-ers* (1977), and *Qilaluganiatut/Whale Hunting* (1977). Gil Cardinal's work includes *Fos-ter Child* (1987), *The Spirit Within* (1990), and *Totem: The Return of the G'psgolox Pole* (2003). Loretta Todd took over from Obomsawin to make *The Learning Path* (1991) (White 2002, 381), part of the series *As Long as the Rivers Flow* (Tamarack Produc-tions and the NFB), and went on to direct *Forgotten Warriors* (2007); she also made *Today Is a Good Day: Remembering Chief Dan George* (1998) and *Kainayssini Imani-staisiwa: The People Go On* (2003).

20. Deer's films are *Mohawk Girls* (2005) and *Club Native* (2008), Tarbell's is *To Brooklyn and Back: A Mohawk Journey* (2008), and Boileau made *Last Call Indien* (2010) and *The Dep* (2015).

21. See Rosa 2002 for a detailed look at that NFB program.

22. Diamond discusses *Atanarjuat* at the end of his documentary, and its effect is clearly framed as the culmination and the pinnacle of Diamond's search for an authentic portrait of indigenous people in film.

23. See, for example, Darrell Varga's contribution to *The Cinema of Canada* (White 2006), as well as the analyses in Raheja (2010) and Knopf (2008).

24. See Santoro 2013 for an analysis of Niro and Durand's work.

25. The Indian Act was first passed in 1876 and has been amended a number of times since. Its most recent iteration can be accessed online at the Government of Canada's Justice Laws website, http://laws-lois.justice.gc.ca/eng/acts/i-5/.

26. Barnaby cites *The Upturned Stone* by Scott Hampton as influencing the animation sequence as well as the style and story of his film.

27. The Mi'gmaq language, also called Mīkmawísimk, has a number of dialects, including Listuguj, which is apparently hard to understand for those not from Barnaby's own community. In the RFYG press kit, Jeff Barnaby explains and contextualizes the term *matnaggewinu* this way in his director's statement: "There are three kinds of Indians that have lived to see the 21st century. There are the ones that . . . lead fully integrated Western lifestyles. There are the ones [who integrated] into a welfare state and look to the people around them to co-sign their broken lives: 'I am Indian therefore I deserve your pity.' Then there are the Indians that have made it their business to make sure that the culture and the languages have survived—the omega man Indians. Every beating they take recharges their fuel cells, and instead of tapping out they dust themselves off . . . and just move forward. We are all of us survivors, descendants of this Indian. Otherwise we wouldn't be here. In Mi'gMaq we call this person *matnaggewinu*, a warrior."

28. It bears noting that the last residential school closed in 1996. See the Canadian Broadcasting Corporation's "A Timeline of Residential Schools, the Truth and Reconciliation Commission," available at www.cbc.ca/news/canada/a-timeline-of-residential -schools-the-truth-and-reconciliation-commission-1.724434/.

29. Jeff Barnaby, telephone interview with Miléna Santoro, June 11, 2014.

30. They also boast of international outreach to twenty-six communities from ten different nations outside of Canada, notably in Bolivia, Panama, and Peru.

## Selected Chronology of Canadian and Quebec Indigenous Films

| | |
|---|---|
| 1922 | *Nanook of the North*, Robert J. Flaherty (non-Native director) |
| 1968 | *Ballad of Crowfoot*, Willie Dunn |
| 1969 | *Charley Squash Goes to Town*, Duke Redbird |
| 1969 | *These Are My People*, Roy Daniels, Willie Dunn, Michael Mitchell, and Barbara Wilson |
| 1969 | *You Are on Indian Land*, Mort Ransen (non-Native director) |
| 1971 | *Christmas at Moose Factory*, Alanis Obomsawin |
| 1972 | *The Other Side of the Ledger: An Indian View of the Hudson's Bay Company*, Willie Dunn and Martin Defalco |
| 1973 | *Starblanket*, Donald Brittain (non-Native director) |
| 1973 | *Cree Hunters of Mistassini*, Tony Ianzelo, Boyce Richardson (non-Native directors) |

| | |
|---|---|
| 1974 | *Our Land is Our Life*, Tony Ianzelo and Boyce Richardson (non-Native directors) |
| 1975 | *Natsik Hunting*, Mosha Michael |
| 1977 | *Asivaqtin / The Hunters*, Mosha Michael |
| 1977 | *Qilaluganiatut / Whale Hunting*, Mosha Michael |
| 1977 | *Mother of Many Children*, Alanis Obomsawin |
| 1980 | *Le Pays de la terre sans arbre*, Pierre Perrault (non-Native director) |
| 1983 | *Mémoire battante*, Arthur Lamothe (non-Native director) |
| 1984 | *Incident at Restigouche*, Alanis Obomsawin |
| 1987 | *Foster Child*, Gil Cardinal |
| 1990 | *The Spirit Within*, Gil Cardinal |
| 1990, 1991 | *La Conquête de l'Amérique*, Arthur Lamothe (non-Native director) |
| 1991 | *As Long as the Rivers Flow.* Series of five documentaries, including *Tikinagan*, directed by Gil Cardinal; *The Learning Path*, directed by Loretta Todd; *Starting Fire With Gunpowder*, directed by David Poisey and William Hansen. Produced with support of the National Film Board of Canada; Telefilm Canada; Ontario Media Development Corporation; TV5; TVOntario; The Canadian Studies Secretariat of the Secretary of State, Canada; Teck Corporation. Distribution: Icarus Films, New York. www.icarusfilms.com. http://tamarackproductions.com/AsLongAsTheRiversFlow.php/. |
| 1993 | *Kanehsatake: 270 Years of Resistance*, Alanis Obomsawin |
| 1994 | *Dance Me Outside*, Bruce McDonald (non-Native director) |
| 1996 | *Le Silence des fusils*, Arthur Lamothe (non-Native director) |
| 1998 | *Kanata: L'héritage des enfants d'Aataentsic*, René Sioui Labelle |
| 1998 | *Honey Moccasin*, Shelley Niro |
| 1998 | *Today is a Good Day: Remembering Chief Dan George*, Loretta Todd |
| 2000 | *Atanarjuat / The Fast Runner*, Zacharias Kunuk |
| 2002 | *Bearwalker*, Shirley Cheechoo |
| 2003 | *Attache ta tuque!*, Denis Boivin (non-Native director) |
| 2003 | *Totem: The Return of the G'psgolox Pole*, Gil Cardinal |
| 2003 | *Kainayssini Imanistaisiwa: The People Go On*, Loretta Todd |
| 2004–2017 | Wapikoni mobile shorts, www.wapikoni.tv |
| 2005 | *From Cherry English*, Jeff Barnaby |
| 2005 | *Mohawk Girls*, Tracey Deer |
| 2006 | *Waban-Aki, peuple du soleil levant*, Alanis Obomsawin |
| 2007 | *Forgotten Warrior*, Loretta Todd |
| 2007 | *The Colony*, Jeff Barnaby |
| 2008 | *To Brooklyn and Back: A Mohawk Journey*, Reaghan Tarbell |
| 2008 | *Club Native*, Tracey Deer |
| 2008 | *Ce qu'il faut pour vivre*, Benoît Pilon (non-Native director) |
| 2009 | *Reel Injun: On the Trail of the Hollywood Indian*, Neil Diamond |
| 2010 | *Last Call Indien*, Sonia Bonspille Boileau |
| 2010 | *Kissed by Lightening*, Shelley Niro |

| 2010 | *File Under Miscellaneous*, Jeff Barnaby |
| 2011 | *Mesnak*, Yves Sioui Durand |
| 2012 | *La Légende de Sarila*, Nancy Florence Savard (non-Native director) |
| 2013 | *Rhymes for Young Ghouls*, Jeff Barnaby |
| 2013 | *Uvanga*, Marie-Hélène Cousineau (non-Native director) |
| 2014 | *Maïna*, Michel Poulette (non-Native director) |
| 2014 | *3 Histoires d'Indiens*, Robert Morin (non-Native director) |
| 2015 | *Le Dep*, Sonia Boileau |
| 2016 | *Avant les rues*, Chloé Leriche (non-Native director) |
| 2017 | *Hochelaga, Terre des âmes*, François Girard (non-Native director) |

## Bibliography

Adams, James. 2014. "*Rhymes for Young Ghouls* Director Likes to Lean on Other Art Forms." Interview with Jeff Barnaby. *The Globe and Mail*. January 30. Accessed July 8. www.theglobeandmail.com/arts/film/rhymes-for-young-ghouls-director -likes-to-lean-on-other-art-forms/article16616782/.

Anderson, Benedict. (1983) 2006. *Imagined Communities*. London and New York: Verso.

Barnaby Jeff. 2013a. Director's Statement. In *Rhymes for Young Ghouls Press Kit*, 3–4. Accessed February 17, 2014. www.prospectorfilms.ca/.

———. 2013b. "Five Major Influences from Jeff Barnaby." *Tribeca Film Institute Blog*. Accessed July 8, 2014. www.tfiny.org/blog/detail/5_major_influences_from_jeff _barnaby/.

Beard, William, and White, Jerry, eds. 2002. *North of Everything: English-Canadian Cinema Since 1980*. Edmonton: University of Alberta Press.

Brittain, Donald, dir. 1973. *Starblanket*. Montreal: National Film Board of Canada.

Canadian Broadcasting Corporation. 2008a. "A Timeline of Residential Schools, the Truth and Reconciliation Commission." Accessed July 8, 2014. www.cbc.ca /news/canada/a-timeline-of-residential-schools-the-truth-and-reconciliation -commission-1.724434/.

———. 2008b. "Wapikoni Mobile: Giving First Nations Youth a Voice through Film." Accessed June 6, 2014. www.cbc.ca/cinqasix/film/2014/03/08/wapikoni-mobile -giving-first-nations-youth-a-voice-through-film/.

Cardinal, Gil. n.d. "The Aboriginal Voice: the National Film Board and Aboriginal Filmmaking through the Years." Accessed March 6, 2013. www.nfb.ca/playlists /gil-cardinal/aboriginal-voice-national-film-board-/.

Diamond, Neil, dir. 2009. *Reel Injun: On the Trail of the Hollywood Indian*. Montreal: Rezolution Pictures Inc., National Film Board of Canada.

Ginsburg, Faye. 1999. "The After-Life of Documentary: The Impact of *You Are on Indian Land*." *Wide Angle* 21, no. 2 (March 1999): 60–67.

Gittings, Christopher. 2002. *Canadian National Cinema. Ideology, Difference and Representation*. London: Routledge.

Government of Canada. 1969. *Statement of the Government of Canada on Indian Policy*. [Also known as the White Paper.] Accessed January 11, 2018. www.aadnc -aandc.gc.ca/eng/1100100010189/1100100010191/.

Graham, Laura R. 2016. "Toward Representational Sovereignty: Rewards and Challenges of Indigenous Media in the A'uwe̅-Xavante Communities of Eténhiritipa-Pimentel Barbosa." *Media and Communication* 4, no. 2: 13–32.

Indian Chiefs of Alberta. 2011. "Citizens Plus." *Aboriginal Policy Studies* 1, no. 2: 188–281.

Jenkins, Henry. 2006. *Convergence Culture: Where Old and New Media Collide.* New York: New York University Press.

King, Thomas. 1990. "Godzilla vs. Post-Colonial." *World Literature Written in English* 30, no. 2: 10–16.

Knopf, Kerstin. 2008. *Decolonizing the Lens of Power: Indigenous Films in North America.* Amsterdam: Rodopi.

Krupa, Mark. 2011. "An Interview with Jeff Barnaby." *Montreal Serai.* Accessed March 8, 2013. http://montrealserai.com/2011/02/12/an-interview-with-filmmaker-jeff-barnaby/.

Lever, Yves. 1995. *Histoire générale du cinéma du Québec.* Montréal: Boréal.

Lischke, Ute, and David T. McNab, eds. 2005. *Walking a Tightrope: Aboriginal People and Their Representations.* Waterloo: Wilfrid Laurier University Press.

MacKenzie, Scott. 2000. "Mimetic Nationhood. Ethnography and the National." In *Cinéma and Nation,* edited by Mette Hjort and Scott MacKenzie, 241–59. New York: Routledge.

Marshall, Bill. 2001. *Quebec National Cinema.* Montreal: McGill-Queen's University Press.

McIlroy, Brian. 2006. *"Kanehsatake: 270 Years of Resistance."* In *The Cinema of Canada,* edited by Jerry White, 173–81. London: Wallflower.

Melnyk, George. 2004. *One Hundred Years of Canadian Cinema.* Toronto: University of Toronto Press.

Monk, Katherine. 2001. *Weird Sex and Snowshoes and Other Canadian Film Phenomena.* Vancouver: Raincoast.

Morris, Rosalind C. 1994. *New Worlds From Fragments: Film, Ethnography, and the Representation of Northwest Coast Cultures.* Boulder: Westview Press.

National Film Board of Canada. 2011. "Our History: The NFB Foundation: 1939." Accessed July 17, 2012. www.nfb.ca/history/about-the-foundation/.

———. 2017. "New Filmmaking." Accessed January 11, 2018. http://onf-nfb.gc.ca/en/about-the-nfb/the-nfb-%20today/new-filmmaking/.

Obomsawin, Alanis. 2005. "Alanis Obomsawin-Interview by Micol Marotti." *American Indian Magazine* (Spring): 36–41. www.nativenetworks.si.edu/eng/rose/obomsawin_a_interview.htm/.

Peterson, Leighton. 2014. "Made Impossible by Viewers Like You: The Politics and Poetics of Native American Voices in US Public Television." In *How Television Shapes Our Worldview,* edited by Deborah A. Macey, Kathleen M. Ryan, and Noah J. Springer, 247–65. New York: Lexington.

Pick, Zuzana M. 2003. "'This Land is Ours'–Storytelling and History in *Kanehsatake: 270 Years of Resistance.*" In *Candid Eyes: Essays on Canadian Documentaries,* edited by Jim Leach and Jeannette Sloniowski, 181–96. Toronto: University of Toronto Press.

Rabb, J. Douglas. 2011. "The Master of Life and the Person of Evolution: Indigenous Influence on Canadian Philosophy." In *Hidden in Plain Sight: Contributions of Aboriginal Peoples to Canadian Identity and Culture*, vol. 2, edited by Cora J. Voyageur, David R. Newhouse, and Dan Beavon, 198–220. Toronto: University of Toronto Press.

Raheja, Michelle H. 2010. "Visual Sovereignty, Indigenous Revisions of Ethnography, and *Atanarjuat (The Fast Runner)*." In *Reservation Reelism: Redfacing, Visual Sovereignty, and Representations of Native Americans in Film*, 190–220. Lincoln: University of Nebraska Press.

Rosa, Maria de. 2002. "Studio One: Of Storytellers and Stories." In *North of Everything: English-Canadian Cinema Since 1980*, edited by William Beard and Jerry White, 328–41. Edmonton: University of Alberta Press.

Santoro, Miléna. 2013. "The Rise of First Nations' Fiction Films: Shelley Niro, Jeff Barnaby and Yves Sioui Durand." *American Review of Canadian Studies* 43, no. 2 (June): 267–82.

Starblanket, Noel. 2010. "A Voice for Canadian Indians: An Indian Film Crew (1968)." In *Challenge for Change: Activist Documentary at the National Film Board of Canada*, edited by Thomas Waugh, Michael Brendan Baker and Ezra Winton, 38–40. Montreal: McGill-Queen's University Press. Kindle edition.

Stewart, Michelle. 2007. "The Indian Film Crews of Challenge for Change: Representation and the State." *Canadian Journal of Film Studies* 16, no. 2 (Fall): 49–81.

Varga, Darrell. 2006. "Atanarjuat: The Fast Runner." In *The Cinema of Canada*. Edited by Jerry White, 225–33. London: Wallflower.

Voyageur, Cora J., David R. Newhouse, and Dan Beavon, eds. 2011. *Hidden in Plain Sight: Contributions of Aboriginal Peoples to Canadian Identity and Culture*, vol. 2. Toronto: University of Toronto Press.

Wapikoni Mobile. 2018. "Wapikoni in Brief." Accessed January 11, 2018. www.wapikoni .ca/about/who-are-we/wapikoni-in-brief.

Waugh, Thomas, Michael Brendan Baker, and Ezra Winton, eds. 2010. *Challenge for Change: Activist Documentary at the National Film Board of Canada*. Montreal: McGill-Queen's University Press. Kindle edition.

White, Jerry. 2002. "Alanis Obomsawin, Documentary Form and the Canadian Nation(s)." In *North of Everything: English-Canadian Cinema Since 1980*, edited by William Beard and Jerry White, 364–75. Edmonton: University of Alberta Press.

———, ed. 2006. *The Cinema of Canada*. London: Wallflower.

Zéau, Caroline. 2006. *L'Office national du film et le cinéma canadien (1939–2003): L'éloge de la frugalité*. Brussels: Peter Lang.

# Postface

Indigenous Experience and Legacies

# 10

## Travels of a Métis through Spirit Memory, around Turtle Island, and Beyond

DAVID T. MCNAB

I taught my first university course in Canadian history in the midst of the infamous White Paper brought in by then minister of Indian Affairs Jean Chretien, later Canada's prime minister, which was ostensibly designed to assimilate "Indians" in Canada in 1970. Having now worked on indigenous issues for more than forty-five years, I find that to write on the subject of "becoming Indigenous" is ultimately multidimensional and highly complex. In a recent program on Aboriginal Peoples Television Network on Buffy Sainte Marie (*Catch the Dream Bios with Adam Beach* 2014), she described best the idea of "becoming Indigenous" as being that one is born indigenous and "made in the Creator's image." My approach to this question is simply based on stories and storytelling through indigenous knowledge from a precolonial perspective. As other contributors to this volume highlight, such an alternative to Eurocentric perspectives is in good company. After all, most of my working life has not at all focused on scholarship and teaching on innovative approaches to the plethora of issues involved in indigenous matters. I have rather spent my time (since it appears to me that is where the real needs were) on nitty-gritty community issues on the ground rather than on metaphysical or other cosmic divinations. As former chief Gary Potts of the Temagami First Nation in northeastern Ontario has written simply and profoundly: "The Land is Boss" (Potts 1999, vi). It is not "we as human beings" who control things, much less nature. Nature includes human beings (contrary to the OED definition), and I have come to see it as a "conjoining of Mindscape and Landscape" (McNab 2013, 1).

The subject of the "Becoming Indigenous, Asserting Indigeneity" symposium that inspired this volume is far too complicated and beyond my understanding. After all, when you know that you are born indigenous, your spirit walk within your community is all about asserting indigeneity, so why would you want to spend any time at all on the topic of becoming indigenous? Frankly, I do not know the answer to that question. However, one of the reviewers of this chapter commented wisely that indigenous is a category that emerges out of colonial encounters and that indigeneity is not an identity that indigenous people inherently have. The logic here is that individuals are first human (of course), Métis, Anishaanabe, Kaqchikel, Aymara, or whatever (the *group* into which they are born) and secondarily indigenous. However, as a Métis (meaning in Cree "the other son/daughter," being one of mixed ancestry), I can only speak from my own experiences and tell my story and that of my family and its history (McNab 2007, 21–37). So I will tell you stories, so as to avoid complications and complexities, that focus on only two things on Turtle Island: spirit memory and islands and their connections to transnationalism—both indigenous and European (McNab 2012, 67–80).

Today, there are over 650 First Nations in Canada alone and perhaps many more Métis and non-status communities as well, so I cannot address all of their issues as "Indians" under Canada's Indian Act, and even less can I address those of the Inuit communities in the Far North. If you speak only about pan-Indian identities, you give lie to the enormous diversities in languages, cultures, and people within Canada (and across its borders) today (Lischke and McNab 2005, 1–10). This latter approach is the primary weakness of Canada's indigenous policies through the Indian Act, which still exists as a federal government statute that is both racist and colonial, if not imperial, from an indigenous perspective (McNab 2009a, 99–115).

In every course I teach at York University, I state in the first class that as an indigenous human being, I am a very lucky person, and I pause to let that sink in. Most indigenous men in Canada are dead or in prison by the time that they are fifty years old. Life for us is, to quote Thomas Hobbes's *Leviathan* (1651), "nasty, brutish and short." So I am very, very lucky to be here. Quite a few years ago now, I had a conversation on this subject with a good friend of mine who lives on a reserve in Canada. The starting point was that if you know you are indigenous, there is nothing to do about your situation since you do not become so. It simply becomes a matter of performing indigeneity. Bernard Perley has written that "my daily practice of Indigenous experience is my manifesto for critical Indigeneity" (2014, 32). This process begins when you come into this world from the world of spirits. It is not a linear progression, nor is it entirely either a positive or a negative undertaking. You are born into this natural world from the spirit world as such, and you have an intimate understanding of the landscape in which you are born, as suggested by N. Scott Momaday in his memoir *The Names* (1976, 4). My acquaintance tackled the issue (as most do logically) by asking the question, "who would ever want to become an indigenous person?" He also cited many examples of indigenous people who wanted to accomplish the opposite objective: how not to look indigenous by making themselves look "white" by, for example, literally scrubbing themselves with bleach or other noxious substances to do away with their brown skin. The objective was to blend in and to look "white" so that they could then escape the racism, prejudice, unemployment, and the poverty of being an "Indian," which are meted out to you by the larger society on Turtle Island if you are indigenous being, something that is especially true after 9/11 and the advent of "Homeland Security."

Thomas King, a prodigious indigenous writer, has written, based on his own experiences on Turtle Island and elsewhere, that in the twenty-first century indigenous peoples are simply here in the Americas as "Inconvenient Indian(s)." More succinctly, he has argued that "Indians" are today viewed bleakly as either "invisible" or, better yet, as "dead" (2012, 77–98). To me it is clear after forty years that the initiative to counter this narrative of erasure has to continue to come from First Nations. Perhaps it is time to ask the question or questions related to not becoming Indigenous. As Thomas King has also written in *The Truth about Stories*, "that's all we really are." We may wish to probe the multidimensional and dynamic lives of indigenous individuals in the past, present, and the future to see what makes them "tick" and to discover the "Native Narrative" (King 2003, 4), if such a monolithic thing can be said to exist.

My "Native narrative" is quite simple, though it has taken me into some fascinating places, all of which have many stories. My life has been all about asserting Métis resistance and sovereignty while being free and independent, adhering to my ancestors' ways through spirit memory across seven generations. This path is quite natural as a human being, and after all, indigenous people are human beings. They are not at all like Charles Darwin's specimens under glass. However, a word of warning. I cannot speak to you of what I have not experienced, such as, for example, life on the reserve, poverty, alcoholism, residential schools, the "sixties scoop," and posttraumatic stress disorder. Some of our elders tell us that if we have a happy childhood, it may be different later on and vice versa. Everyone's life is different, and that goes for indigenous people too, for they are not categories of thought. There are many names, families, clans, communities, nations, and confederacies, all with multidimensional, multiple, dynamic cultures and languages on Turtle Island. Within such complexity, to become indigenous is a learning process of giving back and sharing based on trust and mutual respect. What I record here is only one story of a Métis in the process of being an indigenous human, whose life has been shaped by many islands (Wagamese 2005).

I suggest that one should consider a precolonial approach to Métis thought and knowledge. I teach using this perspective at York University, since most of my students (or their parents/grandparents) are international and indigenous from all over the world. This philosophical notion has been well described by the late Vine Deloria Jr. in his distinctly spiritual precolonial idea of *The World We Used to Live In* (2006). Deloria posited correctly that we are consumed by "modernism" and by an "uncritical acceptance" of it, including Euro-American knowledge systems. We cannot see that "higher spiritual powers are still active in the world." As a result, we "need to glimpse the old spiritual world that helped, healed, and honored us with its presence and companionship." He also wrote that in the twenty-first century we "need to see where we have been before we see where we should go, we need to know how to get there, and we need to have help on our journey." This wisdom was written in Deloria's last book before his passing in 2005 (2006, xix).

It will also be recalled, from Anishinaabe prophecy, that the Métis, as a cultural "rainbow people (of mixed descent)," will assist us "on our journey" in the present and in the future (Simpson 2013, A15). Precolonial indigenous thought systems of spirituality are seemingly incompatible with the modernism of the twentieth and twenty-first centuries based on the material character of Euro-American knowledge systems. Deloria's thought forms the basis for the primary argument of this paper: that Métis voices are being reclaimed. Spirit memory is the process by which Métis families and communities continue to operate in international, transnational and hemispheric contexts (McNab 2012, 67–80).

One of the first steps in the recognition of spirit memory is discovering who we, as Métis, are, and where our places are. In Cree *Métis* means accurately "the other son/daughter" (Barkwell 2001, 127). The French word *Métis*, however, originally comes from the Latin word *miscere* which, simply but profoundly, means "to mix" in English. The historical meaning of Métis was the mixing of many peoples from all over the globe with the indigenous people of this land since at least the fifteenth century. Thus, the Métis, through their ubiquitous family connections, have always been part of an international community right into the early twenty-first century (Lischke and McNab 2007, 1–9). They came not just from the Canadian West— the former Red River community—as so often has been portrayed in Canadian nationalist historiography. They came also from the north, and from the west to the east and to the south, across international borders. In the mid-nineteenth century, non-Aboriginal observers regarded the Métis as having a new and distinctive society separate from either First Nations or non-Aboriginal peoples. Let me illustrate this point by telling a story through my reflections on my own Métis family experiences which are transnational and based on islands, which are sacred for indigenous people (Lischke and McNab 2007, 21–37).

### A Story from Tierra del Fuego (The Land of Fire)

Early in 2010 (after the 150th anniversary of Darwin's *Origin of the Species*), I visited one of the places where the *Beagle* had visited in the 1830s—the archipelago of islands across the Strait of Magellan—

Tierra del Fuego in Patagonia. At Ushuaia on Cape Horn, the local museum seemed to me the best hope of finding some reference to the great English scientist Charles Darwin and the *Beagle*. There it was as I entered—Darwin's room on the third floor! Bingo! Darwin is hated here by the local indigenous people—Tehuelches—who had their own separate museum in a different place in this southernmost city. Darwin did not paint a flattering portrait of these "Indians" of the misnamed Patagonia (referring to the large clumsy foot of the indigenous inhabitants who were believed to have been giants). So I visited the Darwin room and, except for the plaque above the entrance to this room, there was not one picture or even a reference to him or the *Beagle*. The only "inhabitants" in the Darwin room were penguins.

The local indigenous people had the last laugh at Darwin and his nineteenth-century science. There was of course no reference at all to Darwin or the *Beagle* in their local indigenous museum. I asked our tour guide (who was of mixed descent) about the "Indians." She said that they were all "unfortunately exterminated long ago." To prove her point, she took us to the local cemetery to show us where the last "Indian" was buried. Invisible or dead: too much I believe is made out of categories and becoming indigenous by those who are not. Indigenous peoples, like all human beings, are simply indigenous. They resist becoming anything else in someone else's category. They resist, survive, and are still here in the Americas. They wish to be free and independent and to exercise their own sovereignty in their own multidimensional and dynamic ways. They choose to do so in their own places on Turtle Island.

### A Story Overlooking the Toronto Islands

To use N. Scott Momaday's words in *The Names*, "events take place" (1976, 142). In the fall of 2012, events *took* place. I reside in a place overlooking the Toronto Islands. It was a full moon on Monday, October 29. I was driving home after a day at my university during Hurricane Sandy. Heading south toward Lake Ontario just after 6 p.m., although I was moving slowly, my 4 × 4 red truck hit a patch of water on the Don Valley Parkway. I hydroplaned and lost control. I turned around completely three times and ended up with the back end of my truck against the concrete guardrail facing the sacred direction of west. The place was a six-lane highway on a sacred site overlooking the Don River and the Toronto Islands. Despite it being rush hour, I collided with no one, and I was completely unhurt. It was like being in an abbreviated time capsule in that place. I started my truck again and drove home. I was in a state of shock. My old red truck was totaled ten years almost to the day that I got it. What did this event mean, and was it a sign? What could I learn about this story and the place? Why had I not traveled from Turtle Island back into the land of the spirits? This event, among others, has guided me in connecting with my spirit memory, at moments like islands in time, where time and place have deep resonance for those who listen to their stories.

## A Story of Borikén—the Island of the Brave People

Before I had time to contemplate this sign and its meaning (the elders tell us that some of us are clearly slower learners than others, and I am the slowest learner of all), I was on my way to present a paper on "The Rights of Indigenous People with Disabilities" at the American Studies Association in San Juan, Puerto Rico (an island with a rich port or harbor) where it will be recalled that Columbus landed in 1493. I should mention that I had a stroke almost a decade ago (on February 19, 2007) when I was on a research trip to Central America visiting Mayan sites in El Salvador, Honduras, and Guatemala, so I have more than a passing acquaintance with disability issues. I first saw this clearly on Sunday, February 17, 2007, when I had a sweat with a Mayan shaman in El Salvador. He provided us with a clear picture of what it was like to have lived in precolonial Americas and moreover what had been wrought after Columbus came to the "New World." He almost erased the decade of my book learning in the 1970s leading to my doctorate in history with what amounted to a precolonial framework.

Two days later (on Tuesday, February 19, 2007), I was attempting to make a digital photograph of the Agua Volcano, a water volcano that has not erupted since the arrival of Columbus, near Escuintla in Guatemala, the day after I visited the ruins of the Mayan city of Copán in Honduras. I never took this picture since I had a stroke at precisely the same time. I found myself being cared for by Mayan doctors in a storefront hospital named Genesis. No Western-trained doctor could explain why I had the stroke. The Mayan doctor told me cheerfully that I when I became well I would go back to work in six months. And he was right, I did.

On November 16, 2012, 127 years to the day that Louis Riel (an American citizen) was hanged for treason against the Canadian nation-state, I presented my paper in San Juan. And, the next day, at almost precisely the same time as my accident with the truck a few weeks before, I fell coming out of the shower in our hotel room onto the unforgiving Spanish tile floor. I broke my wrist in two places and also fractured my femur, which required a total hip replacement. After surgery on the island, I flew back to Toronto and recovered fairly quickly. I was assisted by a physiotherapist in a sacred place in Toronto (then known as Hillcrest Hospital), a Mi'kmaq medicine woman of mixed descent, whose family originally came from Fortune Bay on the island of Newfoundland.

Fascinating events do indeed take place. They form the Native narrative from the truth about transnational stories, which come from islands as sacred places (Lischke and McNab 2007, vii–viii). Again it raises the issue why one would want to become an indigenous person. Perhaps Washington DC is a safer place for Métis? After all, here is where Riel had his Métis vision of sovereignty, freedom, and independence "hiking up a mountain [likely Mount Vernon] near Washington, D.C." The Métis author Joseph Boyden describes "the same spirit who visited Moses 'in the midst of cloud and flame' appearing to Louis. 'Rise, Louis David Riel, you have a mission to accomplish for the benefit of humanity.'" After his vision near Washington, Riel became "a prophet of the New World" (Boyden 2010, 83–84). Riel's "Native narrative" shaped the Canadian Confederation by bringing Manitoba into it in 1868–70, thereby changing, or at least mitigating, the nationalistic historical myth of the impact on the Canadian nation-state of the "civil war" of 1812 (Taylor 2010, 6–10).

Riel's prophecy that the Métis, his people, would arise again about one hundred years after his death is certainly being affirmed with the *Powley* Supreme Court of Canada decision of 2003. This ruling recognized the hunting rights of the Métis community at Sault Sainte Marie in Ontario and also applies to the rest of Canada. Now this precedent-setting decision on Métis rights has been reinforced by the Supreme Court of Canada's April 2016 *Daniels* decision (9–0) recognizing and declaring the Métis as equals under Canada's constitution and as a federal government responsibility under the British imperial legislation known as the British North America Act of 1867. This legislative progress reminds me of the importance of indigenous narrative and its visionary value as well as its role as spirit memory.

## Inchbuie (Yellow Island) in the Dochart River in Killin

Like many Métis now residing in Canada, my family dates back to the late eighteenth century on my mother's side. My father, John McNab, was born in Buckhaven, Scotland, and came to Montreal, Canada, with his parents when he about six years old in 1929. Many of the chiefs of the McNab clan are buried on the ancient island of Inchbuie on the River Dochart in Killin, Scotland. I revisited the place, on this island that dates back to the Iron Age, about six years ago. My father never went back to the place of his birth, but he loved the Canadian outdoors and especially northern Ontario. He married a Métis woman in 1946 whose family came from the north of Canada near Pine Tree Island (Cumberland House, Saskatchewan), and my father was adopted thereby according to Métis custom. As the firstborn, it is not surprising that all of my research has involved spirit memory about islands and their history.

## A Story from the Bear River

My maternal grandparents were also influential in my childhood, growing up along the Bear River. The Métis have a distinct history as the first "true Canadians," as my maternal grandmother always told me. Mabel was a proud Kennedy, born thirteen years after the hanging of Riel. But she never forgot, and she passed on that mixed heritage to me. The Métis are the offspring of trade and diplomacy and, as such, continue to be an international and a transnational people.

I reflect now that I was also growing up Métis under the guidance of my maternal grandfather, Edward Huehn (1898–1967), who was of both German and Onondaga descent from the former Six

Nations Reserve. He was the first person to teach me, at the age of four, how to remember, by focusing on an image and saying its meaning four times. In his basement in Kitchener in the 1950s, I learned many things about the day-to-day use of indigenous tools, some of which I believe dated back to the nineteenth century. Indigenous knowledge is, after all, a practical everyday reality. I accepted that this urban indigenous world was part of my existence. One thing was missing, however—an indigenous language. Instead I grew up surrounded by English and German. How could it have been otherwise?

### A Story from Allumette Island (Kichesipirini—People of the Great [Ottawa] River)

In the early 1950s, my family spent one entire summer in a log cabin on the Ottawa River where my father was working as a construction foreman on the renovations to the military base at Camp Petawawa near Pembroke during the Cold War. The camp was intended to guard the new Chalk River nuclear facility close by. In the way were the dispossessed Algonquin people who had formerly lived for thousands of years on Allumette Island on the Ottawa River. Our log cabin overlooking the Ottawa River was located in an Algonquin settlement. We had fun playing with their children that summer. We were unaware of the fact that they were going to be once again removed from their place. One day, we took our father's homemade cedar strip motorboat over to Allumette Island, where we spent the day playing. On the high bank I found an Algonquin burial site, and the hair stood up on the back of my neck. Many years later I realized that I had found the grave of my maternal great-great-great-grandmother, Sarah Stevens (1809–c. 1858), an Algonquin woman and a relative of Chief Peter Stevens, whose family was originally from Allumette Island (Lawrence 2012, 38–53). In about 1833, Sarah was "married" to William Kennedy (1814–90), then a Métis Hudson's Bay Company fur trader, originally from Pine Tree Island at Cumberland House in present-day northeastern Saskatchewan. Now Allumette Island is covered over by an expensive subdivision, though the Algonquin cemetery was relocated to Fort William on the Quebec side of the Ottawa River. Recently, I visited that place and paid my respects to her spirit.

## A Story from the Bear (Grand) River

The next stop on my travels was at the Bear River (now called the Grand) on the former Six Nations Reserve, where I currently reside. This place is now called Waterloo. In the mid-1950s, I took my first course in Canadian history in public school there. The curriculum was distinctly colonial and imperial, with University of Toronto Professor of Education George E. Tait's *From Breastplate to Buckskin: A Story of Exploration and Discovery in the Americas* (1953) as our textbook. However, our teacher was Jim Moses from the Six Nations. He was in his early twenties, just out of teacher's college (he is now in his eighties, residing in Kitchener, Ontario). He taught us physical education and Canadian history. In his history classes, we were baffled. Mr. Moses would assign us a section in a chapter from Tait's text to read for our homework. We would come into his class, and he would never, ever mention anything in the text. He talked to us about the indigenous history of Canada and put it on the blackboard, and then we would have to copy it into our workbooks. At the end of each topic, he would ask us to read the next section from Tait. He never talked or discussed the textbook. He taught us Haudenosaunee philosophy and teachings of the Great Law and, in effect, the two-row wampum. The two-row wampum has been defined as a "bed of white wampum shell beads symbolizing the sacredness and purity of the treaty agreement between the two sides":

> Two parallel rows of purple wampum beads that extend down the length of the belt represent the separate paths travelled by the two sides on the same river. Each side travels in its own vessel: the Indians in a birch bark canoe, representing their laws, customs, and ways, and the whites in a ship, representing their laws, customs, and ways. In presenting the Gus-Wen-Tah to solemnize their treaties with the Western colonial powers, the Iroquois would explain its basic underlying vision of law and peace between different peoples as follows: "We shall each travel the river together, side by side, but in our own boat. Neither of us will steer the other's vessel." (Williams 1999, 4)

This wampum belt was initially given by the English to the Haude-nosaunee to cement the treaty entered into at Albany in 1664. The Haudenosaunee people were the "grandfathers" to the First Nations of the Western Confederacy (Johnson 1755, RG 10, Volume 1822, 35). In retrospect, Jim Moses passed this living history to me as spirit memory.

However, our class never caught on to this indigenous wisdom. After ten months, he simply asked us who he was. Of course, being abysmally slow learners, none of us knew. Some brave students put up their hands and answered him saying that he was Spanish, Mexican, Portuguese. He could hardly contain his anger. He went out of the room for what seemed an interminable length of time. About twenty minutes later, after he had cooled down, he came back and simply told us that he was a Mohawk from the Six Nations. Although it was the last afternoon of school before the summer break, I have never forgot-ten that moment. And it was instrumental in my thinking about his teachings about the Great Law of Peace, including the two-row wam-pum, the indigenous history of Canada, and the Métis role in it.

In subsequent years, during the late 1950s and 1960s, I met many indigenous children my age every summer when we were in the "north." In the natural world, you cannot "escape," since it is formed in the world of the spirits before you enter this life. We are part of nature. The land is the "boss" and it does shape you wherever you may be. This happy childhood literally changed overnight one day early in June 1967, when my father was killed by a drunk driver in Kitchener, leaving his wife and five children alone, with me the eldest. Our family became fragmented and has remained so, much like Maria Campbell's (among others) when her mother died (Camp-bell 1973).[1] Maria Campbell's Métis story of loss and fragmenta-tion in *Halfbreed* has many resonances with my own. You are born indigenous. Becoming indigenous is a living process, if you are one. And life rarely follows a linear path or an easy one. My memories are like islands on my spirit journey that remind me of my place.

## A Story from the Spirit of Pine Tree Island (1846–1975)

Spirits in the stories I am telling came to me often in the form of events taking place as well as through written documents. It was in Cambridge, England, in May 1973 that I discovered the subject of my doctoral dissertation, "Herman Merivale and the British Empire," simply by letting the catalog cards fall in the Cambridge University Library. The cards fell on the first edition of Merivale's *Lectures on Colonization and Colonies* (1841). It led me to William Kennedy and my family history through an original petition written and signed by him in 1846.

More than thirty-seven years ago, I was in the Public Record Office, then on Portugal Street in central London. On one of my last days there, I think it was Friday, August 8, 1975, at about 1 p.m., I turned a folio in CO 6 (British North America) records. There, in the miscellaneous records filed alphabetically in the "K" file, I touched the first page in the Métis William Kennedy's handwritten petition of 1846 (published in 1847) on behalf of the "Inhabitants of Rupert's Land." I immediately felt an electric-like jolt that went up my right arm that touched the page, and the hair stood up on the back of my neck. A Métis voice was speaking directly to me. It was an original document written by my great-great-great-grandfather Kennedy (1814–90) to the secretary of state for war and the colonies.

When I read the minute (a note placed on the correspondence) that Herman Merivale, the permanent undersecretary of that office, had written on this petition, I became very angry. Merivale dismissed the petition because he assumed that it could have only been written by a missionary, since the indigenous people of Rupert's Land were illiterate. Merivale was wrong. My ancestor and his nephew Alexander Kennedy Isbister (1822–83) were highly educated in Canada and Britain. They wrote that petition, and moreover, they, in the decade that followed, took away the Hudson's Bay Company's monopoly and license to trade in Rupert's Land, which they saw, quite rightly, was and had always been illegal. It led the way to the formation of nineteenth-century Manitoba as an indigenous place within the nation-state of Canada.

I have never forgotten that defining moment in my life. I was in the seat of the former British Empire because I had had to leave my country. In 1971 there was no one in Canada to supervise my doctoral research on nineteenth-century Canadian indigenous policy. Ironically, I found myself in England, studying under an Africanist.

In those days, no one thought that Canadian indigenous history was possible because Canadian scholars claimed—erroneously—that there were no written documents, since we were illiterate. But the written records were there, as well as the spirits within the spirit memory of the Métis family stories. Was it the spirit in the stories that were handed down to me as part of my family history of the Kennedys? I believe that it was spirit memory (Lischke and McNab 2007, 21–37).

Thereafter, my travels led me to many places—Corner Brook, Conne River, and Flat Bay, on the island of Newfoundland in 1977–78, and to the world of treaties and land rights in Toronto, and elsewhere. Then I followed my spirit memory to other places such as Toronto (1978–present), where my Métis great-great-great-grandfather had lived in the 1850s. Bear Island and the Temagami land claim followed. In 1981 I came to the Third Stopping Place (Bkejwanong—"the place where the waters divide," also known as Walpole Island), where I have visited for over thirty years. Oka followed in the summer of 1990, and then Churchill on Hudson Bay in 1992. I have in essence gone "home" to the Métis community of Saugeen Shores (Southampton) since 2004.

### A Story from Toronto—The Gathering Place

I really got to know the Métis historian Olive Patricia Dickason (1920–2011) in Toronto in the 1990s. She was a formidable scholar and also a good friend. We finished our doctorates in the same year (1978), and we may have been among the very first Métis historians to obtain our doctorates in Canada's history. Olive's PhD was from the University of Ottawa, and mine was from the University of Lancaster in England. I was a mere callow youth of thirty; Olive was fifty-seven. We were from two different generations.

However, except at conferences in western Canada in the 1980s, until a 1994 conference at Walpole Island I had never met her on a personal level (McNab for Nin.Da.Waab.Jig 1998). We were working at different places in Canada. I was teaching at Waterloo Lutheran (later Wilfrid Laurier), then at Memorial University's Regional College in Corner Brook, and then later (from 1979 to 1991) working for the provincial government in Toronto. At the 1994 Walpole

Island conference, we told each other stories about the "bad old days" going back to the early days both before and after Jean Chretien's White Paper of 1970. It was then we were literally told that the indigenous history of Canada did not exist because "everyone knew that Indigenous people only had oral traditions and no written records." Thus, it followed that indigenous people had no history. In 1994, we laughed at that a priori false assumption, but it was a real obstacle back then. In the years that followed the White Paper, we challenged that notion by invoking spirit memory.

Olive was lucky (or more likely highly experienced) in that she found a supervisor, Professor Cornelius Jaenen, a Belgian historian, who would take her on as a doctoral student. On the other hand, even though I was accepted at a number of Canadian universities, I found no one who would supervise my work. Fortunately, I was accepted at Oxford, Cambridge, and Lancaster. I was forced to leave Canada without any funding and to enroll at the University of Lancaster under Professor John M. MacKenzie, now professor of Imperial History emeritus, who had some acquaintance with indigenous oral traditions from the history of southern Africa. Later, Olive and I realized we had graduated with our doctorates in history at the same time. Olive was hired to teach Canadian history by the Department of History at the University of Alberta in 1976. She always told me that she was only allowed to teach Canadian history courses but never was asked to teach the indigenous history of Canada. However, she also ended this story with the mischievous smile telling me that she taught every course as indigenous history.

Our relationship became more permanent in 1997 when Olive joined the council of the Champlain Society, with its headquarters in Toronto. On the council, I was the government historian and Olive was the token indigenous historian. It was fascinating being a part of the society's council and a little unnerving as indigenous people. We shared many stories after these council meetings since I, as Olive's "chauffeur," drove her to and from the society's meeting places to her daughter's house in Toronto. Olive had quite a Métis sense of humor, and she was very sharp in questioning everything, including me.

Issues in the writing of the indigenous history of Canada consumed us both. Olive would begin the conversation by stating that a number of the nonindigenous reviewers of her written work would sometimes comment on why she had only included the written documents. Where, they would ask, were the indigenous oral traditions? Since she was "Native," it was assumed by nonindigenous scholars that she would have abundant access to its many diverse forms. Such comments were completely misplaced, since indigenous oral traditions are rooted in the land as family and community stories, as "spirit memory" (Lischke and McNab 2005, 189–214). Respect must be shown for the oral traditions and the community and family histories.

Flowing from this discussion, Olive and I would always talk about two other issues: how to address oral traditions in our written work without disrespecting the stories, and what was ours to tell or not. The second issue was how to incorporate the oral traditions and the stories which we wrote, as writing by its very nature changes their inherent form. These were fundamental issues that we knew how to approach on a specific case-by-case basis. However, it was also an argument without end because of the independence and sovereignty of oral traditions. These stories were often juxtaposed with the written records. Needless to say, we never reached a conclusion on these issues. The Supreme Court of Canada did so in its judgment in the Delgamuukw case (1997), which stated the oral traditions should be given equal weight with the written record before the Canadian courts.

I left the Champlain Society's council in 2000, having served twenty-two years on it, and our paths did not cross again for a few years. In 2003, with Olive still in Ottawa and now retired, I became the first Hudson's Bay Company visiting professor in the School of Canadian Studies at Carleton University. One of the conditions attached to that appointment was that I had to put together a symposium on Métis studies in March of 2003. The first thing I did was to phone Olive and ask her to be the keynote speaker. Initially, she was reluctant, citing her age of eighty-three years. I talked Olive into accepting the assignment. The symposium was, somewhat auspiciously, held the day after the *Powley* case was heard (March 19) by the Supreme Court of Canada. This timing was completely unplanned since there was no scheduling apparent for the hearing of the court case when the dates for the symposium were set. I would like to think that they were echoing each other.

Our well-attended symposium focused on many Métis studies issues. We attempted to answer at least some of these outstanding questions in the context of Métis history. Olive spoke about her life as a Métis woman, entitled "Out of the Bush: A Journey to a Dream." It was very well received. Olive was so modest that when I invited her to submit the piece for publication in a forthcoming book (which was eventually published in 2007, entitled *The Long Journey of a Forgotten People: Métis Identities and Family Histories*), she protested that she would not be able to produce a "research piece" but only something based on her "personal experiences" (Dickason, email to author, May 12, 2003). Of course, it became the first chapter in *The Long Journey*.

In our introduction to the volume, "We Are Still Here," Ute Lischke and I described this chapter as a tribute to Olive and her work: "As a Métis historian, Dickason has done much in her own historical writings to break the silence" about indigenous histories and "to give voice in written form to them. She is herself a watershed in Canadian historical writing" about indigenous peoples and "has been prominently recognized in the First Peoples Hall in Canada's National Museum of Civilization for her work," next to Louis Riel. "She has received a National Aboriginal Achievement Award and the Order of Canada [as well as many honorary degrees]. Dickason's magisterial volume, *Canada's First Nations, A History of Founding Peoples from Earliest Times*, first published in 1992, . . . has made an enormous impact on the process in which the multiplicity and distinctiveness of Aboriginal voices, including those of the Métis, are heard" (Lischke and McNab 2007, 6). Olive literally led the way to show Canadians how "our history is far more ancient and complex than has generally been acknowledged."[2]

My last story about Olive is one from the heart. Before *The Long Journey* appeared in the summer of 2007, I had a precolonial experience in Central America in late February 2007. I had been in rehab in Toronto as an inpatient when I learned that Olive had been trying to track me down for a number of weeks. This time she was not successful, so she wrote me a letter asking me to call her. I called her early in April and identified myself. I explained that I had had a stroke, was incapacitated on my right side, could not walk, and was confined for the moment to a wheelchair. Olive listened to me patiently and then said to me that she wanted me to undertake the fourth edition of her magnificent book *Canada's First Nations: A History of Founding Peoples from Earliest Times* (2009). I was, of course, both apprehensive and fearful. But at the same time I had to say "yes" to her. Olive was very happy, and we got together in August 2007, when I was able to travel to Ottawa.

My family later told me that this activity was the best thing I could have undertaken for my recovery after the stroke. The fourth edition was completed before the deadline put forward by Oxford University Press. Olive Dickason was a top-notch researcher, an incredible historian, a wonderful human being with a sharing Métis spirit, among many other things. She also had the capacity to heal me. This experience I will never forget.

### The Broken Manitoba Treaty and Resistance

What do all these stories, and their Métis spirits, mean in the end? Thirty-five years before Olive was born in the Red River "colony"— now Winnipeg—Riel was hanged in Regina in 1885. We still know very little about the Métis both before and after the death of Riel (McNab 1978, 21–38). It is said by Canadian nationalist historians that the Métis were dispersed to the west and the north. I do not believe this overly simplistic historical myth. For one thing, we were always in the area to which we allegedly "dispersed" since we were the first true Canadians.[3]

Many Métis continued to reside in southern Manitoba because that is where they lived and held property. For example, William Kennedy, born at Pine Tree Island, Cumberland House, in 1814, had already built his stone house on the banks of the Red River in the 1860s, before the first Métis resistance movement of 1869–70. It still is standing there to this day as a provincial historical site. My point is that the stereotypes of the Métis are wrong; things were considerably more complex. Some of the Métis voices were "lost" after 1885 through the breaking of the 1870 Manitoba Treaty, yet the spirit in these stories still remains intact.

That treaty had brought the Métis homeland of Manitoba into the Canadian Confederation in 1870 by federal legislation. This treaty was a direct consequence of the Métis resistance since at least the 1840s, which was fought by, among others, my great-great-great-grandfather and his nephew, first against the Hudson's Bay Company and then the British Empire, literally bringing down the company and ending its informal and illegal "empire of trade" and creating a new "homeland" for the Métis and other First Nations. The racist war that was waged by the first prime minister of Canada, Sir John A. MacDonald, a colonial born British imperialist, for fifteen years against the Métis (as well as other First Nations), dismantled and broke the Manitoba Treaty. That treaty is still being contested in the Canadian courts. In addition, there was also the racism that ensued in the embodiment of the Indian Act of 1876, which purged many of the Métis from the treaties.

I was in Ottawa on March 8, 2013, two blocks away from the Supreme Court of Canada building, when the court reached its decision on Section 31 of the Manitoba Act (which is part of Canada's constitution), finding in favor of the Métis. The Supreme Court declared its judgment that the federal government had breached its constitutional obligation (but not its fiduciary duty) on behalf of the honor of the Crown to the Métis when it did not deliver 1.4 million acres of land owed to the children of the Métis since 1870. While the Supreme Court did not issue such a fiduciary declaration in its decision, it has the power to do so. Hopefully, this decision will lead to constitutional reconciliation through negotiations and to a renewed Manitoba Treaty under Section 31 between the Métis nation and the government of Canada. Thereby, one aspect of Riel's prophecy will be fulfilled.

Olive's generation and the one that preceded it—the Métis children spoken of above—were tempered by the historical fact of the racism that followed the hanging of Riel. If the Canadian nation-state could do such a thing to the Métis "father of Canadian Confederation," then what it would do with the rest of the Métis in the context of the racism after 1885? So for a time Métis voices were stilled, and they literally hid the fact that they were Métis. Beginning in the 1970s, the spirit memory came back to persons of my generation, and we knew that we had to act, no matter the personal, family, or community costs.[4] The direct impact and the legacy of the Métis resistance movements of 1849, 1869–70, and 1885, fought by negotiation and force of arms to protect their sovereignty and land and natural resource rights, has been substantial in the history of the Métis and in Canada's colonial history.

The events of 1885 had some considerable effect on the federal government's indigenous policy as it developed through the administration of that policy and the Indian treaties in Canada. For example, before 1885, Métis in Ontario were involved in treaty negotiations and, in some cases, participated in them as Métis communities (McNab 2012, 71). After 1885, with their leader hanged as a traitor and many others hiding out of fear of racism, they continued to participate in the treaty-making process. The Métis nonetheless gradually became less influential in federal and provincial government legislation and policies. For example, they were treated as individuals, not as identifiable Métis communities or as a "new nation," and often did not even participate as individual Métis, only as "Indians." Through the 1885 revisions to the Indian Act of 1876, ignoring their communities, sovereignty, and land rights directly as a response to the armed Métis resistance of 1885, federal government policy for Métis became a policy of exclusion of their citizenship based on an increasingly homogeneous and racial view of Métis as Indians.[5] Like the "Indians" and the Inuit, the Métis also suffered physical and sexual abuse in the residential schools that were set up to assimilate them. The cultural survival of the Métis is thus a testimony to the strength and vitality of their culture and traditions, as the *Powley* judgment of 2003 has signified.

As I noted briefly earlier in this story, the *R. v. Powley* decision, handed down on September 19, 2003, was the first Canadian Supreme Court judgment to address the question of whether Métis communities can possess Aboriginal rights pursuant to subsection 35(1) of the Constitution Act of 1982. Despite Canada's constitution, the Métis have not been not recognized as a nation by the federal or the provincial governments since the Confederation of Canada in 1867. The Supreme Court ruled that the Métis community of Sault Sainte Marie possesses a constitutionally protected right to hunt for food (see Hele's chapter in this volume for more of this history). The Supreme Court articulated a test for Métis Aboriginal harvesting rights, thereby allowing for the possibility that such rights might exist elsewhere in Canada, while setting some parameters around who might exercise these rights (Lischke and McNab 2007, 1–10).[6] In responding to that decision, the federal government of Canada is currently engaged in a joint process with provincial and territorial governments and Métis leaders. The first step is to reclaim our Métis voices and to rediscover the spirit memory of our families— our ancestors—through distinct Métis knowledge in an international and transnational context.

Even with the *Powley* victory as well as the 2016 *Daniels* decision, Métis land rights are still today in a precarious balance between negotiation and litigation, between being subject to passive and active resistance movements and non-Aboriginal governments' policies and inactions. What is certain is that Métis people have much outstanding land and resource (as well as other) grievances, flowing from a more than two-hundred-year-old treaty-making process that is flawed and that must be renewed both in time and over time. Tenaciously, Métis people hold on to their concept of their sovereignty as a free and independent people. They have rights flowing from their title to land and resources as well as their inclusion in the Canadian treaty-making process. The objective is to become sovereign again as a free and independent self-governing people.

Let us return now to our issue of what does it mean to become an indigenous person. Why have our lives been "nasty, brutish, and short"? It was not so when Hobbes wrote these words in 1651. Will it always be so in the twenty-first century? I think that the answer for the Métis people lies in the spirit of prophecy, which has always been a primary component of the spirit memory of Métis history. I cannot suggest anything for other indigenous people. For the Métis, this situation has begun to change and move toward us being, as Riel said, "free and independent" as we once were, now over a century after Riel's death. For example, on Tuesday, January 15, 2008, Statistics Canada released its latest census on Aboriginal peoples in Canada, which was compiled in 2006. The population of the Métis between 1996 and 2006 nearly doubled to a total estimated figure of 389,785. Urbanization among indigenous people is increasing steadily (Dickason with McNab, 2009, 451–53). The answer to our survival also lies in the particular history of the Métis as one of resistance and sovereignty.

## Becoming Indigenous: A Story about Tecumseh

After I had finished writing and presenting this paper at Georgetown University in March of 2013, my Métis travels continued through the summer and fall of 2013. This time it was fortunately without incident or injury. In the spring I was invited to take part in a major gathering which was to celebrate and rekindle Tecumseh's vision at Bkejwanong on the two-hundredth anniversary of Tecumseh's passing at the Battle of Moraviantown on October 5. This celebration was to honor, during the two-hundredth anniversary of the War of 1812, the events surrounding the death of Tecumseh who was (as noted below) the "Great Leader of the Confederacy of Nations, a war chief, a statesman and an orator, who struggled to protect the Confederacy's sovereignty over its lands and waters." Tecumseh's remains are buried in a cairn overlooking the Saint Clair River on Walpole Island. This event was the highlight of the summer since in July, I (with Paul-Emile McNab, my youngest son) was asked by Walpole Island Heritage Centre to assist in the research and to write the words for the historical plaque, which would be unveiled on October 1, 2013 in a rededication ceremony hosted by the Walpole Island Soldiers Club at the Third Stopping Place. Obviously, the community was also involved in this process so as to include the oral traditions of Walpole Island, since Tecumseh's lieutenant, Chief John Nahdee, was responsible for protecting Tecumseh in battle and then for protecting his bones after he passed away to the spirit world.

I worked at my paper on Tecumseh over the summer, focusing on the significance of Tecumseh's vision for the twenty-first century. The paper was entitled: "'We are determined to defend our lands': Tecumseh and the British Imperial (and Canadian) Myths of Protection and Citizenship," and it was delivered on September 30. I concluded that Tecumseh's vision of sovereignty lives on in the early twenty-first century in contradistinction to the myths of protection and citizenship propounded for well over two hundred years by the

British imperial and the Canadian governments. Tecumseh's vision is now being rekindled at the place where he was buried in 2013.

Before the ceremony began on a day when the sun shone brightly in a cloudless, blue sky, Eric Isaac, an elder from Walpole Island, told me a story about Tecumseh. From an early age, Tecumseh, long celebrated as a great chief and a powerful warrior, was an indigenous human being who was disabled. His right leg was shorter than the left. Tecumseh built a wooden box (with a hole and a rope he tied to the box), which he used regularly to mount his horse when traveling or riding into battle or otherwise. As a human being, Tecumseh was able to overcome his disability and become an outstanding indigenous person whose vision and memory would live on after his travels in the natural world were over.[7]

Later that morning, the historical plaque was unveiled, and Tecumseh's vision and his memory were celebrated at an international gathering. The words on the plaque stated:

> Tecumseh was the Great Leader of the Confederacy of Nations, a war chief, a statesman and an orator, who struggled to protect the Confederacy's sovereignty over its lands and waters. Tecumseh fought valiantly in the War of 1812 and in the Battle of the Thames. It is believed that Chief Oshawanoe retrieved Tecumseh's remains hidden near the battlefield and placed them on St. Anne Island. Chief Joseph White, his stepson Silas Shobway, and the Walpole Island Soldiers Club cared for Tecumseh's bones through the generations. Overlooking the lands and the waters of Bkejwanong Territory, Tecumseh's remains were placed in this cairn on August 25th, 1941. This final resting place was rededicated on October 2, 2013 in honour of the bicentennial of the War of 1812. Tecumseh's spirit, his memory, and his legacy live on today.

Tecumseh, disabled and a human being, had become indigenous in both body and in spirit and in our memory. His spirit, his memory, and his legacy live on today.

### Retrospect

Métis history in the twenty-first century will be interdisciplinary, international, and transnational, leading to and being part of a new hemispheric and transnational approach based on Métis knowledge and thought.[8] Many prominent Métis have been linked through intermarriage, land, and trading relationships. They have made significant contributions to Canadian society and culture in the fields of indigenous knowledge, medicine, law, politics, literary and historical studies; mediating indigenous land, resource, and treaty rights issues; and by participating in international trade and trading. There have always been educated Aboriginal people using both their oral traditions and the imposed European-based knowledge systems. Their stories simply have remained untold because they have not been published or made known. An approach to remedy this, which I have tried to prefigure in this essay, will give voice to the Métis and document, through the intersection of oral traditions and the written records, their significance and value.

This new Métis history will focus on spirit memory, as a form of Métis knowledge, including both the stories and the spirits in the stories themselves. This approach to stories and storytelling, using the cultural intersection of Métis oral traditions with the written and archival records in the Canadian context, will build on Métis knowledge, which literally comes from places. For example, the Métis writer Louise Erdrich's collection of stories *The Last Report on the Miracles at Little No Horse* opens with the following statement by Nanapush about the framework of creation: "Nindinawemaganidok. There are four layers above the earth and four layers below. Sometimes in our dreams and creations we pass through the layers, which are also space and time. In saying the word nindinawemaganidok, or my relatives, we speak of everything that has existed in time, the known and the unknown, the unseen, the obvious, all that lived before or is living now in the worlds above and below" (Erdrich 2001, i). The words "all my relations" conveys the family or clan social structure and organization whence the stories and their spirits come to indigenous people as knowledge. Métis voices—of the "other son/daughter"—have that knowledge if we care to listen to and understand the spirit memory, and the spirits, in their stories.

## Notes

Turtle Island is the name used for North America by several indigenous peoples and Native activists, including the poet Gary Snyder, whose 1974 anthology, *Turtle Island*, won a Pulitzer. He more recently penned "The Rediscovery of Turtle Island" in *At Home on the Earth: Becoming Native to Our Place: a Multicultural Anthology.*

1. Consider also Olive Dickason's family, when her husband left her in the 1950s and she became a single mother with a job as a journalist. Olive's children were placed in foster care until Olive bought a house in Toronto, and they were returned to her (personal communication with Olive Dickason, May 12, 2003).

2. Olive fittingly ended her first chapter with these words:

> Perhaps as a consequence of these events, the period following the Second World War witnessed the beginning of a change in Canadian attitudes towards First Nations, a change that continues to develop. There is a growing level of acceptance on the part of the general public, manifested by a greater willingness to acknowledge First Nations as founding members of the Canadian nation. The growing number of Native studies courses at Canadian universities testifies to this. There is a project afoot to adapt my book for grade school use, and another to produce a thirteen-part school television series based on this book for educational purpose. In other words, Canadian Native studies is growing, and at a rapid rate. I could go on from here, but I think my point has been made. Our First Nations played and continues to play a fundamental role in the creation and shaping of Canada. Our history is far more ancient and complex than has generally been acknowledged. These personal reflections are my journey as a Métis woman out of the bush to a dream (Dickason 2007, 19).

3. Obviously, we were of mixed indigenous descent.

4. For example, after the events of Oka in the summer of 1990 in which the Canadian army was brought in to end the Mohawk resistance at the Kahnawake and Kanehsatake territories, I was blacklisted and remained unemployed for twelve years.

5. The first Canadian citizenship was only passed into law in 1947, and Métis, "Indians," and Inuit were not recognized under that legislation until 1960. "Indians" in the United States were recognized by legislation in 1924.

6. "The test is that there must be a historically identifiable Métis community prior to the time at which Europeans effectively established political and legal control over a particular area. A Métis community was defined as a 'group of Métis with a distinctive collective identity, living together in the same geographic area and sharing a common way of life'" (Teillet 2007, 65).

7. I am very grateful to Eric Isaac for giving me permission to tell this story given my own disability; after my stroke my right leg is shorter than my left.

8. At York University I taught the first graduate course in Humanities in Métis Knowledge and Thought in 2015. The framework for this approach would be both hemispheric and global.

## Bibliography

Archibald, Jo-ann. 2008. *Indigenous Storywork: Educating the Heart, Mind, Body, and Spirit.* Vancouver: University of British Columbia Press.

Barkwell, Lawrence J., Leah Dorion, and Darren R. Préfontaine, eds. 2001. *Metis Leg-*

*acy: A Metis Historiography and Annotated Bibliography. Vol. 1.* Winnipeg: Pemmican Publications.

Boyden, Joseph. 2010. *Louis Riel and Gabriel Dumont.* Toronto: Penguin.

Campbell, Maria. 1973. *Halfbreed.* Lincoln and London: University of Nebraska Press.

*Catch the Dream Bios with Adam Beach.* 2014. "Buffy Sainte Marie" episode. First broadcast by APTN. Stonecast Pictures. http://catchthedream.tv/.

Deloria, Vine, Jr. 2006. *The World We Used to Live In: Remembering the Powers of the Medicine Men.* Golden CO: Fulcrum Publishing.

Dickason, Olive Patricia. 2007. "Out of the Bush: A Journey to a Dream." In *The Long Journey of a Forgotten People: Métis Identities and Family Histories.* Edited by Ute Lischke and David T. McNab, 13–19. Waterloo: Wilfred Laurier Press.

——— „ with David T. McNab. (1992) 2009. *Canada's First Nations: A History of Founding Peoples from Earliest Times.* 4th ed. Toronto: Oxford University Press.

Erdrich, Louise. 2001. *The Last Report on the Miracles at Little No Horse.* New York: HarperCollins.

Foster, John E. 1978. "The Métis: The People and the Term." *Prairie Forum* 3, no. 1 (Spring): 79–91.

Glick Schiller, Nina, Linda Basch, and Cristina Blanc-Szanton, eds. 1992. *Towards a Transnational Perspective on Migration: Race, Class, Ethnicity, and Nationalism Reconsidered.* New York Academy of Sciences.

Hobbes, Thomas. 1651. *Leviathan.* London: Andrew Crooke.

Johnson, Sir William, Superintendent of Indian Affairs, Letter of June 23rd, 1755. RG 10, Indian Affairs, Volume 1822, 35. National Archives of Canada.

King, Thomas. 2003. *The Truth About Stories: A Native Narrative.* Toronto: House of Anansi Press.

———. 2012. *The Inconvenient Indian: A Curious Account of Native People in North America.* Toronto: Doubleday.

Lawrence, Bonita. 2012. *Fractured Homeland: Federal Recognition and Algonquin Identity in Ontario.* Vancouver: University of British Columbia Press.

Lischke, Ute, and David T. McNab, eds. 2005. *Walking a Tightrope: Aboriginal People and their Representations.* Waterloo: Wilfrid Laurier University Press.

———, eds. 2007. *The Long Journey of a Forgotten People: Métis Identities and Family Histories.* Waterloo: Wilfrid Laurier University Press.

———. 2009. "Introduction." In *Sacred Landscapes,* edited by Jill Oakes, Rick Riewe, Rachel ten Bruggencate, and Ainslie Cogswell, vii–viii. Winnipeg: Aboriginal Issues Press.

McNab, David T. 1978. "The Colonial Office and the Prairies in the Mid-Nineteenth Century." *Prairie Forum* 3, no. 1 (Fall): 21–38.

———. 2004. "Borders of Water and Fire: Islands as Sacred Places and as Meeting Grounds." In *Aboriginal Cultural Landscapes,* edited by Jill Oakes and Rick Riewe, 35–46. Winnipeg: Aboriginal Issues Press.

———. 2007. "A Long Journey: Spirit Memory and Métis Identities." In *The Long Journey of Canada's Forgotten People: Métis Identities and Family Histories,* edited by Ute Lischke and David T. McNab, 21–37. Waterloo: Wilfrid Laurier University Press.

———. 2009a. "A Brief History of the Denial of Indigenous Rights in Canada." In *A History of Human Rights in Canada*, edited by Janet Miron, 99–115. Toronto: Scholarly Publishing.

———. 2009b. "Métis Identities in Louise Erdrich's *The Painted Drum* (2004)." In *Sacred Landscapes*, edited by Jill Oakes, Rick Riewe, Rachel ten Bruggencate, and Ainslie Cogswell, 155–69. Winnipeg: Aboriginal Issues Press.

———. 2009c. *No Place for Fairness: Indigenous Land Rights and Policy in the Bear Island Case and Beyond*. Montreal: McGill-Queen's University Press.

———. 2009d. "Thomas King's Storytelling and Humour: Hunting and Healing." In *Sacred Landscapes*, edited by Jill Oakes, Rick Riewe, Rachel ten Bruggencate, and Ainslie Cogswell, 65–73. Winnipeg: Aboriginal Issues Press.

———. 2012. "Métis Voices and Sovereignty: Reflections on Métis Resistance to Imperial Layers of Colonialism in Canada." In *Comparative Indigenous Identities of the Américas: Toward a Hemispheric Approach*, edited by M. Bianet Castellanos, Lourdes Gutiérrez Nájera, and Arturo J. Aldama, 67–80. Tucson: University of Arizona Press.

———. 2013. "Indigenous Voices and Spirit Memory in the Journals of Ezhaaswe (c. 1848–1929), Indian Missionary." In *Indigenous Voices and Spirit Memory*, by David T. McNab, Ute Lischke, Patsy McArthur, Paul-Emile A. McNab, Maureen Riche, Katie Peterson, and Stephane McLachlan, 1–10. Winnipeg: University of Manitoba Aboriginal Issues Press.

———. 2015a. "Historic Saugeen Métis Treaty-Making in the 19th Century: The Significance of the Pierre Piche Wampum Strings of 1818." In *Tecumseh's Vision: Indigenous Sovereignty and Borders since the War of 1812*, edited by Ute Lischke, David T. McNab, and Paul-Emile McNab, 17–28. Winnipeg: Aboriginal Issues Press.

———. 2015b. "Indigenous Persons, with Disabilities, and the United Nations Declaration of Indigenous Rights in Canada." In *Tecumseh's Vision: Indigenous Sovereignty and Borders since the War of 1812*, edited by Ute Lischke, David T. McNab, and Paul-Emile McNab, 159–78. Winnipeg: Aboriginal Issues Press.

McNab, David T., ed., for Nin.Da.Waab.Jig. 1998. *Earth, Water, Air and Fire: Studies in Canadian Ethnohistory*. Waterloo: Wilfrid Laurier University Press.

Merivale, Herman. 1841. *Lectures on Colonization and Colonies*. London: Longman, Orme, Brown, Green, and Longmans.

Momaday, N. Scott. 1976. *The Names*. Tucson: University of Arizona Press.

Perley, Bernard. 2014. "Living Traditions: A Manifesto for Critical Indigeneity." In *Performing Indigeneity: Global Histories and Contemporary Experiences*, edited by Laura R. Graham and H. Glenn Penny, 32–54. Lincoln: University of Nebraska Press.

Potts, Gary. 1999. Foreword. In *Circles of Time: Aboriginal Land Rights and Resistance in Ontario*, by David T. McNab, vi. Waterloo: Wilfred Laurier University Press.

Saul, John Ralston. 2008. *A Fair Country: Telling Truths About Canada*. Toronto: Penguin.

Simpson, Jeffrey. 2013. "Quebec, Meet Your Neighbour Ontario." *Toronto Globe and Mail*. February 5. A15.

Snyder, Gary. (1969) 1974. *Turtle Island*. New York: New Directions.

———. 1999. "The Rediscovery of Turtle Island." In *At Home on the Earth: Becoming*

*Native to our Place: A Multicultural Anthology*, edited by David Landis Barnhill, 297–306. Berkeley: University of California Press.

Tait, George E. 1953. *From Breastplate to Buckskin: A Story of Exploration and Discovery in the Americas*. Toronto: Ryerson Press.

Taylor, Alan. 2010. *The Civil War of 1812*. Toronto: Random House.

Teillet, Jean. 2007. "Winds of Change: Métis Rights after Powley, Taku, and Haida." In *The Long Journey of a Forgotten People: Métis Identities and Family Histories*, edited by Ute Lischke and David T. McNab, 55–78. Waterloo: Wilfrid Laurier University Press.

Wagamese, Richard. 2005. *One Native Life*. Madeira Park BC: Douglas and McIntyre.

Williams, Robert A., Jr. 1999. *Linking Arms Together: American Indian Treaty Visions of Law and Peace, 1600–1800*. New York: Routledge.

# CONTRIBUTORS

**Waskar Ari-Chachaki** is a historian of nineteenth- and twentieth-century Latin American nation-states and how they intersect with indigenous peoples and coloniality; his work particularly emphasizes race, ethnicity, gender, and sexuality. His book, *Earth Politics: Religion, Decolonization, and Bolivia's Indigenous Intellectuals*, was published in 2014 by Duke University Press. He is now working on a study of indigenous women, land tenure, and Aymara epistemologies in the private and public spheres from 1825 to 1971. Waskar is associate professor of history and ethnic studies and Latin American studies at University of Nebraska–Lincoln.

**Luis Fernando Granados**, of the Universidad Veracruzana, Xalapa, holds a PhD in history from Georgetown University (2008). He has taught at the University of Chicago, Universidad Nacional Autónoma de México, Universidad Iberoamericana, and Skidmore College, as well as at the Michigan-Cornell-Pennsylvania Program in Seville. He is the author of *Sueñan las piedras: Alzamiento ocurrido en la ciudad de México, 14, 15 y 16 de septiembre, 1847* (2003) and *La sombra de Santo Domingo: Apuntes para una historia de la revolución popular novohispana* (forthcoming). He is also the coeditor of the history blog *El Presente del Pasado* (http://elpresentedelpasado.com/).

**Karl S. Hele** is a member of the Garden River First Nation. He was the director of First Peoples studies at Concordia University before joining the Canadian Studies Program at Mount Allison University as an associate professor of First Peoples studies in the School of Community and Public Affairs. He has served as the joint editor of the

*Algonquian Proceedings* and has edited *Lines Drawn upon the Water* and *The Nature of Empires and the Empires of Nature*. He contributes a column on regional history to the *Sault Star* and occasional articles to *Ansihinabek News*. He has presented and published several papers on the history of the Anishinaabe and Métis communities in the Sault Sainte Marie region.

**Susan Kellogg** is professor of history and director of Latin American studies at the University of Houston. She is the author of *Law and the Transformation of Aztec Culture, 1500–1700*, published in 1995 by University of Oklahoma Press, and *Weaving the Past*, published in 2005 by Oxford University Press, as well as numerous articles, including most recently "The Mysterious Mothers of Alva Ixtlilxochitl: Women, Kings and Power in Late Prehispanic and Conquest Tetzcoco," in *Género y arqueología en Mesoamérica: Homenaje a Rosemary A. Joyce*, which she coedited with María J. Rodríguez-Shadow. Her current research and writing focuses on the lives and writings of several early colonial indigenous and mestizo writers of the Basin of Mexico region.

**Erick D. Langer** is professor of history in the Edmund A. Walsh School of Foreign Service at Georgetown University and faculty director of the master's program in the Center for Latin American Studies. His research interests include contemporary indigenous movements, frontier missions, and the role of indigenous peoples in the nation-building process in Latin America. He is the author of many books, including *Economic Change and Rural Resistance in Southern Bolivia* (Stanford, 1989) and *Expecting Pears from an Elm Tree: Franciscan Mission on the Chiriguano Frontier in the Heart of South America* (Duke, 2009), and is the editor or coauthor of five other books. He is also the editor in chief of *Gale World Scholar: Latin America and the Caribbean*, an online resource. Langer is presently working on a book exploring the indigenous role in the economic development in the south-central Andes during the nineteenth century.

**David T. McNab** is a Métis historian who has worked for more than thirty-five years on indigenous land and treaty rights issues in Canada. He is a professor of Indigenous thought and Canadian studies in the Department of Equity Studies and Humanities in the

Faculty of Liberal Arts and Professional Studies at York University, in Toronto. He has also been a claims advisor for Nin.Da.Waab. Jig., Walpole Island Heritage Center, Bkejwanong First Nations since 1992. In addition to over ninety articles, David has published *Earth, Water, Air and Fire: Studies in Canadian Ethnohistory* (ed., 1998) and *Circles of Time: Aboriginal Land Rights and Resistance in Ontario* (1999), as well as the coedited *Blockades and Resistance: Studies in Actions of Peace and the Temagami Blockades of 1988–89* (2003), *Walking a Tightrope: Aboriginal People and their Representations* (2005), and *The Long Journey of Canada's Forgotten People: Métis Identities and Family Histories* (2007), all with Wilfred Laurier University Press. In 2009 he published the fourth edition (with Olive Patricia Dickason) of *Canada's First Nations* (Oxford University Press) and also published *No Place for Fairness: Indigenous Land Rights and Policy in the Bear Island Case and Beyond* (McGill-Queens University Press). In 2013 he coauthored *Indigenous Voices and Spirit Memory* with Aboriginal Issues Press. He is currently working on the fifth edition of *Canada's First Nations* and a book project on Canada's North tentatively entitled "'Arctic Prescription': William Kennedy's (1814–90) Search for Sir John Franklin in 1851–55."

**Susan Elizabeth Ramírez** holds the Neville G. Penrose Chair in History and Latin American Studies at Texas Christian University in Fort Worth. She is the author of several books, including *Provincial Patriarchs: Land Tenure and the Economics of Power in Colonial Peru* (1986); *The World Upside Down: Cross-Cultural Contact and Conflict in Sixteenth-Century Peru* (1996 and 1998); *To Feed and Be Fed: The Cosmological Bases of Authority and Identity in the Andes* (2005); and *Al servicio de Dios y Su Magestad: Los orígenes de las escuelas públicas para niños indígenas en el Norte del Perú en el siglo XVIII*. She continues her research on Native cultures in the contact era and the impact of the Bourbon Reforms under Bishop Baltazar Jaime Martínez Compañón on the indigenous peoples of Peru.

**Miléna Santoro** is an associate professor specializing in Quebec studies and film and media studies at Georgetown University. Her publications include *Mothers of Invention: Feminist Authors and*

*Experimental Fiction in France and Quebec* (McGill-Queens University Press, 2002), the coedited volume *Transatlantic Passages: Literary and Cultural Relations between Quebec and Francophone Europe* (McGill-Queens University Press, 2010), and articles on the literature and culture of Quebec, Canadian First Nations filmmakers, Francophone women novelists, and women in the profession. She coedited the June 2013 special issue on *Québec Cinema in the 21st Century* for the *American Review of Canadian Studies*, where she served as associate editor (2008–2015). Her other positions include associate editor for the *International Journal of Canadian Studies* (2006–10, 2014–2017), executive council member of the Association for Canadian Studies in the United States (2011–2015), member of the editorial board of *Quebec Studies* (2010–), executive committee member of the Modern Languages Association Division on Francophone Literatures and Cultures (2015–2019), and president of the International Association of Quebec Studies (2015–2018). She is currently working on a monograph, *Encountering America in Quebec Cinema since 1960*. In 2017 she was awarded the Grand Prix de la Francophonie by the Festival de la Francophonie of Washington DC and the Quebec Ministry of International Relations and la Francophonie's Médaille hommage 50e.

**Lynn Stephen** is distinguished professor of arts and sciences, professor of anthropology, and director of the Center for Latino/a and Latin American Studies at the University of Oregon. Her scholarly work has centered the impact of globalization, migration, nationalism, and the politics of culture on indigenous communities in the Americas. Her research also highlights the importance of indigenous epistemologies and their theoretical and methodological contributions. Other major research focuses on gender, Mexican immigration, and the history of Latino communities spread across multiple borders through her concept of transborder communities. She has a strong commitment to collaborative research and to projects that produce findings that are accessible to the wider public. Her most recent books include *Transborder Lives: Indigenous Oaxacans in Mexico, California, and Oregon* (Duke University Press, 2007); *We Are the Face of Oaxaca: Testimony and Social Movements* (Duke University Press, 2013) with an accompanying website: http://faceofoaxaca.uoregon.edu/introduction/; and *Otros Saberes: Collaborative Research on Indigenous and Afro-Descendent Cultural Politics* (coedited with Charles R. Hale, School for American Research Press, 2013) available at http://lasa.international.pitt.edu/members/special-projects/files/OtrosSabereslasa.pdf.

# INDEX

CPSIA information can be obtained
at www.ICGtesting.com
Printed in the USA
LVHW01*2159180918
590552LV00006B/87/P

9 781496 206626